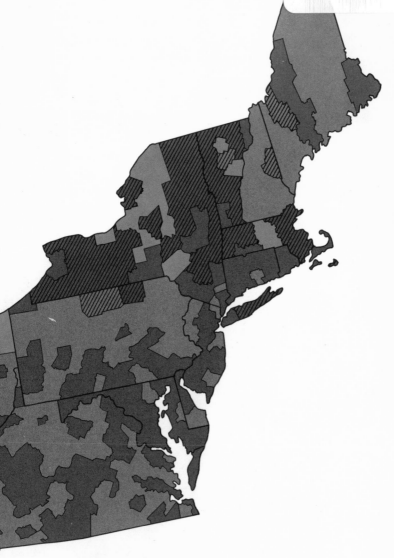

ELECTION OF 1848:
POPULAR VOTE BY COUNTIES

Van Buren plurality

Van Buren won 20% of vote

Cass plurality

Taylor plurality

FREE SOIL

WITHDRAWN

FREE SOIL

The Election of 1848

Joseph G. Rayback

THE UNIVERSITY PRESS OF KENTUCKY

TO
Arthur C. Cole
MENTOR & FRIEND

Standard Book Number: 8131-1222-2

Library of Congress Catalog Card Number: 79-111514

Copyright © 1970 by The University Press of Kentucky

A statewide cooperative scholarly publishing agency serving Berea College, Centre College of Kentucky, Eastern Kentucky University, Kentucky State College, Morehead State University, Murray State University, University of Kentucky, University of Louisville, and Western Kentucky University.

Editorial and Sales Offices: Lexington, Kentucky 40506

Contents

Preface

Historians generally evaluate the administration of James K. Polk as one of the more significant in American history. It was a period in which the major issues that divided the nation during the Jackson–Van Buren administrations were redebated: the Federal financial structure, the tariff, Federal aid to internal improvements. For each of these issues the nation determined upon an essentially Jacksonian solution and in a sense concluded the Jacksonian Era. It was a time when the nation peacefully annexed Oregon. It was also a period of war with Mexico—a war highly unpopular among and bitterly opposed by some elements, primarily in the East, and a war that ended with the annexation of the vast regions west of the Rio Grande and "completed" the process of "rounding out the continent" that had begun with the purchase of Louisiana.

It was, in addition, a period when new issues began to appear in strong enough force to demand solution. Chief among them was the problem of slavery. In Polk's administration the argument over slavery shifted from a demand for abolition to a demand for limitation of its expansion. Although the shift had started during the election campaign of 1844, it was the Mexican War, the prospect of annexing territory, and the introduction of the Wilmot Proviso in Polk's administration that made limitation of the area of slavery the major issue of American politics, a predominance it maintained until South Carolina seceded from the Union in 1860. In short, it was during Polk's administration that many of the developments of the American past were completed and the dominant political movement of the future was started. Viewed in this way, as a period of both ending and beginning, Polk's administration was a dividing point in American history.

This conjunction made the period one of considerable political turmoil. Older politicians accustomed to past alignments struggled to maintain the old political balances; younger politicians (the age gap was actually only fifteen years), while recognizing the importance of the past, sought to meet the new rising issues, one of which—slavery—so strongly aroused antagonistic emotions and ideologies as to threaten the disruption of political parties and even of the Union.

As is normal in American politics, the contest between contending elements and forces inevitably centered upon the campaign to elect the next president. My purpose in this book is to relate and analyze that campaign from its origins in the early days of Polk's administration to the election of Zachary Taylor.

The early portion of the 1848 campaign to name a new president might be called politics, old style. It involved the efforts of ambitious men or their friends or both to discover possible support and, without too much exposure, to place themselves or their favorites in a favorable position for an active campaign. Much of the maneuvering at this stage was submerged and was allowed to surface only when some advantage might be gained. The campaign was based upon personalities. There were seldom any commitments; in fact, almost no thought was given to principles and issues. It was the kind of a campaign that can develop only when the aspirants are already well known and the issues are those of the past. It could have lasted a long time, but it ended abruptly, even before the congressional elections of 1846, with the introduction of the Wilmot Proviso and the "discovery" of Zachary Taylor by southern Whigs at the head of the army in northern Mexico.

It took nearly half a year for these two not unconnected events to make a large impact. But in that time it became clear that the nation was joining in a conflict over the future of slavery in the territories and that it had a presidential candidate with unknown principles who was sweeping to victory almost without a contest. Although undercover maneuvering by presidential hopefuls continued, the larger part of the campaign to elect a president now came into the open—in full view of the public.

By far the greater part of this book is devoted to the campaign after it became open to the public. It was during this period that the interplay between politicians and the electorate influenced potential candidates and the action of parties; the public used the arguments and events of the period to make its decisions.

To a very large degree my focus in the campaign has been directed on the Wilmot Proviso because, as the sources clearly reveal, the efforts to advance, check, compromise, evade, reverse, embrace, or repel the principle involved in the Proviso—Free Soil—had the greatest, sometimes the overwhelming, influence upon the party structures, the selection of candidates, and the final results of the campaign.

Free Soil brought the conflict-ridden Democratic party of New York to the point of disruption, gave the Conscience Whigs of Massachusetts an issue upon which a reform movement could be based, and provided Liberty party leaders such as Salmon P. Chase the opportunity to move toward the creation of an antislavery league. Until his untimely death, Free Soil helped make Silas Wright a major contender for the Democratic nomination. Reaction to Free Soil, in both the North and the South, caused leading Democratic contenders such as James Buchanan, George M. Dallas, and Lewis Cass to seek middle ground and led Levi Woodbury to keep carefully quiet. Among Whigs, appalled by the possible consequences of the issue, it produced efforts to push it into the background, affecting the candidacies of John McLean, Thomas A. Corwin, Daniel Webster, Henry Clay, and Winfield Scott. In the South, reaction to Free Soil started a southern political movement, which John C. Calhoun was prepared to lead but which was absorbed by Zachary Taylor's candidacy. The threat to southern interests in Free Soil gave Taylor's aspirations their strongly sectional bias.

Free Soil was the unbidden guest at the nominating conventions. It was the issue around which dissenting and discordant elements from the Democratic, Whig, and Liberty parties united at Buffalo into the "Free Democracy"—in a sense the climax of political developments during the Polk administration. Free Soil became "the issue" of the postconvention campaign, claimed by all parties in the North, disclaimed by both parties in the South. When the public went to the polls in November 1848, it not only elected a president but also made two decisions concerning the future of slavery in the territories, one immediate and one long-term. Free Soil made the presidential campaign of 1848 one of the most significant in American history.

A number of people, too many to designate by name, have helped make this book possible. Of them I particularly wish to express my thanks to my best critic, analyst, proofreader, and copyreader—my wife, Virginia McKay Rayback.

Chapter One

The Early Contenders

The presidential campaign of 1848, like several presidential campaigns before and like most of those that followed, began almost as soon as the results of the election of 1844 were known. As might be expected, it began earliest among the close political friends and associates of former aspirants in the defeated party—among the Whigs who were unembarrassed by their own party leader in the White House, who might lay claim to future support.

In a measure, Henry Clay, as the party's latest candidate and as the Great Embodiment of Whig principles, had to be given consideration. Clay, however, had retired to the seclusion of his Kentucky estate, bitterly disappointed over his defeat by the less widely known James K. Polk. Although faithful followers showered messages of sympathy and continued loyalty upon him and wealthy personal and political friends sought to lighten his burdens by removing the heavy mortgage that weighed upon his property, even his most devoted adherents dared not look forward to another contest under his tattered banner. In late 1844, Clay, veteran of many political campaigns and a thrice-defeated presidential candidate, was an old man at sixty-five. At best, his friends could only hope that he might enjoy a few more years of quiet contentment. Clay himself saw only the "walks of private life" stretching before him.[1]

The first Whig to enter the contest for party nomination was John McLean of Ohio, postmaster general under both Monroe and John Quincy Adams, and since 1829 an associate justice of the United States Supreme Court. McLean had been a contender for the 1844 nomination until it became evident that Clay's preconvention strength was too great to overcome; when friends had suggested him as a possible running mate, he had declined.[2]

Exactly when McLean became an active contender is difficult to determine. In late November 1844 his longtime friend Calvary Morris inquired about his intentions: "What is to be done? Shall we give up all as lost & retire from the field in disgust or shall we make an effort to put down the 'Dictators' & take command of our own forces?"[3] McLean probably took up the challenge, for by early spring of 1845 an observer in New York City reported that his friends were "covertly" at work.[4] At this stage his campaign, aimed in part at the party's old managers, held out a vague prospect of success. There were early indications that Whig leaders such as Senator John M. Clayton of Delaware, Reverdy Johnson of Baltimore, Joseph Trumbull of Hartford, and Amos Lawrence of Boston were sympathetic; that there was "no doubt of Vermont"; that McLean had support in western Pennsylvania; and that he was the "talked of candidate in Detroit."[5] There was also some evidence that he might expect aid from "the moderate part of the Democratic party."[6]

First indications of possible organized support, however, came not from the party, but from the "Nativists," a group which had become fearful of the growing influence of foreigners, particularly unnaturalized foreigners, in elections. To curb that influence, the Nativists had proposed that the term for naturalization of foreigners be extended from five to twenty-one years, that states be denied the power to enfranchise the foreign-born before they were naturalized, and that laws be enacted requiring registration of all voters in order to prevent multiple voting, a practice in which Nativists were convinced that foreigners under the guidance of Democratic ward heelers often indulged.

In January 1845 various leaders among eastern seaboard Nativists, in

---

[1] The rather funereal attitude of many Whigs toward Clay's future was well expressed in the address made by Judge Joseph R. Underwood early in December 1844 when the Kentucky electors made a pilgrimage from Frankfort to Ashland: "In the shades of Ashland may you long continue to enjoy peace, quiet and the possession of those great faculties which have rendered you the admiration of your friends and the benefactor of your country. And when at last, death shall demand its victim, while Kentucky will contain your ashes, rest assured that old and faithful friends . . . will cherish your memory and defend your reputation" (Henry Clay, *Works of Henry Clay: Comprising His Life, Correspondence and Speeches,* ed. Calvin Colton, Federal Edition [New York, 1904], 3: 14–19 [hereafter cited as *Clay's Works*]).

[2] McLean's 1844 campaign is detailed in Francis P. Weisenburger, *Life of John McLean: A Politician on the United States Supreme Court* (Columbus, Ohio, 1937).

[3] Morris to McLean, 20 November 1844, John McLean Papers.

[4] Nicholas Carroll to Mangum, 29 April 1845, in Willie Person Mangum, *Papers of Willie Person Mangum,* ed. Henry T. Shanks (Raleigh, N. C., 1955), 4: 287 (hereafter cited as *Mangum Papers*).

[5] Elisha Whittlesey to McLean, 11 July 1845, James Dunlap to McLean, 29 November 1844, McLean Papers; William H. Seward to Thurlow Weed, 24 July 1845, in William H. Seward, *William H. Seward: An Autobiography,* ed. Frederick Seward (New York, 1891), pp. 771–72.

[6] William Miner to McLean, 25 January 1845, McLean Papers.

the interest of rescuing the nation "from the grasp of foreign Ecclesiastical politicians" and of preserving "the purity of the Ballot Box," asked McLean his attitude toward the Nativist platform. To all queries McLean returned adequate replies.[7] Indeed, his opinion on the subject of restricting alien voting was so completely satisfactory that one of his followers found it necessary to warn Nativist leaders against a nomination. "I took the occasion," he reported, "to intimate the great injustice they might do to you by asking to identify you closely with their political objects, thus separating you perhaps from more general and more extensive association. I pointed out . . . that you were their natural ally and friend, but could not be their exponent or agent." In short, the Nativists were an unpopular element; their endorsement of the Judge might have proven to be a kiss of death.[8]

The Nativists made no nomination because there was another Whig candidate in the field who was also attracting attention—General Winfield Scott, the man who had carried New York's vote into the Whigs' Harrisburg convention of 1839 and who also had been a contender for nomination in 1844.[9] The development of Scott's early candidacy is more obscure than that of McLean's. It was apparently in the making by March 1845, when Thomas Corwin, senator from Ohio, could report from Washington that Scott looked "ten feet high."[10] Occasional comments in the correspondence of politicians and in the editorial columns of the press during the summer and fall of 1845 also indicated that a Scott movement was underway.

When Congress met in the winter of 1845–1846, the movement became public knowledge. "Ion," the correspondent of the Baltimore *Sun,* later reported that Scott "was constantly surrounded by Whig statesmen and politicians of the highest eminence. The most distinguished of the Clay Whig Senators were his constant companions." Congressional approval also became apparent early in January 1846 when various senators

<hr />

[7] F. C. Messinger to McLean, 15 January 1845, Jesse Mann to McLean, 10 February 1845, McLean to Messinger, 25 January 1845, McLean to Mann, 14 February 1845, McLean Papers.

[8] P. W. Richards to McLean, 24 February 1845, Samuel Whitcomb to McLean, 3 July 1845, McLean Papers. McLean evidently had no personal objection to a Nativist nomination (McLean to Whittlesey, 9 August 1845, Elisha Whittlesey Papers).

[9] Scott was endorsed by two Nativist newspapers in late 1844 (*Cincinnati Herald-Philanthropist,* 13 November 1844 [hereafter cited as *Cincinnati Herald*]). No biographer of Scott has provided an account of his 1844 movement.

[10] Corwin to Oran Follett, 13 March 1845, in L. Belle Hamlin, ed., "Selections from the Follett Papers," *Quarterly Publication of the Historical and Philosophical Society of Ohio* 9 (1914) : 85 (hereafter cited as "Follett Papers").

(among them John M. Clayton, John J. Crittenden of Kentucky, and Willie P. Mangum of North Carolina) arranged a private dinner to launch his candidacy. Over the convivial board the "cream" of Whig politicians pronounced Clay "hors de combat," and by "unanimous assent" named Scott the party candidate for the next contest. "So great was the joy and enthusiasm of the assembly, at the happy and unanimous conclusion," "Ion" continued, "that they embraced each other in mutual exultation at what appeared to be a certainty of success." Plans were made to "announce the General as the chosen candidate," and a short while later his *Life and Times* appeared fresh from the press.[11]

The Scott movement quickly gathered strength in the country. Reports of Scott strength appeared in many quarters, and it was even rumored that Clay had given the candidacy his blessing.[12] By the summer of 1846, however, the movement had ended. It was Scott himself who was responsible.

On 11 May, shortly after news arrived in Washington of the attack by Mexican troops upon American forces outside Matamoros, President Polk received almost unanimous authorization to carry on the war "commenced by the acts of the Republic of Mexico." Two days later he gave Scott command of the army, expecting him to hasten to the scene of war. Scott, however, realized only too well that a decisive military campaign could not be conducted without preparation. It would be August, he pointed out, before volunteers could reach the Rio Grande; moreover, they would arrive coincidentally with the rainy season, when effective military operations would be impossible. He recommended, therefore, that American troops be stationed at some healthful points in the United States during the summer, where they could be given rudimentary training, and then be dispatched to the Mexican border ready for action on 25 September. He himself proposed to leave Washington in sufficient time to make a thorough inspection of preparations and to arrive at the Rio Grande just before the troops.[13]

Such procrastination disgusted Polk; through William L. Marcy, secretary of war, he warned General Scott to "proceed very soon to his post" or be removed from command. A sharp epistolary exchange followed between Marcy and Scott. In the course of the correspondence Scott revealed one reason why he hesitated to leave Washington: he

[11] Baltimore *Sun,* 25 October 1847. See also Seward to Weed, 4, 6 January 1846 (Seward, *Autobiography,* pp. 771–72).

[12] *Cleveland Plain Dealer,* 6 May 1846.

[13] Justin H. Smith, *War with Mexico* (New York, 1919), 1: 196–99. It should be noted that Scott's reasoning proved accurate. It was not until the fall of 1846 that Taylor engaged in a second round of battles with the Mexican army.

feared a political attack. "I do not desire," he confessed, "to place myself in the most perilous of all positions, a fire upon my rear from Washington, and a fire in front from the Mexicans." Simultaneously, a copy of one of Scott's private letters turned up at the White House. In it Scott indicated that he did not expect to exercise any authority over the appointment of officers for the new army. The commissions, he insinuated, were to be used to "pay . . . western democrats. Not an eastern man, not a graduate of the Military academy and certainly not a Whig would obtain a place under such proscriptive circumstances." The president was enraged. Privately denouncing Scott as "recklessly vindictive" toward the administration and as "violently partisan," Polk excused him from his command at the front and ordered him to remain in the discharge of his duties in Washington.[14]

Whig members of Congress, sensing a possible political coup, at once demanded an explanation. Not unwillingly, Polk made public in a message to the Senate the correspondence between Marcy and Scott. A political sensation followed. At one point in his exchange with the secretary of war, Scott had revealed his extreme devotion to duty by remarking that his lunch had consisted merely of a "hasty bowl of soup."[15] Democratic editors, ignoring whatever merit there was in Scott's case, instantly pounced upon the statement to parade it before the country in dozens of hilarious versions to which the nation rocked with laughter. Poems, broadsides, and stinging banter were aimed at the hapless general. One Democratic journal suggested: "As the universal Whig party were once successful with a 'hard cider' candidate, what may they not do with a 'soup candidate.' Thousands eat soup who never would be made to guzzle hard cider. Let the old soup eater cast off his regimentals . . . and . . . take to the field (political) with his spoon and ladle. An army of 'spooneys' would arise at his command." In such an atmosphere the proud banner of Old Fuss and Feathers began to droop; his presidential prospects quickly withered and appeared to die. As the Boston Courier aptly remarked, General Scott had "committed suicide on the point of a goose quill."[16]

[14] James K. Polk, Diary of James K. Polk during His Presidency: 1845 to 1849, ed. Milo M. Quaife (Chicago, 1910), I: 408, 414, 416, 419, 424 (hereafter cited as Polk's Diary); Niles' National Register 70 (13 June 1846): 231–32 (hereafter cited as Niles' Register).

[15] Niles' Register 70 (13 June 1846): 233.

[16] Cleveland Plain Dealer, 17 June 1846; Boston Courier, 15 June 1846. The Tri-Weekly Nashville Union remarked on 2 July 1846: "There never was so signal an instance of felo de se, as that done upon himself by Gen. Scott" (hereafter cited as Nashville Union). See also Zachary Taylor to Richard C. Wood, 24 June 1846, in Zachary Taylor, Letters of Zachary Taylor from the Battlefields of the Mexican

As might be expected, the Scott movement affected McLean's candidacy. Even in its early stages, it worried one of McLean's supporters sufficiently for him to urge that steps be taken to place McLean's name quickly before the public. "It is of importance," he argued, "that your star should be above the horizon ere the time is far spent, that public attention should not be attracted by planets of less magnitude." He suggested that the Indiana Whig Convention of January 1846 would be a suitable place to start McLean's ascent into the political firmament.[17] As General Scott's movement became public, other friends of McLean began to warn him that Scott was making inroads upon his support, even in Ohio, and that McLean was being pushed into the background. After a meeting of Whigs in Huntingdon, Pennsylvania, urged McLean to accept a vice-presidential nomination on a ticket headed by Scott, the Judge's supporters increased their importunities for a public announcement of his candidacy.[18]

McLean refused to panic. He learned that Joseph Chandler, editor of the influential *United States Gazette* of Philadelphia, favored him and that ex-Governor Charles S. Morehead of Kentucky regarded him as the strongest candidate; he was still being assured that "a vast proportion of the Whigs of the Union" preferred him "as their leader and the representative of their principles."[19] He would not permit any demonstrations on his behalf because, he believed, any such action would merely serve to expose him needlessly to the ruthless attacks of other aspirants.[20]

After Scott's decline the agitation to bring McLean into the open abruptly ceased.[21] His position quickly began to improve. During the late summer and fall of 1846 various correspondents reported that "a very excellent feeling" toward him existed in Massachusetts, that Millard Fillmore was friendly, that Tyler's former secretary of war, John C. Spencer, and his former postmaster general, Francis Granger (both leaders of New York's Anti-Masons, who had not supported Clay), and

---

War (Rochester, N. Y., 1908), p. 17 (hereafter cited as *Taylor Letters*); Anthony Butler to Crittenden, 15 June 1846, in Ann Mary Crittenden Coleman, ed., *Life of John J. Crittenden, with Selections from His Correspondence and Speeches* (Philadelphia, 1871), 1: 247 (hereafter cited as *Crittenden*).

[17] Humphrey Marshall to McLean, 19 November 1845, McLean Papers.

[18] Daniel H. Whitney to McLean, 6 January 1846, George Fisher to McLean, 15 February 1846, James E. Harvey to McLean, 24 April 1846, Miner to McLean, 24 April 1846, ibid.

[19] H. Lincoln to McLean, 23 April 1846, John Teesdale to McLean, 23 March 1846, ibid.

[20] McLean to Lewis C. Levin, 26 April 1847, ibid.

[21] The last suggestion that McLean make his candidacy public came from Judge Humphrey H. Leavitt (Leavitt to McLean, 2 July 1846, ibid.).

Judge Robert T. Conrad of Philadelphia openly espoused his cause. He was the favorite of a majority of members in the Ohio, Michigan, and North Carolina legislatures. In Ohio he was "stronger than the Whig strength by from 10 to 20,000 votes." He would be supported by the Seward wing in New York and the Websterians in New England, by the "*best* citizens and men of property," and by the "moral and religious community" that had looked with disfavor upon Henry Clay because he was "a gambler, . . . fond of wine, and other intoxicating drinks . . . and . . . too much addicted to great gallantry among females of all climes and colors."[22]

With his growing popularity, however, came the slowly developing opposition that the Judge had foreseen. McLean's campaign to secure a nomination was centered around the vices of the spoils system; his followers everywhere condemned the "proscription" of the Polk administration and promised a reform if McLean secured the presidency. But this kind of campaign soon gave rise to the rumor that McLean had declared that he would "never . . . consent to turn any man out of office for opinion's sake." His opponents began to argue that this sort of attitude would result in a continuation of Democrats in office—an interpretation that found no favor with hungry Whig office seekers. Objections also arose to McLean's "Methodistical cant," which one of Mangum's correspondents warned would lose the Whig ticket as many votes as the bitter sectarianism of Theodore Frelinghuysen had cost it in 1844. The party could not afford to nominate another "Psalm-Singing Candidate."[23]

Such opposition, however, was regarded as unimportant by McLean's supporters, primarily because it was not attached in any way to another candidate. In late 1846, as a matter of fact, there appeared to be no other serious aspirant for the Whig nomination. A few of McLean's informants occasionally noted that Clay was still very strong among the ward workers of New York City and Philadelphia, but there was no movement on his behalf. They likewise reported no enthusiasm for Daniel Webster, a perennial possibility in New England.

Other Whig prospects had been proposed. During 1845 several leaders

[22] Harvey to Mangum, 25 August, 22 September, 24 October 1846, Willie P. Mangum Papers; Harvey to McLean, 30 August, 3 November 1846, James B. Mower to McLean, 14 November 1846, Miner to McLean, 19 December 1846, Z. Pilcher to McLean, 21 December 1846, McLean Papers; *Cleveland Plain Dealer,* 18 November 1846; *Chicago Democrat,* 24 November 1846.

[23] R. H. Williams to Colonel Sawyer, 25 July 1845, Dunlap to McLean, 29 November 1846, McLean Papers; A. H. Sheppard to Mangum, 21 May 1846, George C. Collins to Mangum, 12 July 1846, Mangum Papers.

of the party suggested that John J. Crittenden was potentially the most available candidate. The men who made these suggestions were generally Clay devotees, such as William J. Graves of Louisville, who believed that the old man had run his last race and who regarded Crittenden as his heir apparent, or Joseph L. White of New York City, who hoped that Clay might still "consent to run against his consent" and felt the need to advance some "*real* Whig" to combat the force of the McLean and Scott movements if Clay refused to enter the contest a fourth time. Crittenden, however, was apparently completely involved in the Scott movement and gave no encouragement to any suggestion that he throw his own hat into the ring. Similar suggestions made shortly after the decline of Scott's candidacy met with the same reaction. Crittenden did not appear to be a candidate.[24] Another of General Scott's early congressional supporters who was importuned to enter the race after Scott's position had deteriorated was John M. Clayton, Delaware's favorite son. But Clayton was opposed to his own candidacy and even refused to allow any of his correspondence to be published, lest it might be inferred that he desired "to court public observation."[25]

A third early congressional supporter of Scott, Willie P. Mangum, was in a somewhat different category. Mentioned very early as a possible running mate for either McLean or Scott, he appeared to be "obviously pleased" with the notice.[26] At the same time, there were some, chiefly outside North Carolina, who felt he deserved a better position on the Whig ticket; it was not improbable that Mangum was willing to be considered for the lesser post in order to keep his name before the public. This strategy was suggested to him early in 1845 by Nicholas Carroll, a fellow North Carolinian who was an executive in a New York insurance firm. He proposed that Mangum be presented "as second" on any ticket that might be formed. In that position he could not be attacked; when the inevitable quarrel between McLean's and Scott's supporters oc-

[24] Graves to Crittenden, 16 February 1845, White to Crittenden, 29 September 1845, John J. Crittenden Papers; Coleman, *Crittenden,* 1: 247-48, 259. See also George R. Poage, *Henry Clay and the Whig Party* (Chapel Hill, N. C., 1936), p. 154 (hereafter cited as *Clay*).

[25] Washington *National Intelligencer,* 22 September 1846 (hereafter cited as *National Intelligencer*); Clayton to Timothy Childs, 23 November 1846, John M. Clayton Papers.

[26] Philadelphia *North American,* 8 July 1846 (hereafter cited as *North American*); *Cleveland Plain Dealer,* 29 July 1846; Nashville *Republican-Banner,* 10, 16 October 1846 (hereafter cited as Nashville *Republican*); Mower to Mangum, 2 August 1846, Harvey to Mangum, 24 October 1846, Mangum Papers; James Graham to William Graham, 20 February 1846, in William Alexander Graham, *Papers of William Alexander Graham,* ed. J. G. de Roulhac Hamilton (Raleigh, N. C., 1960), 3: 106-7 (hereafter cited as *Graham Papers*).

curred, Mangum's friends could "step in as mediators and heal the breach by naming *our second* as the *general first*." If such a scheme existed, it was ended by Scott's political suicide; Mangum thereafter seemed content to have his name connected with McLean's. Accordingly, the Judge's supporters could not regard Mangum as a serious contender for the presidency, even though an occasional voice suggested that he should be considered.[27]

But if McLean had no apparent opponents for nomination in late 1846, there were some developments that caused alarm among his followers. One was an anti-McLean movement in Ohio, whose major figure was Thomas Corwin, the state's junior senator. Evidence of a Corwin movement had been reported to the Judge in late 1844, but little attention was given it until the autumn of the following year, when the Wagon Boy was nominated for the presidency at a dinner party in Philadelphia.[28] Although McLean's adherents considered Corwin's candidacy "little short of madness," privately denounced his followers as "numskulls," and claimed that their number was limited to a few young men of the "ultra school," they were nevertheless forced to admit that the movement was a threat. At first it had appeared dangerous because of its apparent connection with the Scott campaign, in which some included Corwin as Scott's running mate. When Scott's star faded from the political scene, however, reports revealed that Corwin had gathered a considerable following of his own throughout the middle Atlantic states and Ohio and that he was using it not for himself but to deny McLean a nomination.[29] A friend of the Judge explained that Corwin men would support anyone but McLean because if McLean were nominated, no other Ohioan—meaning Corwin—could expect to be named for the presidency in any "reasonable time." Corwin had to stop McLean to protect his own future aspirations.[30]

It was probably this Corwin threat that led to the next developments

[27] Carroll to Mangum, 19 March 1845, Collins to Mangum, 24 March 1846, Mangum Papers; Collins to Mangum, 14 July 1846, in Shanks, *Mangum Papers,* 4: 445–46; *North American,* 8 August 1846.

[28] Miner to McLean, 8 December 1844, McLean Papers; *Cleveland Plain Dealer,* 8 October 1845.

[29] Leavitt to McLean, 29 December 1845, Morris to McLean, 4 December 1845, 12 September 1846, Miner to McLean, 3 January, 11 February, 24 April, 28 September 1846, Harvey to McLean, 24 April 1846, McLean Papers. William Bebb's election as governor of Ohio in 1846 was regarded as a Corwin victory.

[30] Robert Young to McLean, 25 December 1846, McLean Papers. Interestingly, Corwin denied any attempt to supplant McLean in Ohio (Corwin to William Greene, 30 March 1847, in L. Belle Hamlin, ed., "Selections from the William Greene Papers," *Quarterly Publication of the Historical and Philosophical Society of Ohio,* 13 [1918]: 18 [hereafter cited as "Greene Papers"]).

in McLean's campaign. Late in January 1847 friends of the Judge issued a call, signed by more than "300 Merchants, Manufacturers & Mechanics," for a McLean mass meeting in Pittsburgh. This gathering of "Democratic, Anti-Masonic and Whig citizens" endorsed McLean's candidacy, an action which the Judge believed would check the effort to name Corwin.[31] Shortly thereafter "many Members of Congress" recommended him to the Whig National Convention through the columns of the *Washington Fountain* as "an eminently qualified candidate for the next Presidency," and a "memoir" of him was published in Philadelphia.[32] So impressive was McLean's strength in Washington that the Baltimore *Sun* of 29 January 1847 scornfully pronounced him "the favourite of the wire-workers." The Judge was now squarely before the public.

In Democratic ranks, development of presidential movements among friends and associates of aspirants proceeded somewhat more slowly than among Whigs. There was one obvious reason: the party's titular leader occupied the White House, and much doubt existed as to his future intentions. When he accepted the party nomination in 1844, Polk had announced that if elected he would "enter upon the discharge of the high and solemn duties of . . . office with the settled purpose of not being a candidate for re-election." While the statement seemed clear enough, Democrats could readily recall that Jackson, too, had pledged himself to one term. Moreover, some undoubtedly knew that Polk had told his old friend Cave Johnson, who became postmaster general, "I said nothing to commit the party upon the *one term* principle, but expressed simply my own determination."[33] Such a statement could have meant that Polk would take a second nomination if pressed by the party; it could also have meant that he would look with disfavor upon any rival movement.

This latter interpretation was given credence by the fact that Polk had informed prospective members of his cabinet that he would "take no part between gentlemen of the Democratic party" who aspired to the succession; he requested members of his political family to observe the same line of conduct and added, significantly, "Should any member of my cabinet become a Candidate for the Presidency or Vice Presidency, . . .

---

[31] Dunlap to McLean, 15 January, 6 February 1847, Leavitt to McLean, 24 January 1847, McLean Papers; Baltimore *Sun*, 26 January 1847; McLean to Teesdale, 6 February 1847, John Teesdale Papers; McLean to Mangum, 30 January 1847, Mangum Papers.

[32] Baltimore *Sun*, 1 February 1847; *Baltimore Clipper*, 8 February 1847.

[33] Eugene I. McCormac, *James K. Polk: A Political Biography* (Berkeley, Calif., 1922), p. 259.

it will be expected . . . that he will retire from the Cabinet." Shortly after his inauguration the *Washington Madisonian* announced, "as if by authority," that anyone who agitated the succession "before three years" would "incur the President's displeasure."[34] Although such covert threats of proscription undoubtedly caused party aspirants to hesitate before launching any campaigns that would cause a breach with the White House, it did not stay their ambitions nor stop the activities of their supporters and friends; moreover, it did not long check those who for one reason or another had grievances against the president.

One of the first to make known his possible aspirations was Polk's secretary of state, James Buchanan. The Pennsylvanian had been an avowed candidate for the 1844 Democratic nomination until it became evident that the forces behind a renomination for Martin Van Buren were too strong to overcome; he had then withdrawn from the race, and no amount of pressure from his supporters could induce him to change his mind—even when it became evident that the adoption of the two-thirds rule by the 1844 Democratic National Convention had checked the Van Buren movement.[35] Nevertheless, he had secured some support in the 1844 convention, and knowledge of that support must have made him realize that he was a possibility for 1848. He stated his recognition of the situation in his reply to Polk's request for a pledge against agitation of the succession. He pointed out that he "would not & could not" accept the State Department "at the expense of self-ostracism." "My friends would unanimously condemn me were I to pursue this course," he explained. "I cannot proclaim to the world that in no contingency shall I be a candidate for the Presidency in 1848."[36]

That Buchanan's friends expected him to be a contender became evident in the spring of 1845, when Polk offered him one of the vacancies on the United States Supreme Court, and the rumor promptly arose that Buchanan would resign from the cabinet to accept the offer. Some suggested that he stay in the cabinet as the best place from which to conduct a presidential campaign; others suggested that he go to the

[34] Polk to Buchanan, 17 February 1845, in James Buchanan, *Works of James Buchanan: Comprising His Speeches, State Papers, and Private Correspondence,* ed. John B. Moore (Philadelphia, 1909), 6: 110 (hereafter cited as *Buchanan's Works*); Duff Green to Calhoun, 26 March 1845, in Chauncey S. Boucher and Robert P. Brooks, eds., *Correspondence Addressed to John C. Calhoun: 1837-1849* (Washington, D. C., 1930), p. 288 (hereafter cited as *Calhoun Correspondence*).
[35] The best accounts of the Buchanan movement in 1843-1844 are in Charles M. Snyder, *The Jacksonian Heritage: Pennsylvania Politics, 1833-1848* (Harrisburg, Pa., 1958) (hereafter cited as *Jacksonian Heritage*); and Philip S. Klein, *President James Buchanan* (University Park, Pa., 1962).
[36] Buchanan to Polk, 18 February 1845, in Moore, *Buchanan's Works,* 6: 112.

bench, "from which some of our next Presidents will be taken."[37] Although Buchanan informed Polk that he would rather be chief justice than president, he declined the offer. Later rumors of his impending resignation to take some other post produced the same kind of reaction and the same result. Buchanan never resigned, even after asking Polk on one occasion for an immediate appointment to the bench. Indeed, the continual rumors of his impending resignation raised the question of whether or not they may have been part of the effort to keep his name before the public; one of his political enemies suggested that the rumors were "all smoke:—a method of keeping up his importance resorted to by his partisans."[38]

There was other evidence that Buchanan was a possible aspirant. One supporter very early advised him to prevent any "misunderstanding" with the administration of Francis Shunk, governor of Pennsylvania, whose support he would need to secure a favorable state delegation to the next convention; others kept him well informed about the efforts of his enemy Vice President George M. Dallas to secure control of Federal patronage in Philadelphia, where Buchanan was reputedly weak and where a base for an anti-Buchanan movement could be established.[39] Buchanan himself exerted strenuous efforts to secure control of all Federal patronage in Pennsylvania, leading Polk to complain as early as January 1846 that Buchanan was being false to his promises: "He accepted his place in my cabinet under the written pledge . . . that during his continuance in it he would not become a candidate for the Presidency, and yet it is manifest that he desired to control my patronage with that view."[40] In the early spring of 1846 Polk also saw a presidential maneuver in Buchanan's shift from a rather moderate position concerning American claims to all of Oregon, which the secretary of state was even then in the process of negotiating, to a more belligerent attitude:

[37] George F. Lehman to Buchanan, 26 March 1845, Peter S. Sumworth to Buchanan, 15 July 1845, James L. Barbour to Buchanan, 19 July 1845, Isaac E. Holmes to Buchanan, 13 April 1845, Robert Letcher to Buchanan, 22 October 1845, James Buchanan Papers.

[38] Quaife, *Polk's Diary*, 1: 98–99, 189–90, 200–201; 2: 1–2; Daniel Webster to Fletcher Webster, 27 January 1846, in Daniel Webster, *Writings and Speeches of Daniel Webster*, National Edition (Boston, 1903), 16: 443 (hereafter cited as *Webster's Writings*); Edward Johnston to Buchanan, 12 August 1846, Buchanan Papers; Dallas to his wife, 14 June 1846, George M. Dallas Papers.

[39] Henry Welch to Buchanan, 18 September 1845, Lehman to Buchanan, 26 March 1845, Buchanan Papers.

[40] Quaife, *Polk's Diary*, 1: 200–201. See also 1: 183–85, 189–90, 220, 488–89; 2: 202.

He recently mentioned to me, that Gen'l Cass . . . was making political capital by insisting on our extreme rights on the question. . . . Within a few days past it is pretty manifest to me, that Mr. Buchanan has manifested a decided change of his position, and a disposition to be warlike. His object . . . is to supercede Gen'l Cass before the country, and to this motive I attribute his change of tone and the warlike character of his draft of my proposed message. I think he is governed by his own views of his chances for the Presidency.[41]

That Polk's suspicion was probably correct was indicated in a letter to Buchanan from Albany, New York, where the Pennsylvanian's correspondent had been discussing his prospects: "The Oregon correspondence shed new light on the claims which your friends advanced in your favor. You have gained and are still gaining hourly."[42]

Buchanan was probably not the only member of Polk's official family who had aspirations for higher office. Early in the new administration there were speculations concerning Robert J. Walker, who as senator from Mississippi had led the successful southern movement against Van Buren's quest for a renomination at the Democratic convention of 1844. Walker had become secretary of the treasury, a position that gave him a strong hand in the dispensation of the department's not inconsiderable patronage; there were some who were certain he was using that patronage on his own behalf. He was also related by marriage to Vice President Dallas, and there were those who saw in this relationship the making of a movement to give him either first or second place on the next presidential ticket.[43]

But most early presidential aspirants among Democrats appeared outside Polk's cabinet. Among them was the vice president. Onetime United States senator, political rival of Buchanan, and strong man of the party in Philadelphia, Dallas was generally considered to be the leader of the Van Buren element in Pennsylvania, and his nomination for the vice-presidency in 1844 after Silas Wright had declined was regarded as

[41] Ibid., 1 : 297. Secretary of the Navy George Bancroft agreed with Polk's opinion (1 : 299).

[42] C. L. Ward to Buchanan, 14 March 1846, Buchanan Papers.

[43] Samuel Medary to Van Buren, 22 May 1845, Martin Van Buren Papers; L. Sanders, Jr., to Crittenden, 20 September 1846, Crittenden Papers; Andrew Jackson to Polk, 2 May 1845, in Lyon G. Tyler, Letters and Times of the Tylers (Williamsburg, Va., 1896), 3 : 162 (hereafter cited as Tylers) ; S. Penn to Calhoun, 26 June 1845, in Boucher and Brooks, Calhoun Correspondence, pp. 298–300; Concord New Hampshire Patriot and State Gazette, 1 January 1846 (hereafter cited as New Hampshire Patriot).

an effort to placate the disappointed supporters of the former president.

While evidence indicating that there was a Dallas movement is slight, there is little doubt that one existed. Buchanan's correspondents found it obliquely in Dallas's unsuccessful efforts to control Federal patronage in Pennsylvania; in the late summer of 1845 they found it more directly when they discovered that the "friends of Dallas" were agitating the succession in the rural areas of Pennsylvania. Polk apparently sensed the movement. Dallas himself indirectly revealed his aspirations in letters to his wife which showed distress—"a most dangerous choice"—over Buchanan's appointment to the cabinet; he also disclosed his maneuverings in 1846 when he suggested to Polk the appointment of Governor Francis Shunk, whom Dallas supporters regarded as friendly to Buchanan, to a Federal office to "promote the harmony of the Democratic party in Penna."[44]

Another Democrat occasionally mentioned in 1845 as a possible contender for nomination was Silas Wright, governor of New York. A respected leader for many years of the Democratic party in the United States Senate and widely recognized as Van Buren's first lieutenant, he had been nominated for the vice-presidency by acclamation at the party convention in 1844, as compensation to the New York Democracy for the rebuff given Little Van. Wright had declined; he did not want a position which he compared to that of "the hearse behind the black pony"—an obvious indication of his feeling that the Democratic ticket was doomed to defeat. But he had then been persuaded to resign his seat in the Senate and to accept leadership of the Democratic forces in the Empire State in their effort to salvage the party from the consequences of Van Buren's rejection and Polk's nomination.

In the contest that followed, Wright, as candidate for governor, rolled up a majority twice as large as that secured by the national ticket; indeed, there were some who believed that Wright had carried Polk to victory.[45] The event, of course, was widely noticed: it established the New Yorker as a strong and popular figure, so strong in fact that one of McLean's supporters thought the Judge could win against "any Competition" but that of Silas Wright.[46]

---

[44] Lehman to Buchanan, 26 March 1845, Welch to Buchanan, 18 September 1845, Buchanan Papers; Dallas to his wife, 22 February 1845, Dallas Papers; Quaife, *Polk's Diary*, 2: 260-61.

[45] For an account of Wright's involvement in the campaign of 1844 see John A. Garraty, *Silas Wright* (New York, 1949) (hereafter cited as *Wright*).

[46] Charles W. Cutler to Bellamy Storer, 26 November 1844, McLean Papers. The respect of the Whigs for Wright's strength is well illustrated by a letter Carroll

Despite this strength, it was not until 1846 that Wright's name was mentioned with any frequency as a possible contender. In March of that year one of Buchanan's correspondents learned during a tour of New York that the Van Buren wing was advancing Wright for the presidency; in May, Secretary of War Marcy learned that political intrigues were being plotted to secure Wright's nomination. By September the movement had proceeded far enough to lead newspapers from as far away as Georgia and Tennessee to conclude that Wright would be the next choice of the Democratic party.[47] Meanwhile, Wright gave no indication that he thought of himself as a contender; he was deeply involved in his duties as governor of New York and in the entanglements of New York's Democratic politics. Moreover, unlike most other possible candidates, he was facing a campaign for reelection.[48]

Perhaps the most widely recognized Democratic aspirant for the 1848 nomination in the early years of Polk's administration was Lewis Cass, senator from Michigan. Long a political figure—as governor of Michigan Territory, as Jackson's secretary of war, as minister to France, and as a United States senator—Cass had been at the front of the anti–Van Buren movement in the Democratic convention of 1844.[49] Cass's campaign for delegates in 1844 had laid a firm foundation for his possible candidacy in most states of the Northwest.

In Ohio, which had remained loyal to Van Buren, a Cass faction began to form late in 1844 to prevent the expected appointment of a Van Buren man, Samuel Medary, as postmaster general. Early in the following year this faction was enlarged by the accession of some "Softs," advocates of paper money and opponents of the state's banking laws, which provided that no bank could begin operations until all of its capital had been paid in gold and silver and which also provided for the individual liability of stockholders and officers of the banks for losses

---

wrote to Mangum on 18 September 1844: "Silas Wright is nominated for Governor. He is the strongest man the destructives *can* boast—he is the hardest man for us to beat. . . . With *any other* nomination our success was assured" (Shanks, *Mangum Papers*, 4: 180–81).

[47] Alexander Gardiner to Mrs. John Tyler, 22 February 1846, in Tyler, *Tylers*, 2: 453–54; Corwin to Follett, 20 August 1846, in Hamlin, "Follett Papers," 10 (1915): 88; Ward to Buchanan, 14 March 1846, Buchanan Papers; W. L. G. Smith to Marcy, 6 May 1846, William L. Marcy Papers; *Savannah Daily Republican*, 1 September 1846 (hereafter cited as *Savannah Republican*); Nashville *Republican*, 4 September 1846.

[48] The best account of Wright's governorship is in Garraty, *Wright*, pp. 334–84.

[49] There are accounts of Cass's role in the 1844 convention in Andrew C. McLaughlin, *Lewis Cass* (Boston, 1891); and Frank B. Woodford, *Lewis Cass: The Last Jeffersonian* (New Brunswick, N. J., 1950) (hereafter cited as *Cass*).

suffered by depositors. The Softs believed that Senator William A. Allen was using his position to channel patronage to the "Hards," supporters of "the constitutional currency of gold and silver" and of strict banking laws.[50] Cass's position in the Buckeye State continued to improve during the year, largely, as Allen was informed, because of "his age, his *fancied* military services in The Last War, his services abroad, together with his Western position."[51]

Cass's "Western position" also became important in other northwestern states. Polk's failure to appoint a northwesterner to his cabinet and a feeling that the Northwest had not been given its fair share of lesser appointments made many an office seeker turn to Cass as a man who would correct the situation.[52] In addition, there was the Oregon issue: "Fifty-Four Forty" was a popular cry in the Northwest—even Whigs supported it—and Cass identified himself completely by his votes and speeches in the Senate with the advocates of extreme American claims. Polk and others maintained that Cass took this stand because it provided him with "his best chance of reaching the Presidency." The favorable reaction in the Northwest was good evidence that Cass's pretensions were well advanced by his position. He also attracted support among some elements in New York and favorable attention in "Virginia and . . . large portions of the South."[53]

Thus there was no doubt that Cass was an active aspirant for the Democratic nomination. During 1846 he was constantly writing to influential politicians in all sections of the nation for names of newspapers and "prominent Democrats" to whom he could send copies of his speeches on Oregon. In late 1846 he indirectly admitted his candidacy to his friend Henry N. Walker. While he protested that he never expected "to feel better in public life" than he did in his current position and that

---

[50] Thomas Drake to Allen, 14 December 1844, G. B. Flood to Allen, 22 December 1844, James Hough to Allen, 4 January 1845, H. V. Wilson to Allen, 9 April 1845, H. C. Whitman to Allen, 23 November 1845, William H. Allen Papers; Edgar A. Holt, "Party Politics in Ohio: 1840–1850," *Ohio Archeological and Historical Publications* 37 (1928): 560–64; 38 (1929): 111–12 (hereafter cited as "Party Politics in Ohio").

[51] Whitman to Allen, 26 January 1848, Allen Papers.

[52] Corwin to Follett, 7 March 1845, in Hamlin, "Follett Papers," p. 83; *Boston Daily Atlas*, 6 July 1846 (hereafter cited as *Boston Atlas*); Whitman to Allen, 23 November 1845, Allen Papers.

[53] John Niles to Welles, 15 December 1845, Gideon Welles Papers; Joseph Cable to Allen, 24 June 1846, Whitman to Allen, 26 January 1846, Allen Papers; Silas M. Stilwell to Daniel S. Dickinson, 17 March 1847, in Daniel S. Dickinson, *Speeches, Correspondence, etc., of the Late Daniel S. Dickinson, of New York*, ed. John R. Dickinson (New York, 1867), 2:382 (hereafter cited as *Dickinson*); Quaife, *Polk's Diary*, 1:154; 2:264–65.

he would be "as happy a man as our country affords" if he could be allowed quietly to serve out his term in the Senate, at the same time he cautioned against any premature action by his friends: "I am under the decided impression that no demonstrations should be made in Michigan in my favor at present." The time was not ripe. "In the present state of things if one portion of the party push a man the other will assuredly oppose him. It is therefore better to leave time for public opinion to develop." By this time, however, Cass's aspirations were well enough known for him to be assigned a vice-presidential running mate, General William O. Butler of Kentucky.[54]

While it was clear that Cass was a candidate, it was also obvious that his support was not overwhelming. As Gideon Welles pointed out, his partisans in Congress were not numerous. Despite the fact that Cass had a "good deal of ability and tact," was a tolerable debater, an elegant writer, and had received "some experience as a statesman," his supporters were fewer than might have been expected. What injured him among his fellow congressmen, Welles believed, was "his want of courage, his timidity, his fear of responsibility." On every occasion he appeared to be "more anxious" to know how he was affected by his votes than how his votes would affect the country. There was, moreover, a "want of definiteness in his character." While he and his friends "try to identify him with the Democratic party and its principles," the Yankee politician declared, "there is a vagueness as concerns his own principles and opinions—an impression that he merely supports measures because others do, whose support he wants, and not from hearty conviction and honest zeal."[55]

Besides this lack of support in Congress, Cass had strong enemies in the Northwest—the devoted supporters of Van Buren, many of whom were certain that "all the intrigues" against Van Buren at the 1844 Democratic convention had been spawned by the Michigander. Determined to keep Cass out of the White House, some of them turned to William Allen of Ohio, who became the *New York Herald*'s announced candidate in 1845. As one of Allen's friends pointed out, many were raising the cry "The West, the long neglected & the mighty West" to advance the fortunes of Cass. It was necessary, therefore, to present

[54] Cass to Aaron Hobart, 20 June, 2 September 1846, Lewis Cass Papers (Clements); Cass to A. O. P. Nicholson, 22 September 1846, Lewis Cass Papers (Burton); Cass to McClelland, 4, 21 September 1846, Robert McClelland Papers; Cass to Pierce, 2 September 1846, Franklin Pierce Photostats; Cass to Walker, 26 December 1846, Henry N. Walker Papers; *Chicago Democrat,* 15 December 1846.

[55] Welles to [?], 27 February 1847, Welles Papers. See also Daniel Mallory to Mangum, 22 December 1845, Mangum Papers.

"another Western man" to meet the threat: "Lewis Cass must be beat. He can only be beat by a Western man. I say William Allen of Ohio must be the man." But Old Fog Horn refused to be enticed. While he informed Polk that he did not favor Cass, at the same time he announced that he was not a candidate.[56]

Another Democrat who may have been an early aspirant for the nomination was Levi Woodbury of New Hampshire. Long an "examplar" of the Democracy in New England, a member of the cabinet in both the Jackson and the Van Buren administrations, Woodbury was in the Senate when Polk was inaugurated. Both his relatives and his friends promptly started to advise him of ways to advance his prospects. One suggested that he accept an appointment as minister to England because it would enable his supporters to give him "a splendid dinner in Boston" which would "strengthen" his chances for the presidency; another suggested that he become acquainted with the Democrats in the southern tier of counties in New York and the northern tier of counties in Pennsylvania, where the people, "mainly from the New England States," held "the balance of power in President making." Still others advised him to cultivate the Calhoun element because there was evidence that it was willing to make an alliance.[57]

What Woodbury thought of this advice has not been recorded. However, if he had any hope of securing the support of the Calhoun element, it must have been slight, for at this stage John C. Calhoun was himself a contender. The name of the South Carolinian—twice a vice president, twice a cabinet member, ofttimes a United States senator, and an 1844 hopeful—had appeared on the list of presidential aspirants shortly after Polk's election.[58] At the time, many of Calhoun's friends and some of his

[56] John Lane to Van Buren, 25 March 1846, Van Buren Papers; Columbus *Ohio Statesman*, 28 November 1845 (hereafter cited as *Ohio Statesman*) ; Whitman to Allen, 23 November 1845, Allen Papers; Quaife, *Polk's Diary*, 1 : 300.

[57] Charles W. Woodbury to Levi Woodbury, 21 April 1845, Seth Salisbury to Levi Woodbury, 1 May 1845, J. T. Tasker to Levi Woodbury, 3 January 1846, Charles L. Woodbury to Levi Woodbury, 13 January 1846, Levi Woodbury Papers. Calhounites' interest in Woodbury was indicated in a letter from W. A. Harris to Calhoun, 4 August 1845; "Mr. Woodbury," he wrote, "was the only man in the Senate "upon whom we can depend" (Boucher and Brooks, *Calhoun Correspondence*, p. 311). See also John B. Lamar to Cobb, 8 June 1846, in Ulrich B. Phillips, ed., *Correspondence of Robert Toombs, Alexander H. Stephens, and Howell Cobb* (Washington, D. C., 1913), p. 81 (hereafter cited as *Toombs, Stephens, and Cobb Correspondence*).

[58] All of Calhoun's biographers have dealt with his efforts to win the Democratic nomination in 1844. See Herman E. von Holst, *John C. Calhoun* (Boston, 1882) ; Gaillard Hunt, *John C. Calhoun* (Philadelphia, 1908) ; William M. Meigs, *The Life of John Caldwell Calhoun*, 2 vols. (New York, 1917) ; Arthur Stryon, *The Cast-Iron Man: John C. Calhoun and American Democracy* (New York, 1935) ;

enemies believed that the movement to annex Texas before the inauguration of the new administration was part of a maneuver to keep him in
the cabinet "in order to prepare for accession in 1848."[59]

When the South Carolinian was forced to retire, returning to his
home at Fort Hill to tend to his broken health and his long-neglected
private affairs, many predicted that his ambitions would create a party
revolt in the near future.[60] Joseph Gray, editor of the *Cleveland Plain
Dealer,* voiced the prevailing Democratic opinion early in the Polk
administration when he declared that Calhoun's retirement had produced
"the most painful suspicion" that his "fancied wrongs" would "ere long
burst forth in open disaffection." True, he admitted, "Mr. Calhoun
leaves the cabinet, leaves Washington, and leaves his friends without
uttering one word of complaint, but he also leaves without a word of
commendation. This very *silence* is ominous! It is idle to suppose that he
retires from a field of thirty years labor, where his ambition has figured
incessantly . . . to the solitude and simplicity of private life without
casting a 'long and lingering look behind.' "[61]

For his own part, Calhoun denied any "hostile feelings" toward Polk.
"It is no grievance to me, personally," he informed Robert M. T. Hunter
of Virginia, that Polk "did not invite me to remain. . . . If he had, I

Margaret L. Coit, *John C. Calhoun: American Portrait* (Boston, 1950) ; Charles
M. Wiltse, *John C. Calhoun, Sectionalist: 1840–1850* (New York, 1951) ; Gerald
M. Capers, *John C. Calhoun, Opportunist: A Reappraisal* (Gainesville, Fla., 1960).
Except for Stryon, who hints at them, and Capers, who affirms them, none relates
Calhoun's later ambitions. In this account I have followed my own findings,
published as "The Presidential Ambitions of John C. Calhoun, 1845–1848," *Journal
of Southern History* 14 (August 1948) : 331–56 (hereafter cited as "Calhoun's
Presidential Ambitions").

[59] John Fairfield to Van Buren, 21 December 1844, Van Buren Papers. See also
Niles to Van Buren, 30 December 1844, Niles to Welles, 24 December 1844, W. S.
Holabird to Niles, 20 November 1844, Welles Papers; Sam Vinton to Greene, 15
December 1844, in Hamlin, "Greene Papers," 14 (1919) : 19; Hammond to William
McDuffie, 27 December 1844, Daniel I. McCord to Hammond, 12 December 1844,
James H. Hammond Papers; James A. Seddon to Robert M. T. Hunter, 16
November 1844, in Robert M. T. Hunter, *Correspondence of Robert M. T. Hunter,
1826–1876,* ed. Charles Ambler (Washington, D. C., 1918), p. 73 (hereafter cited as
Hunter Correspondence).

[60] In the spring of 1845 a number of politicians, either from the South or
otherwise associated with Calhoun, came to the conclusion that Polk's administration was dominated by Van Buren men (James Graham to William Graham, 20
March 1845, in Hamilton, *Graham Papers,* 3:33; C. L. Woodbury to Levi
Woodbury, 15 March 1845, Woodbury Papers). So strong was this belief that
Calhoun's best biographer appears to accept it as fact (Wiltse, *Calhoun,* 3:
227–28).

[61] *Cleveland Plain Dealer,* 26 March 1845. See also Daniel Webster to Fletcher
Webster, 12 March 1845, in *Webster's Writings,* 16: 431.

would not have accepted."[62] In spite of such attempts at concealment, Calhoun's associates knew he had been "deeply wounded," and they expected that they would soon be summoned "to kick up a 'damned fuss generally.'"[63]

That Calhoun and his close supporters were rightly suspected of the highest ambitions soon became privately evident. In May 1845 Franklin H. Elmore, president of the Bank of South Carolina, arranged a gathering at his home to decide how Calhoun's presidential interests could best be advanced. The meeting concluded that "for the *present*" it would be wisest for Calhoun to remain in private life.[64] What Calhoun thought of the advice is unknown; in mid-May, however, he disclosed his ambitions and a plan to achieve his goal in a letter to an unidentified recipient, perhaps Richard K. Crallé, editor of the *Lynchburg Virginian*. He proposed the creation of a movement against the system of nominating presidential candidates in convention, where his hopes had often foundered. When such a movement had been sufficiently developed in the South,

> then my friends if they should choose to present my name as the proper candidate in opposition to the Convention Candidate, may do it with success. . . . If we are resolute and determined, the office-seekers and office-holders will succumb. . . . With them a half-loaf is better than none; and prospect of success is better than no prospect. In no other way . . . can we succeed. The mercenary corp will never permit power to be put in my hands, if they can elect another. . . . But had rather see me elected than an opponent from whom they have nothing to hope.[65]

Whether Calhoun's friends acted upon these instructions is impossible to determine, but gradually, almost imperceptibly, a Calhoun movement began to appear. In June 1845 Joel R. Poinsett informed Van Buren that "the spirit which stalked abroad over this land in 1830–32" was being "conjured up" and that those behind it could "only be conciliated by a cordial, open and undivided support of their candidate for the succession."[66] By early autumn there were indications of a strong Calhoun current. From Virginia came reports that he was gaining strength every day, even among Whigs. In Baltimore "all the Tyler men . . . and

[62] Calhoun to Hunter, 26 March 1845, in Ambler, *Hunter Correspondence*, p. 75.
[63] James M. Walker to Hammond, 22 March 1845, Hammond Papers.
[64] Dixon H. Lewis to Calhoun, 9 May 1845, in Boucher and Brooks, *Calhoun Correspondence*, pp. 293–94.
[65] Calhoun to [?], 16 May 1845, in Ambler, *Hunter Correspondence*, p. 78.
[66] Poinsett to Van Buren, 2 June 1845, Van Buren Papers.

the disappointed and to be disappointed Polk men" favored him. In New York City, among the "Young Democracy" represented by Fernando Wood, there was support for Calhoun which one friend suggested would ripen "into a confidence and enthusiasm that no selfish or designing combination of corrupt partizans could ever remove."[67]

In late 1845 Calhoun accepted election to the Senate, a step that may have been taken at the behest of friends outside South Carolina who felt the need of congressional leadership and who insisted that he would thus be able to bring himself more directly before the public. The immediate effects appeared beneficial. Calhoun's opposition to the "all of Oregon" movement found hearty response in various quarters. Crallé reported that the Calhoun forces were in "high spirits" in Virginia; indeed, they were beginning to worry about excessive "cordiality" on the part of the Whigs. In Georgia one informant disclosed a steadily increasing movement among states' rights wings of both parties "to rally" to him. Further evidence of support came from Connecticut, from Pennsylvania, from the free-trade Whigs of New York City, from the friends of Edward M. McLane of Delaware, and from Florida. The election of Robert M. T. Hunter and John Y. Mason as senators from Virginia early in 1847 appeared to foretell a long series of victories for the Calhoun forces.[68] The South Carolinian reflected this attitude in a letter to his son-in-law in January 1847: "My friends think I never stood higher, or stronger than I now do. Time has justified the wisdom of my course."[69]

In all these efforts to promote contenders for the presidential nominations during 1845–1846, there was one significant omission: almost no

[67] H. W. Conner to Calhoun, 28 September 1845, Crallé to Calhoun, 23 September 1845, Fernando Wood to Calhoun, 26 December 1845, in John C. Calhoun, *Correspondence of John C. Calhoun*, ed. J. Franklin Jameson (Washington, D. C., 1900), pp. 1057, 1052, 1066 (hereafter cited as *Calhoun Correspondence*); Robert Beale to Calhoun, 31 August 1845, in Boucher and Brooks, *Calhoun Correspondence*, p. 303.

[68] James S. Barbour to Calhoun, 26 June 1845, Harris to Calhoun, 4 August 1845, Crallé to Calhoun, 3 May 1846, W. C. Daniell to Calhoun, 2 April 1846, Edward J. Black to Calhoun, 22 February 1846, Samuel Bishop to Calhoun, 11 June 1846, James B. Sawyer to Calhoun, 10 July 1846, in Boucher and Brooks, *Calhoun Correspondence*, pp. 298, 301–2, 343–44, 338–39, 326, 348–49, 351–52; James Hamilton to Calhoun, 12 October 1846, F. W. Byrdsall to Calhoun, 14 February 1847, in Jameson, *Calhoun Correspondence*, pp. 1090–91, 1093, 1104; Tallahassee *Floridian*, 2 January 1847 (hereafter cited as *Floridian*); *Daily Richmond Enquirer*, 16 January 1847 (hereafter cited as *Richmond Enquirer*).

[69] Calhoun to Thomas G. Clemson, 30 January 1847, in Jameson, *Calhoun Correspondence*, p. 700. See also Calhoun to Henry A. S. Dearborn, 2 July 1846, Calhoun to Lewis S. Coryell, 7 November 1846, Calhoun to Mrs. T. G. Clemson, 21 November 1846, pp. 700, 709–10, 713.

attention was given to principles and issues. McLean and Calhoun expressed opposition to the prevailing maldistribution of patronage; Calhoun opposed the convention system of nominating presidential candidates; Buchanan, Cass, and Calhoun put forward positions on the Oregon issue. But there were no revelations of more far-reaching attitudes. However, the situation was of short duration. Events of late 1846 and early 1847 caused major changes—both in men and in attention given to measures.

Chapter Two

The Wilmot Proviso

The event that caused the greatest change in the campaign was the introduction of the Wilmot Proviso late in the first session of the Twenty-ninth Congress. On 8 August 1846, President Polk requested Congress to appropriate $2 million to enable him to bring about a speedy termination of the war with Mexico. Since he expected that an adjustment of the boundary between the two republics would probably be the chief obstacle to establishment of a peace, he suggested that a settlement might be expedited if "we . . . pay a fair equivalent for any concessions which may be made by Mexico." Under such circumstances, he thought, it would be wise to place a sum of money into his hands "to be advanced, if need be," to the Mexican government upon its ratification of the treaty. This arrangement, he contended, would avoid any inconvenience which might be met if all payments were delayed until the Senate should approve a treaty and Congress should make appropriations for the whole amount that might be involved.[1] A bill appropriating $2 million was immediately introduced into the House of Representatives by James J. McKay of North Carolina.

To those who opposed the war on partisan grounds and to those northerners who regarded the war as a southern conspiracy to extend the limits of slavery, the proposition looked like a grandiose scheme "to purchase California, and a large part of Mexico to boot."[2] After a brief recess and a short, stirring session of debates, Congressman David Wilmot, Democrat from the Bradford district of Pennsylvania (a region strongly influenced by emigrants from New England) submitted an amendment:

> *Provided,* That as an express and fundamental condition to the acquisition of any territory from the Republic of Mexico by the United States, by virtue of any treaty which may be negotiated with them, and to the use by the Executive of the moneys herein appropriated, neither slavery nor involuntary servitude shall exist in any part of said territory, except for crime whereof the party shall first be duly convicted.[3]

Almost no effort was made to defeat the amendment; the bill and the Proviso both passed the House, 87 votes to 64. But the measure received no consideration in the Senate, where it reached the floor an hour before the end of the session; because of some misunderstanding concerning time, it was talked to death by one of its professed friends, John Davis of Massachusetts.[4]

Initial reaction to the Proviso revealed a nation strangely indifferent to the issue presented. In the South, where after the election of 1844 many were concerned over the growing strength of abolitionism, it was given very little attention. A few South Carolina newspapers were mildly alarmed, but even the *Pendleton Messenger,* reputed to be Calhoun's journal, was at first inclined to dismiss the issue. Later it announced that the South "would not yield an inch" beyond the Missouri Compromise line.[5]

In the North there had been plentiful indications of opposition to the further extension of slavery before the introduction of the Proviso;

[1] James D. Richardson, comp., *Compilation of the Messages and Papers of the Presidents* (Washington, D. C., 1896–1899), 4: 459–60.

[2] See Charles B. Going, *David Wilmot: Free-Soiler* (New York, 1924), p. 75 (hereafter cited as *Wilmot*).

[3] *Congressional Globe,* 29th Cong., 1st sess., p. 1217. There was a slight amendment (Going, *Wilmot,* pp. 101–2). President Polk called the Proviso "mischievous and foolish." He wondered "what connection slavery had with making peace with Mexico." Later he informed Wilmot: "I did not desire to extend slavery, that I would be satisfied to acquire by Treaty from Mexico the Provinces of New Mexico and the Californias, and that in these Provinces slavery could probably never exist" (Quaife, *Polk's Diary,* 2: 75, 289).

[4] Going, *Wilmot,* pp. 101–5. In later years questions concerning the authorship and motivations of the Proviso arose to plague historians. It was claimed by some—among them John B. McMaster, Hermann E. von Holst, and Henry Wilson —that Jacob Brinckerhoff, Democratic representative from Ohio, had prepared the amendment, and then because he realized that his known antagonism to the administration would preclude his recognition on the floor, he persuaded Wilmot, a man of excellent standing with the administration because of his vote for the Walker Tariff, to submit it (John B. McMaster, *History of the People of the United States from the Revolution to the Civil War* (New York, 1910), 7: 451; Hermann E. von Holst, *Constitutional and Political History of the United States* (Chicago, 1881), 3: 87; Henry Wilson, *History of the Rise and Fall of the Slave Power in America* (Boston, 1874), 2:16 (hereafter cited as *Slave Power*); Alexander H. McClure, *Recollections of a Half-Century* (Salem, Mass., 1902), p. 36). Wilmot's biographer has ably disposed of all doubts on the question (Going, *Wilmot,* pp. 130–41). For accounts of Wilmot's motives see Clark E. Persinger, "The Bargain of 1844 as the Origin of the Wilmot Proviso," *Annual Report of the American Historical Association* 1911: 187–97; and Richard R. Stenberg, "Motivations of the Wilmot Proviso," *Mississippi Valley Historical Review* 18 (1932): 535–41.

[5] James Hamilton to Hammond, 9 December 1844, Armistead Burt to Hammond, 20 December 1844, Hammond Papers; Philip M. Hamer, *Secession Movement in South Carolina, 1847–1852* (Allentown, Pa., 1918), pp. 1–2.

expressions of this opposition had come chiefly from New England and from the Yankee Belt in declarations similar to that of the *Cleveland Plain Dealer:* "The West has but to say that *no more slave territory shall be annexed to the Union,* and the dark tide of slavery will be stayed. . . . Let the motto be written on the back of every man's vote when the question arises—'NO MORE SLAVE TERRITORY.' "[6] It was this latent antislavery sentiment that had provided the popular foundation for the Proviso. Yet, introduction of the measure did not appear to increase interest in the issue during 1846. Local Whig conventions in Michigan avowed their determination to "wage an endless war against further extension of Slave Territory," and a Democratic journal in New Hampshire announced: "We regard Slavery as a great moral, social and political evil—as a foul blot upon our national escutcheon—an evil which must sooner or later be removed; and we believe that not only the cause of humanity, but the interest and permanent prosperity of the South would be advanced by the abolition of Slavery."[7] Although these sentiments were typical, they were no more numerous, no more fervent than earlier expressions upon the issue. There was, in short, no spontaneous outburst of antislavery sentiment in the North among either Democrats or Whigs.

Nevertheless, antislavery sentiment ran deep in the northern conscience. The *Newark Advertiser* expressed it well: "If public sentiment at the North is properly manifested there is an end to the extension of the area of slavery. . . . It is one of the things about which there is an almost entire concurrence of opinion among reflecting men of every party and degree in the free states."[8] This sentiment was apparently fully revealed to northern congressmen during the fall elections; when Congress reconvened for its lame-duck session in December 1846, it became obvious that there were many members determined to push an antislavery program to its bitter end.

Early in January 1847 Congressman Preston King, Democrat from the Saint Lawrence district of northern New York, requested permission to introduce a substitute for the "Two Million Bill," with the Proviso attached. His application was refused. He renewed his request during a discussion of Charles J. Ingersoll's motion to make the "Three

[6] *Cleveland Plain Dealer,* 24 June 1846. See also Theodore C. Smith, *Liberty and Free Soil Parties in the Northwest* (New York, 1897), p. 107 (hereafter cited as *Liberty and Free Soil Parties*).

[7] *Detroit Daily Advertiser,* 29 September 1846 (hereafter cited as *Detroit Advertiser*); *New Hampshire Patriot,* 10 September 1846.

[8] *Newark Daily Advertiser,* 8 January 1847 (hereafter cited as *Newark Advertiser*).

Million Bill" the special order of business for 8 February. After a sharp contest over parliamentary rules, King was allowed to read his proviso, the duplicate of Wilmot's, which he announced he would offer as an amendment to Ingersoll's bill when it came up for consideration. On 8 February the fateful appropriation was brought to the floor of the House; before King's proviso could be introduced, the opponents and defenders of the "firebrand" amendment launched into a heated discussion of its merits. The debate raged for a full week, steadily growing more violent as the passions of southern partisans rose to fever pitch in their attempts to protect the interests of their section. But the provisoists would not be denied; on 15 February, in a House shrouded in most "solemn silence," Hannibal Hamlin of Maine succeeded in wording a proviso that met all objections to "irrelevant and incongruous amendments." The new proviso was broader than the original:

> There shall be neither slavery nor involuntary servitude in any territory on the continent of America which shall be hereafter acquired by or annexed to the United States by virtue of this appropriation or in any other manner whatever except for crimes whereof the party shall be duly convicted.

The Hamlin proviso was attached to the Three Million Bill by a vote of 116 to 83. The contest in the House was over.[9]

In the nation at large, however, the struggle had just begun. The furious congressional debates of February 1847 quickened latent antislavery sentiment throughout the North; the rank and file of both parties, who had revealed little interest in abolitionism, immediately expressed their intense zeal for the effort to limit the boundaries of slavery. Among Democrats closely allied to the Polk administration there was some tendency to denounce the Proviso as a "mischievous" measure concocted by the Whigs to obstruct the prosecution of the war, but even this group confessed its approval of the Proviso's ultimate objective.[10] The depth of the antislavery sentiment which the Proviso debate revealed was disclosed in the action of northern state legislatures. During the first three months of 1847 nine states (New Hampshire,

[9] The "Three Million Bill" had the same purpose as the "Two Million Bill," appropriation of money to pay for territory which might be acquired from Mexico. The debates in the House are well described in Going, *Wilmot*, pp. 159–201.

[10] Philadelphia *Pennsylvanian*, 15 January, 15 February 1847 (hereafter cited as *Pennsylvanian*); *Boston Daily Times*, 12 March 1847 (hereafter cited as *Boston Times*); *Boston Post*, 13 March 1847; Iowa City *Iowa Capitol Reporter*, 24 March 1847 (hereafter cited as *Iowa Capitol Reporter*); W. J. Hammersley to Welles, 26 February 1847, Welles Papers.

Vermont, Massachusetts, Rhode Island, New York, New Jersey, Pennsylvania, Ohio, and Michigan) gave the principle of slave limitation their official sanction by requesting their representatives and instructing their senators in Washington to vote in favor of the Proviso. Maine added itself to the list in the following summer.[11]

So obvious a threat to the extension of slavery created widespread alarm in the South. In the border states some newspapers were inclined to dismiss the Proviso as insignificant because, as the *Nashville Union* expressed it, the measure could be "rescinded at any future session of Congress." But this view was not shared by many. More typical was the apprehension enunciated by the *Charleston Mercury,* which maintained that the Proviso was meant to degrade the slaveholding states. Under its provisions, it warned, the South would become "a portion of the Union to be tolerated only—not to be cherished, not to be held as sharing in joint sovereignty the empire of the continent. Our increase is to be stifled, our state institutions to be denounced in legislative acts in Washington and like a caged debtor we are to give bonds not to go out of the jail bounds." The unanimity with which members of both parties from the nonslaveholding areas had supported restriction of slavery, moreover, convinced even moderate southerners that they could not "expect justice" from the North. The solution, therefore, lay with themselves. "It behooves the whole South," the Whig *North Carolina Register* declared, "to cast about, and decidedly and unflinchingly resist any and every project which must inevitably tend to advance the unholy and mischievous purposes of those who have openly and willingly violated the Missouri compromise. . . . It is time for party distinctions to sleep, and for the South to present a united front."[12]

This kind of plea was to have considerable effect upon the presidential campaign in the South. The first to benefit was Calhoun. Apparently he was not at first alarmed by the implications of the Proviso. In fact, he seemed pleased that "Wilmot's proposition" would do much to disrupt both parties.[13] When Congress reconvened in December 1846, he began to display greater interest. "It is understood," he informed his daughter, "that the north is united on Wilmot's proposition. . . . The present indication is, that the South will be united in opposition. . . . If they

[11] The legislatures of New Hampshire, Vermont, Massachusetts, Rhode Island, New York, and Ohio were controlled by Whigs; the others were Democratic.

[12] *Nashville Union,* 6 March 1847; *Charleston Mercury,* 14 January 1847; Raleigh *North Carolina Standard,* 28 February 1847 (hereafter cited as *North Carolina Standard*).

[13] Calhoun to Coryell, 7 November 1846, in Jameson, *Calhoun Correspondence,* pp. 709–10.

regard their safety they must defeat it even should the union be rent asunder."[14] Not until the Proviso appeared in the Senate, however, did Calhoun decide that the time had come to bring the whole slavery question "to a final decision."[15]

On 19 February 1847 he introduced in a series of resolutions the famous doctrine which was to become the southern position on the issue of slavery extension. The territories, he maintained, were the "joint and common property" of the several states; Congress had no power to make laws which would deprive any state of its "full and equal rights" therein, or which would prevent citizens of any of the states "from emigrating, with their property," into these territories, or which would preclude the formation of any constitution which the people of the territories should adopt as "best calculated to secure their liberty, prosperity, and happiness" when they applied for admission into the Union. How the South would act if these rights were denied, he could not foretell. But as a southerner and a cotton planter, he proclaimed, "I would rather meet any extremity upon earth than give up one inch of our equality. . . . The surrender of life is nothing to sinking down into acknowledged inferiority."[16]

The resolutions, which were never acted upon, met with instant approval among many southerners. The legislature of the Old Dominion approved Calhoun's propositions so vigorously that for a while thereafter they were known as the "Virginia resolutions." In South Carolina the press, led by the *Charleston Mercury,* called for action: "It is time that we should say to those who . . . insist that Slavery is to be introduced into no territory . . . that . . . we should like to see what measures, they in their wisdom would propose, to compel us to [a] surrender of our rights, and an abandonment of our property."[17]

Two days after he returned to Carolina following the adjournment of Congress, on 9 March 1847, Calhoun took over the leadership of a movement to unite the South in defense of its peculiar institution. At a meeting that filled to overflowing "every nook and cranny" of the spacious New Theatre in Charleston, he announced his program for the South.

He pointed out that after what had occurred in the past year, it was

[14] Calhoun to Mrs. T. G. Clemson, 27 December 1846, in John C. Calhoun, *Works of John C. Calhoun,* ed. Richard K. Crallé (New York, 1854–1855), 4: 328.
[15] Calhoun to Clemson, 19 March 1847, in Jameson, *Calhoun Correspondence,* p. 720.
[16] *Congressional Globe,* 29th Cong., 2d sess., p. 455. Thomas Hart Benton denounced the resolutions as "a string of abstractions."
[17] Hamer, *Secession Movement,* p. 5; *Charleston Mercury,* 9 March 1847.

"almost idiotic to doubt that a large majority of both parties in the non-slaveholding States" had determined "to appropriate all the territories of the United States . . . to the entire exclusion of the slaveholding States." Although he admitted that the North had the numerical power to accomplish its purpose, the South, he maintained, had ample means of defense. Not only was the Constitution on its side, but also there were many in the free states willing to defend the rights of the slaveholders under that instrument.

He recognized that under existing circumstances these friends would be overwhelmed in the struggle of northern parties to secure the abolitionists, whose support was necessary to achieve victory. However, he contended, "if we should act as we ought—if we by our promptitude, energy, and unanimity, prove that we stand ready to defend our rights and maintain our perfect equality, as members of the Union, be the consequences what they may; and that the immediate and necessary effect of courting abolition votes by either party, would be to lose ours, a very different result would follow." Those who were not inclined to violate the Constitution and who were not disposed to see the Union endangered would rally to the aid of the South. The northern parties which expected to secure the presidency through the assistance of the abolitionists would be forced to drop their courtship of that faction and align with the slave states.

How was this happy result to be achieved? Obviously, it would not come about through the existing system, for so intent were the parties in their struggle to secure the presidency that even slaveholding politicians were willing to see the wooing of the abolitionists continue if it meant control of government offices. To accomplish their object southern states would of necessity have to absent themselves from the national conventions, where they were in a minority and could easily be outvoted by delegates determined to divest the South of its "just and equal rights in the public domain." The safety of the slaveholding states, then, rested on their unanimity in the coming presidential elections; "all party distinctions" among southerners had to cease. Only union on a single proslavery candidate would insure the security of the slave interests.[18]

The initial response to Calhoun's proposal was enthusiastic approval. In South Carolina, editors and politicians who could logically expect that Calhoun would be the candidate of a southern party quickly threw their strength behind the movement for southern unity. "No fellowship with provisoists" became their war cry. "We lend ourselves to no paltering

[18] *Niles' Register* 72 (3 April 1847) : 73–74.

with Wilmot provisos," the *Mercury* exclaimed, "nor the authors, nor the abettors, nor the accessories—nor with any who hold fellowship with those who would degrade the section we live in and the institutions of our state." This meant that the South would have to absent itself from the "convention caucuses," where the enemies of slavery controlled a majority of the delegates. Throughout the state carefully engineered public meetings called for a southern convention to unite the slave interests upon a common platform of resistance. Plans were made to establish a newspaper in Washington which would "represent southern views on the subject of SLAVERY—Southern views of Southern Rights and interests growing out of, and connected with this institution."[19]

Outside South Carolina, initial reaction also proved highly encouraging. In May, Democratic state conventions in Alabama and Georgia announced their unqualified approval of the Calhoun doctrine. Governor Albert Gallatin Brown of Mississippi indicated that his state would oppose cooperation with any northern party which did not pledge that the candidate selected would not only be sound on the slavery issue "but beyond the *taint* of suspicion." In Florida the editor of the *Tallahassee Journal* nominated Calhoun as the candidate for the presidency best fit to represent southern views.[20] So encouraging were all these reports that by mid-April 1847 Calhoun was showing evident signs of pleasure. "The Old Hunkers," as he called his opposition in the Democratic party, had been destroyed. He was joyful that they could never again be "resuscitated," while he, who had "sustained the democratick party for the last ten years," was unchanged.[21]

Calhoun's pleasure was short-lived. Southern reaction to his proposal for united action on the slavery issue under the banner of a true champion of southern institutions aroused his enemies—and they were abundant. Many had long suspected that he was making a last effort to secure the presidency. Among them was "Veritas," Washington correspondent of the *Boston Atlas,* who voiced a common belief when he declared in the summer of 1846 that Calhoun's denunciation of conven-

[19] *Charleston Mercury,* 23 March, 5, 12 April 1847; Laura A. White, *Robert Barnwell Rhett: Father of Secession* (New York, 1934), p. 92; J. W. Hayne to Hammond, 31 March 1847, Hammond Papers; Calhoun to Duff Green, 9, 28 March, 19 April 1847, in Jameson, *Calhoun Correspondence,* pp. 718–20, 722–25, 727–28.

[20] Hamer, *Secession Movement,* p. 12; *Augusta Constitutionalist* quoted in *Charleston Mercury,* 20 May 1847; Jackson *Mississippian,* 30 April 1847 (hereafter cited as *Mississippian*) ; *Tallahassee Journal,* 20 March 1847.

[21] Calhoun to Clemson, 11 April 1847, in Jameson, *Calhoun Correspondence,* p. 726. Calhoun's use of the term "Hunkers" was not in accordance with the prevailing meaning. He meant the Van Buren–Wright–Blair–Benton wing of the party, with which he also identified Polk.

tions as "packed juries" and the "slaves of Cabals" revealed that he would be presented as an "independent candidate" with the expectation that the election would be thrown into the House, where Whigs might be expected to unite for him in preference to a "more ultra partizan." President Polk several times recorded his opinion that Calhoun was being destroyed by presidential ambitions.[22]

But no direct attack was made upon Calhoun's movement until after the "Vindicator" affair. In early February 1847 the Senate took up the "Ten Regiment Bill," a measure increasing the army to carry on the war with Mexico. Calhoun made a bitter attack upon the measure and helped in its defeat. A few days later the *Washington Union* printed an article signed by "Vindicator," entitled "Another Mexican Victory." It was a violent attack upon Calhoun. On the following day Senator David L. Yulee of Florida, a Calhoun lieutenant, introduced resolutions to exclude the editors of the *Union*—meaning Thomas Ritchie—from the floor of the Senate, and the newspaper's reporters from the galleries. The resolutions passed when the senators from Florida and South Carolina, Calhoun included, joined the Whigs to make a majority.[23]

The incident aroused the almost unanimous indignation of Democratic editors. One castigated Yulee as a "worthy descendant of the Grand Turk"; others hastened to read Calhoun and his henchmen out of the party. Many agreed with "Halifax" of the *North Carolina Standard,* who charged that the attack on Ritchie was part of Calhoun's presidential maneuvers. Calhoun, he declared, wished "to be returned to the House . . . as one of the highest candidates." Before he could accomplish this, however, "the moral influence of Thomas Ritchie with the South" had to be broken; expulsion from the Senate was one way to accomplish that purpose.[24]

If such were the case, the results, especially in Virginia, where Ritchie boasted a powerful influence through the *Richmond Enquirer,* were far removed from expectations. Hardly had the news reached the state when rumors arose that Calhoun's friends there were "seeking . . . an opportunity to make a respectable retreat." Both the Democratic state convention and the party's state central committee issued addresses condemning Ritchie's expulsion. Anti-Calhoun candidates captured most of the Dem-

[22] *Boston Atlas,* 1 July 1846; Quaife, *Polk's Diary,* 1: 344, 426; 2: 371.

[23] Charles H. Ambler, *Thomas Ritchie: A Study in Virginia Politics* (Richmond, Va., 1913), pp. 266–68.

[24] *Mobile Register and Journal,* 17, 20, 25 February, 1 March 1847 (hereafter cited as *Mobile Register*); *Savannah Republican,* 1 March, 3 May 1847; *Savannah Daily Georgian,* 20 February 1847 (hereafter cited as *Georgian*); *Cleveland Plain Dealer,* 24 February 1847; *Washington Union,* 15 February 1847; *North Carolina Standard,* 24 February 1847.

ocratic congressional nominations, and even where, as in Richmond, a known Calhounite was named, the local convention announced that his nomination did not grant "any color of approval of the political course of the Hon. J. C. Calhoun, or any pledge to support him for the presidency."[25]

Thus, even as Calhoun was organizing his southern movement, opposition was beginning to develop. After his Charleston speech the opposition became vociferous. Calhoun's policy, the *Washington Union* declared, looked "to his own views, to his own aspirations, to the gratification of the ruling passion of his life." The *Mississippian* was scathing in its denunciation of Calhoun for "courting collision upon this deprecated, awful and monstrous" slavery issue. The more moderate *Floridian* declared that it could see no necessity for a southern party: "We do not see the benefit to be derived. . . . The whigs and democrats are already united on this [slavery] question. . . . As we are indissolubly united on this point, what are we to gain by surrendering all our cherished principles and forming a party, based alone, on opposition to the North. . . . For ourselves, we are not yet ready to give up our democratic creed."[26]

Along with such criticism, Calhoun began to receive reports that his third-party dreams were hopeless. From Alabama, Alexander Bowie, former chancellor of the state, informed him, "There is no political event we desire more than to see you elevated to the presidency—yet, with your known principles and feelings, we scarcely believe such an event possible." By the end of summer, Joseph W. Lesesne, writing from Mobile, confirmed the judgment. With the press in the hands of the regular party organization, the people could not be convinced of the necessity of forming a third party. In Georgia, too, the great mass of Democrats were strongly inclined "to their old ways of temporizing with

[25] Baltimore *Sun*, 19 February 1847; *Richmond Enquirer*, 26 February, 19, 25 March 1847. Beverley Tucker's comment at this point was most appropriate: "Mr. C—— is certainly an extraordinary man. A man of wonderful powers and profound political knowledge—but no statesman. A man of infinite address in his intercourse with individuals, but utterly without tact when he comes to deal with men in masses. . . . With the most upright intentions he cannot preserve his perpendicular for six months together: eager for public favor, he always finds out the most unpopular side of every question; and devoted to consistency, shows it by always setting his face against the wind, let blow from what quarter it may. . . . He is certainly the most unskillful leader of a party that ever wielded a truncheon." Tucker added, "Mr. C's misfortune is a fixed idea concerning the presidency" (Tucker to Hammond, 13 March 1847, Hammond Papers).

[26] *Washington Union*, 16 March 1847; *Mississippian*, 12 March 1847; *Floridian*, 7 August 1847. See also *Boston Post*, 8 April 1847; *Albany Evening Atlas*, 2 April 1847 (hereafter cited as *Albany Atlas*); *Pennsylvanian*, 29 March 1847.

principles, and postponing necessary and ultimately inevitable issues."[27]

An undercurrent of opposition developed even in South Carolina. The Whigs and the sprinkling of old Van Buren men, such as Joel R. Poinsett, could be expected to react, but they were too few to create a serious obstacle.[28] It was the friends of former governor James H. Hammond, among whom Calhoun was regarded as a "millstone" around the neck of the state, who provided the chief resistance. Hammond denounced Calhoun's Charleston speech as a desperate attempt "to revenge himself" on those who would "not run him for the Presidency." William Gilmore Simms condemned him as a victim of presidential ambitions, pointing out the "remarkable contradiction" between his "scornful denunciation" of the executive chair as an object of interest for twenty years and the "sudden change" to a policy in which the state was informed that the presidency was "the interest paramount to all others." Among this faction, as Hammond revealed, the attempt to organize a third party was considered "utterly abominable," the most "fatal" of a long list of blunders the South had already committed, the most certain method of destroying the entire institution of slavery.[29]

With such a fear running through the South, it was not amazing to see Calhoun's fortunes fade rapidly in the summer of 1847. Politicians close to him in South Carolina continued their agitation for a southern convention, and Calhoun himself urged that the issue be forced upon the North,[30] but the bouyant feeling was gone. By June, Calhoun had given way to despondency. "All that remains for me," he despairingly informed Duff Green, "is to finish my course with consistency and propriety." He was grateful for the efforts his friends had made, but he realized that the obstacles to his candidacy under a third party were too great to overcome.[31] Meanwhile, impressed by the futility of their efforts, his friends had turned their attention to another candidate who appeared to promise protection for southern institutions—General Zachary Taylor.

[27] Alexander Bowie to Calhoun, 3 April 1847, in Jameson, *Calhoun Correspondence*, pp. 732–33; Joseph W. Lesesne to Calhoun, 21 August 1847, Black to Calhoun, [June–December 1847], in Boucher and Brooks, *Calhoun Correspondence*, pp. 39, 380–81. See also Crallé to Calhoun, 18 April 1847, Hamilton to Calhoun, 24 April 1847, in Jameson, *Calhoun Correspondence*, pp. 1112, 1117.

[28] Poinsett to Van Buren, 4 June 1847, Van Buren Papers.

[29] McCord to Hammond, 12 December 1844, Hammond to Simms, 22 February, 1, 19 April 1847, James Hammond to M. C. Hammond, 26 February 1847, Simms to Hammond, April 1847, Hammond Papers.

[30] Hamer, *Secession Movement*, pp. 11, 12–13; *Niles' Register* 73 (23 October 1847): 127.

[31] Calhoun to Green, 20 June 1847, in Jameson, *Calhoun Correspondence*, pp. 723–33.

Chapter Three

The Hero of Buena Vista

Credit for "discovering" Zachary Taylor at the head of the American army below the Rio Grande was claimed by several contemporary political leaders, among them John J. Crittenden, Alexander H. Stephens, and Thurlow Weed.[1] But the credit more rightfully belonged to the people. Taylor's initial and apparently spectacular victories over Mexican forces at Palo Alto and Resaca de la Palma on 8 and 9 May 1846 made an instantaneous impression upon the popular mind.

As early as 11 June a large meeting of New Jersey citizens gathered on the old battlefield at Trenton to name the hero as the "People's Candidate" for the presidency; this was, significantly, the first popular nomination of the presidential campaign.[2] A few days later an assembly in New York City was persuaded from following a similar course only by the persuasive rhetoric of J. Watson Webb, editor of the New York *Courier and Enquirer*. Webb argued that, save for Taylor's victories, the country knew little about the man. He confessed that the "modest manner" in which his dispatches chronicled those victories "indicated a fitness for the Presidency," but he warned, "once put him in nomination . . . once array him against the administration in power—once compel all the supporters of the administration to look upon him as a political rival—a Whig candidate for the Presidency—and his chance will dwindle down to nothing." Webb counseled delay until the time was ripe for "the people" to bring him forward.[3]

During the summer, when military operations in Mexico were suspended, such spontaneous movements ceased. Public attention did not again fasten on the General until September, when it became evident that he was about to engage the enemy. The battle occurred at Monterrey on 24 September; it was another important victory, whose aftermath proved equally important. The terms that Taylor granted to the Mexicans were extremely liberal. He had permitted the badly defeated Mexican army to retire from the field, with its arms and accouterments, without demanding the customary parole; he had also agreed to an eight-week armistice, giving the Mexicans an opportunity to re-form their shattered lines.[4]

When the situation became known, a storm of criticism arose. Officers in the field, the administration, and the press of both parties censured the leniency of the terms of capitulation. General Scott reported that they "came very near causing Taylor to be recalled."[5] Although President Polk continued him in command because "public opinion" seemed to indicate that he was "entitled" to it, he began to nurse a growing suspicion of Taylor's competence. A short while later Polk instructed General Robert Patterson, one of Taylor's subordinates, to occupy the defenseless province of Tamaulipas. Taylor's bitter protest against the order provoked Polk to great anger. Because he believed that Taylor was seeking a pretext for a quarrel that would enhance his presidential prospects, the president held his peace. But he lent a favorable ear to

[1] Crittenden to Albert T. Burnley, 8 January 1848, in Coleman, *Crittenden,* I : 290; Richard H. Johnston and William H. Brown, *Life of Alexander H. Stephens* (Philadelphia, 1884), p. 224 (hereafter cited as *Stephens*) ; Alexander H. Stephens, *Recollections of Alexander H. Stephens,* ed. Myrta L. Avery (New York, 1910), pp. 21–22. Weed's claim is in his autobiography. In the middle of June 1846—two or three weeks after the Battle of Resaca de la Palma, when the Scott movement had just collapsed—Weed, according to his own account, was introduced to Taylor's brother on board a Hudson River steamboat. In the conversation that followed he learned that the General "neither knew nor cared anything about parties" but did entertain "strong prejudices." He was said to be a firm admirer of Henry Clay and was "strongly prejudiced against General Jackson"; his antipathy to foreign manufactures, moreover, was so pronounced "that he would not wear a coat except made from American cloth, nor a button upon his coat that had been imported." Weed remarked that such *"prejudices"* were quite as important and practical as *principles"* and then to the incredulous amazement of his companion declared, "If your brother goes through the Mexican war as he has commenced it, he will be the next President of the United States" (Thurlow Weed, *Autobiography of Thurlow Weed,* ed. Harriet A. Weed [Boston, 1883], p. 371) (hereafter cited as *Autobiography*). Weed's seriousness became evident a few days later when he made a similar announcement in his newspaper (*Albany Evening Journal,* 18 June 1846). Weed, however, did not develop Taylor's candidacy; neither was he an enthusiastic supporter.

[2] *Niles' Register* 70 (20 June 1846) : 256. The *Register* dated the meeting 11 May, which is probably an error. News of the battles at Palo Alto (8 May) and Resaca de la Palma (9 May), at a time when four days were needed to transmit news from New Orleans to Washington, could not have reached New Jersey in two days.

[3] *Morning Courier and New York Enquirer,* 18 June 1846 (hereafter cited as New York *Courier*).

[4] Justin H. Smith, *War with Mexico* (New York, 1919), I : 259–61.

[5] Scott to Crittenden, 19 October 1846, Crittenden Papers. In his memoirs Scott claimed that Crittenden had urged Taylor to engage in battle at Monterrey (Winfield Scott, *Memoirs of Lieutenant-General Scott, L.L.D.* [New York, 1864], p. 392).

Scott's plan to shift the scene of military action from northern Mexico to Veracruz.[6]

Polk's suspicions concerning Taylor's presidential prospects were partly correct. The General, against his will, was rapidly becoming a presidential candidate. The two men who were probably most responsible for the development were John J. Crittenden and Alexander H. Stephens.

Crittenden was an example of that element in the Whig party which preferred Clay "to all [other] men for the Presidency." At the same time, he was convinced that a fourth contest under Clay's banner, assuming that Clay was able, would only hazard another defeat.[7] This conviction had at first turned his hopes to Scott, but after Old Fuss and Feathers had destroyed his prospects with his own pen, Crittenden found his attention drawn to the American commander in Mexico, whose possibilities were made forcibly apparent by the spontaneous demonstrations in the East.

Various politicians and private citizens had urged Taylor to become an aspirant before Crittenden entered into the situation. Taylor had dismissed these suggestions with scant courtesy. As he told his son-in-law Dr. Richard C. Wood he did not want the presidency and would never be a candidate for the office even if it were offered without opposition. Moreover, he pointed out, any action that would single out a political unknown—who had spent all his adult life in the rude garrisons of the frontier, who knew nothing about civil affairs, and who had never cast a vote—in preference to tried Whig statesmen, was an idea "too visionary to require a serious answer." The whole movement, he maintained, would serve only to embarrass him in the successful prosecution of the war.[8]

[6] Polk recorded in his diary on 5 September 1846: "Gen'l Taylor, I fear, is not the man for the command of the army. He is brave but he does not seem to have the resources or grasp of mind enough to conduct such a campaign. . . . He seems to obey orders, but appears to be unwilling to express any opinion or take any responsibility upon himself. Though he is in the country with the means of knowledge which cannot be possessed at Washington, . . . he gives no information to aid the administration. . . . He is, I have no doubt, a good subordinate officer, but from all the evidence before me I think him unfit for the chief command" (Quaife, *Polk's Diary*, 2: 119). See also pp. 139–40, 227, 229–30, 236, 243, 249–50.

[7] Coleman, *Crittenden*, 1: 290.

[8] Taylor to Wood, 30 June 1846 in *Taylor Letters*, pp. 21–22. See also Weed, *Autobiography*, p. 573; Taylor to a group of Philadelphia politicians, August 1846, in *Albany Atlas*, 24 April 1847; Taylor to George Folsom, 14 August 1846, in *Niles' Register* 71 (12 September 1846): 20–21. Taylor at this time hoped that Scott would be the Whig nominee (Taylor to Wood, 4 August 1846, in *Taylor Letters*, p. 34).

It was Crittenden, an old friend and a distant kinsman, who changed Taylor's mind, perhaps with the assistance of Crittenden's friend Albert T. Burnley, a former resident of Frankfort living in New Orleans.[9] Crittenden suggested to Taylor that his own preferences should not be the decisive factor; he asked only that Taylor say nothing that would prevent the people from selecting him to lead the nation out of the sorry circumstances into which the reckless expansionist course of the Polk administration had plunged it. Still unconvinced of his fitness for the task, Taylor gave a reluctant consent.[10] He expressed his attitude in a letter to Dr. Wood dated 10 December 1846:

> Could I reach the presidency by announcing publicly my wishes to that effect, I certainly would never arrive at the same; at the same time I will not say I would not serve if the good people were imprudent enough as to select me; but I would prefer at the end of the present war, in a great measure to retire from the bustle of public life, & to pass the few days or years which may be alotted to me in quietness if not in retirement.[11]

Taylor, in short, had consented to a draft.

Alexander Stephens's original role was a different one. The congressman from Georgia represented that element among southern Whigs who went home to campaign for reelection in the summer of 1846 fully realizing the meaning and consequences of the antislavery sentiment which the northern wing of the party had revealed when the Proviso had been introduced. They hoped to safeguard the interests of the South by selecting as the party candidate a southerner and a slaveholder who, they believed, would prove an uncompromising champion of slavery in the controversy which they expected would soon come to a head.[12]

It was this sectionally conscious element which took the first steps to

[9] I have found it impossible to date precisely Crittenden's first approach to Taylor. The first letter from Taylor to Crittenden that I found is from Camargo, dated 1 September 1846 (Crittenden Papers). The same letter is in Coleman, *Crittenden*, 1: 251, dated 15 September 1846. Crittenden's relationship with Burnley and with other residents of New Orleans in the Taylor camp can be found in Holman Hamilton's excellent biography, *Zachary Taylor: Soldier in the White House* (New York, 1951) (hereafter cited as *Taylor*); and Albert D. Kirwan, *John J. Crittenden: The Struggle for the Union* (Lexington, Ky., 1962), pp. 200–223.

[10] Poage, *Clay*, p. 154. While such letters were undoubtedly exchanged, I have not been able to find either Crittenden's suggestion or Taylor's consent.

[11] Taylor to Wood, 10 December 1846, in *Taylor Letters*, p. 76. In Hamilton, *Taylor*, p. 40, the letter is dated 10 November 1846.

[12] Johnston and Brown, *Stephens*, p. 215; Arthur C. Cole, *Whig Party in the South* (Washington, D. C., 1913), p. 126 (hereafter cited as *Whigs in the South*).

organize a Taylor movement. At the opening of the second session of the Twenty-ninth Congress in December 1846, Stephens, who may have known that Taylor would consent to a draft, secured the formation of a "Taylor-for-President" club in the House. Its comparatively youthful adherents were promptly named "Young Indians." Besides Stephens, its charter members included William Ballard Preston, Thomas S. Flournoy, and John S. Pendleton of Virginia; Robert A. Toombs of Georgia; and Henry A. Hilliard of Alabama. Two northerners, Abraham Lincoln of Illinois and Truman Smith of Connecticut, gave the rolls a necessary nationwide touch.[13]

The organization of a congressional machine to advance Taylor's candidacy came at a propitious moment, just as the rift began to widen between Polk and his general in Mexico. In late November word that Scott was about to take the field began to circulate. Whigs immediately suspected a politician's plot to supersede Taylor or to play Scott against him.[14] Such suspicions were reinforced early in 1847, when Polk requested Congress to authorize the appointment of a lieutenant general to take full charge of operations in the field, and Thomas Hart Benton announced on the floor of the Senate that he would be the recipient of the "Field Marshall's baton." At almost the same time it became known that Scott had taken a portion of Taylor's forces for an attack on Veracruz; a short while later two administration congressmen, Orlando B. Ficklin of Illinois and Jacob Thompson of Mississippi, threatened to prevent passage of resolutions thanking Taylor for his heroic leadership, by launching a movement to censure him for the Monterrey capitulation.[15]

In late January 1847 Taylor's letter to General Edmund P. Gaines was published. In it Taylor justified the terms granted at Monterrey on the grounds that the administration had not provided him with sufficient men, supplies, or means of transportation to carry the campaign any further.[16] Since the letter also contained information concerning Taylor's

---

[13] Avery, *Stephens*, pp. 21–22; Poage, *Clay*, pp. 157–58.

[14] Smith, *War with Mexico*, 1: 354; *Pennsylvanian*, 16 January 1847; *Richmond Enquirer*, 4 February 1847. Even Taylor, who had once urged Scott to take the command which was rightfully his, saw in the movement an act of political chicanery (Zachary Taylor to Colonel Joseph P. Taylor, 8 February 1847, Zachary Taylor to Jefferson Davis, 27 July 1847, Taylor Papers).

[15] *Congressional Globe*, 29th Cong., 2d sess, pp. 295–99, 433.

[16] The text of the letter is in *Niles' Register* 71 (30 January 1847): 342–43. Taylor did not intend the letter for publication (73 [19 February 1848]: 384). Marcy, it should be noted, opposed Scott's action to weaken Taylor (Marcy to Prosper M. Wetmore, 21 March 1847, Marcy Papers).

future operations, the administration issued a reprimand, warning him that further revelation of military secrets would subject him to court martial.[17]

This accumulation of apparently hostile actions brought a roar of rage from the Whig press against the "unceasing and malignant character of the attacks made upon the old Hero, by the carpet-knights and back-stairs chivalry at Washington."[18] For several months Whig editors paraded evidence of administration "perfidy" before the public.[19] In the meantime, they also began to single out for special attack the administration's failure to reinforce Taylor at Saltillo, where the American army had encamped after the battle at Monterrey and upon which, it was soon learned, General Santa Anna was advancing with a gigantic force. Although Democratic journals assured the nation that Taylor was fully equipped to meet any attack, the reiterated Whig alarms gradually created a high state of anxiety. Rumors of disaster, of a fearful massacre, of a complete annihilation of American forces spread throughout the country. Nor were Whigs above heightening public fears by insinuating that a great catastrophe had been planned by James K. Polk and his minions to rid themselves of Taylor.[20]

Then, at the very end of March, the deep gloom that had settled on the nation was suddenly lifted by news of another great victory at Buena Vista. The glad tidings were received at New Orleans on the twenty-eighth; fleet horses of the famed pony express, maintained by the Baltimore *Sun,* sped the news to Richmond, Virginia, where it arrived late on the night of the thirty-first and was winged by telegram throughout the northeastern and New England states. By April first the reports had reached nearly every large town in the nation. The first reaction was

---

[17] Smith, *War with Mexico,* 1: 356. Polk and other administrative leaders regarded the letter as a bid for the presidency (Quaife, *Polk's Diary,* 2: 359; Baltimore *Sun,* 25 January 1847).

[18] *Savannah Republican,* 28 January 1847.

[19] *Boston Atlas,* 29 January 1847; *Nashville Whig,* 2 February 1847; *Nashville Union,* 6 February 1847; Nashville *Republican,* 10 February 1847; *Vicksburg Weekly Whig,* 10 February 1847 (hereafter cited as *Vicksburg Whig*). Silas Wright believed that the administration's hostility to Taylor "would give him an aid and render him a service that his friends could not do" (Wright to Van Buren, 7 January 1847, Van Buren Papers).

[20] Some Whig journals had started this kind of rumor before the Monterrey campaign. The *North American* of 19 September 1846, for example, charged that Taylor "was deliberately offered up to the fire-eyed maid of smoky war, all hot and reeking." See also 14 January, 2 February, 22, 27 March 1847; *Washington Union,* 30 March 1847. Polk, taking cognizance of the rumors and charges, recorded, "If Gen'l Taylor is in any danger . . . it is in consequence of his having in violation of his orders, advanced beyond Monterrey" (Quaife, *Polk's Diary,* 2: 444).

one of incredulity: to many the news was a cruel April Fools' Day joke. But confirmation soon followed, and the prevailing pessimism gave way to a mad delirium of rejoicing.[21]

After the first paroxysm of joy had passed, a happy nation turned to shower its gratitude on the General, whose genius, according to Whig journals, had accomplished a military miracle. That sentiment favorable to Taylor had been building throughout January and February was abundantly clear. One of Mangum's correspondents found him "extremely popular" in New Orleans. James A. Harvey reported the "prevailing inclination" in Lexington, Kentucky, was for him. The *Iowa Reporter* revealed a Taylor-for-president movement in the Hawkeye State. Caleb B. Smith learned that the Indiana Whig Convention of January 1847 had contained a large minority favorable to the General. Alert agents of John McLean found strong sentiment for a "drum and fife" candidate in all the major eastern cities. Moreover, "MANY MEMBERS of the Senate and House of Representatives" had submitted Taylor's name to the favorable consideration of the Whig National Convention through the columns of the *Washington Fountain*.[22]

But such indications were slight compared to the developments after Buena Vista. Like a gigantic tidal wave out of the Gulf of Mexico, a movement to name Taylor the "People's Candidate" for president swept across the nation; Whig editors and politicians, somewhat amazed at the swelling enthusiasm, leaped into the current to ride it to its limits.

Here and there Whig journals such as the Philadelphia *North American* and the *Savannah Republican* protested that the "zeal" of the party was outrunning its "discretion," that nominations by newspapers were "arrogant and unwise."[23] But such statements were drowned in the chorus that proclaimed the virtues of the "Hero of Buena Vista" and the reasons he deserved the nation's support.

A few editors frankly based their arguments on Taylor's military glory, such as the editor of the Nashville *Republican-Banner,* who on 31 May 1847 admonished the people "to reflect upon the debt of gratitude" due the gallant commander for his "heroic valor" in battle. Others carefully pointed out that his military glory was not their only reason for

[21] *Georgian,* 30 March 1847; *Richmond Enquirer,* 31 March 1847; *North American,* 1 April 1847.

[22] E. J. Foster to Mangum, 8 February 1847, Mangum Papers; Harvey to McLean, 12 October 1846, McLean Papers; *Iowa Capitol Reporter,* 3 March 1847; John H. Bradley to Smith, 16 January 1847, Caleb B. Smith Papers; Mower to McLean, 2 January 1847, R. Peters to McLean, 6 January 1847, Whitcomb to McLean, 4 February 1847, Richards to McLean, 5 February 1847, McLean Papers; Baltimore *Sun,* 30 January 1847.

[23] *North American,* 3 April 1847; *Savannah Republican,* 15 April 1847.

supporting Old Zack. There were more tangible reasons. The *New Orleans National* declared:

> May our hand be paralyzed if we ever for such reason alone, advocate the claims of any man to civil office. We consider General Taylor's civil qualifications far outshine those connected with his military history brilliant as it is. . . . It is his patient endurance, his prudence of speech displayed under obstacles most unnecessarily thrown in his way, and singularly calculated to try his spirit; it is his purity of character, it is his modest appreciation of his own merits; it is his correctness of judgement shown in selecting his friends and advisors; it is his stern integrity, the marked simplicity of his habits, and his singleness of purpose in all matters relating to his country; it is the atmosphere that tangibly surrounds him impresing all that he is a true Republican, a honest man, that calls upon us and the whole nation to . . . assist in his elevation to the highest office in the gift of a free and enlightened people.[24]

Occasionally a journal announced that its favorable attitude was the "result of knowledge that Gen. Taylor was heart and soul a Whig, a noble, disinterested and devoted Whig."[25] More frequently, Whig editors called for approval of their candidate because his election would "destroy the monster party," or as the New York *Courier* maintained, because General Taylor was "not popular with the political demagogues and officeseekers" who made politics a trade and who feared the elevation of an honest man.[26]

Throughout the slave states the Taylor movement was especially enthusiastic. Hardly an expression of disapproval was heard as editor after editor, meeting after meeting announced a preference for the Old Hero. By midsummer, sixteen of twenty-eight Whig papers in Maryland and seventeen of twenty-eight in Virginia had avowed an undying devotion to Old Zack, and the Whig state conventions in Maryland and Georgia had given him a formal nomination. The movement made deep inroads into southern Democratic ranks as well. In Kentucky and Tennessee large nonpartisan meetings saw prominent Democrats climb upon the Taylor bandwagon. Louisiana, Mississippi, Alabama, and Maryland Whigs found so many of their former opponents eager to support Taylor that they readily agreed to drop their party label to combine in "neutral" and "independent" nominating assemblies. In Georgia only the

---

[24] *New Orleans National* quoted in *Baltimore Clipper*, 18 June 1847. See also *New Orleans Commercial Bulletin*, 7 April 1847; *Detroit Advertiser*, 14 April 1847.
[25] *North American*, 13 April 1847. See also Nashville *Republican*, 23 April 1847.
[26] New York *Courier*, 14 April, 27 June 1847. See also *Baltimore Clipper*, 18 June 1847.

parliamentary skill of Congressman Howell Cobb prevented a nomination by the Democratic state convention.[27]

The explanation for this sudden zeal, which for the moment threatened to obliterate party lines in the South, is simple. To many the halo of military glory that surrounded Taylor was reason enough for enthusiasm. William R. King, former senator from Alabama, fully recognized this situation in a letter to Buchanan: "The Whigs are playing a skillful game in seizing upon Genl. Taylor. . . . Full well do they know that such is the military enthusiasm of the American people that they can be led to the support of a successful general without inquiring into his political principles, or his qualifications. . . . But what are we to expect from the masses."[28]

Among more thoughtful southerners, however, Taylor's ownership of slaves was the deciding point. The *New Orleans Bee* aptly expressed the attitude: "One reason the South should . . . sustain General Taylor for the Presidency with great unanimity is because his nomination affords us a final and unlooked for chance of electing a Southern man to office. . . . When it is considered that both the great parties at the North court the antislavery faction; that both are opposed to the extension of slavery . . . the importance of placing at the head of the Government one who from birth, association and conviction, is identified with the South and who will uphold her rights and guard her from oppression cannot fail to strike every candid mind." Taking this view, it argued that Taylor's election had become "a matter of vital moment to the slaveholding portion of the confederacy." The *Florida Sentinel* stated the idea even more succinctly: "Just as long as the Wilmot Proviso is an open question, WE ARE FOR A SOUTHERN MAN AND A SLAVEHOLDER FOR THE PRESIDENCY."[29]

[27] See *Niles' Register* 72 (24 April, 10 July, 14 August 1847): 128, 294, 375; 73 (2, 23 October, 13 November 1847): 79, 126, 172; Baltimore *Sun*, 20 April, 13 May 1847; *Baltimore Clipper*, 24 April, 21 July, 10, 19 August, 24 December 1847; Baltimore *Republican and Argus*, 19 June 1847 (hereafter cited as Baltimore *Republican*); *Washington Union*, 4 June 1847; *Richmond Enquirer*, 3 July 1847; *North Carolina Standard*, 23 June, 7, 14 July 1847; *Savannah Republican*, 2, 3 July 1847; Nashville *Republican*, 12 April, 5 July, 13 October 1847; *Vicksburg Whig*, 5 May 1847; *New Orleans Commercial Bulletin*, 8, 19–22, 26, 29, 30 April, 3, 20, 29 May, 28 June, 22 July, 11 August 1847; New Orleans *Daily Picayune*, 11 July, 30 October 1847 (hereafter cited as New Orleans *Picayune*); *Boston Atlas*, 21 April, 21 June 1847; *Boston Post*, 28 June 1847; New York *Courier*, 12 July 1847.

[28] King to Buchanan, 11 June 1847, Buchanan Papers.

[29] *New Orleans Bee* quoted in *Pennsylvanian*, 12 May 1847; *Florida Sentinel* quoted in *Boston Times*, 13 November 1847. See also *Vicksburg Whig*, 28 July 1847; *North Carolina Standard*, 1 September 1847.

Among those to whom the logic of this argument appealed very strongly were the followers of Calhoun. Rumors that the South Carolinian had abandoned his own candidacy and was urging his friends to unite on Taylor appeared as early as April 1847.[30] The restlessness of his devotees indicated that these reports had some foundations. Even while the Calhoun movement was still high, the *Charleston Mercury* revealed its interest in Taylor by protesting against the support he was receiving from northern Whigs. "Are they not aware that he is a Southern man, a slaveholder, a cotton planter?" it demanded. "Do they suppose him . . . so lost to self respect as to endorse the Wilmot abolition Proviso, which by implication denounces him and every other slaveholder as infamous and unworthy the association of citizens of the free States?"[31]

Evidence of Taylor sentiment among his own associates was quickly revealed to Calhoun. From New Orleans James Hamilton reported that the most intelligent of the Carolinian's partisans in that city were inclined to surrender Calhoun's claims to those of the General because they believed he alone would "enable the Country to relieve itself of the conjoint and infamous burdens of Hunkerism and abolitionism." In these opinions Hamilton concurred and suggested that Calhoun take immediate steps to organize "a New National Republican party" on a basis broad enough to admit both the "Crittenden Whigs" and the South Carolina faction.[32] Crallé of Virginia and Elmore of South Carolina offered similar counsels; Calhoun's editorial supporters lent subtle encouragement.[33]

Although Calhoun recognized the strength of Taylor's position, regarded him as a likely "anti-convention" candidate, and privately disclosed that he would "be content" to see Old Zack elected, he declined to give any coalition movement his aid or even to express publicly his favor for the General.[34] But Calhoun's silence did not restrain his followers. Throughout the summer of 1847, as it became apparent that Calhoun had failed to bring southern Democrats to his standard and that the states'

[30] Baltimore *Sun,* 12 April 1847; *Niles' Register* 72 (17 April 1847): 112; Quaife, *Polk's Diary,* 2: 470.

[31] *Charleston Mercury* quoted in *New Hampshire Patriot,* 29 April 1847.

[32] Hamilton to Calhoun, 24 April 1847, in Jameson, *Calhoun Correspondence,* p. 1118.

[33] Crallé to Calhoun, 18 April 1847, ibid., pp. 1114-15; Elmore to Calhoun, 16 May 1847, in Boucher and Brooks, *Calhoun Correspondence,* p. 376. The *Charleston Mercury* of 13 May 1847 stated the motive: "What his opinions are on the great questions of constitutional controversy—the Tariff, Bank and Internal improvements—we know not. . . . He is true and sound on the Wilmot Proviso."

[34] Calhoun to Clemson, 6 May, 24 July 1847, in Jameson, *Calhoun Correspondence,* pp. 728-29.

rights Whigs on whom he had counted were rallying en masse under
Taylor's banner, a number of his lieutenants announced their allegiance
to the man whom Beverley Tucker described as "a God-send" to the
South. John A. Campbell of Mobile expressed their motive when he
declared that "it was a profound conviction" of Calhoun's inability to
check the threat of the antislavery forces that had induced him to throw
in his lot with the Taylor movement.[35]

In the free states the Taylor movement, though widespread, did not
blanket the entire section. In the Northwest large meetings in Cincinnati
and Detroit attested to the General's popularity among the commercial
element. Strong support was manifested in Iowa, where Whigs gathered
in a statewide mass convention to nominate Taylor for the presidency; in
Illinois, where the *Sangamo Journal,* official organ of the party, and
fifty-six delegates to the state constitutional convention proclaimed Old
Zack their favorite candidate; and in Indiana, where the *State Journal* at
Indianapolis threw its weight behind the movement that had been disclosed earlier in the year, and where Cass men began to desert their
erstwhile hero for the more glamorous victor of Buena Vista.[36] In New
York, Taylor sentiment revealed itself all along the course of the Erie
Canal and particularly in New York City, where it appeared among the
"sound and conservative men who had rarely taken part in political
affairs" and among petty tradesmen. "I have seen on the Ice Carts, and
other vehicles drawn about the city," one observer reported, "the portrait
of General Taylor, well painted on the tail board. . . . It is on the
butcher's stall, it is in the market places. It is on the fishstands. It is on
cigar boxes and divers other places." Support for the movement also
appeared among such Tyler Democrats as ex-Senator Nathaniel P.
Tallmadge, whose support of the General was considered highly significant because he had never been found on the losing side amid all the
fluctuations in party fortunes the nation had witnessed since the advent
of Andrew Jackson.[37]

[35] Tucker to Hammond, 13 October 1847, Hammond Papers; Campbell to
Calhoun, 20 December 1847, in Jameson, *Calhoun Correspondence,* pp. 1153–54.

[36] *Niles' Register* 72 (17, 24 April 1847) : 97, 128; *Detroit Advertiser,* 7, 21 May,
17 July 1847; Detroit *Daily Free Press,* 12 July 1847 (hereafter cited as Detroit
Free Press) ; *Baltimore Clipper,* 6 April 1847; *Sangamo Journal,* 8 April 1847;
Chicago Democrat, 14 September 1847. John Lane wrote rather gleefully to Van
Buren from Vincennes: "As for Gen'l Cass . . . most of his political friends have
gone over to Taylor. Breaking one's sword is not equal to a battle gained like that
of Buena Vista" (Lane to Van Buren, 22 August 1847, Van Buren Papers).

[37] G. W. Clinton to Dickinson, 14 April 1847, in Dickinson, *Dickinson,* 2 : 405;
Niles' Register 72 (24 July 1847) : 334; Harvey to Mangum, 18 August 1847,
Mangum Papers; Mower to McLean, 16 August 1847, McLean Papers; New York
Courier, 12 July 1847.

McLean was the chief victim of the Buena Vista movement in these areas; his followers, it seemed, found the appeal of the victorious general well-nigh irresistible. In Ohio so many of his supporters deserted his standard that Thomas B. Stevenson, editor of the *Cincinnati Atlas,* pronounced McLean politically dead. "Galvinism," he informed ex-Governor Robert Letcher of Kentucky, "could hardly resurrect a grin from his earthly cause." In New York a similar development, catalogued in the letters of McLean's correspondents, finally led the faithful but realistic James B. Mower to suggest that the Judge's best course would be to climb on Taylor's bandwagon, where an opportunity might be presented to direct its course or where he might be able to place himself in a position to secure a cabinet post.[38]

The tide that thus apparently swept away the tenuously rooted McLean candidacy in Ohio and in New York also rolled across eastern Pennsylvania and New Jersey. In this area Taylor enthusiasm rivaled, if it did not excel, that in the South. The Whig press declared almost unanimously for Old Zack; scores of counties held Taylor nomination meetings. In Philadelphia, Taylor sentiment appeared particularly high. Observers reported that the movement there was "almost universal," that all but one Whig journal had "hoisted the military flag." A nomination meeting proved so large and enthusiastic that the *United States Gazette* suggested that the Whig Executive Committee be charged with the duty of selecting a vice-presidential candidate, since a national convention was unnecessary.[39]

As in the South, both states contained large numbers of Taylor supporters among Democrats. Pennsylvania, moreover, boasted the only statewide organization of Taylor Democrats in the nation. Led by United States Senator Simon Cameron, who claimed that Taylor was a Democrat, the organization included on its central committee such prominent men as Richard Vaux, collector of the Port of Philadelphia; ex-Congressman Henry A. Muhlenberg; ex-Governor David R. Porter; and Tyler's former secretary of war, James M. Porter. Although political observers regarded this development either as an effort on Cameron's part to repay a political debt to the Whigs, who had been instrumental in securing his election to the United States Senate, or as an effort to

[38] Stevenson to Letcher, 23 April 1847, Stevenson to Crittenden, 1 May, 20 June 1847, Crittenden Papers; Teesdale to McLean, 4 May 1847, Mower to McLean, 17 June, 3 July, 16 August 1847, McLean Papers.
[39] *Niles' Register* 72 (17, 24 April, 31 July 1847): 112, 118, 340; *Philadelphia Inquirer* quoted in *New Orleans Commercial Bulletin,* 22 July 1847; *Newark Advertiser,* 15 April, 20 September 1847; Peters to McLean, 3 May 1847, McLean Papers; *North American,* 11 May 1847.

destroy Buchanan's position within the Democratic party, the movement showed surprising strength—a strength attested to by the attendance of great numbers of the Democratic rank and file at the mass convention held in Harrisburg in July to organize a campaign to secure the Democratic presidential nomination for Taylor.[40]

When Taylor supporters looked over the political scene in midsummer of 1847 and saw how readily their candidate had taken hold of the popular imagination in a few short months, how effortlessly he had pushed all other movements into the background, their hopes rose to dizzy heights. Nothing, they believed, would prevent his nomination by the Whigs. The most cautious Taylor editor and many a Democrat acknowledged the probability; the more exuberant Whigs pronounced his election a certainty.[41] Their attitude was well expressed at the outset of the Taylor boom by a Kentuckian visiting Baltimore, who, when told that Old Zack had to win the approval of the Whig National Convention before he would be a candidate, exploded into profanity. "Convention be damned," he roared, "I tell ye General Taylor is going to be elected by *spontaneous combustion.*"[42]

But this sanguine element was destined to receive some rude shocks. Although it was not apparent, few Democratic editors gave aid and sustenance to the enthusiasm of the Taylor Whigs. The first onrush of the Buena Vista movement had stunned many of them into silence, but those who had not lost their voices quickly revealed the inconsistencies that Taylor's candidacy presented. While they carefully refrained from attacking the General directly, they did not hesitate to arraign the motives of the Whigs. At first they questioned Taylor's Whiggery, demanding to know "when or where he ever expressed a single political opinion" and by what right Whigs used him as a party "hobby horse."[43] He was, they claimed, more a Democrat than a Whig. "As a large cotton planter," the *Richmond Enquirer* pointed out, he was directly interested

[40] *Newark Advertiser*, 29 May, 17 June, 11 August 1847; *Pennsylvanian*, 1 June 1847; Harvey to Mangum, 18 August 1847, Mangum Papers. There are brief accounts of the Cameron movement for Taylor in Henry R. Mueller, *Whig Party in Pennsylvania* (New York, 1922), p. 143 (hereafter cited as *Whigs in Pennsylvania*); and Snyder, *Jacksonian Heritage*, p. 209.

[41] See for example Daniel Webster to Fletcher Webster, 25 April 1847, in *Webster's Writings*, 18: 239; Buchanan to General James Shields, 23 April 1847, Buchanan to Henry Wise, 15 June 1847, in Moore, *Buchanan's Works*, 7: 345–46; Marcy to Wetmore, 25 April 1847, Marcy Papers; New York *Courier*, 6 September 1847; Nashville *Republican*, 14 April 1847; *Richmond Enquirer*, 9 August 1847; *New Orleans Commercial Bulletin*, 11 August 1847.

[42] *Niles' Register* 72 (24 April 1847) : 128.

[43] *Richmond Enquirer*, 21 April 1847; *Chicago Democrat*, 20 April 1847; *Louisville Daily Democrat*, 21 July 1847 (hereafter cited as *Louisville Democrat*).

in "the benefits of free trade" and could not be regarded "as an advocate of . . . a protective tariff." Indeed, the *Milledgeville Federal Union* of Georgia contended that he was identified with the Democratic party "in all its measures, its triumphs and its glory." He was *"undeniably a Democrat of the purest water."* His nomination, said the Baltimore *Republican,* would be the most satisfactory and triumphant vindication that Polk could ask.[44] By what species of rationalization could Whigs claim him?

In a short time Democratic editors developed more embarrassing questions. What, many asked, had become of Whig opposition to military candidates? Had not Henry Clay begged the Almighty God to visit the land "with WAR, with PESTILENCE, with FAMINE, with any scourge other than military rule or a BLIND AND HEEDLESS ENTHUSIASM" for the military renown of Old Hickory?[45] Yet, the Detroit *Free Press* declared, "the same men who denounced Jackson's unfitness, because he girded on his sword to protect the frontier inhabitants from the tomahawk and scalping knife of the savage foe—because he protected New Orleans from plunder, her beauty from pollution, are now clamorous for the nomination of General Taylor." If it was wrong to elect Jackson "because of his military education," the *Free Press* concluded, "with how much more force does the objection lie against Gen. Taylor, whose education has been entirely of a military character—whose whole life has been spent in a garrison or camp?"[46]

How, furthermore, the Democrats asked, could northern Whigs, who had "such a holy horror of slavery," who had "shed crocodile tears over the sufferings of the poor slave," and who had "preached, spoken, written, prayed, and sworn against the extinction of slavery," how could they select for their standard bearer a man who was himself "A SLAVE OWNER—A SLAVE TRADER—A SUGAR AND COTTON PLANTER OF THE SOUTH"?[47] It was impossible to believe that even Whigs would violate so many of their avowed principles and accept as a candidate a man with whom they had nothing in common. Yet their activities belied this.

What explanation could be made? Obviously, Democratic editors agreed, the whole movement was nothing more than a mad and reckless effort by "party hacks, intriguants and spoilsmen" to ride into power on the military glory that rightfully belonged to the nation.[48] Perhaps, the

---

[44] *Richmond Enquirer,* 6 April 1847; *Milledgeville* (Ga.) *Federal Union* quoted in *Savannah Republican,* 13 May 1847; Baltimore *Republican,* 5 April 1847.

[45] *Pennsylvanian,* 6 May 1847.

[46] Detroit *Free Press,* 15 June 1847.

[47] *Ohio Eagle* quoted in *Cleveland Plain Dealer,* 21 April 1847.

[48] *New Orleans Delta* quoted in *Boston Times,* 28 April 1847.

Democrats also suggested—and Whigs such as Eustis Prescott and Judge McLean agreed—the Whigs were using the military popularity of General Taylor with the hope of carrying state and congressional elections in the autumn of 1847. But "as to any intention of making him President," the *Louisville Democrat* declared, "it's all nonsense." Whigs used his name, the *Baltimore Sentinel* and other journals explained, "only to prevent a disbandment of their forces and to fill up their diminished ranks with the requisite number of recruits, and when *that* is accomplished *they will cast him adrift* and try to smuggle some other Whig champion into the Presidency *on the strength of his well earned popularity.*"[49]

At any rate, this adoption of Taylor made it apparent that the cardinal points of Whig policy—the protective tariff, the bank, and the old land-distribution scheme—had "gone to the limbo of 'obsolete ideas,'" buried forever by the votes of the electorate. In the South, of course, the *Chicago Democrat* declared, this did not matter much. Nobody there cared "for anything but the extension of slavery," in which it was admitted General Taylor had a personal interest. But what of the North? Did not Zack Taylor's candidacy mean that "Old Whiggery" had reached its "last gasp"?[50]

Taylor Whigs did not hear these scathing charges without making reply. Though they were unable to show any recorded evidence of Old Zack's Whiggery, they could, as did the *North American* on 28 April 1847, maintain and reiterate that there "was not in the country a more ardent Whig, one more devoted to *all* the principles recognized by the party than General Taylor." Democratic claims upon the General were entirely without foundation, they insisted; the administration's zealots had no other object than to destroy the Old Hero, as they had already tried so unsuccessfully to do on the field of battle.[51]

Democrats, the *New Orleans Bee* explained, had been "accustomed to make and unmake political idols, not worshipped to be sure by the million, but placed upon the altar of democracy to be adored by the devout and credulous votaries of the faith." But, it warned, "because a

[49] Prescott to Calhoun, 23 August 1847, in Boucher and Brooks, *Calhoun Correspondence*, p. 390; Harvey to Mangum, 3 June 1847, Mangum Papers; *Louisville Democrat*, 9 February 1847; *Baltimore Sentinel* quoted in *Mobile Register*, 31 July 1847. The *Pennsylvanian*, the Baltimore *Republican*, the Indianapolis *Indiana State Sentinel* (hereafter cited as *Indiana State Sentinel*), the *Iowa Capitol Reporter*, the *North Carolina Standard*, the *Nashville Union*, and the *Mississippian* all made the same charge.

[50] *Washington Union*, 5 July 1847; *Chicago Democrat*, 27 April 1847; *Pennsylvanian*, 17 May 1847.

[51] *Albany Evening Journal* quoted in *Washington Union*, 30 April 1847.

Van Buren and a Polk were fabricated out of most unpromising materials, and converted for the nonce into heroes and exalted beyond the rest of the nation, it does not follow that the converse of the proposition holds good," namely, that Democrats could "strip merit of its plumage and hurl genius and patriotism down in the mires of party ribaldry."[52] As for the insinuations of northern Democratic journals concerning Taylor's views on slavery, the *Albany Evening Journal* corrected them in two lines of type: Old Zack was "not only opposed to any extension of slave territory," but he regarded slavery "as one of the incident evils of our otherwise free government."[53]

Political developments during the summer of 1847 gave the General's opponents new grounds for assault. At the beginning of the Buena Vista movement, James W. Taylor, editor of the *Cincinnati Signal,* had addressed an editorial letter to his namesake. In it he had condemned any attempt by either party to monopolize the General's glory for selfish purposes, or "to cast the mantle of his military fame and private virtues over the excesses and corruptions" which disfigured the politics of the day. The time was ripe, he declared, when some popular figure would refuse to accept the foul toga of party, "take independent ground, and become president of the people!" Both Whigs and Democrats were at the moment in a state of utter confusion as to their next standard bearer. Amid this general chaos it was feared that the election would be thrown into the House—"a result greatly to be deplored." The popular will, therefore, chose to abandon party strife, and "take breath under the administration of an independent president."

But before the people would consent to the election of General Taylor, the *Signal* editor declared, it would be necessary to know the principles upon which he would conduct the government. For fifteen years the nation had been divided "on most exciting topics." Fortunately, these subjects no longer agitated the public; they no longer provided points for radical disagreement. There was one principle, however, upon which Taylor had to declare his position—that of executive pressure on Congress.

There were questions approaching, which the people wished to settle in their own way without executive interference. The editor announced:

> The American people are about to assume the responsibility of framing the institutions of the Pacific States. We have no fears for the issue, if the arena of high debate is the assemblies of the people

[52] *New Orleans Bee* quoted in *Niles' Register* 72 (24 July 1847): 334.
[53] *Albany Evening Journal* quoted in *Washington Union,* 30 April 1847.

and their representative halls. The extension to the continent beyond the Rio Grande of the ordinance of 1787 is an object too high and permanent to be baffled by presidential vetoes. All that we ask of the incumbent of the highest office under the constitution is to hold his hand, to bow to the will of the people as promulgated in legislative forms, and restrain the executive action in its appropriate channels! Give us an honest administration of the government, and an end to all cabals of a cabinet—all interference from the White House—designed to sway or thwart the action of the American people. If such simplicity and integrity should guide the administration of General Taylor, the north and west would yield to it a warm support and a hearty approval.

In late June the *Signal* published Taylor's reply, in which he indicated that because his duties in his mission "against the common enemy" were heavy, he would have to be briefer than courtesy demanded. He also apologized that he did not feel himself "at liberty" to discuss the "subjects of public policy" suggested in the editorial letter "till the end of the war." Nevertheless, he expressed his "high opinion and decided approval of the sentiments and views embraced in your editorials." Although he had "not . . . the slightest aspiration" for the "high honor and responsibilities" of the presidential office, he acknowledged that he was "not prepared to say that I shall refuse if the country calls me to the presidential office." At the same time, he wanted to make it clear "that I can and shall yield to no call that does not come from the spontaneous action and free will of the nation at large and void of the slightest agency of my own. . . . In no case can I permit myself to be a candidate of any party, or yield myself to any party schemes."[54]

During the next two months letters of similar import from Taylor's pen reached the public eye. Most important were those to a "gentleman of Lansingburgh," New York; to Dr. Edward Deloney of Clinton, Louisiana; and to the "Democrats" of Clarksville, Tennessee. In all of them he reiterated the declaration that he "would not be the candidate of a party or party clique" and that he would accept the presidency only if elected "by the spontaneous and unanimous voice of the people."[55]

The *"Signal* letter" fell like a bombshell into the camp of the Whigs;

[54] The complete editorial letter and Taylor's reply, published in most major journals of the day, are readily available in *Niles' Register* 72 (3 July 1847) : 288.

[55] The Lansingburgh, Deloney, and Clarksville letters are in *Niles' Register* 72 (24 July 1847) : 333; 72 (21 August 1847) : 389; 73 (25 September 1847) : 63. Taylor's sincerity in his position can be seen in his private letters (Taylor to Dr. Wood, 9 May, 13 July, 27 September 1847, in *Taylor Letters,* pp. 99, 100, 113–14, 134–36; Taylor to his brother, 9 May 1847, Taylor Papers; Taylor to Crittenden, 15 May, 1 November 1847, Crittenden Papers).

the letters that followed only added to their consternation.[56] In Washington the *National Whig,* organ of the Taylor movement, immediately pronounced the *Signal* letter a forgery, "offspring of none but a mean, lying fellow who would steal your purse or stab you in the back, if an opportunity only offered of doing so without detection," and it promised that the "scoundrels who had been instrumental in this infamous act" would be "ferreted out" and hung on "gallows as high as Haman's."[57] When the editors of all the Cincinnati newspapers jointly announced that they had examined the letter and had found it genuine,[58] a thunder of Whig disapproval burst forth. The *Pittsburgh American* stated the reaction most succinctly: "The result is inevitable. *General Taylor cannot be the candidate of the Whigs, unless the Whigs* ABANDON ALL THEIR PRINCIPLES."[59] The *Richmond Times,* one of his original supporters, observed that if Taylor adhered to his nonpartisan position, the Whigs could not be expected to surrender their organization and their principles to elevate him to the presidency. The Whigs had rendered him "the homage of enthusiastic admiration." They had rallied "as one man" in Congress and in the country to defend his reputation from "ungenerous insults." Almost unanimously they had looked forward with pleasant anticipation to the time when they would reward him with the highest station in the civil government. However, the *Times* declared a little sadly, if Taylor chose to decline an honorable testimonial of their gratitude because they would offer it as Whigs, it could not see that the Whigs had any other recourse than to accompany him to the retirement he coveted. "There are others," the *Times* pointed out, "who descry nothing to revolt at in receiving the concerted support of the whig party of the Union."[60]

To the Democrats who saw this confusion in Whig ranks, the *Signal* letter offered a great opportunity. Throughout the nation they promptly interpreted the letter to mean that Taylor had repudiated the Whig attempt "to use him, his name, and services, to promote political ends." They expected "to hear no more of Zachary's being a good Whig, a Whig sound in all principles of the party, a Clay whig, a Whig of the right stamp."[61]

[56] *Washington Union,* 16 July 1847; Detroit *Free Press,* 9 July 1847.
[57] *National Whig* quoted in *Daily Albany Argus,* 5 July 1847 (hereafter cited as *Albany Argus*).
[58] The articles of the Cincinnati editors are in *Washington Union,* 2 July 1847.
[59] *Pittsburgh American* quoted in Baltimore *Republican,* 10 July 1847.
[60] *Richmond Times* quoted in *Niles' Register* 72 (10 July 1847): 294. The press was full of similar announcements, gleefully reprinted by the Democratic journals, sorrowfully by the Whig press.
[61] Detroit *Free Press,* 3 July 1847.

In the South, Democratic editors denounced the letter because it committed Old Zack "to the doctrine of prohibiting slavery in any territory" thereafter acquired by the United States. "When great men —Southern men and slaveholders—yield a tame assent to this frightful doctrine," the *Mississippian* mourned, "the institution of slavery will have become weak indeed."[62]

The Democratic press also took the occasion to warn those of the party who had been seduced by the siren call of the Buena Vista movement. Principles, not men, were the cardinal plank of the party. No Democrat could support the General until assured that he was in favor of all the measures of the Democracy. "The principles of our party, being, as we believe, the very best that human wisdom can devise for the good and prosperity of our country," the *Intelligencer* of Lancaster, Pennsylvania, declared, "why should we abandon them for those, whatever they may be, of one who, as yet, has made no declaration of his views upon any of the great questions that concern the national government, save that he is a 'no-partyman?'" Democrats who felt "any symptoms of the Taylor mania," the *Buffalo Republic* admonished, would do well to "reflect upon the fate of all those factions of the party" that had "forsaken their faith and run after strange Gods."[63]

Taylor editors, placed on the defensive, waged a gallant struggle against this sudden turn in the contest. In the South, most expressed indifference over the problem of Old Zack's Whiggery. Some, such as the *Savannah Republican,* dismissed the issue with the confession that it was unable to understand why the position taken by Taylor "should alienate the Whigs from his support." We prefer "to sustain the hero even more strongly," it declared, "because of his manly determination to ascend the Presidential chair with unfettered hands, as a freeman should."[64] Others, such as the *New Orleans Commercial Bulletin* of 24 July 1847, directing attention to Taylor's apparent antiextension views, hastened to assure their slaveholding brethren that any supposition that Taylor meant to sacrifice "one jot, or one tittle" of southern rights was an "absolute absurdity."

Farther north, where Whiggery was more important, party journals

[62] *Mississippian,* 16 July 1847. Taylor later informed Jefferson Davis that he had not intended to endorse the Wilmot Proviso (Taylor to Davis, 16 August 1847, Taylor Papers). Stevenson of the *Cincinnati Atlas* informed Crittenden that James Taylor of the *Signal* had "no idea" that the General "meant to endorse the Wilmot Proviso" (Stevenson to Crittenden, 1 September 1847, Crittenden Papers).

[63] *Lancaster Intelligencer* quoted in *Washington Union,* 12 August 1847; *Buffalo Republic,* 14 August 1847.

[64] *Savannah Republican,* 14 July 1847. See also *Vicksburg Whig,* 14 July 1847; *Nashville Whig* quoted in *Washington Union,* 20 July 1847.

revealed a greater concern over Taylor's orthodoxy. The Baltimore *Republican* reconciled the matter by maintaining that nonpartisanship was "of the essence of Whig principles," and the New York *Courier* condemned the whole argument as an obvious attempt to distort the General's language: "We have no doubt whatever that Gen. Taylor is a WHIG. . . . In his elevation to the Presidency, *Whig principles* would enjoy a gratifying victory." That "all the OFFICES of the national government would be filled by noisy partisans:—that the infamous doctrine that *public office is a party spoil,* would prevail, as it has prevailed in twenty years," the *Courier* declared, "we do not believe." The whole tenor of Taylor's letters revealed only that he would not "yield himself to party schemes," that eagerness to reward party service would never with him "outweigh devotion to the public good," that he would never be made "the President of a party, subject to its dictation, the tool of its purposes, or the mere agent of its decrees." This was, of course, "the spirit and the temper" which the Whigs had always claimed as their own. Taylor's declaration was, therefore, conclusive evidence that he was "thoroughly and heartily a WHIG,—not a clamorous, selfish, unscrupulous advocate for the ascendancy of the Whig party, at any sacrifice of principles and character, but a firm, disinterested advocate of the best and loftiest principles which the Whigs as a body" had always professed.[65]

All argument upon the subject ended abruptly with the appearance early in the autumn of two more of Taylor's letters, one to Joseph R. Ingersoll of Philadelphia, the other to Dr. F. S. Bronson of Charleston. Although in both he reiterated his determination to run only as a candidate of the people, he declared himself "a whig, not an ultra partisan Whig, but a decided Whig" and further disclosed that if he had voted at the last election, a privilege he had never exercised, he "most certainly" would have cast his vote for "Mr. Clay."[66] As the *Richmond Whig* declared, such statements removed "all doubts as to his political affinities"; the Whig contention had been proven, Taylor partisans maintained, by the best evidence which the case admitted.[67] At the same time, the evidence meant a loss of Democratic support. Taylor might be

---

[65] Baltimore *Republican,* 9 July 1847; New York *Courier,* 9 July 1847.

[66] Only a résumé of the Ingersoll letter was published at first; the full text was not made public until February 1848 (see *Niles' Register* 73 [23 October 1847, 26 February 1848] : 126, 407). The complete Bronson letter, in most journals published only in part, is in *National Intelligencer,* 5 October 1847. See also Taylor to Wood, 5 August, 14 September 1847, in *Taylor Letters,* pp. 122, 130, in which Taylor affirms privately that he would have voted for Clay; and Hamilton, *Taylor,* p. 45, for an analysis of Taylor's opinions.

[67] *Richmond Whig* quoted in *Richmond Enquirer,* 23 October 1847.

dubbed "the PEOPLE'S CANDIDATE," the *Mobile Register* of 8 January 1848 declared, "but he will, in despite of the transparent artifice, by which men can no more be deceived than can mice by the trick of covering one of their number with meal, be regarded as the WHIG CANDIDATE."

There was one political element, the Native Americans, upon which the whole furor concerning the General's party affiliation had no effect. Before Taylor's appearance as a candidate, that party appeared to favor the pretensions of Judge McLean, though there had been some sentiment for Scott, Mangum, and Senator William S. Archer of Virginia, and the party chairman, Peter Sken Smith, had sounded the positions of Clay and Calhoun.[68] Taylor's popularity, however, had swept many of the Natives into the Buena Vista movement. Men such as Lewis C. Levin, Nativist congressman from Philadelphia, viewed the development with considerable alarm, revealing a fear that the nation was moving in the direction of "military despotism." His friends, "the *conservatism* of the country," were among the few who remained loyal to McLean; they even proposed to keep the Judge before the public by nominating him without any pledges at the national convention of the party to be held at Pittsburgh in May 1847. McLean refused the honor.[69] The Levin faction, accordingly, decided to await future developments, especially when it found that the few delegates, "not more than twenty all told," who attended the Pittsburgh meeting were controlled by the "military wing" of the party. They succeeded in postponing nominations until fall.[70] When the "national" Native American convention met at Philadelphia in September, however, even Levin had been seized by the prevailing fever. By a unanimous vote the party "recommended Gen. Zachary Taylor" as the People's Candidate for the presidency with General Henry A. S. Dearborn of Massachusetts as his running mate.[71]

Nativist action, however, ran completely counter to the general political trend. In spite of the heroic work of the Whig press, the publication

[68] Smith to Calhoun, 24 April 1847, in Jameson, *Calhoun Correspondence,* pp. 1116–17; Clay to Smith, 2 April 1847, Henry Clay Papers; Baltimore *Sun,* 13 September 1847; Mueller, *Whigs in Pennsylvania,* pp. 144–45.

[69] Smith to McLean, 16 March 1847, Levin to McLean, 17 April 1847, McLean to Levin, 26 April 1847, McLean Papers.

[70] C. Darragh to McLean, 12 May 1847, Levin to McLean, 12 May 1847, ibid.

[71] *Niles' Register* 73 (25 September, 2 October 1847) : 62, 79. Peter Sken Smith had asked Taylor if he would accept a nomination. Taylor replied in part: "I would not, while the country is involved in war, and while my duty calls me to take part in the operations of the enemy, acknowledge any ambition beyond that of bestowing all my best exertions toward obtaining an adjustment of our difficulties with Mexico" (*Niles' Register* 72 [24 July 1847] : 334).

of the *Signal* letter "and its thousand subsequent daguerrotypes" was followed by reports that Taylor's popularity had begun to decline all over the North. In New York the change was most clearly revealed at Albany, where the Buena Vista movement lost the powerful support of Thurlow Weed, and at the spas which wealthy Whigs were wont to frequent in summer. In Philadelphia James Harvey reported "a radical change," and in Pittsburgh, where Taylor's singular appeal had won over many McLean men, observers declared that the "Taylor fever" had not only abated but had disappeared. From the Northwest came similar accounts. In Ohio the *Cleveland Herald* and every other Taylor paper in the state hauled Old Zack's flag from their mastheads. Thomas B. Stevenson reported from Cincinnati that very few politicians north of the Ohio River regarded Taylor's chances "with any respect." In Indiana, Taylor delegates to the Whig State Convention were reduced to a mere handful; in Wisconsin the *Madison Express,* state organ of the Whigs, deserted the cause. Even Virginia journals, which had joyfully flocked to the Taylor standard, began to backslide.[72]

Undoubtedly, among the reasons for the decline in Taylor's strength during the late summer of 1847 were his letters, which in varying degrees had disaffected both Whigs and Democrats who had originally joined his movement. At the same time it was also evident that the greatest loss of Taylor strength occurred in those quarters that had not been attracted by the Buena Vista "madness"—in the strongholds of those elements that were opposed to the Mexican War and to the extension of slavery. At first they had been relatively inarticulate, but the pressure of the Taylor tide brought them a measure of solidarity, and their voices gradually developed into a loud chorus of antagonism. The *Signal* letter offered them an opportunity for a concerted drive against the principles represented in Taylor's candidacy, and they did not neglect it. At the same time they seized upon the situation to push forward with ever increasing vigor their own separate program—the restriction of slavery to its existing limits.

[72] *Albany Evening Journal* quoted in *Niles' Register* 73 (25 September 1847): 63; Harvey to Mangum, 18 August 1847, Mangum Papers; Harvey to McLean, 1 August, 20 September 1847, Dowling to McLean, 4 February 1848, McLean Papers; *New York Tribune*, 31 July 1847; Stevenson to Crittenden, 1 September 1847, Crittenden Papers; E. Fisher to Calhoun, 22 August 1847, in Boucher and Brooks, *Calhoun Correspondence*, p. 394; "E." to Smith, 30 January 1848, Smith Papers; Milwaukee *Daily Wisconsin,* 27 July 1847 (hereafter cited as *Daily Wisconsin*) ; *North Carolina Standard,* 7 July 1847. Taylor was evidently apprised of the trend (Taylor to Wood, 27 September 1847, in *Taylor Letters,* p. 135).

Chapter Four

Antislavery Forces:
The Democrats

The antislavery movement that developed in the Polk administration and became a major force in the presidential campaign of 1848 had diverse origins and motives. Much of the story is familiar. The movement became political in 1833 when the American Anti-Slavery Society started a petition campaign for the abolition of slavery in the District of Columbia. When a Democratic House of Representatives—urged in part by southerners who were angered by the criticism of their peculiar institution and in part by those who wanted relief from the flood of petitions—adopted a resolution to table such petitions in 1836, the movement broadened. It became a campaign to repeal the gag rule; it also became a campaign against slaveholders, the enemies of free speech.

In Congress the campaign was taken over by a handful of northern Whigs, led by John Quincy Adams, to whom the gag spelled tyranny, and by Joshua Giddings, congressman from the Western Reserve of Ohio, where abolitionism had become a potent political force. Aided and abetted by other northern congressmen in both parties, many of whom had no higher motive than a desire to embarrass the administration, the Whigs ultimately secured a repeal of the gag rule in 1844. The campaign had several effects. It produced the impression, deserved or not, that northern Whiggery was tarred with the brush of abolitionism. More important, it helped develop an antislavery and antislaveholder attitude among northern people.

Meanwhile, a faction within the American Anti-Slavery Society organized the Liberty party at Warsaw, New York, in November 1839. The party enjoyed little success. Immediate abolition of slavery was too extreme a program for the American electorate to accept. In 1840 its candidate for the presidency, James G. Birney, secured only 7,000 votes; although that number grew in 1844 to 62,000, it was less than 3 percent of the total votes cast. Nevertheless, Liberty men had an effect. They were the first to raise a concerted outcry against the annexation of Texas as a slaveholders' conspiracy to extend slavery.

Northern Whigs who had early opposed the annexation of Texas exploited the charge. Whig hostility to annexation was based upon a combination of factors: upon the traditional northeastern opposition to westward expansion, which had been expressed after the annexation of Louisiana in the Hartford convention and in the Foot Resolution, and upon a very reasonable fear that annexation would be followed by war with Mexico. Furthermore, there were areas, particularly in New England and in the Yankee belt, where Whigs honestly believed that annexation was a slaveholders' conspiracy. All these elements used the conspiracy charge effectively to increase votes for northern Whig congressional candidates in 1844.

Some of the same attitudes toward the Texas issue—attitudes reflected in Van Buren's opposition to annexation—appeared among northeastern Democrats in 1843–1844. The need to maintain party unity had pushed these attitudes into the background during the 1844 presidential campaign. But they came into sharp focus in New Hampshire shortly after Polk's election and developed in a way that was to form the pattern for the whole political antislavery movement of Polk's administration.

The man who began the developments in New Hampshire was John P. Hale, a two-term congressman, generally regarded as a particular friend of the workingmen of Portsmouth. In January 1845 the state legislature, controlled by Democrats, requested him to support the joint resolution before Congress for annexation of Texas. Hale, already an official candidate for reelection in the congressional contest to be held in March, hesitated and then announced his opposition to annexation on the grounds that it would extend the area of slavery. He informed Franklin Pierce, chairman of the Democratic State Central Committee, of his decision and simultaneously disclosed his opinions to his constituents in a letter ultimately published by the *New Hampshire Patriot*. In the public letter Hale pointed out that his position was contrary to that of the Democratic party and that he could not allow people to vote in ignorance of the fact. In all fairness, therefore, he was forced to instruct his friends who favored annexation to cast their ballots for some other candidate.[1]

The alternative thus placed before the electorate presented a serious

---

[1] Hale to Pierce, 18 January 1845, Franklin Pierce Papers; *New Hampshire Patriot,* 23 January 1845.

challenge to the leaders of the party in the Granite State. One of them stated the situation briefly and clearly. Friends in Dover, he informed Hale, had received the letter with deep regret, "not . . . because you happen to hold views different from them on the Texas issue, but that you have thought it proper to place your election in March . . . on this simple question alone, knowing that if acted upon it must certainly divide if not ruin the Democratic party."[2] The problem arose out of New Hampshire's unusual electoral system, whereby all congressmen were elected at large; there was a danger that the vote which Hale might normally expect to poll would be so widely scattered among opposition candidates that the whole Democratic congressional ticket would be defeated. The potential disaster had to be prevented.

Accordingly, after a rapid canvass of reaction to the letter convinced party leaders that Hale would find little support among Democrats, a special state convention met at Concord on 12 February 1845.[3] The convention erased Hale's name from the ballot and substituted the name of John Woodbury. The issue, as far as the New Hampshire Democracy was concerned, was not slavery extension; it was Hale's arrogant assumption that he could dictate the issue upon which the election would turn.[4]

Hale could have withdrawn, but he received assurances of secret support from Whigs such as Charles Robbins of the *New Hampshire Courier* and from Liberty men such as Amos Tuck—some of whom were already thinking in terms of a future coalition—and he stayed in the race.[5] Though he received only 7,800 votes at the polls in March, they were sufficient to prevent the election of Woodbury. A second contest was scheduled for September. During the intervening six months, Hale gradually gathered a following among antislavery Demo-

[2] Joseph H. Smith to Hale, 21 January 1845, John P. Hale Papers.

[3] Pierce to George Atherton, 18 January 1845, Pierce Photostats; Pierce to Levi Woodbury, 20 January 1845, Woodbury Papers.

[4] Pierce privately informed the insurgent congressman: "If you had felt constrained to oppose annexation in any form in which it might finally be presented to the House, if you had spoken against it & voted against it, it would have been a matter of regret to the great body of your Democratic friends, but stil it would not have been made a ground of opposition to your re-election" (Pierce to Hale, 24 January 1845, Pierce Papers). See also *New Hampshire Patriot*, 13, 20 February 1845. Roy F. Nichols, *Franklin Pierce: Young Hickory from the Granite Hills* (Philadelphia, 1931), pp. 135–38, gives an excellent brief analysis of the party situation (hereafter cited as *Pierce*).

[5] Robbins to Hale, 15 March 1845, Tuck to Hale, 23 January 1845, Hale Papers. See also E. Hurd to Hale, 22 January, 3 February 1845, Daniel Root to Hale, 27 January 1845, Tuck to Hale, 5, 18 February 1845, L. H. Parson to Hale, 18 February 1845, J. W. W. Colby to Hale, 20 February 1845, I. S. Palmer to Hale, 26 February 1845, J. H. Higgins to Hale, 1 March 1845.

crats and among elements who nursed grievances against the "State House Gang," captained by Pierce. Organized as the Independent Democrats, they established a newspaper in Concord. The Liberty party gave unofficial support by withdrawing its candidate; many Whigs provided covert aid.[6] Although the Texas question had been settled, slavery extension remained the issue. Hale's vote increased slightly in the three-cornered race; a third contest in November also ended without a decision. At the end of 1845 the struggle in the state had reached a stalemate.[7]

During the following winter the informal combination of the Hale forces and the Liberty party was transformed into a firm coalition by the joint nomination of an abolitionist, Nathaniel L. Berry, as its gubernatorial candidate. Hale also accepted a joint nomination, for the state assembly. A vigorous contest followed. With Hale's political matyrdom as the main issue, the coalition won enough votes to prevent any gubernatorial candidate from securing a majority. Under New Hampshire law, election of the governor then devolved upon the state legislature. Before it convened, the Independent Democrats and the Whigs reached an "understanding."[8] When the legislature met in June 1846, the "unholy alliance," which controlled the body, elected Anthony Colby, a Whig, as governor by a count of 146 votes to 135; it gave Hale a six-year term in the United States Senate; and it named Joseph Cilley, an abolitionist, to a short Senate term.[9]

This alliance dominated the state for the rest of the year, until its strong federalism and its adoption of the radical doctrines of the abolitionists drove many of Hale's followers back into the Democratic party, which recovered its long-standing ascendancy in the spring of 1847. The return to Democratic control did little to weaken the antiextension movement, however. The Democracy, obedient to popular pressure, had adopted the Wilmot Proviso as its own property; like the Independents, the regular Democrats were committed in 1847 to a war against the further spread of slavery.[10]

[6] D. S. Palmer to Hale, 13 April 1845, ibid.

[7] Much of the material on these three campaigns is taken from the *New Hampshire Patriot,* 20 March, 8 May, 12, 19 June, 17, 31 July, 4 September, 2, 16, 30 October, 6 November, 4, 25 December 1845.

[8] The "understanding" provided not only for the election of Anthony Colby and Hale, but also for the continued advancement of Ichabod Goodwin, a Whig, as a congressional candidate, in order to develop him for the future (Palmer to Hale, 2 February, 21 March 1846, Samuel Webster to Hale, 17 April 1846, A. Cass to Hale, 23 April 1846, Hale Papers).

[9] See *New Hampshire Patriot,* 15 January, 14 May, 4, 11, 18 June 1846.

[10] See the statement of "15 Independent Democrats" and the Democratic party's antiextension platform, ibid., 24 December 1846, 4 November 1847.

The furor and division that the Texas issue created within the New Hampshire Democracy was not matched in any other state Democratic organization until after the second introduction of the Wilmot Proviso, when the smoldering antislavery feeling that had existed in the North during the summer of 1846 burst into life. Why northern Democrats delayed so long in revealing their attitude is difficult to understand and to explain. Perhaps it was because northern thoughts upon the issue had not been clearly formulated: Wilmot had not stated the issue as it affected the common man.[11] It was not until the second introduction of the measure that the issue was stated in simple terms, in the words of Preston King: "If slavery is not excluded [from the territories] by law, the presence of the slave will exclude the laboring white man."[12] Within the year it was stated in another fashion by Walt Whitman. The issue, he announced in the columns of the *Brooklyn Eagle,* was between *"the grand body of white workingmen, the millions of mechanics, farmers, and operatives of our country,* with their interests on one side—and the interests of the few thousand rich . . . and aristocratic owners of slaves at the South, on the other."[13] In such terms, defined as a struggle between free white labor and slave plantation labor in which the freedom, dignity, and opportunities of the white laboring man were at stake —terms which the average northerner could readily understand—the Proviso became an immediate issue. Throughout the North, Democrats who feared for their liberties demanded that the old issues be pushed into the background, that all political questions be reduced to the one issue of the future freedom of white labor.

The manifestations of this demand were most apparent and most bitter in the camp of the New York Democracy, where the pressure forced a ten-year-old feud between "radicals" and "conservatives" into open warfare.[14] Differences between the factions had originated over such issues as the re-charter of the Second Bank of the United States, distribution of the surplus, the specie circular, state banking laws, the Independent Treasury System, and the financing of canal construction. They were differences based on principle. The radicals revealed a gener-

---

[11] Wilmot declared later: "I would preserve for free white labor a fair country, a rich inheritance, where the sons of toil, of my own race and color, can live without the disgrace which association with negro slavery brings upon free labor" (Going, *Wilmot,* pp. 98–100, 174).

[12] Jabez Hammond, *Life and Times of Silas Wright* (Syracuse, N. Y., 1848), pp. 706–7.

[13] *Brooklyn Eagle,* 1 September 1847.

[14] The terms, of course, are inexact, but there is little question about the composition and principles of the factions to which they were attached.

ally restrictive economic outlook and a suspicion of monopoly, loose banking practices, paper money, and speculation; they became the spokesmen for most of the state's small farmers and mechanics. The conservatives voiced the more expansive attitude of those elements among New York's commercial and financial interests which had not joined Whig ranks.

Until 1843, when William C. Bouck became governor, this division among New York Democrats had caused a major problem only once— when conservatives, under the leadership of Lieutenant Governor Nathaniel P. Tallmadge, bolted the party over Martin Van Buren's proposal for an Independent Treasury and allowed the Whigs, led by William H. Seward, to take control of the state in 1838. Throughout this early period the radicals dominated the party.

The situation changed in Bouck's administration. Bouck threw his support to the conservatives, and a contest for party control developed. The division widened to the point where each faction recognized its own journalistic spokesman in Albany: radicals looked to the *Atlas,* edited by James M. French and William Cassidy, and conservatives to the *Argus,* edited by Edwin Crosswell. The two factions also acquired distinct names: the radicals were called Barnburners; the conservatives were called Hunkers.[15]

The strained relations between the two factions,[16] however, did not prevent their united support of Van Buren's campaign to recapture leadership of the Democratic party and to secure another presidential

[15] There are many explanations of the two names. Whigs insisted that the name *Barnburner* had been fastened to the radical wing because its actions were similar to the barnburning tactics of the Rhode Island Dorrites; Hunkers claimed the word was used because the faction was mean enough to burn down barns in order to get the nails. A more logical explanation is that the name grew out of an insulting remark which likened the policy of the radicals to that of a legendary Dutch farmer who burned down his barn to rid it of rats. The name *Hunker* is equally difficult to trace. Some declared that the word was used to ridicule the conservatives' strenuous efforts to get a large "hunk" of the spoils of office; others thought it was a corruption of the Dutch slang word *hanker,* freely translated as greedy." Neither term was in common use before 1843. It is interesting that Calhounites used the term *Hunker* to describe almost any of their enemies in the Democratic party.

[16] The best contemporary account of the radical-conservative conflict is in De Alva S. Alexander, *Political History of the State of New York* (New York, 1906), 2: 126-44 (hereafter cited as *New York Political History*). Later accounts include Herbert D. A. Donovan, *Barnburners* (New York, 1925), pp. 15-47; and Arthur M. Schlesinger, Jr., *The Age of Jackson* (New York, 1945), pp. 74-305 passim, where it is related to the national scene. All three books are biased in favor of the radicals. See also Ivor D. Spencer, *The Victor and the Spoils: A Life of William L. Marcy* (Providence R. I., 1959), pp. 53-122 passim, for an account with a more "conservative" point of view.

nomination in 1844. Few ventured objections to the state's endorsement of his candidacy. Although many of the Hunkers were secretly disaffected because of Van Buren's Independent Treasury policy, and although some even arranged meetings in the interests of Calhoun and the former vice president, Richard M. Johnson of Kentucky, almost all the Democratic newspapers of the state carried Van Buren's name on their mastheads.[17]

In Baltimore both factions gave Van Buren their unanimous vote. When he lost, the Hunkers accepted the outcome with a hearty cordiality. But the Barnburners, who believed they had discovered evidence of treachery among their conservative associates, returned home filled with discontent and a sense of injustice.[18] Nevertheless, they temporarily submerged their feelings and set out to carry the Democratic ticket in the Empire State. In order to aid the cause of the Democratic party and to bolster their own political position in the state, they suggested that Silas Wright, their leader in the United States Senate, replace Bouck as the party's gubernatorial candidate. Bouck, they maintained, did not deserve reelection, because he had been false to Democratic principles; besides, his reputation was too weak to aid the Democratic presidential ticket against Clay. Although Wright discouraged the movement to draft him and although the Hunkers waged a vigorous campaign to retain Bouck, the Barnburners, aided by Van Buren, succeeded in their objective.[19] Wright's election by a majority twice the size of Polk's attested to the wisdom of their course. The Barnburners turned expectantly to Polk for their reward.

Everyone, including the president-elect, acknowledged that Polk was indebted to "Mr. Van Buren and his friends" for his victory in New York, the vote of which was "indispensable to . . . success."[20] Everyone expected that such service would be repaid with a major cabinet post, and Polk acted according to expectation. Although he may have been

[17] Donovan, *Barnburners*, pp. 52–53.

[18] Ibid., pp. 53–55.

[19] It was Van Buren who recommended that the state convention use Wright's name without his consent (Harry Rogers to Van Buren, 27 December 1844, Van Buren Papers).

[20] Polk to Benjamin F. Butler, 25 November 1844, in William A. Butler, *Retrospect of Forty Years, 1825–1865, by William Allen Butler*, ed. Harriet A. Butler (New York, 1911), p. 146. See also Gideon Welles to Van Buren, 13 November 1844, Samuel Medary to Van Buren, 4 January 1845, Van Buren Papers. In the following account of Polk's negotiations with Wright, Van Buren, and other New York Democrats, I am largely following my article, "Martin Van Buren's Break with James K. Polk: The Record," *New York History* 26 (January 1955): 51–62.

aware that the New Yorker could not be induced to desert his post in Albany, he offered Wright the Treasury.[21] When Wright politely refused, Polk turned to Van Buren. Admitting that his own knowledge of Empire State politics was meager, he informed the ex-president that he wanted a New Yorker at the head of the State Department or the Treasury Department and asked him to suggest suitable persons for both posts.[22] With evident delight Van Buren, in a letter dated 18 January 1845, recommended Benjamin F. Butler, attorney general in Jackson's and his own cabinet, as the "best man in the country" for the State Department. If Butler should not prove satisfactory, he suggested that the Treasury be given to Churchill C. Cambreleng, former chairman of the House Ways and Means Committee, or to Azariah C. Flagg, New York state comptroller, whose reputation as a public financier in the state stood "higher . . . than that of any man" who had held office before him. Wright also recommended Butler and Flagg.[23]

More than a month elapsed before Polk again communicated with Van Buren. During this time the president-elect, still in Nashville, offered the State Department to Buchanan, for reasons which are unrecorded in the pertinent letters of the day but which may be deduced from the fact that Polk owed a political debt to Pennsylvania. Then he moved his headquarters to Washington, where he learned that several factions and individuals were ready to battle against the rumored appointment of Butler or Flagg. Cave Johnson reported the situation succinctly: "The whole force of Calhounism and Cassism threatened open war."[24] More-

[21] Francis W. Pickens informed Polk that Wright was committed to remain in the governorship (Pickens to Polk, 5 November 1844, James K. Polk Papers). But Polk could have ignored this information, since Pickens had no important New York connections. Preston King informed Cave Johnson that Wright would not take a place in the cabinet, and Johnson so informed Polk (Niles to Welles, 29 December 1844, Welles Papers; Johnson to Polk, 6 December 1844, Polk Papers). Polk could not have received Johnson's letter before he sent his offer to Wright on 7 December 1844. Moreover, there is an indication that Polk had a high regard for Wright and genuinely wanted him in the cabinet (John O'Sullivan to Van Buren, 28 March 1845, Van Buren Papers). On the other hand, Marcy was well aware that Wright would not accept a cabinet post (Marcy to Wetmore, 10 November 1844, Wetmore to Marcy, 16 November 1844, William L. Marcy Papers).

[22] Polk to Van Buren, 4 January 1845, Van Buren Papers.

[23] Van Buren to Polk, 18 January 1845, Wright to Van Buren, 17 January 1845, ibid.

[24] O'Sullivan to Van Buren, 28 March 1845, ibid. Some of Polk's problems with cabinet appointments and with patronage are outlined in Henry B. Learned, "Sequence of Appointments to Polk's Original Cabinet: A Study in Chronology, 1844–1845," *American Historical Review* 30 (1924): 79–80; and Norman A. Graebner, "James K. Polk: A Study in Federal Patronage," *Mississippi Valley Historical Review* 38 (March 1952): 613–32. More recent and more con-

over, there was another major candidate for the Treasury, Robert J. Walker. As Polk explained in his letter to Van Buren of 22 February 1845: "The South had in advance of my arrival . . . united on a distinguished gentleman from that section of the Union for that office. *Indiana* and a portion of some other Western States—had joined them —in earnestly pushing the appointment of the same gentleman." Polk said he surrendered to this pressure because he "became convinced—that if I did not—great and extensive disaffection would prevail." However, he continued, he still wanted a New Yorker in the cabinet as secretary of war; the question was, who should it be? Cambreleng and Flagg had been mentioned only for the Treasury and presumably would not be suited for any other department. Would Butler or William L. Marcy be satisfactory for the War Department?[25]

The suggestion that Marcy was being considered probably astonished Van Buren. Measured by Barnburner standards, the ex-governor was not a true Jacksonian; he had revealed that fact during the controversy over the specie circular. In November 1844 he had declined a chance to fill out Tallmadge's unexpired term in the Senate. According to current rumors, moreover, he had moved from the political arena to the presidency of a Wall Street trust company. It was generally conceded that his political career was over. Where did he fit into the picture?

Marcy, it appears, had never allowed the offer of a Wall Street post to interfere with his desire for further public employment, and his close associates knew it. His agents (Daniel S. Dickinson, elected a United States senator early in 1845, Congressman George C. Strong, Bouck, and Crosswell) had reached Washington in January. Armed with a recommendation from a portion of the New York legislature, they had quietly urged his claims on the Treasury, because it was well known that the post had been assigned to a New Yorker. After the office was filled, they transferred their attention to the War Department.[26] In spite of

---

clusive accounts are in James P. Shenton, *Robert J. Walker: A Politician from Jackson to Lincoln* (New York, 1961), pp. 58–63 (hereafter cited as *Walker*); and the excellent work by Charles G. Sellers, *James K. Polk, Continentalist: 1843–1846* (Princeton, N. J., 1966), pp. 162–208 (hereafter cited as *Polk*). Sellers relates Polk's problems not only to the warring factions within the party but also to the Texas annexation issue. Notice should also be taken of Eric Foner, "Wilmot Proviso Revisited," *Journal of American History* 56 (1969): 262–79.

[25] Polk to Van Buren, 22 February 1845, Van Buren Papers. Polk's relations and negotiations with Barnburner and Hunker politicians—from Polk's point of view— are related in Sellers, *Polk*, pp. 173–80, 184–86, 196–204.

[26] The whole movement for Marcy is well documented in the Marcy Papers: see J. D. Stevenson to Marcy, 8 November 1844, 2 March 1845, Wetmore to Marcy, 8, 16 November 1844, Marcy to Bouck, 28 November 1844, Marcy to Wetmore, 10

warnings that Marcy's name was being advanced by a faction hostile to Van Buren and Wright, Polk was favorably impressed by Marcy's agents, and his letter to the ex-president reflected that fact.[27]

Polk's letter, which clearly revealed the political machinations that had deprived New York of two major cabinet posts, infuriated Van Buren. On 27 February, his son Smith started for Washington with his reply. In it Van Buren denounced the appointments Polk had already made as "a concession to a selfish influence proceeding from other quarters and directed against New York." This influence had "received its most efficient impulse from the same Indiana delegation" that had worked for a nomination which would have overthrown the party "if New York had not stepped aside." He predicted that knowledge of these developments would incense New York Democrats.

As for Polk's request for advice, Van Buren was precise: "There is no time to consult Mr. Butler, but . . . the danger of your making a fatal mistake in this State [is] so imminent that I take upon myself the responsibility of replying for Mr. Butler that he will accept the War Department if it is tendered to him."[28] Before this letter reached him, Polk, alarmed because his cabinet was not yet completed, had written directly to Butler, offering him the War office. Without consulting Van Buren or Wright, and against the urgent pleading of his friends in New York, Butler had refused the position and had suggested that Polk give the office to Cambreleng.[29]

Butler's decision was apparently made with the knowledge that Marcy was also a candidate for the position.[30] Accordingly, he persuaded Samuel J. Tilden to rush to Washington to throw his influence against the former governor. On 1 March Tilden went with John L. O'Sullivan, editor of the *Democratic Review,* to see the president-elect; Polk assured them that he would make no further decision on the War Department

November 1844, H. K. Smith to Marcy, 26 November 1844, George C. Strong to Marcy, 18 December 1844, Orville Robinson to Marcy, 20 January, 12 February, 1 March 1845, Daniel S. Dickinson to Marcy, 1 March 1845. The vice-president-elect placed Marcy in the War Department as early as 23 February 1845 (George M. Dallas to William Dallas, 23 February 1845, Dallas Papers). See also Spencer, *Marcy,* pp. 129–36.

[27] Smith Van Buren to Martin Van Buren, 2, 3 March 1845, Van Buren Papers.

[28] Van Buren to Polk, 27 February 1845, ibid. Polk's reaction to this letter is recorded in Quaife, *Polk's Diary,* 3: 74.

[29] Polk to Van Buren, 25 February 1845, Butler to Polk, 27 February 1845, Van Buren Papers. Butler's refusal, as later correspondence reveals, was based on "pecuniary and domestic" considerations (Butler to Van Buren, 28 February 1845, Harriet Butler to Van Buren, February 1845).

[30] Butler, *Retrospect,* p. 147.

until he heard from Van Buren.[31] On the same day, however, he offered the position to Marcy, explaining in a letter to Van Buren that he wanted the office to be occupied by a man of "national reputation," which "Mr. Flagg does not posesss."[32]

On the following day, 2 March, Smith Van Buren arrived in Washington. Before he delivered his father's message, he saw Tilden, O'Sullivan, and John A. Dix, Wright's successor in the United States Senate. He learned that they had warned Polk against appointing Marcy and that Polk had pledged to make no decision on the War Department until he received Van Buren's letter. With this information, Smith Van Buren took his father's communication to the president-elect, who "was very much & very evidently embarrassed" throughout the interview. Polk "took the letter, held it in his hands, turned it about in his fingers without offering to open it & said, *'I wish I had recd this last evening.'* " When he continued to fidget, Smith Van Buren disclosed the contents of the letter, "at which he slapped it with his hand & said, 'It is too late.' " Polk then went on to explain that he had offered two posts to New Yorkers and that both had been refused; with no one to consult and the time for inauguration rapidly approaching, he had been forced to make a decision before it was too late. When Smith Van Buren reminded him of his pledge to Tilden and O'Sullivan, Polk made no reply. The younger Van Buren reported, "I was so disappointed in the result, & so shocked by the transparent indications of his want of faith & his complete *capture* by the rogues that I got out of his way as soon as possible."[33]

On 3 March, Smith Van Buren learned that Congressman Gouverneur Kemble had warned Polk against Marcy's appointment. He also delivered a second letter from his father, a letter of apology for losing his temper, over which Polk revealed considerable relief. But Smith Van Buren had no intention of letting the president-elect rest easily:

> I denounced Marcy to him in good round terms, & in company with Bouck & Crosswell. I thought it best to let him know that we should thereafter call *men* & things by their right names. I told him of Marcy's utter loss of strength in the State—of his holding a commission in his pocket which would withdraw him entirely from politics with the unanimous approbation of the democracy of New York, but that his itchings for politics and his association with the remnants of conservatism had induced him to hold the business

[31] Smith Van Buren to Martin Van Buren, 2 March 1845, Van Buren Papers.
[32] Polk to Van Buren, 1 March 1845, ibid.
[33] Smith Van Buren to Martin Van Buren, 2 March 1845, ibid.

office in abeyance while he took three chances for political posts, 1st. Senator from New York—2d. Judge from Tyler, (both failures) & 3d. a cabinet post from Polk—which if he got would utterly paralyze the party in our state & prostrate the administration & its friends.

He reported that Polk "professed to hear these things for the first time, to be thunderstruck &c. &c. whereas Dix had told him the same thing over & over again," concluding that "he has sold out to Buck—Cass & Walker."[34]

This information, relayed in Van Buren's letters to his father, quickly spread among the Barnburners, who immediately concluded that Polk had never intended to give the War Department to one of Van Buren's friends.[35] Various factors pointed to such a deduction. Polk had not waited, in spite of his promises, for Van Buren's reply to his inquiry about Butler and Marcy before offering the post to Marcy. Despite his plea that he was ignorant about the New York political situation, Polk knew that Marcy's appointment would not fulfill his obligation to Van Buren. The president-elect failed to approach Cambreleng, whom Van Buren had also suggested for a cabinet post, and whom Butler had suggested specifically for the War office. Polk's excuse that he wanted a man of national reputation evaded the fact that Flagg's reputation extended to the Northwest and the deep South, that Cambreleng's reputation was nationwide, and that some of Polk's appointees (George Bancroft, John Y. Mason, and Cave Johnson) could hardly boast such distinction.

Supported by such reasoning, the Barnburners readily agreed with Dix, who declared that New York had been "betrayed." Like Tilden, they were convinced that Polk had been captured by the "quasi-Van Buren men who went with us before Baltimore but deserted us there."[36] Polk tried to assuage the hurt feelings with minor appointments: he selected Bancroft of Massachusetts, one of Van Buren's friends, as secretary of the navy, Cambreleng as minister to Russia, Butler as district attorney for southern New York, and Hoffman as naval officer of the Port of New York. He offered O'Sullivan a new position as assistant secretary of state, and Van Buren both the ministry at London

[34] Smith Van Buren to Martin Van Buren, 3 March 1845, ibid.

[35] Cambreleng charged that Polk's offer to Wright was a "contemptible ruse" (Cambreleng to Van Buren, 13 March 1845, ibid.).

[36] Niles to Welles, 1 March 1845, Welles Papers; Samuel J. Tilden to William F. Havemeyer, 4 March 1845, in Samuel J. Tilden, *Letters and Literary Memorials of Samuel J. Tilden*, ed. John Bigelow (New York, 1908), 1: 26 (hereafter cited as *Tilden Letters*).

and a position on the Supreme Court. None of the appointments and offers changed the Barnburners' opinion, for it was evident that Polk was appointing Hunkers to equally important posts. They continued to believe, as Henry Simpson informed Van Buren, that in Washington "the *ban* appears to be put upon every friend of yours."[37]

Barnburners even discerned a motive for the "treachery" committed against New York. Many became convinced with Cambreleng that a bargain had been made between Polk and Buchanan "to run P. a second time & put B. in line for the succession."[38] To accomplish this end it was necessary to destroy the strength of Silas Wright, the logical candidate for the next presidential nomination; that could be done by putting control of Federal patronage in New York into the hands of Van Buren's enemies, of whom Marcy, believed to be a supporter of Lewis Cass, was the chief.[39] Thus convinced, the Barnburners began to look for further duplicity, and it was not long before they found evidence of it in the gubernatorial election of 1846.

Wright's two-year administration was a period of almost continuous conflict between the two factions of the New York Democracy. It started when the party caucus met in January 1845 to decide upon candidates for three senatorial positions: the seat vacated by Wright, whose term ended in March 1849; the seat vacated by Tallmadge, whose term still had several weeks to run; and a new six-year term to end in March 1851. When the caucus met, the Barnburners were already angry because the outgoing governor, Bouck, had temporarily given the unexpired terms to two Hunkers, Daniel S. Dickinson and Henry D. Foster. The caucus produced a bitter wrangle: Foster, whose name was anathema to the Barnburners, at first insisted upon being a candidate for Wright's seat; when he was persuaded to withdraw, the Hunkers refused to concede one of the seats to the Barnburners without a fight. Ultimately the caucus agreed on John A. Dix to replace Wright and on Dickinson for both Tallmadge's unexpired term and the six-year term.

[37] Henry Simpson to Van Buren, 18 March 1845, Van Buren Papers. This attitude was also expressed outside New York (Niles to Welles, 1 March 1845, Welles Papers; Cambreleng to Van Buren, 14 March 1845, Tilden to Van Buren, 29 March 1845, Van Buren Papers; Erastus Corning to Marcy, 12 March 1845, Marcy Papers).

[38] Cambreleng to Van Buren, 14 March 1845, Van Buren Papers. See also Butler, *Retrospect,* p. 148.

[39] George W. Newell to Marcy, 29 March 1845, Marcy Papers. See also a statement issued by Van Buren, 3 March 1845, Van Buren Papers; Van Buren to George Bancroft, 7 March 1845, in Worthington C. Ford, ed., "Van Buren–Bancroft Correspondence, 1830–1845," *Proceedings of the Massachusetts Historical Society* 42 (1909) : 439–40.

Passions flared again when the caucus voted on candidates for five major state offices held by Barnburners. The Hunkers raised no objection to Comptroller Flagg, and their candidate failed by one vote to take over the office held by Attorney General John Van Buren; however, Hunker candidates captured the three other positions—victories that gave them control of the Canal Commission.

Bitter disagreement also developed in the legislature over a Hunker-inspired appropriation for extension of the canal system; over Barnburner amendments to the state constitution, which would have deprived the legislature of the power to create debts; over a Whig-Barnburner measure for a constitutional convention, which Hunkers feared would restore to the electorate the power of making debts; and over a Barnburner effort to remove Crosswell as state printer. In all these quarrels Governor Wright took the Barnburner position. He vetoed the canal appropriation bill, approved the measure calling for a constitutional convention, and supported the attack on Crosswell. Moreover, his appointments to state offices were almost invariably from Barnburner ranks.[40]

Hunker opposition to Wright's renomination appeared in the early summer of 1846 when various journals, led by Crosswell's *Albany Argus* and strongly abetted by newspapers in Foster's home county of Oneida, started to campaign for a western candidate and to write editorials emphasizing old Democratic watchwords such as "one-term principle" and "rotation in office."[41] They also assiduously developed the rumor that Polk and the whole Federal administration were hostile to Wright in particular and to the Barnburners in general—a contention given strength by Polk's appointment in August 1846 of ex-Governor Bouck as head of the Subtreasury in New York City. Their wounds exacerbated, Barnburners responded with cries of anguish and outrage loud enough to reach Washington and to cause consternation. Buchanan decided to take a vacation at Saratoga. Although strongly courted by Hunkers and almost completely snubbed by Barnburners during his holiday, the secretary of state returned to Washington with a remarkably accurate view of the political situation in New York. His report—particularly concerning the charges that Polk was hostile to Wright and was using his patronage against him—so appalled and discomfitted the president that he asked Bancroft to investigate. When the secretary of

---

[40] Surveys of Wright's administration are in Donovan, *Barnburners,* pp. 62–73; and Garraty, *Wright,* pp. 334–84. Garraty suggests that Wright was partly responsible for the widening breach between Barnburners and Hunkers because he failed to recognize that he was not only the governor of New York but also the leader of a political party.

[41] *Albany Argus,* 17, 27, 29 July, 13 August 1846.

the navy confirmed Buchanan's findings, Polk directed his cabinet to use all their endeavors to secure Wright's reelection.[42]

Meanwhile, the New York governor had won a triumphant, almost unanimous, renomination. But Polk's intervention on his behalf during the gubernatorial campaign did no good. Although there was little direct evidence of Hunker maneuverings against Wright, it became clear that the faction was continuing its hostile campaign. In mid-October Wright himself recognized the situation. Surface manifestations, he informed Van Buren, revealed that leading Hunkers were determined to do their worst. "I infer this," he explained, "from the fact that they all predict defeat and that the first class leaders are professing friendship, but constantly fault-finding, while the second class are open-mouthed in opposition."[43]

In an election marked by a sharp drop in the Democratic vote, Wright lost his chair to the able and clever John Young. (However, Wright's running mate, Addison Gardiner, captured the lieutenant governor's post by a substantial margin.) Barnburners reacted spontaneously: their wrath, nourished now by direct evidence of Hunker duplicity, turned first on Crosswell. His was the influence, as Dix pointed out, that "rested like mildew on the work of the campaign, sapping it of enthusiasm, and encouraging Democrats . . . to put in the knife on election day." Equally important, they excoriated "Polk, Marcy, Cass & Co."; with Cambreleng they denounced Polk's appointment of Hunkers to important offices in New York City and in the state as a "significant indication of the guillotine" prepared for Wright. On all sides the unhappy and infuriated Barnburners contended there were signs that the president and his "treacherous crew" had been party to the double-dealing practiced by the Hunkers.[44]

---

[42] Buchanan to Polk, 5, 10 September 1846, Bancroft to Polk, 4 October 1846, Wright to Polk, 18 October 1846, Polk Papers; Wright to Buchanan, 8, 10 September, 30 October 1846, Buchanan to Wright, 9 September 1846, Buchanan Papers; Ransom H. Gillet, *Life and Times of Silas Wright* (Albany, N. Y., 1874), 2: 1656–60, 1662, 1670–71, 1707–12, 1716.

[43] Wright to Van Buren, 16 October 1846, Van Buren Papers. See also Hoffman to Flagg, 1 November 1846, Azariah C. Flagg Papers. Significantly, Marcy had come to the same conclusion (Marcy to Wetmore, 6 September, 11 October 1846, Marcy Papers). See also Harvey to Mangum, 22 September 1846, Mangum Papers.

[44] The *Albany Atlas* found "direct evidence" of a "corrupt bargain" between Hunkers and Whigs in Herkimer (*Albany Atlas*, 10, 30 November 1846). See also John Adams Dix, *Memoirs of John Adams Dix,* comp. Morgan Dix (New York, 1883), 1: 227 (hereafter cited as *Memoirs*); Cambreleng to Van Buren, 30 November 1847, Van Buren Papers; *Buffalo Republic,* 18, 19 November 1846; Van Buren to Blair, 18 November 1846, Francis P. Blair Papers. Barnburners recognized that other factors were involved in Wright's defeat. They specifically

When the state legislature met in January 1847, the short-tempered resentment that the gubernatorial contest had engendered in both factions was still high, and the quarreling was at once renewed with increased acerbity. The issue now was the Proviso. A week after the session began, the Barnburners introduced a resolution instructing the state's senators and requesting the state's representatives to support the Proviso when it was reintroduced in Congress. All legislative action stopped as the estranged wings of the New York Democracy engaged in a bitter, month-long debate on the subject of slavery in the territories, while the Whigs, who held a majority in both houses, looked on in astonished delight.[45]

Even before the debate in the legislature ended in a Barnburner victory, the issue was taken up by the Democratic press with a vigor greater than before. Barnburner journals, proud of their sensitivity to Jacksonian ideals, had earlier disclosed their opposition to the extension of slavery in the controversy over the annexation of Texas. Party needs had caused them to suppress their views. Now, however, they adopted the new manifestation of the extension issue as their own property and exhorted their arguments in favor of the Proviso in emphatic language.

Their opponents promptly charged them with seeking revenge for Van Buren's defeat at Baltimore. Barnburners indignantly denied the charge. The best report of their position ever published appeared in the *Albany Atlas,* their journalistic spokesman. "The democracy of New York," it declared, "do not arraign the South, and hold it responsible for the wrong done at Baltimore. Whatever of misrepresentation of constituencies there was in that body, whatever of injustice and usurpation in setting aside the will of the majority, was shared in by the delegations from the North." There were "no such unsettled account[s] of wrong, and no such resentments, as those who are busy fomenting alienation would represent." The Barnburners' opposition to the extension of slavery was stronger than a plant "forced to premature growth in the hot bed of factionalism and sectionality."

Their convictions, the *Atlas* maintained, were rooted in the character

mentioned his unpopular use of the state's police forces against Anti-Renters, his canal veto, and the use of fraudulent ballots. But they constantly returned to the theme that Hunker defection was *"the* cause" (*Albany Atlas,* 4, 5, 7, 8, 10 December 1846). Polk also concluded that the Hunkers had defeated Wright (Quaife, *Polk's Diary,* 2: 218). On the other hand, the Hunkers charged the Barnburners with defection in several counties (*Albany Argus,* 6, 18, 28 November 1846).

[45] The debates are reported in *Albany Atlas,* 9, 12, 18, 25 January, 1 February 1847.

of slavery itself. "The degradation of labor, which results from a system of compulsory servitude," it explained, "has a contagion that affects with dishonor all who are associated with it." The citizens of the North, who had been taught to look upon labor with pride and respect, were now called upon to decide whether the soil which the arms of American citizens might acquire should "be the field of the extension and elevation of labor, or in being set apart for Slavery, be devoted to influences that degrade and debase it." With the problem thus posed, the answer of all "Northern Democrats" was not to extend slavery "over another rood of free territory."[46]

Hunkers continued to attack the "selfish and sinister" motives of the Proviso's supporters. While careful to condemn any further extension of slavery, they denounced all legislation upon the subject as premature, or as a "mischievous abstraction, fomenting discord and disunion—delaying the action of Congress upon necessary measures and producing no practical good." Whether introduced in good faith "from some *new born* zeal upon the subject of slavery, or designed to revive fallen fortunes by the blending of prostrate elements," they maintained, "the effect . . . must be to embarrass the administration by vexatious delays and weakened counsels and to arouse the hopes and strengthen the hands of a common and lawless enemy."[47]

All through 1847 this debate raged in the Democratic press, growing steadily more vituperative. Hunkers denounced Barnburners as "factious agitators," "African Democrats," and "cornerstone abstractionists"; Barnburners in turn condemned the Hunkers as "sycophants" and "Southern mercenaries" and even threatened to read them out of the party.[48]

Meanwhile, the time for another state election approached—an election made necessary by a constitutional amendment which had taken the power to name high state officials out of the hands of the legislature and had given it to the electorate. Hunkers began their campaign early. Suggesting that harmony required replacement of all men who had been actively connected with either faction of the party, they raised a demand for the scalp of State Comptroller Flagg, a man whom the *Albany Argus* described as a "cormorant for office," "greedy of patronage," "factious," "intolerant," and "an old offender against the peace and usages of the

---

[46] Ibid., 3 February 1847.

[47] Monroe County convention resolutions quoted in ibid., 16 February 1847.

[48] The exchange was unending. Almost every issue of Democratic newspapers contained a barrage of colorful adjectives and charges aimed at the opposition. See ibid., 6, 12 February, 5 March, 19, 27 July, 28 August 1847; *Albany Argus,* 6 March 1847, 10 February 1848 for some of the best examples.

Democratic party."[49] Sensing a repetition of the 1846 treachery, Barnburners leaped to the defense of the comptroller. Some charged that the canal contractors, whose graft Flagg had halted, were behind the move; others discerned the sinister hand of the bankers, whose speculation with depositors' funds he had ended. The attack on Flagg, declared the *Ulster Republican,* originated with the "vampires" who had fattened upon the public treasury before he took office, the "leeches" who had speculated in state contracts and now were forced to labor like common workingmen for their sustenance.[50] Many heaped revilement on Crosswell; the attack of the *Buffalo Republic* was characteristic:

> We regret as much as any Democrat can, the feuds and bickerings which have taken place in the Democratic party. We very well know that no such disturbance took place as long as Mr. Crosswell was let alone in the enjoyment of his thirty or forty thousand dollars per annum of state pap. But that half-million which he received from the state treasury only whetted his appetite for more; and when such Democrats as Mr. Flagg were willing that other Democrats quite as worthy as Mr. Crosswell, should have some of the crumbs of patronage, the long pampered fattling turned his teeth against those who had succeeded in stuffing him, and resolved to prosecute them with ceaseless vengeance.[51]

In the midst of this acrimonious discussion, on 27 August, Silas Wright died of a heart attack at his St. Lawrence County home. To Barnburners his death was a staggering blow.[52] Wright had not only become their candidate for the Democratic presidential nomination, but he was also the key figure in their hopeful effort to recover a once strong position in the nation's party councils. Although his defeat for reelection had disheartened some of his supporters outside New York and he himself had disclaimed any desire for the presidential office, his stature seemed to have grown during the nine months following the election.[53]

---

[49] *Albany Argus,* 16, 21, 24 August, 2, 8 September 1847.

[50] *Buffalo Republic,* 14, 17 September 1847; *Ulster Republican,* 11 August 1847, quoted in *Albany Atlas,* 14 August 1847.

[51] *Buffalo Republic,* 18 June 1847; George W. Thompson to Van Buren, 23 December 1846, J. Bragg to Van Buren, 10 March 1847, Van Buren Papers.

[52] The effect can be gathered from Henry Horn to Van Buren, 30 August 1847, E. A. Maynard to Van Buren, 30 August 1847, Van Buren Papers; Niles to Welles, 13 September 1847, Welles Papers.

[53] See Wright's letter to *Cincinnati Signal,* 29 July 1847; *Niles' Register* 73 (25 September 1847) : 62. Wright's growing stature is illustrated in Henry D. Gilpin to Van Buren, 4 October 1846, Van Buren Papers; Corwin to Follett, 14 February 1847, in Hamlin, "Follett Papers," p. 90; Byrdsall to Calhoun, 19 July 1847, in Jameson, *Calhoun Correspondence,* p. 1121; *Albany Argus,* 21 November 1846;

Agitation of the Proviso issue during the early months of 1847 apparently had strengthened his position. It was generally assumed, as early as August 1846, that Wright favored the Proviso.[54] Indeed, there were many who felt that Preston King's measure had been written in Wright's "own hand," and southerners often maintained that the Proviso had been introduced for the sole purpose of making Wright the northern Democracy's presidential candidate.[55] Inevitably, however, it became obvious that Wright had not made a public declaration. Quizzed by James H. Titus, a minor New York politician, in April 1847, Wright made a private reply: "If the question had been propounded to me at any period of my political life, shall the arms of the Union be employed to conquer, or the money of the Union used to purchase territory now constitutionally free, for the purpose of planting slavery upon it, I should have answered, No!—And this answer to the question is the Wilmot Proviso, as I understand it." He also asked that Titus request William C. Bryant, editor of the *New York Evening Post,* to make public a statement to reveal

> that I am opposed in principle, to the conquest or purchase of territory, now free, for the purpose of incorporating slavery upon it; that I think it an appropriate time to declare that principle when an appropriation is asked to purchase territory; and that such declaration, made at such a time, is not in opposition to the administration unless it be avowed that the administration wishes to acquire territory for the extension of slavery, in which case I would think the administration wrong and the declaration right.[56]

Although Wright's letter to Titus and his public statement were not published until after his death, his position became publicly known; it made him preeminent among antiextension Democrats. At the time of his death, even his opponents conceded his position. The *Floridian,* a Calhounite journal, recognized that he was the choice of "nine tenths" of the Democracy in the northern and eastern states, enough to secure his

Albany Atlas, 12, 14 August 1847; Baltimore *Sun,* 26 February 1847; *Charleston Mercury,* 1 June 1847.

[54] Wright's first expression on the subject apparently was in a letter to Dix on 19 January 1847 (Gillet, *Wright,* 2: 1915–18).

[55] The Washington correspondent of the *New York Evening Post* appears to have originated this idea (*New York Evening Post,* 5 January 1847). See also Nashville *Republican,* 20, 25 January, 1 November 1847; *Charleston Mercury,* 23 March 1847; *New York Tribune,* 7 August 1847.

[56] The letter was printed in many newspapers. I am using the version published by *Albany Atlas,* 23 September, 5 October 1847.

nomination. Whigs admitted that he would have carried off the antislavery wing of their party; some even conceded that he would have defeated Taylor.[57]

Wright's position, in short, had given the Barnburners a national stature, strength beyond their not inconsiderable numbers in New York, and a confidence in the ultimate victory of their principles. Now, in one fleeting moment, the very foundation of their plans to recover their former position had been destroyed. It was not strange that their effort to maintain control of the party in New York temporarily weakened. Though they soon recovered sufficiently to renew the struggle, they were still a sadly disorganized and bewildered faction when the Democratic State Convention met at Syracuse late in September 1847 to choose candidates for major state offices and to draw up a party platform.

Evidence that this momentary lapse of vigilance would be costly to Barnburner hopes quickly became clear when Hunker delegates from seven counties appeared to contest eleven seats, possession of which was needed to control the convention. Although leaders of the contending factions agreed to dispose of the "frivolously contested" seats before organizing, the understanding was ignored by the Hunkers, who, with the aid of the "sham" delegates, installed New York City Postmaster Robert Morris as permanent chairman. On the next day the Hunkers completed their victory by defeating the renominations of Flagg and John Van Buren; they selected a state ticket composed entirely of their own partisans.

Thoroughly outmaneuvered, the frustrated and almost hysterical Barnburners turned to the construction of a platform that would indicate their own position on slavery. They had given warning of their intentions during the selection of a committee on resolutions, when M. V. H. Smith of Wayne County had offered an antiextension resolution for the committee's consideration. After a long wrangle on the rules, the motion had been tabled by a solid Hunker vote. The issue was presented again on Sunday morning, this time as an amendment to the party platform. David Dudley Field tossed in the apple of discord:

> *Resolved,* That while the Democracy of New York, represented in this convention, will faithfully adhere to all the compromises of the Constitution, and maintain all the reserved rights of the States—

[57] *Floridian,* 11 September 1847; Stevenson to Crittenden, 20 June 1847, Crittenden Papers; Teesdale to McLean, 23 September 1847, McLean Papers. See also *Newark Advertiser,* 28 August 1847; *National Intelligencer,* 31 August 1847; *Charleston Mercury,* 17 September 1847. Taylor regarded Wright as his potential opponent (Taylor to Wood, 7 October 1847, in *Taylor Letters,* p. 139).

they declare—since the crisis has arrived when the issue must be met—their uncompromising hostility to the extension of Slavery into territory now free, which may be hereafter acquired by any action of the Government of the United States.

To prevent an accusation that he was opposed to the war, Field hastily added, "I am willing that our victorious standard should be borne to the Isthmus of Darien or planted on the highest peak of the Polynesian Islands, but the soil on which it advances must be free! As free as the untrammeled soil on which I stand."[58]

When the chairman ruled the resolution out of order, "a scene of indescribable tumult arose." For fifteen minutes, reported a correspondent of the *New York Evening Post,* "every member of the Convention and lobby gathered in the center of the room, and gestures, threats, denunciations and discordant noises . . . drowned all attempt at discussion of the question." Cries of "dodging," "recreancy," and "cowardice" filled the air, and high above it all arose the raucous voice of James S. Wadsworth, demanding "justice from the assassins of Silas Wright."[59] By dint of much profanity from the chair, the uproar was quieted and the roll was called, amid the protests of the Barnburners. The chairman, however, refused to announce the vote (which had actually revealed the absence of a quorum), tore up the results, and declared the meeting adjourned.[60]

When news of these proceedings flashed across the state, the rage of the Barnburner rank and file was unbounded. From every quarter came demands for repayment of the treachery "measure for measure," and from Buffalo came a trumpet call for a "CONVENTION of the RADICAL DEMOCRACY." where political connections with the "Conservative Faction" could be formally dissolved. Although they feared a schism, Barnburner leaders soon found the tide irresistable and finally called for a mass meeting at Herkimer.[61]

Late in October 1847 a horde of some four thousand Barnburners descended upon the picturesque New York village to complete the breach with the Hunkers and to adopt a series of principles that not only announced their own position but also, in essence, gave direction to

[58] *Albany Atlas,* 4 October 1847.

[59] *New York Evening Post* quoted in ibid., 4 October 1847.

[60] Complete proceedings of the Syracuse convention are in *Albany Atlas,* 7, 8 October 1847; and *Albany Argus,* 12, 13, 15 October 1847.

[61] Van Buren and Flagg both opposed the Herkimer meeting as "unwise." Van Buren indicated his sympathy for the Proviso, but he feared that the Democratic electorate would not accept it accompanied by a bolt that would give the state to the Whigs (Van Buren to Flagg, October 1847, Flagg to Van Buren, 13 October 1847, Van Buren Papers).

antislavery Democrats throughout the North. Led by Cambreleng and John Van Buren, the ex-president's second son, the assembled multitude repudiated the "fictitious majority" of the Syracuse convention, which, it declared, had disclosed a "corruption" that called for the "rebuke" of every member of the Democracy. They proclaimed the Field resolution, which had been "stifled" at Syracuse, as "an inseparable element of their political creed."

Unanimously shouting agreement, they protested "in behalf of the free white laborers of the North and South . . . in behalf of prosperity and in the name of freedom" against the extension of the institution whose "inevitable concommitant" was the "social and political degradation of the white laborer," and which denied to the masses "that equality of suffrage" inherent in the Democratic system. They also announced a firm determination to vote for "no man" who did not openly subscribe to the principles of the Wilmot Proviso. Finally, they ordered the Barnburner constituents to summon representatives to a convention at Herkimer on 22 February 1848, where the state delegation to the Democratic National Convention would be chosen.[62] In the state canvass that followed, Barnburners "talked of indifferent matters"; on election day the more radical voted a ticket in which they wrote three slogans: "Maintain Freedom," "Rebuke Fraud," and "Remember Silas Wright." The schism was complete.

The antislavery sentiment which caused division in New Hampshire and in New York echoed through most northern Democratic organizations, though it nowhere created the crisis witnessed in those two states. Massachusetts presented an excellent example. There, the party had divided into two factions in 1834. One, led by Marcus Morton, twice governor of the commonwealth, and including George Bancroft, had supported the Jackson–Van Buren program on banks, hard money, and corporate monopolies. The other, led by Benjamin Henshaw, who was personally allied to Boston's commercial and financial interests, had offered covert opposition to the same program. The differences between the two factions had become apparent in 1841 when Henshaw accepted appointment as secretary of the navy from John Tyler; the appointment precipitated a bitter internal feud over principles. But since the party was a clear minority in Massachusetts, directed by the need for a common front against the Whigs, the feud never caused a breach.[63]

Nor did the Proviso issue change the situation. While antislavery

---

[62] *Albany Atlas,* 27 October 1847.
[63] The feud is outlined in Arthur B. Darling, *Political Changes in Massachusetts, 1824–1848* (New Haven, Conn., 1925), pp. 130–312 (hereafter cited as *Political Changes*); and Schlesinger, *Age of Jackson,* pp. 144–76.

sentiment apparently developed considerable strength among the rural rank and file, generally adherents of Morton, it was relatively inarticulate in 1847. The Henshaw faction (ably led by Federal District Attorney Robert Rantoul, Editor Benjamin F. Hallett of the *Boston Times,* and Boston Postmaster Charles G. Greene) had little sympathy for antislavery agitation. Because of its grip on Federal patronage, it was able to dictate a policy that crippled any full consideration of the issue. Some evidence of antiextension feeling within the party was revealed at the Worcester convention of September 1847, where Amasa Walker, the only open adherent of the Morton faction in attendance, introduced a resolution calling upon the Bay State Democrats to announce their "firm and unwavering resistance to any further extension of slavery." As the *Boston Atlas* jubilantly reported, the resolution met with "hisses and unmannered vociferations" and was voted down 367 to 1.[64] Although several county conventions dominated by farmers later incorporated the resolution into their platforms, the Henshaw faction, secure in its position, revealed no concern; Massachusetts Democrats remained united.

Elsewhere in New England, manifestations of antislavery feeling during 1847 were disclosed among Democrats in Maine—where Governor John W. Dana, an ardent supporter of Van Buren in 1844, delivered an inaugural address bristling with antiextensionist principles—and in Connecticut among the friends of ex-Senator John M. Niles, a Van Buren lieutenant in that state. In neither, however, were there any political repercussions.[65]

In the Northwest, antiextensionist feeling was strongest in Ohio. Here, the Hards and the Softs had waged a battle for control of the party ever since the mid-thirties. The contest had never become rancorous, though some Hards charged that many Softs had joined the Whigs to defeat David Tod, the party gubernatorial candidate in 1844.[66]

The introduction of the Proviso did not disrupt party harmony. The Hards, led by Tod, Congressman Jacob Brinckerhoff, and Cleveland Postmaster John F. Spencer, all strong Van Burenites in 1844, immediately proclaimed their approval of the measure.[67] But the Softs of the Western Reserve were not laggards. Indeed, it was a Soft, Editor Joseph Gray of the *Cleveland Plain Dealer,* who appeared as the Provi-

[64] *Boston Times,* 23, 24 September 1847; *Boston Post,* 23 September 1847; *Boston Atlas,* 27 September 1847.

[65] *Boston Atlas,* 24 May 1847.

[66] James Finley to Allen, 11 March 1845, Allen Papers. Holt, "Party Politics in Ohio," 37: 560–64; 38: 111–12, contains the best discussion of Democratic party politics in the state.

[67] Senator William Allen, a Hard, is conspicuous for his absence from the list.

so's foremost advocate. It was he who best expressed the antiextensionist attitude. "We hold that slavery is an evil," he announced, "a deep, detestable and damnable evil; an evil in all its aspects; an evil to the blacks and an evil to the Whites . . . an evil which shows itself in the languishing conditions of agriculture in the South; in its paralyzed commerce; its want of Common Schools,—an evil that stares you in the face from uncultivated fields, and howls in your ears with its horrid din of clanking chains and fetters, and the groans of wretched bondmen."[68] It was an evil whose "dark tide" scores of county conventions and Democratic journals were resolved to halt through the extension of the Ordinance of 1787.[69]

Inevitably, and in spite of the evidence that the Ohio Democracy was overwhelmingly in favor of the enactment of the Proviso, rumors arose that supporters of Cass would endeavor to give the Proviso the "go-by" at the state convention in January 1848. Antislavery men from all parts of the state threatened to bolt—"another Syracuse"—if such an attempt were made.[70] The danger of a rift was eliminated, however, when the "January 8th Convention" unanimously approved a resolution condemning slavery as an evil, "unfavorable to the full development of the spirit and practical benefits of free institutions," and announced that it felt an obligation "to use all power . . . to prevent its increase, to mitigate and finally eradicate" it.[71]

In the other northwestern states Provisoism caused little furor in Democratic ranks. Few expressions of antiextensionist feelings were printed in party journals; when such sentiments were uttered, they condemned the introduction of slavery into the territories not on the usual ground, as a menace to the liberties of white men, but because the extension of slavery would be "repugnant to the *moral* sense" of the nation.[72] The difference in attitude was significant. In one area of the Northwest, however, the normal Democratic attitude was expressed— around Chicago, home of Long John Wentworth, one of the original supporters of the Proviso in Congress. His opposition to extension, indeed to the whole southern philosophy of government, made him the focus of Provisoism throughout Illinois; his newspaper, the *Chicago Democrat,* helped create an antiextension movement among Democrats

[68] *Cleveland Plain Dealer,* 4 March 1848. See also 13 January, 17 November 1847; *Sandusky Mirror* quoted in *National Era,* 9 December 1847.

[69] *Cleveland Plain Dealer,* 20 October 1847.

[70] D. Radebaugh to Van Buren, December 1847; *Cincinnati Herald,* 29 December 1847.

[71] *Cleveland Plain Dealer,* 13 January 1848.

[72] *National Era,* 24 February 1848.

of the northeastern counties of the state, which in its intensity rivaled that of New Hampshire and New York. In 1847, however, the movement was incompletely organized.[73]

Hostility to the extension of slavery into the territories was thus obviously widespread among northern Democrats in 1847. The feeling in most areas ranged from a passive disapproval of the slave institution to a mildly active antagonism to its further spread. But among Hale's following in New Hampshire and among the Barnburners of New York, the antiextensionist sentiment had reached a degree of intensity that resulted in schism. To the Democratic party as a whole the antiextensionist manifestations in these two states were in themselves alarming. The party recognized that it might maintain its national ascendency without the aid of New Hampshire, but not without the united support of New York Democrats. The situation was also alarming because of its potential effects upon other northern Democrats. New York's Barnburners, basing their position on the grounds that extension of slavery was a menace to the liberties of white men and a threat to democratic institutions, had presented the issue in a manner that appealed strongly to the Democratic rank and file. This appeal—evident to an extent among the farmers of central Massachusetts, among Ohio's Hards, and among the Wentworth men in northeastern Illinois—would create an irresistable demand for a positive stand on the issue, a stand that was to divide and destroy the Democratic party.

[73] *Chicago Democrat,* 2 March, 20 April, 7 September 1847. Antislavery feeling was also expressed by the *Jacksonville Prairie Argus* and the *Peoria Press* (*National Era,* 10 June, 8 July 1847).

Chapter Five

Antislavery Forces: The Whigs

The development of an antislavery movement among northern Whigs during the Polk administration proceeded along somewhat different lines than it did among Democrats. In the early months of the new administration the antislavery passions which had been manifested over the Texas issue began to disappear from public view as Whigs recognized that they were "flogging a dead horse." But the attitudes of antislavery Whigs did not change, and their constancy became evident in Massachusetts.

In 1845, Bay State Whiggery was dominated by an uneasy coalition, divided by the ambitions of its important public figures: Abbott Lawrence and Nathan Appleton, both capable and influential spokesmen for the mercantile-banking-textile interests, and both former congressmen; Daniel Webster; Rufus Choate, a former United States senator and the pride of the Massachusetts bar; Edward Everett, former governor and former minister to Great Britain; and Robert Winthrop, a Back Bay social lion and a congressman who was to become Speaker of the House in the Thirtieth Congress. Although some of these men had expressed antislavery feelings, they had also revealed a reluctance to agitate the issue because of the disunity it might create.

But there was another, somewhat younger element that had no such compunctions. It included Charles Francis Adams, the ex-president's second son, who had gained some reputation as a writer and as a member of the Massachusetts legislature; Charles Allen, former member of the legislature and former judge; John A. Andrew and Anson Burlingame, young lawyers; Richard Henry Dana, Jr., a successful lawyer already famous for his *Two Years before the Mast;* Samuel Gridley Howe, well known for his work in prison reform and on the part of the blind and the deaf; Ebenezer Rockwood Hoar, member of the state Senate; John

G. Palfrey, secretary of the commonwealth and former owner-publisher of the *North American Review;* Stephen C. Phillips, former congressman, former mayor of Salem, and educational reformer; Charles Sumner, popular, somewhat iconoclastic lecturer; and Henry Wilson, shoe manufacturer and member of the state Senate. All were destined to write their names on the scrolls of national fame.[1]

Their attitude was expressed in various ways. Late in 1845, when Webster began to threaten retirement from the Senate if his thirty-thousand-dollar debt were not paid, they indicated a determination to name a successor who would work for the "abolition of slavery under the Federal Constitution," a determination which was translated into a resolve to prevent Massachusetts Whigs from ever again supporting a slaveholder for the presidency.[2] The antislavery attitude was again made evident in the late spring of 1846, when Charles Francis Adams, dedicated to the idea of converting his party to a more active position, agreed to edit a new journal, the *Boston Whig*.[3]

The Young Whigs' active campaign to convert their party began obliquely in midsummer of 1846, when Adams criticized Robert C. Winthrop's vote in favor of supplies to carry on the Mexican War as "a positive sanction of the worst acts of the Administration." Shortly afterward Sumner added his criticism, suggesting that Winthrop "was unwilling to be found alone in the company of the truth," or was unwilling to follow truth "in the company of those few men who bore the stain of antislavery." When the *Boston Advertiser* came to Winthrop's defense, Sumner replied through the *Boston Courier* with a series of attacks, culminating on 10 August, in which he condemned Winthrop for approving "the most wicked act in our history," giving sanction "to all the desolation and bloodshed" of a war waged in the interest of slavery. "Blood! Blood!" he shrieked in print, "is on the hands of the representative from Boston. Not all great Neptune's ocean can wash them clean."[4]

---

[1] The most recent studies of these "Young Whigs" are three biographies: David Donald, *Charles Sumner and the Coming of the Civil War* (New York, 1960) (hereafter cited as *Sumner*); Martin B. Duberman, *Charles Francis Adams, 1807–1886* (Boston, 1960) (hereafter cited as *Adams*); and Frank O. Gatell, *John Gorham Palfrey and the New England Conscience* (Cambridge, Mass., 1963).

[2] Charles Sumner to Francis Lieber, 17 November 1845, Charles Sumner to George Sumner, 30 November 1845, in Charles Sumner, *Memoirs and Letters of Charles Sumner*, ed. Edward L. Pierce (London, 1893), 3: 104–5 (hereafter cited as *Sumner*).

[3] Ibid., p. 106; Duberman, *Adams*, p. 111.

[4] The attack began in the *Boston Whig* on 16 July 1846, then shifted to other papers with larger circulation. Sumner's words first appeared in the *Whig*, 22 July 1846, and in the *Boston Courier*, 10 August 1846 (Pierce, *Sumner*, 3: 115–17);

The onslaught upon the Back Bay lion shocked Boston society and brought about Sumner's immediate ostracism. More important, it brought into the open the cleavage that existed within the Whig party of Massachusetts, a division disclosed in the application of the terms "Conscience" and "Cotton" to the two factions that now appeared.[5] It signalled the beginning of a struggle for power, since the Cotton wing of the party, including men with large ambitions that could only be secured with the help of southern Whigs, was not disposed to surrender. Its position was well expressed by the *Boston Atlas*, often a spokesman for the commonwealth's great textile interests. "The whole institution of human slavery is, to us, most perfectly abhorrent," it proclaimed. "We look upon it as a stain and blot on the fame and character of our land. Its existence brands the practical falsehood upon the very first of our claims to be a free people. It is an excresence which ought to be lopped from the body politic, as soon as the operation can sensibly and safely be performed." However, the *Atlas* explained, "we are not willing to give up the Union, on account of the existence of Slavery. . . . Nor do we design, either, to engage in any wild and ill-digested crusade against the whole body of citizens of the slaveholding States, for the reason, solely, that this great and gross evil exists among them."[6]

The differences between the two factions became even more apparent at the Whig convention which met at Faneuil Hall on 23 September 1846. No conflict occurred until the time came for a report of the resolutions committee, at which point the careful arrangements of party managers for a keynote speech from Winthrop were upset by Conscience Whigs' demand for a speech from Sumner.

Winthrop's side of the argument can be found in Robert C. Winthrop, Jr., *Memoirs of Robert C. Winthrop* (Boston, 1897), pp. 53–54. George Ticknor thought that Sumner took his stand to gain notoriety and "to get earlier into power than he could by other tracks which are occupied by older men," and Congressman George Ashmun found personal ambition at the roots of the Conscience Whig movement: "If Phillips could be made Governor, Allen Senator, and Adams Representative from Suffolk, with such small chance for anything less which might fall to Sumner, the trouble over [antislavery within the Whig party] would be at an end" (Donald, *Sumner*, pp. 149–50).

[5] The origin of the terms is obscure. According to George Frisbie Hoar, the names had been suggested in a Massachusetts Senate debate when Thomas G. Cary, a Boston merchant, deprecated a proposed antislavery resolution with the observation that it was likely to make an unfavorable impression in the South and that it would be injurious to Massachusetts business interests. Ebenezer Rockwood Hoar replied that he thought it "quite as desirable that the legislature should represent the conscience as the cotton of the Commonwealth" (George F. Hoar, *Autobiography of Seventy Years* [New York, 1906], 1: 134 [hereafter cited as *Autobiography*]).

[6] *Boston Atlas*, 23 September 1846.

The air was tense as the young literator climbed to the forum to enunciate the principles of his faction. "We are a convention of Whigs," he began rather mildly. And who were the Whigs? "Some say they are supporters of the Tariff; others that they are advocates of internal improvements, of measures to restrict the veto Power, or may be of a Bank." But, he maintained, this enumeration did not do justice to the Whig character. "The Whigs as their name imparts are, or ought to be, the party of Freedom. They should seek on all occasions, to carry out fully and practically the principles of our institutions. Those principles which our forefathers declared, and sealed with their blood, their Whig children should seek to manifest in their acts. The Whigs, therefore, reverence the Declaration of Independence, as embodying the vital truths of Freedom, especially the great truth that 'all men are created equal.'" Such, he trusted, was the Whig party of Massachusetts—a party which refused "to identify itself exclusively with those measures of transient policy" which might become "obsolete ideas," but which rather connected itself with everlasting truths that could "never fade or decay." At the moment, a party inspired by these principles should be alive to evils of great magnitude—"the unjust and unchristian war with Mexico, which is no less absurd than wicked, and beyond this the institution of slavery."

The time had passed when the question was asked, What did the North have to do with slavery? Politically, the North had little interest in anything else. "Slavery is everywhere," Sumner insisted:

> Appealing to the Constitution, it enters the Halls of Congress . . . in disproportionate representation of the Slave States. It holds its disgusting mart . . . in the shadow of the Capitol, under the legislative jurisdiction of the Nation. . . . It sends its miserable victims over the high seas, from the ports of Virginia to the ports of Louisiana, beneath the protecting flag of the Republic. It presumes to follow into the Free States those fugitives who . . . seek our Altars for safety; nay, more, with profane hands it seizes those who have never known the name of slave, freemen of the North, and dooms them to irredeemable bondage. . . . It assumes at pleasure to build up new slaveholding States; striving perpetually to widen its area, while professing to extend the area of freedom. It has brought upon the country war with Mexico. . . . By the spirit of Union among its supporters, it controls the affairs of Government—interferes with the cherished interests of the North, enforcing them and refusing protection to her manufactures,—makes and unmakes Presidents,—usurps to itself the larger portion of all offices of honor and profit, both in the army and navy, and also in the civil department,

—and stamps upon our whole country the character . . . of the monstrous anomaly and mockery, a *slaveholding republic,* with the living truths of Freedom on its lips and the dark mark of Slavery on its brow.

Such a situation, he maintained, had to be ended. Massachusetts did not allow any of its citizens to hold slaves within its borders. Should its citizens, therefore, continue in any way to sustain outside its limits an institution which its laws declared "contrary to natural right, justice, humanity, and sound policy"? The "conscience of good men" told them that if it was wrong to hold a single slave, it was wrong to hold more than one; if it was wrong for an individual to hold a slave, it was wrong for a state; if it was wrong for a state "in its individual capacity," it was wrong "in association with other States." Circumstances demanded consistency. Massachusetts was forced by reason of its own principles "to call for the abolition of slavery" wherever the state's influence could be extended—"everywhere beneath the Constitution and the laws of the National Government." Sumner continued:

> To labor in this cause is far higher and nobler than to strive for repeal of the tariff, once the tocsin to rally Whigs. Repeal of slavery under the constitution and laws of the national government is a watchword more Christian and more potent, because it embodies a higher sentiment and a more commanding duty. . . . It is the duty of the Whigs professing the principles of the fathers to express themselves openly, distinctly, and solemnly against slavery,—*not only against its further extension, but against its larger continuance under the Constitution and Laws of the Union.* . . . Emancipation should always be presented as the cardinal object of our national policy.[7]

The Conscience Whigs greeted this first public announcement of their creed with a roar of approval. Winthrop followed Sumner with a speech that had evidently been planned to keep the party in line with its former action and to arrest the tendency toward a distinct antislavery policy. He emphasized the measures upon which Whigs of the North and of the South agreed and warned against adoption of principles "less broad and comprehensive" than those which united the whole Whig party.[8]

These, however, were the counsels of expediency. Conscience Whigs, fired by the eloquence of Sumner's passionate oratory, waited impa-

[7] Charles Sumner, *Works of Charles Sumner* (Boston, 1875), 1: 304–13 (hereafter cited as *Sumner's Works*).
[8] *Boston Atlas,* 25 September 1846.

tiently for the reading of the long, tiresome resolutions—graced, as they discovered, by a mild antiextension plank—to end.[9] Instantly Stephen C. Phillips introduced an amendment more expressive of their belief:

> *Resolved,* That the Whigs of Massachusetts owe it to their known principles to make the declaration, that they must hereafter be regarded as the decided and uncompromising opponents of slavery; —that they are opposed to its extension beyond the limits of its present existence, and will maintain their opposition at any political hazard, and in disregard of all temporary sacrifices; that they are opposed to its continuance where it already exists, and will concur in all constitutional measures, that can promote its *abolition;*—and that in their political action they will support such men only, as will steadfastly advance, by appropriate measures, these, their principles and purposes.[10]

A stormy debate involving leading members of both factions followed the introduction of the resolution. Nor was the passion confined to the platform; as Sumner's first biographer related, it was "shown on the floor in sullen countenances and angry voices." Confusion was rampant. As it became evident that the antislavery wing, generally made up of delegates from the country, would stand firmly upon its position, there was some fear that the body would break up in disorder. Then, at the height of the turmoil, Daniel Webster entered at the rear of the historic hall. A sudden hush fell over the assembly.

Almost half a century later, Edward L. Pierce, who was present at the time, described the drama: "The great orator, endowed with a marvelous presence . . . walked slowly the length of the hall, the delegates parting as he advanced, and took his seat near the platform. . . . Debate was suspended, the disorder ceased, and all eyes turned on him. Both parties, just now in fierce discussion, rose and joined in loud cheers. . . . The applause was universal and prolonged; and when it subsided the assembly was still." Everyone knew that the Squire of Marshfield was opposed to any agitation of the slavery issue at that time. His mere presence, Pierce declared, "without a word from his lips, had sealed the fate of the amendment."[11]

---

[9] The original platform contained no resolution on the subject of slavery extension. Some attribute its insertion to Ebenezer Hoar (Pierce, *Sumner,* 3: 124n), others to Webster (John Quincy Adams, *Memoirs of John Quincy Adams,* ed. Charles F. Adams [Philadelphia, 1877], 3: 274). The resolutions are in *Boston Atlas,* 24 September 1846.

[10] *Boston Atlas,* 25 September 1846.

[11] Pierce, *Sumner,* 3: 126–27. Claude M. Fuess, *Daniel Webster* (Boston, 1930), 2: 167 (hereafter cited as *Webster*), presents a similar picture.

Although the debate was shortly resumed, it proceeded without its earlier passion. When it was finally silenced, Webster rose to make a brief appeal for harmony. "Others may look to other sources, or rely upon other foundations for their hopes of the country," he declared, "but I confess . . . that at this period of my political life . . . I am full of the feeling that there is but one ground upon which the good men of this country can rest their trust. I see in the dark and troubled night which is upon us, no star above the horizon, but the intelligent, patriotic, *united* Whig party."[12] The Conscience Whigs had been defeated in their first skirmish.

However, the contest had only begun. Antislavery Whigs returned to their constituencies with indignation in their souls. The test of power had not been a fair one. It could not be disguised, Sumner maintained, that "the *heart* of the Commonwealth" was opposed to the position enunciated by *"the spindles."*[13] In Boston the reaction among Conscience Whigs resulted in the nomination of Dr. Samuel Gridley Howe as an independent congressional candidate to oppose the regularly nominated Winthrop. Their action brought the severe castigation of the *Boston Atlas* down upon their heads. Denouncing them as "hot headed theorists," "chimerical abstractionists," "new-fangled political reformers," and "self-styled keepers of the conscience," the enraged journal of the textile interests drummed them out of the party.[14]

The avid antislavery attitude displayed by the Conscience Whigs of Massachusetts had no counterpart in other northern Whig camps in 1846, nor did this situation change in most states after the second introduction of the Proviso in early 1847. New Hampshire Whigs, forced to take advanced ground because of the Hale movement, warmly embraced the measure. Their position, reflecting Democratic party attitudes, was expressed by their usually conservative party organ, the *Concord Statesman.* "The Wilmot Proviso has no more steadfast friends than the Whigs of New Hampshire," it declared. "Come weal or woe . . . No man who does not sanction the 'White Man's Resolution' will receive their votes . . . in the next Presidential contest."[15] In Connecticut, New Jersey, and Pennsylvania, antiextension planks were incorporated with little sign of disagreement into party platforms.

In New York, however, the issue became involved with other internecine feuds. Like their Democratic brethren, Empire State Whigs had

[12] *Webster's Writings,* 13:328.
[13] Pierce, *Sumner,* 3: 129.
[14] *Boston Atlas,* 31 October, 16 November 1846.
[15] *Concord New Hampshire Statesman,* 31 December 1847, quoted in *New Hampshire Patriot,* 15 June 1848

long been divided, though the line of cleavage between Whigs was not so distinct as it was between Democrats. Some of the divisions were caused by frustrated political ambitions. Thurlow Weed was closely involved. Between 1838 and 1844, by one means or another, the editor of the *Evening Journal* had managed in some degree to alienate Millard Fillmore, Francis Granger, John Collier, and John Young—all strong figures in the party. In addition, his covert opposition to Clay's nomination as a presidential candidate, in 1836 and again in 1840, had engendered a feeling of mistrust among the Kentuckian's numerous friends in the state and particularly in New York City.

But not all divisions were based on political ambitions. During William H. Seward's governorship, many Whigs with Nativist proclivities had revealed strong objections to his recommendations for state support of schools for foreigners and to his "truckling" to the Irish Catholic electorate. Whigs with anti-masonic backgrounds, and to a lesser extent Whigs with antislavery attitudes, expressed a distaste for Clay in 1844.[16]

As long as the Whigs had been a minority, the seriousness of these differences had not become public knowledge, but soon after John Young's victory over Wright, a conservative-radical cleavage came to light. Conservatives hated the new governor's anti-rent principles and made little attempt to disguise the fact, but they made no open attack until the judicial elections of June 1847, when two Whig candidates for the state bench who had been endorsed by Anti-Renters were defeated. The conservative press rejoiced. "The pernicious doctrines" of the Democracy with which a "petty faction" had been trying to "infect" the party had been given a signal rebuke. According to James Watson Webb of the New York *Courier,* the election had "sounded the death knell of an unprincipled political clique," a group, declared Erastus Brooks of the *New York Express,* which had supported "arson, robbery, theft, and midnight plunder," excusing those crimes as pardonable errors. No longer, Brooks maintained, would the existence of the Whig party be "jeopardized by its very success."[17]

Weed and Horace Greeley readily recognized themselves as the targets of the attack and returned it in kind. Weed damned by name Webb,

---

[16] The background to divisions in the New York Whig Party, is explained in Alexander, *New York Political History,* 2: 116–26; and two more recent works with differing viewpoints: Glyndon G. Van Deusen, *Thurlow Weed: Wizard of the Lobby* (Boston, 1847), pp. 86–141 passim (hereafter cited as *Weed*); and Robert J. Rayback, *Millard Fillmore: Biography of a President* (Buffalo, N. Y., 1959), pp. 91–159 passim (hereafter cited as *Fillmore*).

[17] New York *Courier,* 30 July 1847; *New York Express* quoted in *Albany Atlas,* 25 June, 4 August 1847.

Brooks, Alexander Seward of the *Utica Gazette,* and Thomas M. Foote
of the *Buffalo Commercial Advertiser* (a Fillmore paper) as the "toad-
spotted traitors" who were responsible for defections that had caused
Whig defeats. The editor of the *New York Tribune* arraigned the same
crew for faithlessness to the party. The two previous elections, Greeley
charged, had

> been signalized by the novel spectacle of a body of Whigs—small,
> indeed, in numbers, but strong in the means of influencing . . . the
> more timid portion of the wealthy—setting themselves deliberately
> to work to defeat the leading Whig candidates on a pretense of
> superior devotion to the cardinal principles of the Whig party. . . .
> Not that a great many Whig votes were actually carried over to the
> candidates of our opponents—that was at once impossible and un-
> necessary. Every purpose was answered when by unsparing denun-
> ciation of our leading candidates as allied with or subservient to
> plotters of anarchy, robbery, and murder, a portion of the Whigs
> had been thrown into perplexity and doubt with regard to this novel
> election—had been induced to hesitate, to grow cold, and finally to
> conclude not to vote at all.

A convention, he concluded, was needed to purify Whig ranks of this
element.[18]

Into this overheated political atmosphere the second Proviso was
introduced. Both Weed and Greeley supported the measure. Weed's
position was characteristic of northern support. The Proviso, he declared, "embodies the deliberate sentiment of the North. That sentiment
cannot be smothered. If its consummation shall rend the Union, responsibility must rest with the South. . . . With one-fourth of the wealth,
and less than that proportion of free representatives, the South has
gradually acquired control of the Senate, and transformed the people of
the North into mere 'hewers of wood and drawers of water' for Slavery." He maintained that the North could make no more concessions:
"The last foot of slave territory has been acquired; and if the issue is to
be no more Slave territory or no Union, the sooner the issue is tried the
better. We have no fears of the result. Freedom will triumph."[19]

Reaction in the conservative press to this kind of attitude was both
oblique and direct. The New York *Courier* continued its attack on
Weed-Greeley partisans as "anti-renters, vote-yourself-a-farm men,

[18] *Albany Evening Journal* quoted in *Albany Atlas,* 26 June 1847; *New York
Tribune,* 31 July 1847.
[19] *Albany Evening Journal,* 2 March 1847.

Fourierites, Radicals, and Abolitionists." It denounced the *Tribune* as the "most dangerous press published in America," devoted to the "propagation . . . of every conceivable radical doctrine" and determined to bring upon the country "all the horrors of the French Revolution." True Whigs, the *Utica Gazette* declared, who were "necessarily the opponents of all radicalism in any and every form," could have no sympathy with such doctrines.[20] Nor could they support the Proviso, that "hydra-headed monster," the spawn of demagogues who would destroy the Union.[21]

With such high passion it might have been expected that a clash over principles would develop at the Whig State Convention, which met in Syracuse in October 1847 to nominate candidates for high offices. But on the surface, at least, all was harmony. The conservative and moderate elements secured most of the nominations; all of these nominees were victorious in the election that followed. The Weed-Greeley partisans, joined by Seward, secured an antiextension plank. Political expediency dictated their course, for the resolution adopted was a verbatim copy of the Field amendment rejected by the Hunkers.[22] Nevertheless, the situation was ominous for the future of the party.

Among Whigs in the northwestern states the Proviso produced no significant political divisions. In Illinois and Indiana, antislavery forces accepted with ill grace the evasion of the issue by state conventions, where they were strongly outnumbered by those who wished to avoid the consequences of new and distracting questions. In Michigan, where the Provisoists foisted an antiextension plank upon the party, conservatives grumbled about inexpediency and warned of alienating the South.[23] But no intraparty feuds developed.

In Ohio a different situation prevailed; hostility to slavery appeared well-nigh universal. In 1847, Whig conventions of every county in the Western Reserve and in the Miami Valley announced their opposition to the acquisition of "any new slave territory." The state convention made it known by a unanimous vote that if additional territory were acquired, Whigs would "demand that there shall be neither slavery, nor involuntary servitude therein, otherwise than for the punishment of crimes." But ordinary antiextension measures did not satisfy Ohio Whigs. Like their counterparts in Massachusetts, they were determined to give their

[20] New York *Courier*, 11, 13 August 1847; *Utica Gazette* quoted in *Albany Atlas*, 4 August 1847.
[21] New York *Courier*, 14 July 1847.
[22] *New York Tribune*, 16 October 1847.
[23] See Arthur C. Cole, *Era of the Civil War: 1848–1870* (Chicago, 1922), p. 55 (hereafter cited as *Era of the Civil War*) ; Smith, *Liberty and Free Soil Parties*, p. 126; New York *Courier*, 24 September 1847.

principles a practical application. In every county of the Reserve and in those bordering on Cincinnati, they resolved to support "no man for President in 1848" who was not a "true friend and an earnest advocate of the Ordinance of 1787"; some even threatened to bolt the party if it named a slaveholder, regardless of his views.[24]

There was no doubt of the identity of the slaveholder against whom Ohio Whigs, indeed all antislavery Whigs, aimed such resolutions. Zachary Taylor was the man. Anti-Taylor sentiment was prevalent in the whole unorganized mass of Whig Provisoists. In Massachusetts the *Boston Courier* objected to Taylor's nomination because "he is a slaveholder. . . . And his sympathies are doubtless attracted to and harmonize with the interests of the peculiar institution." In New York City Greeley explained that his faction was opposed to Taylor because he had been presented as a man whose election would prove "a death blow to all manner of abolition."[25]

The more extreme antislavery Whigs used more intemperate language. In New Hampshire the Hale journal, edited by a Whig, brutally indicted Taylor as a dealer in human flesh: "He has one hundred mothers, with or without babies, for sale in the shambles. *He furnishes Creole Virgins for the 'Hells' of New Orleans.*" In New Jersey the *Trenton News* denounced the Old Hero as "the bloody mushroom of the battlefield." The most extensive abuse came from Ohio, revealing the maniacal fury of the state's Whigs upon the slavery issue. The *Lebanon Star* inveighed against Taylor as "*a man of blood—an executioner in infamous wars—*AN IGNORAMUS IN STATE AFFAIRS." The *Xenia Torchlight* damned him as "a most adroit skull-breaker, throat-cutter, housebreaker, woman and child slayer." His nomination, the *Rossville News* declared, would indicate that the Whigs had reached a level of "moral destitution" in which it mattered but little whom the party supported.[26] Ohio Whigs certainly had no intention of supporting him. The *Cleveland True Democrat* insisted that the Taylor movement was a scheme designed by "leading spirits" of the South to "wheedle the North into his support." He was proclaimed as the People's Candidate, when "in fact

[24] *Cleveland Plain Dealer,* 8, 15 September, 20 October 1847; Holt, "Party Politics in Ohio," 38: 261–62; Smith, *Liberty and Free Soil Parties,* pp. 127–28.

[25] *Boston Courier* quoted in *Boston Times,* 1, 6 April 1847; *New York Tribune,* 14 August 1847. See also Horace Greeley, *Autobiography, or Recollections of a Busy Life* (New York, 1872), p. 211.

[26] *New Hampshire Independent* quoted in *Mobile Register,* 20 July 1847; *Trenton News* quoted in *Mobile Register,* 21 May 1847; *Lebanon Star* quoted in Detroit *Free Press,* 11 February 1848; *Xenia Torchlight* quoted in Detroit *Free Press,* 20 July 1847; *Rossville News* quoted in Baltimore *Republican,* 27 July 1847.

and truth he is the slaveholders' candidate pledged to them and their institutions by every conceivable tie, not the least among which, is the large ownership of slaves himself, besides being opposed to the Wilmot Proviso. The South knew their man, and no matter what others may say . . . he *is* their man." Ohio did not want him.[27] The intensity of this feeling was illustrated by Joshua R. Giddings at a Whig meeting in Ashtabula. "Sooner shall this right arm fall from its socket and my tongue cleave to the roof of my mouth," he announced, "than I will vote for Zack Taylor for President . . . and I think I can say the same for every true Whig of Ashtabula." The enthusiastic response of the assembly indicated that he was not far wrong in his speculation. Among all the state's Whig journals north of Columbus, only the *Cleveland Herald* dared support Taylor.[28]

But antislavery Whig leaders, seeing beyond the passion of their position, recognized that opposition to Taylor's nomination was not enough; they needed a candidate of their own. Almost coincidentally with the great swelling of the Taylor tide, they thought they had found him in the person of Thomas Corwin. What attracted them to Corwin was the speech he delivered on 11 February 1847, in the midst of the senate debate on the Three Million Bill.

In the course of a three-hour oration against the measure, Corwin launched an excoriating attack on the objectives of the Mexican War. He pointed out that the president had declared that he did not expect to hold Mexican territory by conquest. "Why then conquer it?" Corwin asked. "Why waste thousands of lives and millions of money fortifying towns and creating governments if, at the end of the war, you retire from the graves of your soldiers and the desolated country of your foes, only to get money from Mexico for the expenses of your toil and sacrifice? Who ever heard since Christianity was propagated among men, of a nation taxing its people and enlisting its young men, and marching off two thousand miles merely to be paid for it in money?" What was this war, he raged, "but hunting a market for blood, selling the lives of our young men, marching them in regiments to be slaughtered, and paid for, like men and brute beasts?" Horrible as these statements sounded, they were no more than an expression of the plan, "stripped naked," which the president and his cohorts had proposed, a plan which called for a continuation of the conflict until the nation secured an indemnity not only for past but also for present slaughter. "I have no patience with this flagitious notion of fighting for indemnity,"

---

[27] *Cleveland True Democrat* quoted in Detroit *Free Press*, 12 July 1847.
[28] *National Era*, 10 June 1847; *New York Tribune*, 8 May 1847.

Corwin cried, "especially under the equally absurd and hypocritical pretense of securing an honorable peace! . . . If you have accomplished the objects of this war (if indeed you had an object which you dare avow), cease to fight and you will have peace. Conquer your insane love of false glory and you will 'conquer a peace.'" If the commander in chief would not do this, he warned, "I will endeavor to compel him, and as I find no other means, I shall refuse supplies!"

The most often quoted part of Corwin's speech was his sarcastic rejoinder to Lewis Cass's assertion that the United States would soon have twenty million people and needed more room. "If I were a Mexican," Corwin proclaimed, "I would tell you, 'Have you not room in your own country to bury your dead men? If you come into mine we will greet you with bloody hands, and welcome you to hospitable graves!'"[29]

The speech was received with mixed emotions. To Democrats, whose attitude was typified in a demand that Corwin be incarcerated in the Ohio penitentiary for the duration of the war, the oration sounded like the rankest treason.[30] Among conservative Whigs the opinion developed that Corwin had destroyed all his chances for nomination. The reaction of antislavery Whigs was entirely different. Giddings, who heard the speech, jubilantly informed Sumner that the Young Whigs had found a spokesman. In Massachusetts, Wilson and Charles Francis Adams both found "a very large part of the people . . . ready to rally around him." In New York City the *Tribune* and the whole House of Burgundy—the name by which the *New York Mirror* designated the "discordant and multiplied cliques and factions" which made up the Greeley element—proclaimed Corwin as their first choice for the presidency. In Ohio a score of county conventions hailed him as the "people's choice," and in northern Indiana several newspapers raised his name to their mastheads. By midsummer of 1847—at the very height of Taylor's popularity—the Corwin movement had become widespread enough and formidable enough for the Conscience Whigs of Massachusetts to consider a demonstration in his favor.[31]

[29] Isaac Strohm, ed., *Speeches of Thomas Corwin, with a Sketch of His Life* (Dayton, Ohio, 1959), pp. 365–66; Josiah Morrow, ed., *Life and Speeches of Thomas Corwin* (Cincinnati, Ohio, 1896), p. 300.

[30] See Erwin H. Price, "Election of 1848 in Ohio," *Ohio Archeological and Historical Quarterly* 36 (1927): 199 (hereafter cited as "1848 Election in Ohio").

[31] Giddings to Sumner, 11 February 1847, in George W. Julian, *Life of Joshua R. Giddings* (Chicago, 1892), p. 199 (hereafter cited as *Giddings*); Wilson to Giddings, 24 February 1847, in Morrow, *Corwin*, p. 50; Adams to Giddings, 22 February 1847, in Julian, *Giddings*, pp. 199–200; *New York Mirror* quoted in *Cleveland Plain Dealer*, 10 March 1847; Teesdale to McLean, 12 February, 23 September 1847, McLean Papers; *Indiana State Sentinel*, 12 February 1848; Stevenson to Crittenden, 7 September 1847, Crittenden Papers.

But it was precisely the Conscience Whigs who retained a nagging doubt. They were not certain that Corwin had the correct attitude toward the Wilmot Proviso in particular and toward slavery in general. Nor did they have any assurance that he would be willing to bolt the party if it named a candidate unsatisfactory to the antislavery forces.[32] Their doubt was justified, for Corwin's opposition to expansion was based on an attitude different from that of the Conscience Whigs. He opposed the Mexican War not because he feared that it would expand the boundaries of slavery—he believed that slavery could not expand into Mexican territory—but because he regarded it as a catastrophe which was creating unnecessary destruction and heavy debt and, more important, because it threatened to create issues which would divide both the Whig party and the Union.[33] It was not until mid-September 1847, however, that Corwin made his position publicly clear. Called upon to make a speech in Carthage, Ohio, he attacked the abolitionists as fomenters of discord, denounced the Wilmot Proviso as a "dangerous issue" calculated to disrupt the Union, and announced a determination to maintain his party regularity, because only through a united Whig party could dismemberment of the Union be prevented.[34]

Although a few prominent Whigs such as Sumner and Giddings were at first reluctant to accept the meaning of Corwin's speech, the great mass of the antislavery element immediately began a hasty retreat from the Ohioan's banner. Some, such as Greeley, who had earlier wondered about Corwin's fear of "wetting his feet," expressed sadness. Others, such as the *Cleveland True Democrat,* which hauled down "the black flag of Corwin . . . and stamped the traitor's colors in the dust," displayed anger.[35]

The most significant immediate effect was in Massachusetts, where plans for a Corwin demonstration were promptly abandoned, and where Conscience Whigs turned their full attention to developments within the

[32] Conscience Whigs made a number of attempts to persuade Corwin to take a public stand on the Proviso. See Adams to Giddings, 22 February 1847, in Julian, *Giddings,* pp. 199–200; Wilson to Giddings, 24 February 1847, in Morrow, *Corwin,* p. 50; Sumner to Giddings, 25 February 1847, in Pierce, *Sumner,* 3: 141; Sumner to Chase, 12 March 1847, in Holt, "Party Politics in Ohio," 38: 149; and Duberman, *Adams,* pp. 124–25.

[33] For a more detailed analysis of Corwin's position see Norman A. Graebner, "Thomas Corwin and the Election of 1848: A Study in Conservative Politics," *Journal of Southern History* 17 (May 1951): 162–80.

[34] Holt, "Party Politics in Ohio," 38: 156.

[35] Giddings to Sumner, 18 October, 8 November 1847, in Julian, *Giddings,* pp. 211–13; Sumner to Giddings, 1 November 1847, in Pierce, *Sumner,* 3: 154; Greeley to Schuyler Colfax, 1 May 1847, in Allen Nevins, *Ordeal of the Union* (New York, 1947), 1: 203; *Cleveland Plain Dealer,* 27 October 1847.

commonwealth. During 1847 the tensions within the Bay State party remained high; they were marked early in the year by a bitter newspaper controversy over John Gorham Palfrey's refusal to cast his vote for Winthrop in the contest for Speaker of the House, on the grounds that Winthrop was not a true antislavery man.[36]

The year also witnessed the blossoming of Webster's presidential candidacy, an undertaking, James Harvey maintained, in which the Massachusetts orator was "perhaps more zealously enlisted . . . than at any former period of his life."[37] Although New Hampshire Whigs had set the ball rolling by giving him the nomination in October 1846, the ambitions of the "God-Like" Webster were not openly revealed until the following spring, when he began a "grand electioneering tour through the Southern states."[38] His journey was a magnificent attempt to convince the South that he would not disturb the protection accorded to slavery by the Constitution and that he was thoroughly opposed to any action by northern extremists—perhaps by members of his own party—to overthrow the slave institution. His proposition was most plainly enunciated in Savannah. "Our duty," he announced, "is to be content with the constitution *as it is,* to resist all changes from whatever quarter, to preserve its original spirit and original purpose, and to commend it as it is, to the care of those who come after us."[39] However, the trip was not overly successful. It came at a moment when the Taylor movement was at high tide; moreover, southerners were suspicious of Webster. While a few Whig newspapers such as the *Alabama Journal* pronounced him a "politician of peculiar soundness upon southern questions," the majority seemed agreed that he could "never begin to be President."[40]

Nor was the reaction to Webster's southern jaunt entirely favorable in Massachusetts. Some, whom Harvey described as men of experience and character, "justly entitled to hold sway in the [party] councils," showed little favor for a Webster movement. Among them was Abbott Lawrence, who had never forgiven the statesman for his support of the Tyler regime. Lawrence, moreover, had ambitions of his own: he hoped to become Taylor's vice-presidential running mate. Another opponent of Webster was Senator John Davis, a Lawrence supporter, whom Web-

---

[36] Pierce, *Sumner,* 3: 147–48.

[37] Harvey to McLean, 22 September 1846, McLean Papers.

[38] *Mobile Register,* 7 April 1847. Webster's tour is well described in Fuess, *Webster,* 2: 178.

[39] *Webster's Writings,* 4:100.

[40] Montgomery *Alabama State Journal* (hereafter cited as *Alabama State Journal*) quoted in *Mobile Register,* 14 April 1847; *Savannah Republican,* 9 November 1846.

sterians and Conscience Whigs were trying to defeat in an intraparty contest for Davis's senate seat.[41] Equally important was the Conscience Whigs' opposition. Although their hostility was still subterranean, many of them found it difficult to dissuade themselves of the belief that Webster's course at Faneuil Hall had indicated a covert opposition to their whole program. The orator's "truckling" to the slave interests served to confirm this impression. Vague rumors that they would seek to defeat an endorsement of his presidential candidacy at the state convention, which was to meet in Springfield on 29 September 1847, began to circulate.[42]

That there would be trouble at the convention was made evident on the eve of the gathering, when it became known that the various factions had lodged at separate hotels. The antislavery wing had apparently gained delegate strength during the year because of the Proviso agitation that shook the country—a gain that may have been aided by Lawrence forces in the hope that the "African Whigs" would throw their vote against an endorsement of Webster. The antislavery forces were determined to translate what they regarded as the prevailing sentiment of the commonwealth into a concrete platform. However, the Lawrence and the Webster forces were equally resolved to prevent the adoption of any policy that might preclude cooperation with the Whigs of other states; Websterians, moreover, were determined to resist any movement that would compromise the senator's candidacy.

Webster was present to sound the keynote. His opening oration, the high point of his campaign for the presidential nomination, was a thorough arraignment of the Mexican War, a conflict he denounced as unnecessary, unjustifiable, and unconstitutional, founded upon mere "pretexts." With such sentiments Conscience Whigs could readily agree. But Webster also revealed an unmistakable lack of sympathy for their attempt to commit the party to a definitive antislavery position. Though he announced his opposition to any extension of the slave power, he deprecated the Proviso as a "panacea" for the dangers and evils of slavery. "It is not a sentiment to find [sic] a new party upon," he maintained, although "there is not a man in this hall who holds to it more firmly than I do, not one who adheres to it more than another." "I feel some little interest in the matter," he continued, maintaining that he had fully committed himself to the whole Proviso doctrine in 1838. "I must be permitted to say . . . that I do not now consent that more recent

[41] Harvey to McLean, 22 September 1846, McLean Papers; Harvey to Mangum, 22 September 1846, Mangum Papers.
[42] See *Boston Times*, 24, 28 August 1847; *Boston Atlas*, 6 September 1847.

discoverers should take out a patent for the discovery. I do not quite consent that they should undertake to appropriate to themselves all the benefit and honor of it. I deny the priority of their invention. Allow me to say it is not their thunder."[43]

He clearly implied that the "thunder" was his own, and since he had found no reason to make it a cause for disrupting the Whig party, there was no excuse for others to do so. This part of the speech met with the undisguised disapproval of the antislavery element; they registered their opposition by declining to vote on the resolution which recommended Webster to the national convention as Massachusetts' favorite candidate for the presidency. They saved their energy for the more important conflict expected over the party platform.

Although the resolutions presented to the convention contained a satisfactory Provisoist plank,[44] they also demanded the incorporation of an amendment proposed by Palfrey:

> *Resolved,* That the Whigs of Massachusetts will support no men for the office of President and Vice President but such as are known by their acts or declared opinions to be opposed to the extension of slavery.

The problem, as Conscience Whigs now saw it and as Sumner explained in his speech supporting Palfrey's resolution, was how best to express opposition to the extension of slavery. "It is not proposed to interfere with slavery in any constitutional stronghold," he declared, but Whigs had to assert that "the power of the Nation, of Congress . . . shall not be employed for its extension, and that this curse shall not be planted in any territory hereafter acquired." To enforce this principle a mere declaration of position was not sufficient. "Whigs of Massachusetts," he maintained, "must pronounce a sentence of disqualification upon all not known to be against the extension of Slavery." This was the program of the Conscience Whigs. "Whatever the final determination of this convention," he warned, "there are many here who will never yield support to any candidate . . . who is not known to be against the sacramental unction of a 'regular nomination.' " He concluded, "We can not say with detestable morality, 'our party right or wrong.' The time has gone when gentlemen can expect to introduce among us the discipline of the camp. Loyalty to principle is higher than loyalty to party."[45]

Such views met with the vociferous hostility of the Cotton Whigs,

[43] *Niles' Register* 73 (16 October 1847) : 104–6.
[44] Ibid., 73 (9 October 1847) : 84.
[45] *Sumner's Works,* 2 : 56–58, 60–62.

who demonstrated their disfavor with shouts and hisses while Palfrey and Sumner were speaking. Their own attitude was again expressed by Winthrop, who conducted the fight against Palfrey's amendment almost alone, arguing that it would unwisely fetter the action of the commonwealth's delegation to the national convention, that it would create a fatal breach between northern and southern Whigs, and that it would secure the election of a Democratic president, necessarily more obnoxious than a southern Whig. The debate over the proposal continued for hours, growing ever more bitter, until it was stilled by the exhaustion of the delegates. When the vote was finally taken, in the dim uncertainty of torchlight, Conscience Whigs discovered that they had lost again.[46] It had become painfully apparent that some separate action might be necessary to achieve their aims.

In this situation Conscience Whigs, who had been watching the Barnburner-Hunker feud in New York with great interest, fastened their attention hopefully upon the coming Herkimer meeting and upon developments within the Liberty party for signs of a possible nonpartisan movement against slavery extension. When Hale was nominated as the Liberty party candidate for president in October 1847, some Whigs began to consider him as the possible spearhead of an antislavery coalition.

[46] Pierce, *Sumner,* 3: 146.

Chapter Six

Antislavery Forces:
The Liberty Men

While the nation focused its interest upon the threatening disarray of the Democratic and Whig parties during the crucial months of 1847, a significant crisis was also developing within the Liberty party. Abolitionist politicians had emerged from the contest of 1844 with cruelly disappointed hopes. Not only was their total of 62,000 votes lower than they had expected, but also, as many recognized, their impractical activities during that campaign seemed to have put future success out of reach. The party's refusal to take a stand on the Texas issue had cost it votes which could never be recovered. Moreover, it had thoroughly alienated many Whigs. Its stubborn opposition to an endorsement of such apostles of abolition as Joshua Giddings had angered antislavery Whigs; its ambiguous attitude toward Clay had disgusted old-line Whigs. In New York, Whigs blamed the Liberty party for Clay's defeat.[1] James G. Birney's acceptance of a Democratic nomination for the Michigan state legislature convinced many that the Liberty candidate was a stalking-horse for Polk. Horace Greeley's attitude toward the party was typical: "You third party wire-workers forced this man [Polk] upon us instead of the only anti-Texas candidate who could possibly be elected. On your guilty heads shall rest the curse of unborn generations! Riot in your infamy and rejoice in its triumph but never ask us to unite with you in anything."[2]

Evidence that the Liberty party's appeal to the electorate had reached its limits became apparent in the next three years. Although its vote increased to 75,000 in 1846, a figure which included the total votes polled by the Hale machine, the party steadily became more isolated, its agitation less effective and less enthusiastic. In 1847 its vote began to decrease. Although efforts were made in large regional conventions held in

Chicago and Boston to revive its flagging strength, the party continued to sink.

Realizing their failure, Liberty men began to cast about for some formula which would gain new converts to their cause. One such effort, a labored argument reflecting the clerical calling of its author, Lysander Spooner, appeared in a long pamphlet, *The Unconstitutionality of Slavery*. It was an attempt to prove that the United States Constitution was an antislavery document.[3] Spooner's thesis was widely propagated, but except for abstractionists such as Gerrit Smith, philanthropist of Peterboro, New York, the response among Liberty men was not even faint-hearted. Faults in logic were too obvious. Moreover, incorporation of Spooner's doctrine into the Liberty platform would have pushed the party in the opposite direction from which its farseeing men sought to go; it would have contracted, rather than expanded, the party's principles and its following. Introduced for consideration at both the Chicago and the Boston conventions in 1845 and 1846, the doctrine was quickly relegated to obscurity.[4] The reaction of the *Cincinnati Herald-Philanthropist* was a common one: "The propostition that slavery in the States, at least in the original States, is unconstitutional sounds to us about as reasonable as the proposition that Slavery in the French colonies is unconstitutional."[5]

More important than Spooner's doctrine was the movement to transform the Liberty organization into a "general reform" party. Urged unsuccessfully upon Liberty men during the 1844 campaign, the movement was later taken up by Theodore Foster, editor of the *Michigan Signal of Liberty*. Foster pressed the issue upon Birney with considerable fervor: "In organizing the Liberty party we have done well in making abolition of Slavery the great and *paramount* question, and the

---

[1] Something of the Whig attitude toward Liberty men is contained in the following letter: "A low, reckless, Loco, Grog-shop politician will of course brawl, blackguard and lie & stick it so long as it is of any use to do so, but after that he will confidentially admit the truth, and justify the lie upon the ground that it is necessary one half the world should be humbugged & he might as well do part of it as any one else; but the Abolitionists go quite as far in slander and falsehood, and this under the garb of religion; and they will not only stick to their lie after tho' the truth would answer their purpose just as well, but will even then exhaust and pray over it" (James Adams to Hale, 6 October 1846, Hale Papers).

[2] *New York Tribune,* 28 November 1844.

[3] Lysander Spooner, *The Unconstitutionality of Slavery* (Boston, 1845), pp. 26–125 passim.

[4] Henry B. Stanton to Chase, 6 October 1845, Salmon P. Chase Papers; *Cincinnati Herald,* 29 July 1846. Later the Massachusetts Liberty Party Convention adopted the doctrine (*National Era,* 11 February, 4 March 1847).

[5] *Cincinnati Herald,* 10 September 1845.

only test of membership. . . . But there are multitudes of political questions . . . which concern the interests of members of the Liberty party, and the welfare of the whole nation. . . . *Shall these be discussed and acted upon in our Liberty Conventions, or not?"*

Almost all Liberty men, Foster explained, had once belonged to one of the other parties, where it was customary to take action on these questions. Suppose then that a Democrat approached the party and said, "I hate Slavery as bad as you do, and I am ready to join you and vote against it; but in those matters which deeply concern me as a citizen, . . . and are not in the least antagonistic to the antislavery object, I wish the concurrent action of my Liberty friends, and if I join, I shall propose them for the consideration of the next Convention." If this man were told that all action on such issues was outside the party sphere, Foster argued, he would "most probably refuse to join the party which refuses to act at all upon the most important interests of the citizens." If, he continued, the party persisted in refusing to take any action on questions of state policy or on important national questions—the enumeration is illuminating—such as "the reduction of Navy expenses, abolition of West Point Academy, cheap postage etc," the party could not hope to secure a majority of the votes of the nation or even of the free states.[6] Later, in the autumn of 1845, Foster introduced another argument. There were signs from which he inferred that northern Whigs were moving toward an antislavery position, a movement which would gradually cut the ground from under the Liberty party unless it set up its own appeal to the electorate.[7]

The logic of Foster's argument for general reform was apparent. It would direct the party toward an expansionist policy, which its politically wisest men realized was a necessary antidote to the introverted policy followed in the past. As early as January 1845 the Vermont wing had proven its interest in general reform by adopting a resolution calling on the party "to carry out the principles of Equal Rights into all their practical consequences and applications, and support every just measure conducive to individual and social freedom."[8] Birney's response was wholehearted. "We must be prepared to take on ourselves *all* the administration of the government or *none* of it," he informed Lewis Tappan.

---

[6] Theodore Foster to James G. Birney, 7 July 1845, in James G. Birney, *Letters of James Gillespie Birney,* ed. Dwight L. Dumond (New York, 1938), 2: 950–52 (hereafter cited as *Birney Letters*).

[7] Foster to Birney, 16 October 1845, ibid., p. 980.

[8] R. L. Morrow, "Liberty Party in Vermont," *New England Quarterly* 2 (1929): 24.

"A party that does not take the *whole* of it—but seeks a particular object —will soon, in the strife of other parties, become a lost party."[9]

In January 1846, in a long letter to the president of the Michigan Liberty party, Birney threw his weight behind a proposal to put Christian ethics into the government. It was evident, he declared, that the Liberty party could not carry a majority of the people of the free states on the question of slavery alone. "As a party we cannot limit ourselves to the oppressions of the tyrant over his slaves," he maintained. "If we fail to build on our good and maintainable substratum—*the legal and constitutional equality of all men*—other interests in which the people feel a deep concern; if we are not in fact a *reform* party, we will accomplish comparatively but little, and, I apprehend, there is not much use for us here or at this time."

Liberty men had long ceased to look for any advancement of the nation under the leadership of either the Democrats or the Whigs; it would not be long before sensible men within these organizations would also see that the "conflicts in which they were annually called to play their parts" had degenerated into mere scrambles for office. To Birney the parties represented two gamblers, each of them with only half enough to support him in his laziness and extravagance. Therefore, they staked the whole amount together and played for it in order that one might lead the life of a gentleman, while the other was left a loafer and a vagabond. The people were "only the cards" with which the game was played. The American nation had no need of such political parties. Instead, it required a single party made up of just men who were friendly to the Constitution, the "fount of all justice."

To create a government based on justice would require the complete reform of the Federal administration, Birney declared. The Liberty party would have to support certain principles which he proposed for incorporation into its creed: a diminution of the powers and patronage of the president, a reduction and ultimate abolition of the army and navy, a gradual abolition of the tariff and the introduction of free trade, a reduction of the salaries of members of Congress, and their payment by the states rather than the Federal government. Such reforms, he maintained, would transform the government into a concentrated physical force against violaters of justice and thus into a corollary to the government of heaven.[10]

[9] Birney to Lewis Tappan, 12 September 1845, in Dumond, *Birney Letters*, 2: 970–71.

[10] Birney to the President of the Michigan State Liberty Party, 1 January 1846, ibid., pp. 990–96.

This plan—which unconsciously revealed both the failure of the Liberty party's appeal and the fact that the preservation of the party had become important[11]—found instant acceptance among abstractionists such as Gerrit Smith and among many of the Liberty old guard such as Beriah Green and Lewis Tappan.[12]

But there was a third group in the party which offered the plan no support.[13] To them it smelled too much of midnight oil to be useful in practical politics; besides, it was the product of a man whom they viewed as a dead weight on the party. This recalcitrant faction, sometimes known as the Cincinnati Clique, was headed by half a dozen competent Ohioans: Salmon P. Chase, Samuel Lewis, Benjamin Tappan, Leicester King, Dr. Gamaliel Bailey, editor of the *Cincinnati Herald-Philanthropist,* and Stanley Mathews, his successor. The program of the Cincinnati Clique in 1845 was simple: coalition of the antislavery elements within all parties and the formation of a new party.

Among Ohio Liberty men the desire for a broadened platform and for association with all antislavery elements in the nation had been expressed even before the formation of the Liberty party.[14] In 1839 the American Anti-Slavery Society, meeting at Albany, had pledged: "We will neither vote for or support the election of any man . . . who is not in favor of the immediate abolition of slavery."[15] Bailey denounced the formula as too narrow: "In our own state," he pointed out, "the requirements of abolitionists had exclusive regard to the subjects on which candidates, if elected, might . . . be called upon to take some action." To demand something beyond this, he maintained, "is proscriptive in principle, and tends to pervert the ballot box from its only legitimate end—the fulfilment of the will of the people in just legislation under the constitution." It was unreasonable to extract a pledge from abolitionists to refrain from voting for candidates who did not avow themselves in favor of an act entirely beyond their control; he, for one, did not consider himself pledged.[16]

After the official formation of the Liberty party in 1841, Bailey

[11] Later generations might also find some sign of protofascism in the plan.

[12] Lewis Tappan to Birney, 10 March 1846, Gerrit Smith to the Liberty Party, 7 May 1846, Beriah Green to Birney, 23 September, 17 December 1846, in Dumond, *Birney Letters,* 2: 1006–7, 1019–20 note 2, 1027, 1032.

[13] *Cincinnati Herald,* 29 April 1846.

[14] In this account of the Cincinnati Clique I am using the material in my article, "The Liberty Leaders of Ohio: Exponents of Antislavery Coalition," *Ohio State Archeological and Historical Quarterly* 57 (1948): 165–78.

[15] Boston *Emancipator,* 8 August 1839.

[16] *Cincinnati Herald,* 13 August 1839.

continued to protest, pointing out that it was improper to call the Liberty party an "abolition party," since it could not aim at the abolition of slavery anywhere except in the District of Columbia and in the territories. One New Yorker charged that this protest could only be interpreted as "a direct and bold attempt to sell the abolitionists of Ohio to one of the political parties."[17]

Although this charge was probably not entirely accurate, a movement developed in 1842 among the leaders of the party in Ohio to change the entire direction of Liberty affairs. Salmon P. Chase, a long-time friend of the slave but only recently a member of the party, appeared to be the ringleader. He planned simultaneously to broaden the party's base by adopting less extreme principles and to replace Birney as its standard bearer with some more attractive candidate, such as William H. Seward, William Jay, or the aged John Quincy Adams.[18] Although the project failed, it was not forgotten.

After the campaign of 1844, when Birney's friends once more advanced his name, Bailey registered an immediate protest. "The Liberty party," he maintained, "was organized not for the sake of conferring office on particular men, but for the sake of freeing our country from the crime of slavery." Anyone who accepted a party nomination must understand that he thereby derived "no claim . . . upon the future support of the party; so that at subsequent periods, when it became necessary to select candidates the party may be embarrassed with no proscriptive claims, but left *entirely free* to act *at the time,* as circumstances may demand." Although he had no objection to Birney's renomination at a convention which might be called two or three years later, Bailey warned: "If, by action of certain cliques and influences Mr. Birney be placed in such a relation to our cause that a National Convention should feel itself embarrassed, and almost compelled to nominate him, we should then feel ourselves free from all obligations to the party." [19]

By 1846 this sentiment had found lodgement in other quarters as well. From western Pennsylvania, Russell Erret informed Chase that Birney was regarded as a "dead-weight." "It was hard enough for us," Erret declared, "to bear the odium of being Anti-Slavery—to be his supporters against our own sense of propriety, would make us doubly odious. . . .

[17] Ibid., 16 February, 16 March 1842.
[18] Chase to Lewis Tappan, 26 May, 15, 24 September 1842, 15 February 1843, Chase Papers; Chase to Giddings, 21 January 1842, Joshua R. Giddings–George P. Julian Papers. The letter to Giddings is obviously misdated a year early. It is actually an explanation of what happened at the Ohio Liberty Convention in January 1843. See also *Cincinnati Herald,* 1 October 1842, 26 July 1843.
[19] *Cincinnati Herald,* 25 December 1844.

Our men here with very few exceptions *want a new man.*" The same
was true in Indiana and in Illinois.[20]

The program of the Cincinnati Clique was not confined to action
within the Liberty party; its policy was one of coalition with other
antislavery elements as well. Chase had long toyed with the idea of
coalition; as early as 1842 he had suggested to Thaddeus Stevens a
fusion of Liberty men and the Anti-Masons of Pennsylvania.[21] His own
inclination moved him toward the Democratic party, whose doctrines
"so vociferously proclaimed by every orator on every stump and by
every newspaper from every press" were in exact harmony "with the
principles of the Liberty men."[22] Chase had revealed this tendency in his
attempt to change the party name from Liberty to "True Democrat" in
1844.[23] It was his constant hope that the "Jeffersonians" would take a
stand to make fusion possible. From the Whigs, on the other hand, he
expected nothing. "There are more abolitionists in the Whig party than
in the Democratic party," he admitted to Hale, "but I fear that the Whig
party will always look upon the overthrow of slavery as a work to be
taken up or laid aside, like other *measures,* as expediency may suggest;
whereas if we can once get the Democratic party in *motion* regarding the
overthrow of slavery as a legitimate and necessary result of principles, I
would have no apprehension of the work being laid aside until accomplished."[24] If that time ever came, he was ready to give up the Liberty
party.[25]

Early in April 1845 the Cincinnati Clique brought its program into the
open. It issued a call, prepared by Chase and signed by Bailey and Lewis,
for a "Southern and Western Convention of the Friends of Constitutional Liberty." The convention, duly assembled in Cincinnati in June,
adopted the broadest of antislavery principles. None of the resolutions,

[20] Russell Erret to Chase, 9 May 1846, Chase Papers.

[21] James A. Woodburn, *Life of Thaddeus Stevens* (Indianapolis, Ind., 1913), pp.
67–69; Thomas F. Woodley, *Thaddeus Stevens* (Harrisburg, Pa., 1934), pp. 191–93
(hereafter cited as *Stevens*).

[22] Chase to Giddings, 9 February 1843, Giddings–Julian Papers.

[23] William Birney to James Birney, 25 November 1844, in Dumond, *Birney
Letters,* 2: 887. See also Smith, *Liberty and Free Soil Parties,* pp. 88–89, 90; Chase
to Giddings, August 1846, Chase Papers.

[24] Chase to Hale, 12 May 1847, in Robert S. Warden, *Account of the Private Life
and Public Services of Salmon Portland Chase* (Cincinnati, Ohio, 1874), p. 314.
Chase at this point was willing to support Silas Wright as a candidate for president
on a Wilmot Proviso platform (Chase to Preston King, 15 July 1847, in Salmon P.
Chase, *Diary and Correspondence of Salmon P. Chase* [Washington, D. C., 1903],
p. 121) (hereafter cited as *Chase Correspondence*).

[25] Chase to John Thomas, 24 June 1847, Chase to Sumner, 24 April 1847, in
Chase Correspondence, pp. 119, 115–16.

drawn up by Chase, mentioned immediate abolition. Instead, it was resolved that as a "national party" its purpose was "to divorce the National Government from Slavery; to prohibit slaveholding in all places of exclusive national jurisdiction; to abolish the domestic slave trade, . . . and in all proper and constitutional modes to discourage and discontinue the system of work without wages." The convention extended an invitation for "an union of all sincere friends of Liberty and Free Labor" upon these grounds.[26]

During the next two years, coalition with other antislavery elements was more and more frequently mentioned by Liberty men. Several events helped the movement. One was the success of Hale's revolt in New Hampshire. Another was the appearance of Birney's general reform project, which, while attracting some of the old guard, alienated others and made them more amenable to the suggestions of the Ohio leaders, whose program was still directed exclusively against slavery. The erection in Washington of the *National Era,* under the guidance of Gamaliel Bailey, aided immeasurably in spreading coalition doctrines throughout the party. The loss of Birney's services because of a paralytic stroke liberated many of his friends. The failure of the party to make any appreciable gain in the elections of 1846 produced a feeling that some change was necessary. Finally, the introduction of the Wilmot Proviso, causing a minor upsurge of antislavery feeling among the rank and file of the two major political organizations and the fusion of these elements in some local elections, made it apparent that Chase's schemes were not without merit.[27]

By 1847 various leaders outside Ohio had begun to speak in favor of coalition. William Jay, Elizur Wright, Henry B. Stanton, and the editors of the *Michigan Signal of Liberty,* Theodore Foster and Guy Beckley, had become disgusted with the party's adhesion to one idea and had decided to use the "One Idea Power" where it would "tell for the interest of the Slave." They approved of Chase's proposal to form a "national antislavery league," which would be pledged to vote for no man who was not "reliably known to be opposed to the extension of slavery" and "to nominate candidates of their own on independent grounds."[28]

[26] *Cincinnati Herald,* 25 April, 25 June 1845.

[27] Foster to Birney, 30 March 1846, Birney to Liberty Party, 1 September 1846, in Dumond, *Birney Letters,* 2: 1008, 1033–34; Chase to Hale, n.d., in Smith, *Liberty and Free Soil Parties,* pp. 110–11.

[28] *New York Tribune,* 25 March 1846; Elizur Wright to Birney, 8 February 1847, Guy Beckley to *Michigan Signal of Liberty,* 16 March 1847, in Dumond,

From that point, it was easy to fall in with the reasoning of the *Cincinnati Herald-Philanthropist,* which in April 1847 pointed out that it was not unlikely that the antislavery elements represented in the regular parties would be "driven out" and forced to cooperate with the Liberty men. Such a situation, the journal maintained, "ought to modify our own action in the nomination of our candidates. If there is a possibility of such a desirable aid, their reasonable preferences ought to be consulted with our own in the selection of a candidate upon whom the entire Anti-slavery sentiment of the country might unite."[29]

To many old-guard Liberty men, however, the proposition smacked of heresy. Birney denounced the idea as "wild and visionary" and cautioned his friends against throwing aside a "strong weapon" to pick up a "straw."[30] The orthodox view was expounded by the Boston *Emancipator:*

> The Liberty party occupies the only ground on which the battle of the country can be fought with final success. The ground of absolute and uncompromising hostility to slavery. . . . We make no terms with it but that of actual extinction. . . . We are sorry to see some of the Liberty men so easily carried away with the idea, that we can accomplish our end all at once by some bargain, or some management, or some profound political maneuvre, by which the old parties, or a portion of them can be used as tools in our hands. . . . We distrust all such anticipations.[31]

As the coalition issue developed, the party soon became involved in a discussion of the appropriate time to hold a national nominating convention. The coalitionists, dominating every northwestern state but Wisconsin and having a considerable following in the East, demanded a postponement of nominations to the spring of 1848, when "a pretty correct opinion . . . of the tickets, and the final policy of the old parties" could be formed, and Liberty nominations could be shaped accordingly. The diehards, on the other hand, worked for an early meeting in order to "guard against the danger" of subjecting the party to the control of those who wished to avail themselves of its advantages "without sharing its responsibilities."[32]

Birney Letters, 2: 1039, 1057–59 n; Erret to Chase, 31 August 1846, Chase Papers; Chase to Hale, 12 May 1847, in Warden, *Chase,* p. 313.

[29] *Cincinnati Herald,* 21 April 1847.

[30] Birney to Beckley, 6 April 1847, in Dumond, *Birney Letters,* 2: 1059–61.

[31] Boston *Emancipator,* 16 June 1847.

[32] *National Era,* 15 April 1847; Boston *Emancipator,* 12 May 1847.

The coalitionists were supported by most of the major party journals: the *National Era,* the *Bangor Gazette* of Maine, the *Independent Democrat* of New Hampshire, the *Albany Patriot,* the *Utica Liberty Press,* the *Pennsylvania Freeman,* the *Cincinnati Herald-Philanthropist,* the *Michigan Signal of Liberty,* the *Indiana Free Labor Advocate,* and the *Chicago Western Citizen.* Since the advocates of early action could muster only the Boston *Emancipator* and the *Milwaukee Freeman* to their cause, the coalitionists appeared to hold the edge. But they reckoned without the party's central committee, controlled by the old guard. By a strict East versus West vote of seven states to five, and over the strenuous protests of Chase, that body called for a national convention to meet at Buffalo on 20 October 1847.[33] The coalitionists acquiesced, but they served notice that it was "altogether a mistake" to suppose that the call foreclosed all discussion upon the propriety of making any nominations "at that time."[34]

Meanwhile, the fragments of the party that had accepted Birney's general reform program and Spooner's view of slavery as an unconstitutional institution had met as the "Liberty League" under the leadership of William Goodell in a convention at Macedon Locks, New York, early in June 1847. Their "Reasons for Action" contained an apt summary of their conception of political duties:

> Civil Government has no moral right to compromise or postpone the discharge of any one class of its duties for the sake of attending to another class. . . . It is inadmissable in morals and suicidal in policy, to attempt the redress of any moral and political wrongs while tacitly consenting to any other moral and political wrongs, and we hold that individual voters, and political associations of citizens, have no moral right to propose any object or objects short of the discharge of *all* duties of Civil Government, namely the protection of the equal rights of *all men.*

As originally conceived, the Liberty party had been pledged to apply these principles. None of its prominent men had ever "denied that the party was designed to cover the entire field of political responsibility, or assumed that it was not, in the progress of its development, to take

---

[33] *National Era,* 15, 22 April, 13, 20 May, 24 June, 8, 22 July 1847; *Cincinnati Herald,* 21 April, 5 May, 23, 30 June, 7, 21 July, 8 September 1847; Adam Jewett to Chase, 7 June 1847, John Thomas to Chase, 11 June 1847, Chase Papers.

[34] *Cincinnati Herald,* 28 July 1847. See also Chase to Edward Wade, 23 June 1847, Chase Papers; Chase to Leavitt, 16 June 1847, Chase to Sumner, 22 September 1847, in *Chase Correspondence,* pp. 116–23; *New Hampshire Patriot,* 2 October 1847.

ground on other questions besides that of chattel enslavement." However, since the issue of expanding the party platform had arisen, some had appeared who strenuously insisted that *"nothing except the abolition of chattel slavery"* should engage the party's attention. These same men, moreover, were ready to "run *out* of the party, 'just for this once' and *cooperate with the supporters of Slavery."*

No sagacious politician could assume that the Liberty party on such a basis could be a permanent party; activity of this type could only lead to the party's disbandment. Therefore, in order to prevent the Liberty party's "ultimate absorption in one of the other political parties, to the shipwreck of all objects for which it was originally organized, including . . . the defeat, for the present generation, of the anti-slavery enterprize," it was necessary to issue a distinctly enunciated declaration of its position "on *all* the great political questions before the country," in which the rights of citizens and the security of American liberties, as well as the liberation of the slaves, were *"together* involved."[35]

To carry out this purpose the Macedon Locks convention named Gerrit Smith and Elihu Burritt, the "learned blacksmith" of Massachusetts, to its presidential ticket and adopted a long series of resolutions setting forth the doctrines of Spooner and Birney.

The "Nineteen Articles," as the platform came to be known, affirmed the unconstitutionality and antirepublican character of slavery and asserted the right and duty of the Federal government to abolish it in the states. It arraigned the tariff as an "unjust tax" upon one portion of the community for the benefit of another. It denounced all monopolies, caste legislation, and exclusive privileges as "unequal, unjust, morally wrong, and subversive of the ends of civil government." It called for the abolition of the Federal mail monopoly. It demanded the dissolution of secret societies as "combinations and conspiracies of a part of the people against the whole." It pledged support to legislation which would give citizens their "essential . . . right to occupy a portion of the earth's surface," provide landless men with small "parcels" of the public domain as homesteads free from liabilities of debt, and "restrict within proper bonds, the accumulation of landed property." It announced support for any direct tax measure as a means of reducing national expenditures, compelling the dissolution of the army and the navy, and forcing the emancipation of slaves. Finally, it vigorously condemned votes cast for "unprincipled, licentious, dishonest and unjust men" who neither feared God nor respected men, who were enslaved by "spiritual or ecclesiastical

[35] Dumond, *Birney Letters,* 2: 1051–57.

despotism," or who lent their support to religious bodies which were the "apologists and supporters of despotism, especially in the extreme degree of chattel Slavery."[36]

Of the abolitionist newspapers, only the *Albany Patriot* and the *Cortland True American* of New York announced adherence to the new movement. Other journals either regretted or denounced the action taken by the "Macedonians." The *Cincinnati Herald-Philanthropist* found it morally as "impossible for the Liberty party to support Mr. Goodell's universal reform party" as to vote for Democratic or Whig candidates. Joseph G. Lovejoy of Massachusetts pronounced the Macedonians' doctrines "essentially false." "Instead of fastening the stump machine to one stump at a time," he explained, "they go round and tie the rope to every root on seven acres at a time and then cry lustily 'come over and help us.'" Even Elihu Burritt, declining his nomination, rebuked the movement as one that "must result in new divisions upon points extraneous to the great & mighty idea, that all men are born free and equal in a legal sense."[37]

Most Liberty men gave little attention to the general reformers; they were concerned with the more pressing problem of what was to be done at their regular meeting. When the convention gathered at Buffalo in the fall, with Samuel Lewis of Ohio in the chair, three factions quickly appeared: the orthodox old guard, intent upon keeping the party on its former course; the Macedonians, with numbers greatly swelled by unofficial delegates from western New York; and the coalitionists, eager to moderate extreme principles in order to attract more voters and to postpone nominations to a more opportune moment.

The struggle for supremacy among the three groups began over the resolutions. Led by Gerritt Smith, the "universal reformers" attempted three times to include a plank that would declare slavery in the states unconstitutional; in each instance they were defeated. As finally adopted, the platform, while still paying service to the cause of abolitionism, no longer insisted upon immediate abolition of slavery; instead, it called for abolition "by the constitutional acts of the Federal and State governments." The chief plank, moreover, incorporated the principles which

[36] The Nineteen Articles were enclosed in a letter written by William Goodell to Birney from Honeoye, New York, 1 April 1847. (ibid., pp. 1047–51). They were substantially the same as those announced by Gerrit Smith in a letter written on 8 May 1847 to the *Albany Patriot* in reply to that newspaper's request for his platform (William Goodell, *Address of the Macedonian Convention, and Letters of Gerrit Smith* [Albany, N.Y., 1847], pp. 14–15 [hereafter cited as *Macedonian Address*]). Proceedings of the meeting are in *Cincinnati Herald*, 24 June 1847.

[37] *Cincinnati Herald*, 2 June, 18 August 1847; Boston *Emancipator*, 7 July 1847.

had been suggested as a basis for political action by Gamaliel Bailey in 1839: "It is the duty of anti-slavery men in Congress to propose and vote for acts to repeal the Slave Code of the District of Columbia; to repeal the act of 1793, relating to fugitives from service; to provide against the introduction of slavery in any territory, and [to provide for] such other laws as may be necessary and expedient to withdraw the support of the government from slavery, and array the powers of the general government, on the side of liberty and free labor." The platform concluded with the hope that the discouragement of slavery by "national example and recommendation" would result "at no distant day, in the establishment of peaceful emancipation throughout the Union." The coalitionists had won the first victory.

The convention then turned to nominations. The coalitionists—led by Chase, Jay, Henry B. Stanton, Owen Lovejoy of Illinois, Daniel Hoyt of New Hampshire, and Joshua Leavitt of Massachusetts—made a vigorous effort to postpone nominations. Their move was defeated 144 votes to 72[38] by a combination of the orthodox old guard faction and the Macedonians; only the Ohio delegation supported the motion unanimously.

In desperation, the coalitionists threw all their efforts into the nominating canvass. There were only two candidates: Gerrit Smith and John P. Hale. Coalitionists had started to consider Hale in the summer of 1846, shortly after his election to the United States Senate; by the spring of the next year, some of them had openly approached him with the suggestion that he become a candidate. His closest political advisors, such as Amos Tuck, originally advised him to resist a movement on his behalf, and Hale himself confessed that the idea was "repugnant." Nevertheless, coalitionists such as Stanton indicated that they were determined either to have him or to bolt the party. Moreover, the repugnance Hale felt gave way at the death of Silas Wright; he was needed, and he raised no further obstacles to his candidacy.[39] He was nominated overwhelmingly on the first ballot—103 votes to 44—by a combination of the coalitionists and the old guard, who feared and

[38] The Boston *Emancipator*, 27 October 1847, and the *Cincinnati Herald*, 3 November 1847, both reported this tally; it differs from that reported in Smith, *Liberty and Free Soil Parties*, p. 119.

[39] See *Cincinnati Herald*, 22 July 1846, 28 July, 25 August 1847; Boston *Emancipator*, 1, 18, 15 September 1847; Stanton to Chase, 6 August 1847, in *Chase Correspondence*, p. 467; Z. Eastman to Hale, 25 May, 29 June 1847, Stanton to Hale, 6 July, 10 September 1847, Tuck to Hale, 2 August, 11 September 1847, Leavitt to Hale, 9 November 1847, Hale to Lewis Tappan, 12 October 1847, Hale Papers.

detested Smith. As its vice-presidential candidate the party selected Leicester King.[40]

The Liberty press gave Hale's nomination an enthusiastic ratification; only in Wisconsin did a party journal reveal displeasure. "We are slow to believe it necessary to leave the circle of noble men who have been the life of the cause," the *Milwaukee Freeman* declared. "We will put his name at the head of our columns, but do not wish to be considered pledged."[41] Among Macedonians a spirit of protest raged. Birney was so infuriated by the convention's action that he resigned his office in the American and Foreign Anti-Slavery Society when it extended its approval to Hale's nomination.[42] Unwilling to give up their program, the reformers met in Auburn, New York, late in January 1848 to censure the Liberty party severely for "recreancy to principles," to reaffirm their belief in the Nineteen Articles, and for a second time to choose Gerrit Smith as their presidential candidate, with the Reverend Charles E. Foote of Michigan as his running mate.[43] The event was scarcely noticed, for the attention of the Liberty party and of the nation was now drawn to the dramatic effort of Democrats and Whigs to evade or to compromise the Proviso issue.

[40] The complete proceedings are in *National Era*, 4 November 1847.

[41] *Milwaukee Freeman*, 10 November 1847, in Smith, *Liberty and Free Soil Parties*, p. 120.

[42] Birney to Tappan, 10 July 1848, in Dumond, *Birney Letters*, 2: 1108–9. See also Gerrit Smith's attack in *New Hampshire Patriot*, 20 April 1848.

[43] Wilson, *Slave Power*, 2: 112–13.

Chapter Seven

Compromise and Evasion

In the latter part of 1847 even a casual observer of the political developments of the year would have concluded that the Wilmot Proviso was to
become the issue upon which the next presidential election would be
decided. The *Savannah Georgian* stated the fact in the simplest terms:
"The bank is dead, the sub-Treasury in most successful operation, the
principles of free trade firmly established—all these subjects, for the
time being at least, are laid upon the shelf. . . . The only great question
before the country, therefore, is the Wilmot Proviso. This question will
enter into the next presidential canvass, and exert a controlling influence
upon the result."[1]

But the turmoil of the year indicated that the issue would do more
than decide a presidential election, for it also threatened the unity of
both parties. Democrats were more fully aware of the probability of
schism than were Whigs: in the spring and summer of 1847 some
southern Democrats began to espouse the "Alabama Platform," which
was introduced at the Alabama Democratic Convention of March 1847
by William Lowndes Yancey as a test of party orthodoxy. Reaffirming
Calhoun's position as stated in the Virginia Resolutions, it declared the
"natural and indefeasible right of each citizen of every State of the
Confederacy to reside with his property of every description in any
territory" which might be acquired by the arms of the United States or
which was yielded by treaty with any foreign power. The convention
likewise avowed determination to support no men for the offices of
president and vice president who were not "openly and unequivocally"
opposed to the exclusion of slavery from the territories.[2]

The first official approval of these resolutions came from a state
convention of Georgia Democrats held at Milledgeville in July 1847. The
appeal of the Alabama Platform in the South was obvious. As one
journal expressed it: "We would have it distinctly understood, that the
South will not submit to any interference with her peculiar institutions,
that she will not allow her citizens to be deprived of their constitutional

rights, that she will not submit to the domination of a wild act of intolerant fanatics."[3]

The spirit of the resolutions, which were announced earlier than any similar statements from northern Democrats, threatened party unity. Thomas Hart Benton pointed out the danger in a letter to the editor of the *Fayette* (Mo.) *Intelligencer:* "Everybody must see that if this new test shall be adopted by the slaveholding states, there is an end to all political support of northern men in these states; that the present organization of parties must be broken up, and a new party formed, bounded by geographical lines, and resting on the sole principle of slavery propagandism." Such a development, Benton added, would lead inevitably to the destruction of the Union itself.[4]

When northern Democratic supporters of the Proviso began to move toward a test of the Alabama Platform, regular party members became extremely alarmed. In northern and border states, editorial recognition of the danger to the party brought a sudden, apparently concerted effort to cry down the Proviso. It was denounced as "disastrous . . . to Democratic interest," "premature and preposterous," a "mere shadow," "an abstraction—inoperative in itself—carrying with it not the least legislative or practical force the moment the new territory became a state." It was condemned because it threatened to "bring the war to a disgraceful and dishonorable conclusion"; it was attacked as an invasion of the rights of the states.[5]

But denunciation was hardly sufficient; party leaders recognized that it was necessary to provide some alternative to the Proviso that would be satisfactory to all elements and would quiet discord. The remedy that first suggested itself was the extension of the Missouri Compromise line from the western boundary of the Louisiana Purchase to the Pacific coast. This course, argued the *Washington Union,* one of the earliest advocates of such a settlement, would apportion the benefits of the nation as equally as the "dews of heaven."[6] Some southern journals also

[1] *Georgian,* 28 March 1848. See also *Albany Argus,* 8 April 1847; Baltimore *Republican,* 18 August 1847; *Boston Atlas,* 19 November 1847; Niles to Van Buren, 16 December 1847, Van Buren Papers.

[2] John W. DuBose, *Life and Times of William Lowndes Yancey* (Birmingham, Ala., 1892), pp. 213–14 (hereafter cited as *Yancey*).

[3] *Niles' Register* 72 (20 July 1847) : 293; *Georgian,* 1 September 1847.

[4] *Niles' Register* 72 (12 June 1847) : 225.

[5] *Albany Argus,* 17 December 1847; *Louisville Democrat,* 23 November 1847; Baltimore *Republican,* 13 November 1847; *Niles' Register* 73 (18 September 1847) : 45; *Philadelphia Ledger* quoted in *Nashville Union,* 7 October 1847; *Hartford Times* quoted in *Albany Atlas,* 11 August 1847.

[6] *Washington Union,* 28 September 1847.

indicated approval of the policy. But it was not until August 1847 that the idea was given widespread publicity. On the day of Silas Wright's death, Secretary of State James Buchanan spread the program before the country in a letter he sent to the Democracy of "Old Berks" County, Pennsylvania, which had requested his opinion on the Proviso.

Although northern Democrats were "not expected to approve slavery in the abstract," he wrote, they owed it to themselves to leave the question where the Constitution had placed it—in the hands of the states where slavery existed. Nearly three decades earlier, when the nation had been confronted by an agitation similar to that aroused by the Proviso, Congress had settled the issue in a spirit of mutual concession by adopting the Missouri Compromise line. Accordingly, he proposed that the "harmony of the states, and even the security of the country itself" required the extension of the line "to any new territory" which the nation might acquire from Mexico.

He would hold this opinion, Buchanan declared, even if the question of slavery in the new territories were practical. However, he assured his presumably antislavery Pennsylvania constituents, an examination of the subject would reveal that the issue was a mere abstraction. "Neither the soil, the climate, nor the production of that portion of California south of 36 deg 30 min" was adaptable to slave labor. Nor could anyone envision the possibility of establishing slavery in the region east of the Rocky Mountains, where the people were "in large proportion a colored population."

Since the territory was not conducive to slavery and would, he implied, remain free, the Proviso was not of "practical importance." Moreover, agitation for it could produce no other effect than "to alienate the different portions of the Union, to excite sectional divisions and jealousies ; and to distract and possibly destroy the democratic party." As the adoption of the Missouri Compromise had saved the Union from "threatened convulsions" in 1820, so its extension would "secure the like happy result" in 1848.[7]

Almost simultaneously with Buchanan's plan for settling the question of slavery in the territories, support developed for another ingenious proposal, which became known for a time as the doctrine of "popular sovereignty." The idea was first briefly stated by Vice President George M. Dallas at a large meeting in Pittsburgh, where he had gone to build his presidential prospects, on 18 September 1847. "The very best thing which can be done, when all is said upon the subject [of slavery

[7] Moore, *Buchanan's Works,* 7 : 385–88.

extension]," he declared, "will be to let it alone entirely—leaving to the people of the territory to be acquired the business of settling the matter for themselves; for when slavery has no existence, all the legislation of Congress would be powerless to give it existence; and where we find it to exist, the people of the country have themselves adopted the institution; they have the right alone to determine their own institutions."[8]

The inherent appeal in Dallas's proposal became evident shortly after mid-December 1847, when Daniel S. Dickinson, Hunker senator from New York, introduced into Congress a resolution which would have made the vice president's statement the nation's official policy:

> *Resolved:* That in organizing a territorial government for territories belonging to the United States, the principle of self government upon which our federative system rests will be best promoted, the true spirit and meaning of the Constitution be observed, and the Confederacy strengthened, by leaving all questions concerning the domestic policy therein to the legislatures chosen by the people thereof.[9]

A fortnight later the proposal was placed more forcibly before the nation through the publication of a letter which Lewis Cass sent to his friend A. O. P. Nicholson of Nashville, Tennessee.

Cass, it appears, had originally favored the Proviso, but by February 1847 he had concluded that it was "a firebrand thrown among us which threatens the most disastrous results to the party." Moreover, as he informed his colleague from Michigan, Alpheus Felch, he regarded passage of the Proviso as futile. "If we should pass that resolution tomorrow, it would conclude nothing"; when the time should come for organizing territorial governments, "the subject would be just as open for Congressional legislation as though no such resolution had passed."[10]

Something of this attitude appeared in Cass's letter to Nicholson. "The theory of our government," he wrote, "presupposes that its various members have reserved to themselves the regulation of all . . . local institutions"—including the institution of slavery. Congress had no power over slavery in the states; in his opinion, the constitutional clause granting Congress power to dispose of and make all needful rules and regulations respecting the territory and other properties belonging to the United States did not extend its authority over the domestic institutions of the territories.

[8] *Washington Union,* 28 September 1847.

[9] Dickinson, *Dickinson,* 1: 228.

[10] Woodford, *Cass,* p. 245; Cass to Alpheus Felch, 4 February 1847, Alpheus Felch Papers.

In addition, it was most expedient to avoid any issue that would arouse sectional antagonisms. Since Cass feared that any attempt to "engraft the principles of the Wilmot Proviso" upon the legislation of the nation would seriously affect national "tranquillity," he announced that he was "opposed to the exercise of any jurisdiction by Congress" over the matter. The question would be solved most easily by "leaving [to] the people of any territory, which may hereafter be acquired, the right to regulate it themselves, under the general principles of the constitution."

"After all," Cass reasoned, it was generally conceded that the Proviso's prohibition of slavery "could not operate upon any state to be formed from newly acquired territory. The well known attributes of sovereignty, recognized by us as belonging to the state governments, would sweep before them any such barrier, and would leave the people to express their will at pleasure." Was, then, the goal "of temporary exclusion for so short a period as the duration of the territorial government, worth the price at which it would be purchased—worth the discord it would engender, the trial to which it would expose our Union, and the evils that would be the certain consequences?" Besides, there was evidence of all sorts that the territories that might be acquired from Mexico were not geographically suited to support a slave-labor system. If the nation wished to avoid sectional controversy, its wisest policy would be to leave the issue "to the people" who would be affected by it.[11]

Reaction to the statements by Buchanan, Dallas, and Cass soon indicated that each had struck popular chords. Whigs, of course, immediately and rightfully pointed out that all three men were bidding for support in the approaching presidential contest. They condemned Buchanan's statement as a move to secure southern votes at the Democratic National Convention. The Nashville *Republican-Banner* expressed this attitude: "As an aspirant for the Presidency, Mr. Buchanan knew well enough that he stood little chance for the nomination as long as Mr. Wright was in the field, unless he occupied different ground. The Northern Wilmot Proviso men had already indicated their preference for Mr. Wright. What must be done? He could not succeed against the great son of the Empire State, and he knew it; and the idea was a notable one, as he doubtless concluded, to bid for Southern votes by taking the line of the Missouri Compromise."[12]

If such was the purpose behind the Berks County letter, Buchanan's

[11] *Niles' Register* 73 (8 January 1848) : 293–94.
[12] Nashville *Republican,* 22 October 1847. The *New York Tribune,* 4 September 1847, declared: "Mr. Secretary Buchanan . . . has made a large bid for southern support—so large that we are confident that he would never have made it had the death of Silas Wright been known to him before he thus committed himself."

idea nevertheless enjoyed considerable success. In the North, antislavery Democrats condemned the statement as a scheme "to give up all territory" thereafter acquired south of the Missouri Compromise line "to the domination of the slave interest."[13] More moderate elements in the section remained almost silent. However, Buchanan's correspondents in Pennsylvania reported that his letter was "highly approved," gave "universal satisfaction," and received the "warmest approbation." Southern Democrats, evidently ignoring Buchanan's reasoning that nature was against slavery in the territories, also heaped plaudits on the proposal. The *Mississippian* greeted the idea "as the wearied traveler greets an oasis in the desert," and other southern journals responded in a similar fashion. Even the *Charleston Mercury* extended its approval.[14] William R. King reported from Selma, Alabama, that the letter had increased Buchanan's popularity; John Tyler, usually careful in his speculations, concluded that on 1 November 1847 Buchanan was "in advance" of all his competitors in the race for the party's nomination.[15]

Response to the position enunciated by Dallas and Cass was even more cordial and widespread. Indications that a proposition to let the territories decide the slavery question would be acceptable to many Democrats and to some Whigs had become apparent in midsummer of 1847.[16] Dallas's speech served to reveal that his position was ambivalent enough to attract at the same time the support of ardently proslavery newspapers such as the *Richmond Enquirer* and the *Savannah Georgian,* both of which had endorsed the Alabama Platform; moderate southern Democrats such as the editor of the *Louisville Democrat;* journals such as the *Vicksburg Whig;* and antislavery men such as John Wentworth, whose newspaper, the *Chicago Democrat,* hailed the vice president as a fit successor to Silas Wright.[17]

Reaction to Dickinson's resolution disclosed that its chief opposition

---

[13] *Albany Atlas,* 20 September 1847.

[14] Edwin W. Hutter to Buchanan, 29 August, 3 September 1847, Wilson M. Candless to Buchanan, 2 September 1847, Alfred Gilmore to Buchanan, 3 September 1847, John Snyder to Buchanan, 30 September 1847, Buchanan Papers; *Mississippian,* 17 September 1847; *Charleston Mercury,* 4 September 1847.

[15] King to Buchanan, 5 October 1847, Buchanan Papers; Tyler to Caleb Cushing, 1 November 1847, in Tyler, *Tylers,* 2: 460.

[16] *Baltimore Clipper,* 31 August 1847. The New Hampshire Democratic Convention had adopted a popular sovereignty plank in June 1846 (*New Hampshire Patriot,* 18 June 1846).

[17] *Richmond Enquirer,* 19 September, 29 October 1847; *Georgian,* 4 October 1847; *Louisville Democrat,* 29 October 1847; *Vicksburg Whig,* 29 September 1847; *Chicago Democrat,* 26 October 1847. See also Montgomery Moses to Dallas, 23 October 1847, John Marshall to Dallas, 30 October 1847, Dallas Papers. The *Albany Atlas,* 29 September 1847, preferred Dallas's position to Buchanan's.

would come from the Barnburners and from South Carolina extremists. Barnburner objections were voiced by the *Albany Atlas*, which maintained that a territory was "an inchoate state, without population adequate to its government," and therefore "without power to decide upon the institutions under which its future inhabitants would live." The matter was one to be decided temporarily by Congress, permanently by the territory when it entered the Union.[18] Calhounite response was singularly perceptive. "To understand and appreciate the hidden danger of these resolutions," the *Charleston Mercury* explained, "we must bear in mind that the proposed *new* territory is now *free territory*. When annexed it will remain *free*." In short, free labor and slave labor in the territories started on "a most unequal footing." Slavery had yet to be introduced, but the resolutions did not admit it "of *right*." They permitted its introduction, protection, or recognition only "if the people of such territories, with the consent of Congress," authorized it. However, the *Mercury* insisted, evading its obvious fears, such action was within the power neither of the territories nor of Congress. Neither could forbid the entrance of slavery; its existence depended upon the people of the territory when it entered the Union.[19]

More important, reaction to Dickinson's resolution had also revealed that the proposition could be accepted by the less extreme elements of both the North and the South. In the North the *Albany Argus* pointed the way: "In a territory now free, and with climate, soil and tide of immigration, uncongenial to slavery, it is scarcely possible that slavery would be formally declared one of its domestic institutions, while a territory." The same would be true after the territory achieved statehood. In the South a correspondent of the *Mobile Register* reported that Calhoun's "most prominent supporters in Richmond" had joined Democrats to endorse the resolution.[20]

Therefore, by the time Cass wrote the Nicholson letter, it had become evident that his proposition would secure a favorable response from a vast number of the party, who would find it an escape from the disruptive and divisive consequences of the Proviso. Response to the letter quickly confirmed earlier indications. In the North, Barnburners attacked the proposition as a "repudiation of Jeffersonian principles," but many journals gave it their unqualified support. The Henshaw faction in Massachusetts, editors of party journals throughout New England, New York's Hunkers, and newspapers such as the *Pennsylvanian,* the *Phila-*

[18] *Albany Atlas*, 23, 30 December 1847.
[19] *Charleston Mercury*, 31 December 1847.
[20] *Albany Argus*, 20 December 1847; *Mobile Register*, 21 January 1848.

delphia Ledger, and the *Pittsburgh Post* extended their approval. Their attitude was expressed by the *Columbian Register* of New Haven: "We admire the bold avowal of sentiments in this matter, by General Cass,—and we believe that they are identical with at least nine-tenths of the Democracy of New England. We want not slavery in our midst—but we will not . . . hazard the welfare of our glorious Union, by claiming the sole occupancy of a common domain."[21]

In Ohio, Michigan, Indiana, and Illinois hardly an editor ventured to condemn the Nicholson letter. Even Joseph Gray of the *Cleveland Plain Dealer* managed to squirm away from his former near-abolitionist stand. Cass, he argued, had demonstrated that the Constitution afforded a guarantee against the further extension of slavery. Under the Constitution the nation had annexed continuous slave territory *"without changing the relations of* MASTER *and* SERVANT." Accordingly, it must "leave the condition of *free territory* . . . unchanged." Moreover, Cass had shown that "Nature" had placed "an eternal barrier to the existence of slavery in the new territories, by its want of soil and climate adapting it to slave labor."[22] The latter argument was a potent one.

In the South the *Mercury* approached the letter with high perspicacity. "Of all the schemes which have been devised for the . . . degradation of the South, it is by far the most adroit and effectual." Since slavery did not exist in any part of Mexico, and since the inhabitants of that portion which might be annexed by the United States were known to oppose the institution, Cass's proposition would obviously prohibit the entrance of slavery. "He says to the South, you are right," the *Mercury* maintained; "such a restriction as is proposed by Mr. Wilmot is unconstitutional, and cannot be adopted. He says to the North, why raise any unnecessary disturbances! When we get new territory it will be free—slavery will have no existence there—it will be impossible to give it being. The end you have in view will certainly be accomplished, and you can afford to give up the triumph of the argument on principle if you are made certain of the triumph in your application of it to new territory."[23]

But the *Mercury* was in a minority. Most southern Democratic newspapers approved the Nicholson letter as a "statesmanlike production." Territorial control of the institution of slavery, the *Floridian* declared, "is all the South asks." Even some of Calhoun's close friends, such as

[21] *Buffalo Republic,* 6 January 1848; *Boston Times,* 4, 7 January 1848; *Albany Argus,* 4 January 1848; Detroit *Free Press,* 4 January 1848; *New Haven Columbian Register* quoted in *Springfield Illinois State Register,* 11 February 1848 (hereafter cited as *Illinois State Register*).

[22] *Cleveland Plain Dealer,* 20, 21 January 1848.

[23] *Charleston Mercury,* 6, 17 January 1848.

Daniel J. McCord, took issue with the *Mercury*. "Our own ground has been that Congress has no power over the question of slavery, to forbid or to establish," he maintained, "and if we will add new territory we must take the risk of getting such institutions as the people of such acquired territory must bring us."[24] Cass had written well; popular sovereignty proved to be a popular attempt to evade the Proviso issue.

Whig efforts to evade the consequences of the Proviso were not so successful. Like their Democratic opponents, they feared the effect of continued agitation of the issue, particularly in the South, where the *Richmond Whig* illustrated the danger. "We need scarcely say," it declared, "that Whig principles have no more decided and uncompromising advocates than we are; but whenever our political associates of the North shall force upon us the alternative of choosing between Whig principles on the one hand, and Southern rights and institutions on the other, we cannot for a moment hesitate . . . in the course we shall pursue." There was no Democrat in the nation, the journal warned, "to whom we would hesitate to give our cordial and zealous support in preference to any *Whig* who should come before us . . . tainted in the slightest degree with abolitionism."[25]

The threat could not be ignored; something had to be done to unite Whigs in a program acceptable both to the North and to the South. The readiest solution, not proposed by Democrats, was to avoid the issue completely; this policy was anticipated in the resolution that Senator John M. Berrien of Georgia and Congressman Alexander H. Stephens introduced into both branches of Congress in February 1847, at the height of the debate on the Proviso.

Under their resolution, Congress would declare that the war with Mexico was being prosecuted with no intention of dismembering that republic or of acquiring "any portion of her territory." Adoption of this policy, both Berrien and Stephens pointed out, would effectively silence the entire antislavery agitation by removing any need for the application of the Proviso. Southern Whigs at once rallied their strength behind the resolution and secured some aid from northern members, but a large minority of the northern wing refused to abandon either their desire for expansion or their open support of the Proviso, and the "no-territory" resolution failed of passage.[26]

Nevertheless, it became apparent that the principle embodied in the

[24] *Mobile Register*, 27 January 1848; *Floridian*, 15 January 1848; McCord to Hammond, 9 January 1848, Hammond Papers.
[25] *Richmond Whig* quoted in *Charleston Mercury*, 28 October 1847.
[26] *Congressional Globe*, 29th Cong., 2d sess., pp. 228–29, 330, 354, 357, 556.

resolution had struck a sympathetic chord among the rank and file. Southern journals willingly accepted the Berrien-Stephens formula. Their attitude was expressed by the *Vicksburg Whig* of 15 September 1847. "The South will not submit herself to be surrounded by a cordon of free States," it declared. "This position she will never yield, and any lands, acquired from Mexico cannot, with her consent, come into this Confederacy as free States. To be brief the alternative is NO MORE TERRITORY, or AN END TO THE UNION AS IT IS." The South would lose nothing by the "sacrifice," pointed out Waddy Thompson, a former minister to Mexico who had made a study of the territory. Agreeing with several others, he pointed out that the conditions of the soil and climate would make slavery an impossibility in the coveted region.[27] Why, then, endanger the Union for the sake of a mere abstraction?

Although northern Whigs were slower to accept the no-territory proposition, by late summer some had begun to find the remedy to their liking and had turned against the once favored Proviso as a measure without practical value. "It will not prevent any State from establishing slavery *after its admission into the Union,*" Thomas J. Ewing rationalized. On the other hand, the successful application of a "no-Mexican-territory" policy would *"per se"* prevent the extension of the peculiar institution by affording it no ground on which to expand.[28] Equally important, the *Auburn Advertiser* frankly admitted, enactment of the no-territory resolution would deprive northern Democrats of the Wilmot Proviso "hobby horse" and would reduce their "capital in trade" to a degree that would make their defeat at the polls inevitable.[29] *"No territory at all,"* many northern Whigs concluded, was "a ground of just compromise, national, conservative, right and proper in itself,"[30] a remedy that would still all agitation of the slavery issue and prevent disruption of the Union.

As might be expected, Democrats launched a bitter attack upon Whig motives. In both the North and the South, supporters of the Polk administration denounced the movement to abandon all territorial indemnity as a scheme "to prevent the Whig party from having one of its semi-annual quarrels." Southern newspapers assailed the principle as another example of a Whig "compromise with abolition." Adoption of the no-territory policy, the *Richmond Enquirer* declared, would mean that "northern fanatics" had succeeded "in preventing the further exten-

---

[27] *National Intelligencer,* 21 October 1847.
[28] Ibid., 7 September 1847.
[29] *Auburn* (N. Y.) *Advertiser* quoted in *Washington Union,* 10 September 1847.
[30] Thomas B. Stevenson to Crittenden, 7 September 1847, Crittenden Papers.

sion of slavery."[31] Northern Democratic journals were equally condemnatory. They insisted that the "cry of no more territory" came from the South. *"It is the slaveholder's cry,* and is raised for the express purpose of heading off the supporters of the Wilmot Proviso." Adoption of the resolution, the *Boston Post* maintained, would prove that northern Whigs cared "very little about the Wilmot proviso, the Mexican war, the extension of slavery, or anything else, except high prices, fat dividends, and the chances of office in the millennial days of the Whig presidency."[32]

Whigs made no attempt to answer the attacks; they had apparently marked their course, and its evident appeal to the Whig rank and file in both the North and the South made it unnecessary to acknowledge Democratic stings. By mid-autumn the great mass of the party was aligned strongly behind the proposal; Henry Clay's dramatic sanction of the no-territory resolution in his speech at Lexington on 13 November 1847 showed that the alignment was strong indeed.

The Lexington address produced a major change in the Whigs' internal politics: it added Clay's name to the list of those seeking the party leadership. The event was unexpected, because Clay had lived a very quiet life after his retirement in 1844, giving no public sign of political ambition. In the winter of 1845–1846 he had visited New Orleans, and in April 1846 he had appeared in St. Louis on business; although he was gladdened by the enthusiastic reception both cities gave him, he had offered no indication that another nomination would be welcome. His apparent desire to remain in private life was emphasized in December 1846 by his refusal to accept another senatorial term. During the second winter of Polk's administration Clay had appeared again in the Cresent City to make a speech on behalf of the famished Irish, but again he gave no hint or suggestion that he had resumed an active interest in politics.

Nevertheless, his ambitions were apparently reviving. James Harvey, who visited Clay early in the fall of 1846, reported that the old veteran had been greatly encouraged by Whig victories in the 1846 congressional campaign. "Mr. Clay is not without hope for the future," he informed Mangum, "and the recent result [in Pennsylvania] will encourage him

[31] *Georgian,* 8 October 1847; *Richmond Enquirer,* 1 October 1847.

[32] *New Hampshire Patriot,* 8 September 1847; *Boston Post,* 9 October 1847. The *Pennsylvanian,* 6 January 1848, had a different view, that the motive of the Whigs "will spring from their aristocratic principles. . . . They are not so friendly to free government. . . . They know that new countries are apt to be more strong in their support of democratic principles than old ones. Hence, they are opposed, as a general rule to the admission of all new states."

exceedingly. I was at Ashland when Maryland set forth the first note. I can, therefore, estimate what [effect] the others produced."[33]

Clay's reaction to the Taylor movement, which carried off many of his own supporters in the South, was also indicative of his reviving political interest. He was inclined to protest against the Old Hero's candidacy almost from its beginning. He expressed this feeling in a letter to Daniel Ullman, commenting on a Philadelphia meeting which had acclaimed Taylor as the next Whig nominee. The action, he insisted, was "premature, and if generally concurred in by the Whig party, must place it in a false and inconsistent position." The party had long been deliberately committed against the election of a military officer without civil experience to the presidency. "If General Taylor . . . should be elected," Clay warned, "I think we may bid adieu to the election ever again of any man to the office of Chief Magistrate who is not taken from the army. . . . Military chieftain will succeed military chieftain, until at last one will reach the Presidency, who, more unscrupulous than his predecessors, will put an end to our liberties and establish a throne of military despotism."

More important, Clay also disclosed his fear that the Buena Vista movement had seriously affected his own chances. "Up to that battle," he admitted to Ullman, "I had reason to believe that there existed a fixed determination with the mass of the Whig party . . . to bring me forward again." Though he clung to the belief that the "greater portion of that mass" was still favorable to his own candidacy, he was obviously disturbed.[34] He was hurt, moreover, by the evident desertion of many Kentuckians. "I must frankly own to you," he later confessed to Crittenden, "that the movements in K[entucky] have occasioned me some mortification. They wear the aspect of impatience under the ties which have so long bound me to the State and to the Whig party, and an eager desire to break lose from them."[35]

Nevertheless, Clay's belief that there was a large element in the Whig party that wanted him to run again was solidly based. During the first half of Polk's administration John McLean's agents, in particular, found evidence of a deeply rooted loyalty to Clay all over the North and reported that all overtures for support of some other candidate had met with cold refusal. As early as March 1846, Sam Galloway had informed McLean that he would never be able to command the support of those

[33] Harvey to Mangum, 24 October 1846, Mangum Papers.
[34] Clay to Daniel Ullman, 12 May 1847, in Colton, *Clay's Works*, 5: 541–42. See also Clay to Clayton, 6 April 1847, Clayton Papers.
[35] Clay to Crittenden, 26 September 1847, Crittenden Papers.

"who had sworn to live and die by Clay" until the Squire of Ashland had given his consent. Six months later Harvey reported that the "master-spirits" of the New York City wards, whom he described as "the most important personages in regulating the spirits of the masses," were still looking to Clay as the Whig nominee. After the Whigs won the fall congressional campaign, the undercurrent of Clay strength became so evident that some McLean men began to fear the Kentuckian even more than they feared Corwin.[36] Clay also had support in the South. Even in the midst of the Buena Vista fever the *Vicksburg Whig* proclaimed: "While we yield to none in our admiration of Gen. Taylor, we must nevertheless admit that, as regards the Presidency—OUR VOICE IS STILL FOR CLAY."[37]

Manifestations of Clay's following became more apparent after his trip to Cape May, New Jersey, in August 1847. Although the journey was made to repair the Kentuckian's health and spirits, shattered by the death of a son at Buena Vista, the acclamation he received en route, along with the coincidental appearance of the "elite of eastern Federalism" at the watering places he visited, made it clear to Democrats that "Clay's seaward journey" looked "equally to the restoration of his political as well as his physical health."[38]

Whether or not such was the case, the journey at last brought into the open the latent Clay sentiment among Whigs in the northern states. All through New York, Pennsylvania, Ohio, and Illinois, visible evidence of his hold upon the party reappeared. In New York City the Whig Young Men's General Committee foregathered in their annual meeting "to inscribe and blazon on our shields the much loved and long-honored name of Henry Clay." In Pennsylvania, Ohio, and Illinois, county meetings and party journals hailed him with old-time ardor. It quickly became evident, as the *Nashville Union* declared, that Clay's friends were bent on running him for the presidency a fourth time.[39]

This sudden resurgence of Clay support had a serious effect on the Taylor movement in the North. Reports that "Taylor's star" was de-

---

[36] Samuel Galloway to McLean, 4 March 1846, H. H. Sawyer to McLean, 11 February 1847, McLean Papers; Harvey to Mangum, 25 August 1846, Mangum Papers.

[37] *Vicksburg Whig*, 21 April 1847. In the summer of 1847 several southern Whig papers hoisted Clay-Taylor flags.

[38] *Pennsylvanian*, 14 August 1847.

[39] *Niles' Register* 73 (25 September 1847): 62; Poage, *Clay*, p. 162; *New York Tribune*, 25 September 1847; Baltimore *Sun*, 13 August 1847; *Nashville Union*, 28 August 1847. In Ohio the Clay movement seemed so strong that McLean considered joining it (Mower to McLean, 25 October 1847, McLean Papers).

scending came from all quarters. In mid-September James Mower, who had previously found Old Zack's countenance painted all over New York City, informed McLean that during the past week he had not heard "one haloo" for Taylor. Clay's friends, he claimed, had finally succeeded in "dampening the military fever." From Pennsylvania, Harvey reported that the "county editors" had lost their enthusiasm for the Old Hero and were raising the name of Clay to the mastheads of their papers. Similar information came from Iowa and Wisconsin. The tide against Taylor appeared so strong that prominent Clay supporters boldly suggested that the Old Hero come into the Kentuckian's camp.[40] Once more the Great Embodiment seemed to ride at the head of the Whig army. All that remained was to announce his plans for battle.

The announcement was made on 13 November 1847 from the steps of the Lexington courthouse to a large audience that gathered there beneath dismal and threatening skies. Clay's address was an attempt to bring together all the various political threads which Whigs had spun during the Polk administration and to weave them into a pattern designed to unite the party on a common platform. Opposition to the war and the compromise of the slavery issue were the main threads of the cloth.

"War, pestilence and famine, by the common consent of mankind," he declared, were the "three greatest calamities" that could befall the human race, and war, "as the most direful," rightly stood foremost. War unhinged society, disturbed its peaceful and regular industry, and scattered "poisonous seeds of disease and mortality," which continued "to germinate and diffuse their baneful influence" long after conflict had ended. The Mexican War, created by the annexation of Texas and by Polk's order to General Taylor to occupy the disputed territory west of the Nueces River, could have been prevented by "prudence, moderation and wise statesmanship"—by allowing Taylor to remain at Corpus Christi and by opening negotiations with Mexico "in a true spirit of amity and conciliation." The statement that "war existed by the act of Mexico" he branded as a lie. "No earthly consideration," he maintained, "would ever have tempted or provoked me to vote for a bill with a palpable falsehood stamped upon its face." The war had to be brought to an end, and it had to be ended without further annexation, for the addition of one square rod of territory would bring unaccountable evils in its wake.

---

[40] Mower to McLean, 20 September 1847, Harvey to McLean, 18 October 1847, McLean Papers; *New York Express* quoted in *Nashville Union,* 4 November 1847; *Pennsylvanian,* 28 September 1847; *Iowa Capitol Reporter,* 15 September 1847; Taylor to Wood, 27 September, 19 October 1847, in *Taylor Letters,* pp. 135–36, 142–43; Taylor to Crittenden, 1 November 1847, Crittenden Papers.

Annexation would create the necessity for a large standing army to keep the Mexicans in subjection—a method of government that might ultimately be extended over the whole Union; it would bring into the nation a people of different stock and religion, with alien institutions; it would produce in Congress an insurgent party, comparable to the Irish in Parliament, whose object would be to hinder the wheels of legislation; most calamitous of all, it would bring about collision between the North and the South over the peculiar institution of slavery.

Clay had always regarded slavery "as a great evil, . . . an irredeemable wrong for its unfortunate victims." He declared:

> I would rejoice if not a single slave breathed the air . . . of our country. But here they are, to be dealt with as well as we can. . . . Every state has the supreme, uncontrolled and exclusive power to decide for itself whether slavery shall cease or continue within its limits, without any exterior intervention from any quarter. In states where the slaves outnumber the whites . . . the blacks could not be emancipated and invested with all the rights of freemen, without becoming the governing race in the state. Collisions and conflicts between the two races would be inevitable, and after shocking scenes of rapine and carnage, the extinction of the blacks would take place.

He could not, therefore, favor emancipation.

Nor did he believe, because he conceded the injustice of slavery, that he admitted "the necessity of an instantaneous reparation of that injustice." Unfortunately, it was not always safe, practicable, or possible to remedy or repair the inflictions of previous injustice. "Moderation, prudence and discretion among ourselves," he declared, "and the blessings of providence may be all necessary to accomplish our ultimate deliverance from it." The end of slavery could not be accomplished by forcing upon the nation a conflict over its extension, which annexation of Mexican territory was sure to produce.

What, then, was the program to be followed? Clay announced in the resolutions he presented at the end of his oration

> that it is the duty of congress to declare by some authentic act, for what purpose and object the existing war ought to be further prosecuted, that it is the duty of the President, in his official conduct to conform to such a declaration of congress. . . . That . . . we have no desire for the dismemberment of the republic of Mexico, but only the just and proper fixation of the limits of Texas. . . .
>
> That we do positively and emphatically disclaim and disavow any

wish or desire on our part to acquire any foreign territory whatever, for the purpose of propagating, or of introducing slavery from the United States into such territory.[41]

Clay's address met with varied reactions in the northern states. The strongest approval came from the mid-Atlantic area. In New York City two huge meetings at the Broadway Tabernacle and at Castle Garden— the latter described as "the largest the nation had ever seen under one roof"—demonstrated New Yorkers' devotion to the veteran leader by adopting his resolutions verbatim and proclaiming him as their choice for the presidency. Similar meetings occurred in Poughkeepsie and in Trenton, where the *State Gazette* hailed Clay "as the standard bearer of the great Whig army in the coming battle." In Philadelphia a gigantic throng gathered at Independence Square and under the lead of Robert T. Conrad and Joseph R. Chandler of the *North American* pronounced Clay's speech "one of the rarest efforts of genius and patriotism" and adopted his principles as the party platform. The *Albany Evening Journal* maintained that his oration settled the question of the presidency and gave official sanction to the no-territory resolution.[42]

Otherwise, however, the reaction was disappointing. Taylor men immediately, almost instinctively, proclaimed their opposition to the no-territory policy. The New York *Courier* insisted upon the acquisition of San Francisco Bay and the territory north of the Missouri Compromise line, at the least. The *Philadelphia Bulletin* echoed the demand and warned, "If Mr. Clay really advocates the abandonment of all our conquests, and that without any indemnification for the expenses of the war he will find few, but very few to support him. Such a proposition would rend the Whig party into two bitterly hostile factions."[43] When James Mower saw the outburst of sentiment for annexation within his own party, he informed McLean that the people would "not sustain *any* man" entertaining the opinions enumerated in the Lexington address. Clay, he believed, had "intended by them, just to meet public sentiment," but he had "most decidedly" missed it. "The Democratic side of the Mexican war question," he declared, "is the popular side, hence it will be the *right side,* and the one also, that will elect the next Presit."[44]

[41] *Niles' Register* 73 (27 November 1847) : 197–200.
[42] Colton, *Clay's Works,* 3: 73; *New York Tribune,* 18, 25 December 1847; *Trenton State Gazette* quoted in *Washington Union,* 26 November 1847; *North American,* 7 December 1847; Poage, *Clay,* pp. 166–67.
[43] New York *Courier,* 16, 20 November 1847; *Philadelphia Bulletin* quoted in *Nashville Union,* 27 November 1847.
[44] Mower to McLean, 22 November 1847, McLean Papers.

Websterians likewise found fault. The *Boston Courier* maintained that Clay's resolutions "would not bear close scrutiny," but would require "the exercise of a good degree of Mr. Clay's peculiar attribute, namely, the faculty of manufacturing *compromises,* to reconcile some of their discrepancies." In Ohio, protests came from antislavery men who were dissatisfied with Clay's failure to advocate strong and positive action against the extension of slavery. One of McLean's managers reported that the address had not strengthened Clay's chances. "Hardly an individual can be found who wishes him to be a candidate," he declared in December. The pro-Clay sentiment that had revealed itself in early autumn had disappeared from the Buckeye State.[45]

In the South, however, many Whig journals gave Clay's oration their "utter, unqualified, and emphatic approval." The *Vicksburg Whig* even commended the resolution dealing with slavery. "The acquisition of foreign territory," it declared, "either for the purpose of making it slave or free, in order to acquire a balance of power, will assuredly destroy the Union." The North, by "advocating the acquisition of *Free* territory," violated the Constitution, just as the South did by avowing that the object of the war was the "conquest of *Slave* territory." Clay, the *Whig* believed, was seeking to avoid difficulties. By informing the North that the South did not "intend to violate her part of the Federal compromise . . . by conquering territory in order to extend slavery," Clay placed the North under obligation to make a similar pledge. In Georgia the state Senate extended its sanction by adopting resolutions which occupied "pretty much the position of Mr. Clay in his Lexington Speech."[46]

Among southern Taylor supporters, the principles of the address met with strong objections. Moderate newspapers such as the *Richmond Times* announced that they were "not prepared to assent without qualification to the proposition that no annexation whatever" was to be considered, nor did they believe that the Whig party held such a position. "The acquisition of the port of San Francisco on the Pacific, and the intermediate country," the *Times* maintained, "seems to be an almost necessary sequence of the war." The more outspoken *Nashville Whig* went even further: "We go for keeping Upper California and New Mexico at all hazards. We do not think the people of the United States will ever consent, nor do we believe they *ought* to consent, to restore the provinces

[45] *Boston Courier* quoted in *Cleveland Plain Dealer,* 1 December 1847; Miner to McLean, 6 December 1847, McLean Papers; Holt, "Party Politics in Ohio," 38:270.
[46] *New Orleans Commercial Bulletin,* 23 November 1847; *Vicksburg Whig,* 26 November 1847; L. G. Glenn to Howell Cobb, 1 December 1847, in Cole, *Whigs in the South,* p. 121.

of Mexico. We want something more than a 'just and proper fixation of the limits of Texas.' "[47]

Objections were also raised to Clay's condemnation of slavery and to the antiextension bias of his principles. Many claimed, as Robert Toombs later charged, that Clay had "sold himself body and soul to the Northern Anti-Slavery Whigs."[48] On this point, however, Taylor Whigs apparently allowed their Democratic opponents to lead the attack. At any rate, they made no attempt to answer journals such as the *Louisville Democrat,* which accused Clay of trying "to catch abolitionists and Wilmot Proviso men," or the *Savannah Georgian,* which charged him with pandering to the New York Barnburners, whom he allegedly hoped to unite with Whigs into a great northern party that would send him to the White House. Nor did Whigs reply to the *Mississippian,* which arraigned their former chieftain for spreading a net to catch the "whole catalogue of factions and fragments of factions" into which the Whig party was divided.[49] Their silence made it apparent that Taylor men were quite willing to see the "high priest of Whiggery" defamed. Clay's effort to unite his party had missed the mark.

[47] *Richmond Times* quoted in *Richmond Enquirer,* 30 September 1847; *Nashville Whig* quoted in *Nashville Union,* 20 November 1847. Taylor's position on the subject was changeable. As the *Nashville Union* pointed out in July 1847, Taylor had suggested in his letter to General Gaines "that a just indemnity would include no less than the provinces of Tampico, Victoria, Monter[r]ey, Saltillo, Monclava, Chihuahua, Sante Fe, and the two Californias." Taylor later indicated that he was opposed to the acquisition of any territory south of the Missouri Compromise line which might endanger the permanence of the Union by fomenting sectional discord (Taylor to Crittenden, 3 January, 13 February 1848, Crittenden Papers).

[48] Toombs to James Thomas, 16 April 1848, in Phillips, *Toombs, Stephens, and Cobb Correspondence,* pp. 103–4.

[49] *Louisville Democrat,* 15 November 1847; *Georgian,* 22 November 1847; *Mississippian,* 3 December 1847. Clay's supporters may have hoped to win over the Barnburners. After the Lexington address Greeley informed Clay, "Weed says the leading Barnburners of our State are not satisfied with your slavery resolution . . . if you had used 'No more Slave Territory at any rate' they would have supported you" (Greeley to Clay, 30 November 1847, Clay Papers). See also *Albany Atlas,* 16 November 1847.

Chapter Eight

The Contest for Delegates: Democrats

In the early months of 1848 the question of which philosophies would control the Democratic and Whig parties in the approaching national conventions finally became inextricably mixed with the question of which contenders would control the majority of voting delegates. Thus it often becomes difficult to decide whether measures or men were more important and whether the two factors ever can be separated.

The double uncertainty over issues and men was most acute among Democrats. They had been presented with four "solutions" to the issue of slavery in the territories: the Wilmot Proviso, the Buchanan suggestion for extension of the Missouri Compromise line, the Dallas-Cass proposal to leave the issue to the territories, and the Alabama Platform. Each solution had strong supporters and strong opponents. Some solutions were openly proclaimed by leading presidential hopefuls; some had no openly professed champions. In addition, local divisions and personal rivalries and ambitions often combined to make the struggle for delegates exceedingly complex.

The situation in Pennsylvania was one of the most significant. Two of the state's Democratic leaders, Buchanan and Dallas, had early been recognized as contenders for the presidential nomination; each announced his own solution of the slavery issue. But Buchanan and Dallas did not control all Pennsylvania Democrats; a considerable and vociferous number of them, led by Senator Cameron, joined the Taylor movement in early 1847. Moreover, there were democrats, particularly in the counties bordering on New York, who supported the Proviso and preferred Silas Wright.

During 1847 neither Buchanan nor Dallas supporters seemed to make any effort to win over the Taylor wing of the party. While Buchanan's followers, in particular, fretted over the situation, they apparently hoped that the party's rank and file would ultimately recognize the obvious opportunism of the Taylor movement's leaders and that the Taylor fever would cool off.[1] But the Provisoists were another matter. Shortly after its second introduction, it became fairly clear that the Proviso had earned widespread support neither among Democratic nor among Whig politicians in Pennsylvania; both were much more interested in the tariff issue. A few journals in both parties attacked the Proviso. Nevertheless, it was also clear that the Provisoists, since they were relatively concentrated geographically, could conceivably hold the balance of power in a state convention. Accordingly, they were handled gently throughout the summer of 1847.

But the situation changed after reaction to Buchanan's Berks County letter and Dallas's Pittsburgh speech became known. Hostility to the Proviso then became common. The Philadelphia *Spirit of the Times,* a Dallas supporter, damned the Provisoists' agitation of the slavery extension issue as a course calculated to promote a slave insurrection in the South for the benefit of a few "hollow political demagogues" who hoped through continuous excitement to reap some selfish reward. The *Lancaster Intelligencer,* a Buchanan journal, went so far as to suggest that the Pennsylvania legislature repudiate its earlier endorsement of the Proviso.[2] Buchanan agents, perhaps spurred by a knowledge of Wilmot's opposition to their favorite and by a not wholly unfounded fear that Provisoists preferred the vice president to the secretary of state, went to work assiduously to disorganize the Democratic machinery in the northern counties.[3]

Journals of both factions also turned their guns directly upon Wilmot, who, according to the *Montrose Democrat,* became the target of "poignant diatribes, false representations, and disgusting personal abuse." There were charges that the campaign of vilification was assisted by the financial power of the Federal administration, which gave its printing contracts in Wilmot's district to the anti-Provisoist *Tioga Eagle,* a journal characterized by the *Wilkes Barre Farmer* as an "obscure little

[1] Hutter to Buchanan, 3 September 1847, J. Clancy Jones to Buchanan, 12 September 1847, Buchanan Papers.

[2] Philadelphia *Spirit of the Times and Daily Keystone,* 18 January 1848 (hereafter cited as Philadelphia *Times*) ; *Lancaster Intelligencer* quoted in *North American,* 5 January 1848.

[3] *Congressional Globe,* 30th Cong., 1st sess., pp. 304-6; John Reynolds to Buchanan, 20 November 1847, Benjamin Hill to Buchanan, 30 November 1847, 8 January 1848, Asa Dimock to Buchanan, 28 December 1847, C. L. Ward to Buchanan, 28 February 1848, Buchanan Papers.

sheet" which reached as many people as would "an advertisement copied in Chinese and stuck up on a pine tree." Similar tactics were evident elsewhere in the state; as the *Harrisburg Argus* later charged, those journals which were always ready to surrender their principles for lucre "at once obeyed the nod of their master, and without ceremony delivered Mr. Wilmot to the Whigs."[4]

Meanwhile, the contest between Buchanan and Dallas for the election of delegates to the Democratic State Convention continued unabated. Dallas scored the first major victory early in January 1848, when the Philadelphia convention, in which customhouse workers played a large role, gave him the entire delegation by a respectable margin.[5] Thereafter, Buchanan gradually forged into the lead. Rumored to have the blessing of the president—which Polk repeatedly denied in his diary—supported by the *Washington Union* and by a heavy majority of Pennsylvania's party editors, endorsed by the Democratic legislative caucus, his candidacy pushed by a host of workers, Buchanan gathered a large delegation from the rural areas and towns of central Pennsylvania.[6] A month before the convention his supporters claimed 90 of 130 state delegates.

But there was no cheering among his supporters. Dallas had made a much stronger showing in the more populous, underrepresented eastern counties. His editorial supporters, moreover, boasted that his following outside the commonwealth—primarily because of his tie-breaking vote in favor of the Tariff of 1846—was greater than that of his rival; equally significant was their claim that Dallas was the only man who could unite the warring factions in New York. These arguments were expected to have an effect on the contingent of unpledged delegates whom Buchan-

[4] All three newspapers are quoted in Going, *Wilmot*, pp. 237–38, 242–43, 304–5.

[5] Dallas carried ten wards with 47 votes and Buchanan carried seven wards with 38 votes in the city convention. The rise and fall of Buchanan's campaign in Philadelphia is detailed in J. C. Van Dyke to Buchanan, 29 November, 2, 26 December 1847, 5 January 1848, William A. Stokes to Buchanan, 10 December 1847, Sandy Harris to Buchanan, 3 December 1847, J. B. Sutherland to Buchanan, 10 December 1847, Nile A. Stoker to Buchanan, 13 December 1847, 3 January 1848, Henry Welch to Buchanan, 4 January 1848, Buchanan Papers. One apparently minor factor in the Philadelphia campaign was an effort "to hold up Mr. Buchanan as . . . hostile to the Catholic religion" (James Rider to Jno. Nugent, 5 December 1847, ibid.). However, one correspondent reported, "With very few exceptions we shall have the entire Irish population with us" (Van Dyke to Buchanan, 29 November 1847, ibid.).

[6] Baltimore *Sun,* 22 October 1847; *New York Tribune,* 8 January 1848; Quaife, *Polk's Diary,* 3: 217, 350; *Niles' Register* 73 (19 February 1848): 393. The *Pennsylvanian,* in almost every issue between 19 November 1847 and 28 February 1848, added to its list of newspapers and counties which were supporting Buchanan; the list included twenty-nine newspapers and thirty-one county delegations.

an's followers claimed.[7] The campaign for delegates also revealed that Cass had an unsuspectedly strong following in western Pennsylvania and that the Provisoists in the northern counties had not been submerged.[8]

Even more important was the attitude of those delegates who were attached to the Shunk administration. In 1846 and 1847 out-of-state observers usually concluded that Governor Francis Shunk and his followers—who formed a fifth or even a sixth force in the complex Democratic politics of the state—were opposed to Buchanan's candidacy, if not favorable to Dallas's. The evidence indicates that Shunk himself preserved a strict neutrality toward candidates; with some exceptions, his administrative appointees seem to have followed the same rule. This very neutrality became the despair of Buchanan's supporters, who assumed that it meant either antagonism toward their favorite or deceit and untrustworthiness on the part of Shunk.[9] Since there were nearly a score of Shunk men named as delegates, most of whom were counted in the Buchanan column,[10] it was not strange that the Buchanan managers who counted votes were not sanguine about the results.

Nevertheless, when the Democratic State Convention met at Harrisburg early in March 1848, Buchanan was endorsed as the commonwealth's favorite son by 84 votes to 49 for his opponents.[11] Although the vote effectively ended the Dallas movement, Pennsylvania politics were too devious to make this endorsement a clear Buchanan triumph. In the contest for delegates to the national convention (made even more confusing than usual by a proposal to name only Cameron supporters) Buchanan secured only a bare majority; the Dallas-Cass forces secured a minority favorable to Cass—who was also hailed by resolution as a "great and glorious man." These minority delegates were only tenuously pledged to Buchanan. Furthermore, the "Buchaneers' " effort to endorse the Missouri Compromise line as a means of settling the problem of

[7] Philadelphia *Times*, 20, 22 November, 3, 17, 18 December 1847, 12, 31 January, 4 February 1848.

[8] John Coyle to Buchanan, 30 November 1847, Van Dyke to Buchanan, 12 December 1847, Asa Dimock to Buchanan, 28 December 1847, Ward to Buchanan, 20 February 1848, Buchanan Papers; Philadelphia *Times,* 16 February 1848.

[9] Robert Tyler to Buchanan, 18 November 1847, in Philip G. Auchampaugh, *Robert Tyler, Southern Rights Champion: 1847–1866* (Duluth, Minn., 1934), p. 10 (hereafter cited as *Robert Tyler*) ; D. T. Jenks to Buchanan, 26 September 1847, Samuel S. Bigler to Buchanan, 10 December 1847, Alfred Gilmore to Buchanan, 23 December 1847, Welch to Buchanan, 5 January 1848, J. Clancy Jones to Buchanan, 23 January 1848, Ward to Buchanan, 20 February 1848, Buchanan Papers.

[10] Reporters counted twenty "Shunk men" at the convention; of these, twelve voted for Buchanan.

[11] The vote was Buchanan 84, Dallas 34, Cass 10, Van Buren 5.

slavery in the territories was drowned in a chorus of nays; instead, the convention adopted a plank complimenting Dallas and Cass on their suggested solutions to the issue. The convention's results as a whole revealed that Buchanan's position rested on unstable foundations.[12] Endorsement by New Jersey Democrats improved his position only slightly.

In the six northern states west of Pennsylvania an entirely different situation developed. During 1847 it became obvious, as various polls revealed, that every prominently mentioned Democratic contender, and some who were not contenders, had supporters; it also became obvious that in all these states except Ohio Cass's strength was greater than that of all his opponents combined. After the publication of the Nicholson letter, it became clear that Cass's proposal for solving the problem of slavery in the territories enjoyed widespread approval throughout the area.[13] However, it was not complete approval; every state contained Provisoists who were determined to advance their solution of the territorial problem. Accordingly, the issue in each of these states was between Cass and the Nicholson letter on one side, and the Provisoists, handicapped by the lack of a candidate after the death of Silas Wright, on the other.

In four states the Cass forces carried the day almost without a struggle. Democrats in the Michigan legislature endorsed Cass by a vote of 44 to 8, and the state convention named a Cass delegation.[14] The Indiana State Convention selected an unpledged delegation headed by Cass's friend Senator Jesse D. Bright. The Wisconsin and Iowa delegations, also unpledged, contained only men who had announced for Cass. In all four states the conventions gave some kind of approval to the Nicholson letter; in none was a Wilmot Proviso resolution allowed to reach the floor. The Indiana convention, in fact, condemned any effort by Congress to control the local institutions or internal affairs of a territory, as an improper assumption of power, calculated to create

[12] The proceedings of the convention are in *Pennsylvanian*, 6 March 1848. See also Hutter to Buchanan, 5 March 1848, W. B. Sturgis to Buchanan, 11 March 1848, Albert Ramsey to Buchanan, 13 March 1848, Buchanan Papers.

[13] The popularity of the Cass doctrine was reflected by Stephen A. Douglas: "The republic had always allowed the people of a Territory to decide what kind of school system, banking system, tax system and franchise system they should have. Then why not let them decide upon their own labor system?" (Allan Nevins, *Ordeal of the Union* [New York, 1947], 2:31).

[14] Detroit *Free Press*, 31 January 1848. There were some Michiganders, including the eight delegates who refused to endorse Cass, who did not like the Nicholson letter doctrine. One reported: "Were the Genl. not a resident here, an attempt would be made to organize a head against him" (George R. Griswold to Felch, 16 January 1848, Felch Papers).

sectional divisions and thereby to weaken the bonds of the Union.[15]

In Ohio the result was somewhat different. After the death of Silas Wright those Democrats who had supported Wright in preference to Cass drifted steadily into the latter's camp. As Samuel Medary informed Van Buren in December 1847, "Everything seems to be at loose ends. At many of our meetings some one gets up and proposes a resolution [favoring] Genl Cass and it passes without a word."[16] Under the circumstances it was evident, despite the opposition of a small group of diehards such as Benjamin Tappan, Jacob Brinckerhoff, and James Taylor of the *Cincinnati Signal,* that Cass would receive the endorsement of the state party. On the slavery issue, however, there was less passivity. Among Provisoists, who constituted a powerful minority within the party, there was a feeling that the ardent Cass men would attempt "to put down the spirit of freedom" at the convention; some threatened "another Syracuse" and "another Herkimer" if such a step were successful.[17] The outcome was something of a compromise. A rather raucous convention held in Columbus in January 1848 endorsed Cass, but it also recognized the principles contained in the Proviso[18]—a fragile, but workable, temporary solution.

In Illinois the contest was less one-sided. Antislavery Democrats had made great strides during 1847 and the early months of 1848, especially in the region near Lake Michigan. Their growing strength was manifested by the action they took at a Chicago meeting which the chairman adjourned when an attempt was made to offer antislavery resolutions. Led by Thomas Hoyne and Isaac N. Arnold, the Provisoists organized a new meeting on the spot, and after a strenuous oratorical effort they carried a resolution which enunciated their "uncompromising determination to prevent the extension of slavery into territory" which might be acquired.[19]

Despite this evidence of increasing strength, antislavery Democrats easily recognized that they were a minority in Illinois. In January 1848 they began an agitation for the election by districts of delegates to the national convention, a method calculated to give them control of the

---

[15] *Indiana State Sentinel,* 11, 13, 27 January 1848; *Iowa Capitol Reporter,* 23 February 1848; Theodore C. Smith, "Free Soil Party in Wisconsin," *Proceedings of the State Historical Society of Wisconsin, 1894* (Madison, 1895), p. 110.

[16] Medary to Van Buren, 27 December 1847, Van Buren Papers.

[17] Price, "1848 Election in Ohio," pp. 206–7; George C. Gorham, *Life and Public Services of Edwin M. Stanton* (Boston, 1899), 1: 73.

[18] Holt, "Party Politics in Ohio," 38: 176; Stanton to Chase, 16 February 1848, Chase Papers.

[19] *National Era,* 6 April 1848.

delegates from the northern counties. The proslavery state machine, controlled by "Egyptian" politicians, met the campaign with stubborn opposition. A bitter editorial battle between the *Chicago Democrat* and the *Illinois State Register* followed. So violent were the passions aroused that Charles H. Lanphier, editor of the *Register,* suggested that an effort be made "to exclude firebrands from the . . . bosom of [the] Democracy of the State," a proposal that won the approval of several Illinois congressmen who thought it would "purge away the rank inflamation and religious fanaticism" within the party.[20]

A tumultuous state convention met in Springfield in April 1848. The state machine carried everything before it. The district plan of electing delegates was shelved, and the Proviso movement was condemned "as an intemperate . . . and unnecessary agitation" of the slavery issue. Although the state did not specifically instruct its delegation to the national convention to vote for Cass, an informal poll revealed that Cass was favored with 60 votes to 51 votes for eight other candidates; his closest competitor was Levi Woodbury, who secured 25 votes, most of them from the northern counties. Egypt and Cass had won the day, but the contest left a large, unsatisfied antiextension element in the Chicago area.[21]

The contest for delegates among southern Democrats, whose political characteristics were as complex as could be found, also combined issues and men. There were only a few points upon which southern Democrats were relatively agreed. They opposed the Proviso and the nomination of any Provisoist, and they preferred that the presidential nomination go to a northern man.[22] Otherwise, there were deep divisions.

The situation was probably most simple in seven states of the southwest. During the winter of 1847–1848 most of the political activity was undertaken by the supporters of Buchanan and Cass. It soon became evident that Cass and his Nicholson letter doctrine had the same appeal in the Southwest that they had in the Northwest.

In Kentucky, where the prevailing attitude on the subject of slavery was so moderate that the *Louisville Democrat* appealed to the North to

---

[20] *Illinois State Register,* 14, 28 January, 3, 10 March 1848; Cole, *Era of the Civil War,* pp. 54–55.

[21] The complete result of the informal poll was Cass, 60; Woodbury, 25; Buchanan, 8; Van Buren, 7; Polk, 4; Butler, 3; Douglas, 2; Dallas, 1; Worth, 1 (Samuel Treat to A. H. H. Clapp, 25 April 1848, Woodbury Papers; *New York Tribune,* 13 May 1848). The proceedings of the convention are in *Illinois State Register,* 28 April 1848.

[22] *Georgian,* 9 December 1847; *Floridian,* 5 February 1848; *Mobile Register,* 19 February 1848; *Mississippian,* 5 May 1848.

forget the issue because the "newly acquired territories will always be free," the convention named an unpledged delegation regarded as favorable to Cass. Both the former vice president, Richard M. Johnson, and the state's vice-presidential candidate, William O. Butler, were in his camp.[23] The Tennessee convention, which also chose an unpledged delegation, failed to endorse Cass, though his supporters had hoped to secure the state; however, as the *Nashville Union* pointed out, anyone "who witnessed its proceedings, or who mingled with the delegates," knew that Cass was the favorite.[24] Party conventions also named unpledged delegations in Missouri and Arkansas, where expansionist attitudes were stronger than fears for the future of slavery, and in Mississippi, also expansionist but concerned with the rights of slaveholders in the territories. In all three states official Democratic journals indicated a strong preference for Cass, "the great . . . statesman . . . of the growing west."[25]

But at this point the Michigander's domination of the Southwest stopped. Although Cass was well liked in Texas, that state evidently preferred a favorite son, Sam Houston. Louisiana, normally Whig and strongly influenced by the commercial element in New Orleans, was most widely impressed by Buchanan.[26]

Along the upper southern seaboard the situation was also fairly clear. During 1847 and in the winter of 1847–1848, Buchanan, Dallas, and Cass supporters were all active in the area.[27] Here Buchanan was personally most popular, and here his Missouri Compromise line solution to the slave issue received the greatest support. After his victory over Dallas in Pennsylvania, it was generally agreed that he would receive the votes of the unpledged delegations from Delaware, from Maryland,

[23] *Louisville Democrat*, 22 March 1848; Johnson to Cass, 21 April 1848, Cass Papers (Clements). Both Buchanan and Dallas had minor support in Kentucky (*Pennsylvanian*, 19 November 1847, 3 January 1848; Philadelphia *Times*, 3 December 1847). Buchanan apparently had some supporters in the convention as well (Robert A. McAfee to Buchanan, 15 March 1848, Buchanan Papers).

[24] *Nashville Union*, 18 March 1848. Before the convention it was reported that a "decided majority of the Democratic members of the Tennessee legislature" favored a Cass-Butler ticket (*Niles' Register* 73 [19 February 1848]: 393). Buchanan's chief supporters were in the Memphis area (Andrew Butler to Buchanan, 10 January 1848, Buchanan Papers).

[25] *Mississippian*, 8 January, 24 March 1848. There was some Dallas strength in Mississippi (*Buffalo Republic*, 24 January 1848).

[26] Louis M. Sears, *John Slidell* (Durham, N. C., 1925), p. 79. Buchanan's dominant position, however, was strongly contested by Cass, and there were some who supported Dallas (William McGiven to Buchanan, 26 January 1848, Buchanan Papers; Philadelphia *Times*, 30 December 1847).

[27] Dallas's strength apparently developed only in Virginia (Philadelphia *Times*, 27 November 1847).

where the Democratic convention rejected a resolution in favor of Cass, and from North Carolina, where Cass's strength lay in the less populous western counties.[28] Only Virginia appeared undecided. Buchanan managers claimed the support of the state rank and file, but Cass had support among the friends of the influential John Y. Mason, who hoped for a vice-presidential nomination on a Cass ticket.[29]

In the remaining four states of the South (South Carolina, Georgia, Alabama, and Florida), the political circumstances were obscure. Here the supporters of the Alabama Platform were most strongly concentrated; they favored neither the Buchanan nor the Cass solution of the territorial problem.[30] In this area a fourth major candidate, Levi Woodbury of New Hampshire, became an important factor in the Democratic campaign for delegates.

Woodbury's candidacy had developed slowly in New England during 1847. There were recurring reports that his own state would give him an endorsement and that Hannibal Hamlin of Maine and Robert Rantoul, a member of the Henshaw machine in Massachusetts, were working on his behalf. Various Democratic journals, notably the *Boston Times,* reminded the electorate of his sterling qualities; some suggested a Woodbury-Walker ticket. His only competitors in the area were Lewis Cass and Silas Wright. But Cass's followers in New England were few, and when Silas Wright died, Woodbury had New England Democrats almost to himself.[31] It was a good base from which to start a campaign, but it needed considerable expansion both in the North and in the South, where his availability as a "northern man with southern principles" was openly suggested in the summer of 1847.[32]

But where was such expansion to occur? His advisors suggested that support could come from Provisoists who were seeking a northern candidate; from elements in the North that for one reason or another were not favorable or were not committed to Cass, whose strength Woodbury's advisors consistently underestimated; and from those ele-

[28] Baltimore *Sun,* 12 January 1848; *Albany Atlas,* 22 April 1848; *Pennsylvanian,* 22 May 1848; *North Carolina Standard,* 31 May 1848; William W. Holden to Sandy Harris, 13 November 1847, Alex Keech to Buchanan, 20 March 1848, Buchanan Papers.

[29] *Pennsylvanian,* 19 November, 9 December 1847; Charles Neale to Buchanan, 11 February 1848, Buchanan Papers.

[30] H. L. Benning to Cobb, 23 February 1848, in Phillips, *Toombs, Stephens, and Cobb Correspondence,* p. 103.

[31] Charles E. Hamlin, *Life and Times of Hannibal Hamlin* (Cambridge, Mass., 1899), pp. 179–81; Niles to Welles, 4 August 1847, Welles Papers; Baltimore *Sun,* 6 September 1847; Barnes to Woodbury, 19 February 1848, Woodbury Papers.

[32] *Savannah Republican,* 26 June 1847; *Charleston Mercury,* 26 June 1847.

ments in the South that favored neither Buchanan nor Cass nor their solutions to the territorial issue—in short, from among the supporters of the position taken in the Alabama Platform.[33]

To put together such a coalition required the talents of political magicians; nevertheless, it was attempted. While Woodbury alone among the major presidential hopefuls kept publicly silent on the issue of slavery in the territories, his agents operated. In the free states, particularly in the Yankee belt, they emphasized his Northern position —by implication, antislavery. Among politicians in the slave states they apparently claimed that Woodbury honestly believed that neither Congress nor the territories had a right to legislate on the subject of slavery in the territories—a clear indication of his extreme southern position.[34]

The strategy was successful to an extent. New England Democrats loyally announced their support. While his own state's party did not give Woodbury an official endorsement, primarily because its leaders feared reopening the partially healed breach with the Independent Democrats, New Hampshire journals backed him almost unanimously. The Vermont, Maine, and Connecticut state conventions endorsed him. In Massachusetts the Democratic legislative caucus named him its favorite, and the Henshaw press extended cordial support.[35] Significantly, no Democratic convention or caucus in New England expressed an opinion on the subject of slavery.

Among Provisoists the reactions were mixed. There were many who took cognizance of the inevitable rumors and news articles, particularly after the Alabama Democratic Convention in February 1848, to the effect that Woodbury had privately indicated his adherence to the southern position on slavery in the territories. In Maine and Connecticut this element voted against his endorsement. At the same time, the antislavery Morton press in Massachusetts and the Wentworth wing of the Illinois Democracy indicated their favor. Woodbury agents became optimistic about winning over the Barnburners, though some warned that the leadership of that faction suspected his attitude.[36] He also made progress

---

[33] The strategy was to secure commitments in New England before taking action in the South (Charles L. Woodbury to Levi Woodbury, 17 February 1848, Woodbury Papers).

[34] See Luke Woodbury to Levi Woodbury, 28 October 1847, Nathaniel G. Upham to Levi Woodbury, 5 March 1848, ibid.; Niles to Van Buren, 18 April 1848, Van Buren Papers.

[35] Luke Woodbury to Levi Woodbury, 28 October 1847, Charles L. Woodbury to Levi Woodbury, 8 March 1848, Woodbury Papers; New Hampshire Patriot, 6 April 1848; Boston Post, 9 March, 19 May 1848; Boston Times, 22, 27 April, 2, 6, 10 May 1848; Baltimore Sun, 13 May 1848.

[36] John D. Kellogg to Woodbury, 9 February 1848, Charles Y. Deane to

among more moderate northern Democrats. His agents reported some Hunkers in his favor. The *Pittsburgh Post,* a one-time Dallas supporter, endorsed him; two St. Louis newspapers hoisted his flag. Thomas Hart Benton and Francis P. Blair were numbered among his supporters.[37]

It was in the lower Southeast, however, that his candidacy became most significant. The Alabama Democratic State Convention of February 1848 thrust Woodbury into the limelight. The convention reaffirmed the Alabama Platform, asserting the equal right of the South in the territories; it imposed upon itself and its delegation to the national convention a pledge to vote for no men for president and vice president who would not "unequivocally avow themselves" opposed to any restriction of slavery into the territories to be acquired from Mexico.[38]

The convention then considered Buchanan, Dallas, Cass, and Woodbury as possible candidates. At this point William L. Yancey took control. In a long speech concerning the platform and the candidates, he "cut off all hope" for Buchanan, Dallas, and Cass by quoting from their letters and speeches "to show that while they opposed any *federal* action upon slavery, they at the same time admitted that the people of a Territory of the United States—the settlers of it—could make regulations, to exclude slavery from it, before they formed a constitution preparatory to admittance into the union." Such an admission obviously did not meet the prescriptions of the Alabama Platform. On the other hand, he also read extracts from a letter which he "averred to be reliable authority,"[39] indicating that Woodbury was opposed "to *both federal and popular* interference with slavery in the Territories, and that he believed that the people of a Territory could only legislate on a subject when they met to frame a constitution preparatory to admittance as a state into the Union."[40]

Woodbury, 1 March 1848, A. Whitney to Woodbury, 8 March 1848, Samuel Treat to Clapp, 25 April 1848, Woodbury Papers; J. H. Huntington to Welles, 9 February 1848, Welles Papers; *New York Tribune,* 13 May 1848; *Boston Times,* 19 May 1848.

[37] Clapp to Woodbury, 12 May 1848, Woodbury Papers; *Boston Times,* 2, 6 May 1848; William E. Smith, *Francis Preston Blair Family in Politics* (New York, 1933), I: 228 (hereafter cited as *Blair Family*).

[38] The proceedings of the convention are in *Mobile Register,* 21 February 1848.

[39] Some at the convention assumed that the letter was written by Woodbury to Yancey (G. W. Gayle to Buchanan, 16 February 1848, Buchanan Papers). Actually what Yancey read were extracts from a letter sent by Woodbury to Senator Dixon H. Lewis of Alabama; they were relayed by Lewis to Yancey (Yancey to Woodbury, 10 March 1848, Woodbury Papers).

[40] See Yancey's letter to the *Montgomery Flag and Advertiser* explaining his action at the convention (*Washington Union,* 18 May 1848); and his letter to Woodbury of 10 March 1848 (Woodbury Papers).

As Yancey himself declared, the speech checked any movement for Buchanan, the strongest candidate,[41] for Dallas, or for Cass.[42] It did not, however, result in an endorsement of Woodbury. "You could have been nominated with great ease," Yancey afterward informed the justice, if the delegates had possessed "public assurances of your opinions," and if "your friends" had thought "your nomination" would have been "of benefit" outside the South.[43]

Alabama's failure to endorse Woodbury was not apparently harmful to his campaign. Both the Georgia and the Florida state conventions adopted versions of the Alabama Platform. Although they named unpledged delegations, Woodbury's support was strong in both states; Cass was his chief competitor.[44] During the spring, moreover, his candidacy gained popularity. In South Carolina he became the prime favorite. Reports that he was making inroads on Buchanan's following in Maryland, Virginia, and North Carolina and on Cass's support in Mississippi became frequent. All that was needed to make his candidacy even more formidable, particularly in the South, was his personal assurance that he accepted the Yancey position on slavery in the territories.[45]

---

[41] The leader of the Buchanan forces in Alabama was ex-Senator William R. King, whom the convention endorsed for vice president. Buchanan was evidently greatly perturbed by the turn of events in the state, whose endorsement he had expected. His friends were also concerned; they were fearful that the movement for Woodbury would succeed unless Buchanan's opinion on the slavery issue should "fortunately coincide" with Woodbury's. But Buchanan was later assured that the resolutions adopted were "nothing more than an expression of opposition to the Wilmot Proviso" and a declaration "against Genl Cass and Mr. Dallas." He was "in no danger of losing Alabama in the [national] convention" (Gayle to Buchanan, 16 February, 9 March 1848, Buchanan Papers).

[42] Cass's strength in Alabama was greatest in the hilly area of the north (*Mobile Register*, 5 May 1848).

[43] Yancey to Woodbury, 10 March 1848, Woodbury Papers. Yancey and others made attempts to persuade Woodbury, as well as other leading candidates, to make a public declaration of his position, but Woodbury's advisers warned against such an exposure. While Woodbury remained silent until shortly before the convention, his agents, among them his son, apparently continued to give assurances of his "southern position" (Yancey to Buchanan, 2 May 1848, Buchanan Papers; L. E. Dow to Levi Woodbury, 29 February 1848, Dixon H. Lewis to Levi Woodbury, 24 March 1848, L. O. B. Branch to Levi Woodbury, 1 April 1848, Charles L. Woodbury to Levi Woodbury, n.d., Whitney to Levi Woodbury, 13 May 1848, Woodbury Papers.

[44] *Savannah Republican*, 23 May 1848; *Floridian*, 25 March 1848; *Georgian*, 9 May 1848; L. G. Glenn to Cobb, 12 February 1848, in Phillips, *Toombs, Stephens, and Cobb Correspondence*, p. 96.

[45] Samuel R. Brooks to Woodbury, 6 April 1848, Edmund Burke to Woodbury, 24 April 1848, Clapp to Woodbury, 17 May 1848, Woodbury Papers; *Baltimore Clipper*, 21 April 1848; *Mississippian*, 26 May 1848; *New Orleans Delta*, 29 May 1848.

The emergence of Buchanan, Cass, and Woodbury as the leading and fairly equal contenders for the Democratic presidential nomination inevitably raised the possibility of a deadlocked convention. Almost immediately rumors arose that President Polk would enter the race to prevent a breach in the party. The possibility that Polk might be renominated if other Democratic contenders destroyed each other had been raised by John Wentworth as early as October 1845.[46] Despite the president's oft-repeated determination not to run again, even for the sake of party harmony,[47] the belief that he hoped to head the ticket a second time persisted, particularly among his enemies.[48]

Many politicians thought they detected actual evidence of a skillfully conducted Polk electioneering campaign headed by Robert J. Walker. Among them was Senator Allen of Ohio, who, according to Francis P. Blair, claimed that the selection of Baltimore as the site of the national convention was "a cabinet scheme to bring the delegations" to Washington "to be purchased up." Allen further maintained that he had learned "to his complete satisfaction that while almost every member of the cabinet was to appear to engross votes to promote his own advancement to the Presidency, there was at bottom a common design to throw the lot up to Polk, if none of them had a sufficient hand to take it." Cass, he continued, was playing the role of dupe. In Indiana Cass's nomination had been "arrested by an administration order through Bill Brown of the Post Office"; in Tennessee, for whose nomination Cass had been "induced to sacrifice himself in the Nicholson letter," the same game had been played. Polk men were appointed as delegates; they were "uncommitted" so that the Michigander "might be deluded . . . with hope" until he could be betrayed at the convention.[49]

That such a plot existed is extremely doubtful; nevertheless, a second

---

[46] *Chicago Democrat* quoted in *Cleveland Plain Dealer,* 29 October 1845.

[47] Quaife, *Polk's Diary,* 1: 103–4, 248–49, 266, 402–3; 3: 210, 254–57, 420. Denials also came from other sources (*Cleveland Plain Dealer,* 9 April 1845; Edward J. Harlan to Cobb, 3 May 1847, in Phillips, *Toombs, Stephens, and Cobb Correspondence,* p. 87; *North Carolina Standard,* 25 August 1847; *Nashville Union,* 2 May 1848; Philadelphia *Times,* 29 April 1848).

[48] The belief persisted among Calhounites (W. A. Harris to Calhoun, 11 July 1845, in Jameson, *Calhoun Correspondence,* p. 1042; Penn to Calhoun, 23 March 1846, in Boucher and Brooks, *Calhoun Correspondence,* pp. 335–36); among Van Burenites (Flagg to Welles, 17 February 1848, Welles Papers; Niles to Van Buren, 18 April 1848, Butler to Van Buren, 9 May 1848, Van Buren Papers); among northwesterners (Columbus *Ohio State Journal,* 5 February 1848 [hereafter cited as *Ohio State Journal*]; *Illinois State Register,* 24 March 1848); and among Whigs (*Boston Atlas,* 1 July 1846; New York *Courier,* 29 January 1848; *North American,* 8 May 1848).

[49] Blair to Van Buren, 23 January [1848], Van Buren Papers.

dark-horse nomination for Polk was not outside the realm of possibility. Governor Hugh J. Anderson of Maine, Senators Isaac Toucey of Connecticut, Arthur P. Bagby of Alabama, and Hopkins L. Turney of Tennessee, and former Vice President Richard M. Johnson, among others, urged him not to commit himself irrevocably against another term, since the divisions among the aspirants might become so acute that his renomination would become "indispensable."[50]

Thus as the time for the Democratic convention approached, Buchanan, Cass, and Woodbury were without doubt the leading contenders. Buchanan's strength, reckoned at about 80 votes, was based in Pennsylvania, New Jersey, and the south Atlantic seaboard. Cass's support, about 100 votes, came from the western states, north and south. Woodbury, with about 70 votes, depended upon New Englanders and southern extremists.[51] In such a situation there was a distinct possibility that none of the three could unite the convention; in this contingency Polk appeared to be the most important dark horse. But any speculation on the outcome was not complete without considering the situation in New York; in a close contest its 36 delegate votes had the power to make or break any candidate.

[50] Quaife, *Polk's Diary,* 1: 402–3; 3: 266, 319–20, 420, 454–55, 458–59. A few county journals in Virginia and Georgia expressed their preference for Polk (*Savannah Republican,* 24 January 1848; *Baltimore Clipper,* 16 March 1848; Nashville *Republican,* 24 April 1848).

[51] The estimates are my own, based on an evaluation of the strength claimed by admittedly partisan newspapers for their favorites and their opponents around 1 May 1848.

Chapter Nine

The Contest for
Delegates: Whigs

The struggle for delegates among Whig candidates and their associates developed differently from that of the Democrats. In the early months of 1848 the party set aside its efforts to evade the Proviso and turned to indulge itself in the luxury of a battle to the death between Taylor and Clay forces.

The attack of Taylor Whigs upon Clay's candidacy began shortly after Clay's trip to Cape May. The General's campaign managers, who long before had concluded that the Kentuckian could not be a winning candidate, had confined their opinions to private communications as long as the old veteran remained quietly at Ashland, giving no countenance to any movement in his favor. There had been no need to hurt his feelings. In the autumn of 1847, however, when it became apparent that a Clay movement was generating in the North, they forgot their qualms and proceeded to announce their views to the nation.

The strongly pro-Taylor New York *Courier* was among the first to fire a blast at Clay's candidacy. It declared bluntly:

> Whigs with Mr. Clay as their candidate would not have the remotest chance of success. His nomination would throw us at once upon the naked issues of 1844, and would again call into active opposition, all the party bitterness . . . of which he has been the occasion and the object for the last twenty years. . . . The tariff, which was then by far the strongest hold of the Whigs, has been for a time at least withdrawn from the controversy. Under the present tariff the revenue has been large, manufactures have prospered and every branch of industry has met its fair reward. . . . The debt created by the war has postponed the issue concerning the distribution of the Public Lands. A National Bank has become an "obsolete idea." Texas has been annexed and the Oregon dispute has been finally

settled. Upon all these questions, the ground held by the Whigs has been taken from under them.

If the Whigs could not win on these issues in the 1844 campaign, the *Courier* asked, "how, with a candidate whose name would rally parties precisely upon their old dividing line, could we hope for success in '48?"[1]

During the next six months the argument outlined by the *Courier* appeared more and more frequently in the press and in the letters of Whig politicians. Over and over again editors and local leaders reiterated the statement that Clay had no chance of success.[2]

Predictions of calamity did not deter Clay Whigs in their efforts to win the Kentuckian a fourth nomination. Their own efforts were aided markedly by Clay himself, who appeared in Washington in January 1848 to argue the case of *Houston* v. *Bank of New Orleans*. His vigorous and bouyant health impressed the denizens of the nation's capital, where for a month he once more became the honored head of his party. Washington correspondents of Democratic journals chortled over the "cold chill" which his presence gave the Taylor fever and reported a noticeable shift to his standard among the fence-sitters.[3]

From Washington Clay journeyed northward, "pinching fair cheeks" and "kissing thousands of pouting lips" on the way, to Philadelphia in late February and to New York in early March, where he received great civic welcomes.[4] With his appearance in these cities the movement to send him to the White House reached full strength; in New York the activities of his partisans reached new heights. There, as the *New York Express* declared, "the cry of 'Justice to Henry Clay'—so rife in 1844"—was again "swelling in the breeze," coming in from every quarter.[5]

---

[1] New York *Courier*, 6 September, 25 November 1847.

[2] *Richmond Enquirer*, 12 November 1847; Burnley to Crittenden, 11 December 1847, Jno. B. Bibb to Crittenden, 25 December 1847, R. R. Richie to Crittenden, 25 January 1848, Samuel P. Armstrong to Crittenden, 2 February 1848, Crittenden Papers; William H. Bennett to Smith, 8 February 1848, Allen Hamilton to Smith, 28 February 1848, Smith Papers; Alexander H. Stephens to Linton Stephens, 11 January 1848, in Johnston and Browne, *Stephens*, pp. 225–27.

[3] "John Taylor of Caroline" in *Mobile Register*, 21 January 1848. When Clay left Washington, the *New York Herald* reported that a poll of Whigs in Congress showed 90 for Clay, 60 for Taylor, and 25 for others. See also Baltimore *Sun*, 12 January 1848; *Boston Atlas*, 24 January 1848; *Georgian*, 27 January 1848; *Cleveland Plain Dealer*, 7 February 1848.

[4] Clay's trip north delighted Democratic editors, who regaled their readers with accounts of Clay's flirtations with the Whig maids and matrons of the East and his attention to the "model artistes" (*Pennsylvanian*, 11 March 1848; *North American*, 25, 26 February 1848; *New York Tribune*, 11 March 1848).

[5] *New York Express* quoted in *Nashville Union*, 3 March 1848.

Before Clay's arrival, New York City Whigs under the leadership of Greeley had met ten thousand strong at Castle Garden to shout their demand for Clay's nomination. Nicholas Carroll was awestruck by the scene; it convinced him that Clay was the most popular man in the nation. "I saw them literally that night, Christian, Jew & Gentile," he reported to Crittenden. "Beside me stood old Hunker Democrats, Radicals, Natives, Adopted Citizens, Abolitionists, Whigs & besides them old white headed men of wealth and influence, seldom seen outside their doors after nightfall—the merchant—the trader—the ship builder & the ship owner—the cartman—the physician—the laborer & the minister of God—all, all with one voice nominating Henry Clay."[6]

The enthusiasm of the Castle Garden meeting spilled into other eastern areas in the late winter and early spring. State Whig conventions in Rhode Island and Connecticut voiced support for Clay, and several county conventions around Newark, New Jersey, chose Clay delegates. In Philadelphia, Young Whigs foregathered under the leadership of the editorial staff of the *North American* to turn a Clay birthday festival into a meeting that proclaimed the Kentuckian their "first, last, and only" choice for the nation's highest office. The greatest triumph occurred in New York, where impatient supporters, anticipating the usual call to name delegates to the national convention, moved spontaneously in their congressional districts to choose delegates pledged to vote for Clay. Early in April the Whig members of the legislature completed the New York movement by announcing their own support for Clay's nomination.[7] So overwhelming was the sentiment for the veteran chieftain that even the *Courier,* on 5 April, admitted that "nine-tenths" of the New York Whigs preferred "Mr. Clay to any other man for the Presidency."

For a time an equal enthusiasm also appeared in some areas of the South, where previously the tide had run overwhelmingly for Taylor. In Maryland, where the press was strongly pro-Taylor, a small majority of Whig legislators announced for Clay; in Baltimore, the Kentuckian's supporters invaded a Buena Vista meeting, hooted Reverdy Johnson from the speaker's stand, forcibly ejected Taylor men from the hall, and then named Clay delegates to the state convention. Farther south, Whig leaders around Augusta and Macon, Georgia, announced a determination

[6] Carroll to Crittenden, 20 February 1848, Crittenden Papers.

[7] *Louisville Democrat,* 2 February 1848; *Newark Advertiser,* 11, 17 February 1848; *North American,* 5 April 1848; Weed, *Autobiography,* pp. 576–77; *New York Tribune,* 25 March, 15 April 1848. Endorsement by the Whigs of the New York legislature probably occurred because Clay demanded it before he would consent to run (Joseph L. White to Clay, 5 April 1848, Clay Papers).

to vote for Clay and for no other man. From Alabama, where the state's most influential editor, John C. Langdon of the *Mobile Advertiser,* had sworn to vote for Clay until the Kentuckian's death and then to support his executors, there were reports that every Whig meeting in the state had announced for Clay. The *Montgomery State Journal* confessed "with a weary groan" that the overwhelming Taylor sentiment of which it had boasted had "died away."[8]

Nevertheless, it soon became evident that Taylor sentiment in the South was too strong for Clay to overcome. While Clay's supporters and well-wishers were numerous and in various localities were a majority of the electorate, they discovered, when the test was made in those state conventions which met early in 1848, that the party machinery was controlled by Taylor forces.

Nowhere did that fact become more apparent than in Clay's own state. Old Zack's supporters in Kentucky were led by men both friendly and hostile to Clay. Crittenden, Thomas Metcalfe, and ex-Governor ("Black Bob") Letcher were tried Clay men. The Wickliffes, Ben Hardin, and John L. Helm were friends of John Tyler.[9] Their skillful direction of Taylor sentiment during the summer of 1847 had disclosed a preference for the Old Hero in a decided majority of the state's counties.

Clay forces, led by Judge George Robertson and General Leslie Combs of Lexington, fought desperately to offset this advantage during the following autumn, even resorting to the doubtful expedient of issuing a "Secret Circular" to leading Whigs throughout the country, giving the lie to current reports of overwhelming Taylor strength in the Blue Grass State. The circular described Taylor's supporters as "scattered" and "without influence."[10]

When this attempted disparagement was revealed by a "dastardly" Nativist journal in Cincinnati in November 1847, the anger of Taylor men burst all bonds. Letcher reported that two of his friends were "both crazy" with excitement and were determined to "let the Lexington managers see whether they were . . . without influence." A reckless spirit took hold of Taylor Whigs as the time for the state convention approached; everywhere local leaders, incensed by the circular, demanded a showdown. Although men like Crittenden and Letcher preached forebearance—pointing out that a Taylor nomination would

---

[8] *Baltimore Clipper,* 7 February 1848; *Boston Atlas,* 30 March 1848; *Georgian,* 12 February 1848; *Mobile Register,* 23 February 1848; *Richmond Enquirer,* 20 April 1848.

[9] Poage, *Clay,* p. 171.

[10] There is a copy of the "Secret Circular" in the Clayton Papers.

not only "throw everything into Hotch Pot" but would also split the party and turn the state over to the Democrats in the gubernatorial contest—their arguments apparently had no effect.[11]

When the convention met at Frankfort on 22 February, a hot contest between Clay and Taylor adherents over the nomination of a candidate for governor revealed that Taylor forces were in control. When Clay men threatened a bolt, a letter from Crittenden pleading for harmony was read to the delegates. His moderate counsels prevailed; the convention compromised by dividing the state delegates between the contending factions. The country correctly credited Taylor with a major victory.[12]

Old Zack's strength also became evident in Virginia, where a forecast of probable results had become known in December 1847 when a caucus of Whig legislators almost unanimously recommended Taylor as the "most acceptable candidate" within the party. At the state convention, which met on 22 February, the Clay forces, captained by John Minor Botts, fought desperately to forestall a Taylor nomination with a resolution to name an uninstructed delegation. After a twelve-hour battle, however, they surrendered when William Ballard Preston announced that the telegraph had just brought the news that Kentucky had declared for Taylor. As if "struck by lightning," the *Richmond Enquirer* reported, the convention voted down 81 to 27 the resolution to select no candidate and named the Old Hero as its choice for the presidency.[13]

North Carolina Whigs also met on 22 February, but their convention was not a test of strength between candidates. The state party was directed by men unfavorable to the sectionalist trend of the Buena Vista movement, and Taylor partisans had made no serious effort to capture control of the party machinery. Nevertheless, Taylor forces managed to secure election of one of the two delegates at large, an outcome that gave Clay Whigs little comfort.[14]

Meanwhile, these early contests between Clay and Taylor forces had given rise to rumors that each would withdraw in favor of the other for

[11] Letcher to Crittenden, 23 December 1847, 1 January, 16, 21 February 1848, George W. Williams to Crittenden, 25 November 1847, John L. Helm to Crittenden, 11 January 1848, Thomas Metcalfe to Crittenden, 8, 20 February 1848, Crittenden Papers.

[12] John W. Russell to Crittenden, 1 March 1848, Crittenden Papers; *Pennsylvanian*, 28 February 1848; New York *Courier*, 5 May 1848.

[13] *Niles' Register* 73 (1 January 1848): 277; *Richmond Enquirer*, 24–26 February 1848. There was considerable furor among Clay Whigs when it was learned that the "telegraphic news" was false (*Richmond Enquirer*, 8 March 1848).

[14] J. G. de Roulhac Hamilton, "Party Politics in North Carolina, 1835–1860," *James Sprunt Historical Publications* 15 (1916): 114; *North Carolina Standard*, 1 March 1848.

the sake of party harmony. In Clay's case the rumor had begun with the first evidence of a public movement on his behalf, and it was encouraged by editors of Taylor newspapers. George D. Prentice of the *Louisville Journal* probably gave the "news" its initial impetus early in September 1847, when he pointed out: "We know that Mr. Clay at the disastrous close of the last Presidential canvass came unhesitatingly and instantly to the determination never again to be a candidate for the Presidency, unless . . . the whole people of the United States . . . should call him . . . by acclamation." Since it was obvious that he was not being "called . . . by any such acclamation," it could be assumed that he was not a candidate. Although the *Lexington Observer,* regarded as Clay's editorial mouthpiece, categorically denied the truth of Prentice's assumption,[15] the rumor that the Kentuckian would not run continued to grow, reaching a high point when he appeared in Washington and persisting into the spring of 1848.[16]

The rumor was not without foundation, for Clay had several times informed friends that he was willing to be superseded. As late as December 1847 he told Thomas B. Stevenson that he would probably refuse to allow use of his name. "Perhaps that is really best for the country and for me," he confided. "I am most unwilling to be thought to desire a nomination. . . . If better can be done without my name, for God's sake, let me be passed by."[17]

During his sojourn in Washington Clay began to find reasons to change his mind. In mid-February he informed a close Lexington friend that eastern Whigs had begged him not to withdraw his name: "I have been assured that if I did, it would lead to a prostration of the Whig party, especially in the Free States." He had also been assured that there was not a particle of doubt about New York's support in the campaign; if the 1844 returns in that state could be used as a basis for a forecast, his election was certain.[18] Under the circumstances, considering the unwelcome news from Kentucky and Virginia, Clay resolved to resume

[15] *Louisville Journal* quoted in *Niles' Register* 73 (11 September 1848): 19–20; *Lexington Observer* quoted in *Washington Union,* 9 November 1847.

[16] Baltimore *Sun,* 22 December 1847; Detroit *Free Press,* 23 December 1847; *Cleveland Plain Dealer,* 6 January 1848; Nashville *Republican,* 10 January 1848; *Charleston Mercury,* 16 February 1848; *Pennsylvanian,* 25 February 1848.

[17] Clay to Stevenson, 2 December 1847, in Colton, *Clay's Works,* 3: 461. On the eve of the Frankfort convention Letcher informed Crittenden: "I am satisfied Clay won't think of running the race out. I judge from various information and from a few private lines he wrote me—which no one has seen" (Letcher to Crittenden, 21 February 1848, Crittenden Papers). See also Clay to Giddings, 6 October 1847, in Julian, *Giddings,* pp. 208–10.

[18] Clay to H. T. Duncan, 15 February 1848, Clay Papers; Clay to General Combs, 18 February 1848, in Colton, *Clay's Works,* 3: 476–77.

his passive role and to make his decision after he returned home. When he reached Ashland, appeals that he remain in the race persisted. Ohio politicians, led by Governor William Bebb, added their entreaties to those from New York, accentuating the argument that Clay's withdrawal would destroy the Whig party in the North.[19] While he remained silent, his supporters grew anxious. From Cincinnati, Stevenson reported that he was "tortured . . . with inquiries" as to Clay's intentions. "I am literally beleaguered in my office from morn till evening. . . . The doubt on this subject, do what we may to remove it, is extensive ; and its manifestation is distressing here. It despirits and almost paralyzes your friends, and gives boldness to opponents."[20]

On 10 April, five days after the Whigs of the New York legislature had made their endorsement, Clay ended all doubts by issuing a public letter announcing his candidacy. In it he revealed his earlier "disinclination" to enter the race and his determination to make this position known in December. On "reflection," however, he had decided to consult his friends before taking "a final and decisive step." Those friends had changed his mind : "They have represented to me that withdrawal of my name would be fatal to the success, and perhaps lead to the dissolution of the party with which I have been associated, especially in the free States ; that at no former period did there exist so great a probability of my election, . . . that I am more available than any candidate that could be presented to the American people." They had also reminded him of his frequent declaration that "whilst life and health remain, a man is bound to render his best services upon the call of his country." He had therefore decided to allow his name to go before the national convention "in connexion with such others as may be presented to it." He would cheerfully accept the result.

At this point Clay might have stopped, but he could not refrain from adding a message to those friends and fellow citizens who had anticipated that he would decline to be a candidate and had accordingly "avowed a preference for and directed their attention to the distinguished names of other citizens of the United States." To them he took "pleasure in declaring" that he had "no regrets to express—no complaints, no reproaches to make on account of any such preferences." He was persuaded that their actions were "generally founded on honest and patriotic convictions."[21]

Reactions to the announcement could have been outlined in advance.

[19] Clay to Stevenson, 19 February 1848, Bebb to Clay, 4 April 1848, in Colton, *Clay's Works,* 3 : 461, 476–77.
[20] Stevenson to Clay, 8 April 1848, Clay Papers.
[21] *National Intelligencer,* 18 April 1848.

To Democrats, the "pronunciamento" meant that all Whig problems were settled with a stroke of Clay's pen. "We see not how the Whigs can resist this appeal," the *Washington Union* of 15 April declared. "It is an appeal to their honor to stand by their oldest and ablest champion. It is an appeal to their party integrity not to throw all their past professions and principles aside. It is an appeal to their fears not to break up their party organization. . . . The appeal will prevail. Mr. Clay will again be nominated."

Among his supporters Clay's announcement was greeted with delight, but other Whigs responded with mingled expressions of regret, amazement, and anger. Moderate journals questioned his political acumen. "No man has more sincere and devoted friends," the *New Orleans Commercial Bulletin* of 20 April admitted; however, it continued:

> Mr. Clay . . . ought to have remembered no one has more uncompromising, bitter and persevering enemies; that the feelings and prejudices against him . . . have been transmitted to immense masses, almost as heirlooms from a preceding generation, and that his appearance at the head of the Whig column, will at once calm all the differences and divisions in the enemy's camp, and unite the fragments of all parties against him. . . . He has . . . been led into error by sanguine and admiring friends, who crowded around him, and whose feelings and friendship made them mistake the signs of the times, and wrongly interpret the outpourings of high respect and attachment to the *man,* as indications of preference for the politician.

The reaction of James Harvey to Clay's gullibility was more typical. The public letter, he contended, betrayed "a willingness to believe representations" that had not even "plausibility" to recommend them; it revealed "a morbid passion" for the presidency, which nothing but charity could extenuate. "It is evident," Harvey concluded, "that he plays his last card and that desperation guides the venture." But this response was mild in comparison to that of rabid Taylor men such as Cassius M. Clay, who maintained that he had read his kinsman's "epistolary atrocity" with "astonishment and pain." From this group, as the *Mobile Register* reported, came "ominous mutterings of unrestrained anger"; on every side they denounced his action "for its arrogant assumptions and dictatorial spirit."[22] Some of the younger Taylor partisans charged that Clay was the "evil genius of the Party" and openly threatened to bolt if he were the Whig nominee.[23]

[22] Harvey to McLean, 15 April 1848, McLean Papers; *North American,* 15 April 1848; *Mobile Register,* 22 April 1848.

[23] *Mobile Register,* 28 April 1848; Dowling to McLean, 14 April 1848, McLean

Meanwhile, Taylor leaders turned their attention to making their candidate too strong to be defeated at a national convention. To accomplish this end, two matters had to be clarified : the persistent rumors that Taylor would withdraw and the continued questioning of his Whiggery.

The rumor of Taylor's withdrawal had become prevalent during Clay's visit to Washington; as in Clay's case it had good foundations. Taylor had provided it with substance in a letter he wrote to Clay early in November 1847. "I fully agree with you," he wrote, "in the necessity for more deliberation in the selection of a candidate for the Presidency and I truly regret that my name should have been used in that relation. . . . To a mutual friend of ours . . . I stated . . . specifically that I was ready to stand aside, if you or any other Whig was the choice of the party, and that I sincerely hoped that such might be their decision."[24] The friend mentioned was Crittenden, who had been authorized to withdraw Taylor's name at any time before the election. Although Taylor withdrew the authorization in January, Clay simultaneously showed the November letter to James Harvey, who, as "Independent," published the essence of it in the Philadelphia North American.[25] In spite of private denials by Taylor,[26] whose position was relayed to the country by his friends, the rumor would not die, and after publication of Clay's pronunciamento it grew even stronger.

The General's Whig opponents had also opened an attack on his continued unwillingness to avow Whig principles. The assault had died down after the appearance of his notes to Joseph R. Ingersoll and to Dr. Bronson in September 1847, but it was renewed early in 1848, when Clay sentiment was reaching its high point. Demand for proof of Taylor's Whiggery came particularly from the East, but it also appeared in most northern quarters. The New York Express stated the demand in mixed terminology : "We Whigs, at least in this part of the Union are not dogs that we can be led by the halter for any man. We have principles that we cherish and that we love—and if General Taylor personifies these principles, he is an acceptable candidate . . . but to vote for him in the dark . . . is a fatuity we cannot dream of, and that we have been fatally warned against in . . . attempts at that sort of folly."[27]

Papers; Crallé to Calhoun, 19 April 1848, in Boucher and Brooks, *Calhoun Correspondence*, p. 435.

[24] Taylor to Clay, 4 November 1847, in Colton, *Clay's Works*, 5 : 548–49.

[25] *Niles' Register* 73 (19 February 1848) : 393–94. See also Crittenden to Burnley, 17 May 1848, Crittenden Papers.

[26] Zachary Taylor to J. P. Taylor, 10 March 1848, Taylor Papers; Taylor to Wood, 18 February 1848, in *Taylor Letters*, p. 154.

[27] *New York Express* quoted in *Nashville Union*, 3 February 1848.

The attack on Taylor's refusal to take a firm Whig stand was increased by several letters that appeared in February and March 1848. In one, to Colonel A. M. Mitchell of Cincinnati, Taylor announced: "If the Whig party desire . . . to cast their votes for me, they must do it on their own responsibility and without any pledges from me." In another, he accepted a nomination from the "Independents" of Pennsylvania, indicating that his Whiggery was not of that uncompromising nature which his Whig opponents demanded and giving those opponents and nominal friends opportunity to repudiate him.[28] The greatest furor was created by his letter to Peter Sken Smith; in it he accepted the Nativist nomination and announced his determination not to be the "exponent of the views of any party." Acceptance of a nomination from a political sect which one of his editorial supporters denounced as a group of "strait-laced, narrow-minded, one-idead" bigots was enough to damn Taylor in many quarters; his further refusal to avow the principles of any party served only to heap insult upon injury. Reports that his once proud ascendancy in the popular mind had seriously declined became frequent in March and April of 1848.[29]

The situation caused considerable consternation among his supporters, who called for drastic measures. Some move had to be made to right him before the people—a move expressing his position on the questions of the day in a manner that would leave no doubt that he was a Whig. His managers and their friends in Washington and New Orleans responded nobly to the crisis. On 22 April a letter from Taylor to his kinsman Captain John S. Allison of Louisville appeared in the New Orleans papers:[30]

> I confess, whilst I have great cardinal principles, which will regulate my political life, I am not sufficiently familiar with all minute details of political legislation to give solemn pledges to exert my influence, if I were President, to carry out this, or defeat that measure. I have no concealments. I hold no opinions which I would not proclaim to my assembled countrymen, but crude impressions upon matters of policy, which may be right today and wrong

[28] *Cleveland Plain Dealer,* 10 March 1848; *Albany Atlas,* 26 February 1848.

[29] *Richmond Whig* quoted in *Richmond Enquirer,* 28 February 1848; James Harlan to Smith, 5 March 1848, Stevenson to Smith, 6 March 1848, John D. Defrees to Smith, 4 April 1848, Smith Papers.

[30] Authorship of the "first Allison letter" has been claimed by many. The two latest accounts of the preparation of the letter are in my article "Who Wrote the Allison Letters? A Study in Historical Detection," *Mississippi Valley Historical Review* 36 (June 1949): 51–72 (hereafter cited as "Who Wrote the Allison Letters?"); and Hamilton, *Taylor,* pp. 76–81.

tomorrow, are, perhaps, not the best test of fitness for office. One who cannot be trusted without pledges, cannot be confided in merely on account of them. I will proceed, however, now to respond to your inquiries.

First—I reiterate what I have often said—I AM A WHIG, *but not an ultra Whig*. If elected I would not be the mere president of a party. I would endeavor to act independent of party domination. I should feel bound to administer the government untrammeled by party schemes.

Second—The veto power. The power given by the constitution to the Executive to interpose his veto, is a high conservative power; but in my opinion should never be exercised except in cases of clear violation of the constitution, or manifest haste and want of consideration by Congress.

Third—Upon the subject of the tariff, the currency, the improvement of our great highways, rivers, lakes, and harbors, the will of the people, as expressed through their representatives in Congress, ought to be respected and carried out by the Executive.

Fourth—The Mexican War. I sincerely rejoice at the prospect of peace. My life has been devoted to arms, yet I look upon war at all times and under all circumstances as a national calamity, to be avoided if compatible with national honor. The principles of our government as well as its true policy, are opposed to the subjugation of other nations, and the embarrassment of other countries by conquest.

These are my opinions upon the subjects referred to by you; and any reports or publications, written or verbal, from any source, different in any essential particular from what is here written, are unauthorized and untrue.[31]

Unfortunately, by the time the Allison letter reached Washington, whence it was relayed to the northern press, another letter, which Taylor had written to the *Richmond Republican* on 20 April, also appeared in the nation's newspapers. It was written in answer to three questions: Would Taylor accept the nomination of a Whig national convention? Would he withdraw if Clay or any other man were the candidate? Had he ever stated that he favored the Tariff of 1846 or the subtreasury, that he himself originated the war, or that he would select his cabinet from both parties? Old Zack's reply was characteristically terse:

> If nominated by the Whig national convention, I shall not refuse acceptance, provided I am left free of all pledges, and permitted to maintain the position of independence of all parties in which the

---

[31] *Niles' Register* 74 (5 July 1848): 8.

people and my own sense of duty have placed me—otherwise I shall refuse the nomination of any convention or party.

I do not design to withdraw my name if Mr. Clay be the nominee of the Whig National Convention—and, in this connexion, I beg permission to remark that the statements which have been so positively made in some Northern prints to the effect *"that should Mr. Clay be the nominee of the Whig National Convention,"* I had stated *"that I would not suffer my name to be used,"* are not correct, and have no foundation in any oral or written remark of mine. It has not been my intention at any moment to change my position—or to withdraw my name from the canvass, whoever may be the nominee of the National Convention, either of the Whig or Democratic party.

I have never stated to anyone that I was in favor of the Tariff of '46—of the Sub-Treasury, nor that I originated the war with Mexico. Nor, finally, that I should (if elected) select my cabinet from both parties. . . .

Permit me . . . to add that should such high distinction be conferred upon me as that of elevation to the Executive office, the Constitution, in a strict and honest interpretation, and in the spirit and mode in which it was acted upon by our earlier Presidents, would be my chief guards. In this, I conceive to be all that is necessary in the way of a pledge.[32]

Reaction to the two communications was what might be expected. Men already committed to Taylor commended the Allison letter because, as the *Savannah Republican* of 5 May declared, it set "at rest, at once and forever, the numerous misrepresentations put in circulation by persons professing to utter his sentiments" and placed Taylor "fully and fairly before the country" on a platform broad enough "to bear all who preferred patriotism to party."

Clay Whigs, who ignored the letter to Captain Allison, except to suggest that there was "more artifice in it, than ever originated in Taylor's own mind,"[33] turned their attention to the letter published in the *Richmond Republican*. Their attitude was well stated by the *Lynchburg Virginian*:

Can Gen. Taylor, in the face of the declaration, that he will, in any event, be a candidate, receive the nomination of the Philadelphia Convention? We answer, without the least hesitation, NO—unless the members of that body *be wanting in respect for themselves and*

[32] *Washington Union*, 6 May 1848.
[33] *Mobile Register*, 27 April 1848.

the Whig party. We should really consider it an *insult,* to bring before it, as a candidate for the nomination, the name of one who says, if you choose to nominate me on my own conditions, well ! !— If you do not, I shall notwithstanding be a candidate. In our view, therefore, Gen. Taylor has virtually placed himself beyond the pale of the Whig party as such, and the convention, in our opinion, cannot possibly entertain the question of his nomination.[34]

Precisely what effect the effort to set Whigs aright concerning Taylor's Whiggery had on the party it is impossible to determine, but the effect on another element, the Taylor Independents, was very clear. When the Taylor boom had first swept the country, "no-party" movements of statewide proportions had generated in Louisiana, Mississippi, Alabama, Tennessee, Kentucky, Maryland, and Pennsylvania. Aided by Taylor's repeated statements that he was not a party candidate, these movements had become so vigorous that many Whigs, particularly in the South, began to reckon with the possibility of nominating the General without calling a convention. As late as January 1848 the *Baltimore Clipper* announced that it could see no necessity, "on the part of the friends of General Taylor, whether whigs or democrats," of holding a national convention to bring him before the people. "He is already a candidate and will remain so," the *Clipper* argued, "whatever may be the position of this or that convention. He stands as the people's candidate for the Presidency, forced into that position by the spontaneous voice of the people—and his chances of being elected is [*sic*] better without than with a party conventional nomination."[35]

After the Whig congressional caucus summoned a national convention, making a party nomination necessary, and after Clay's strength began to make itself felt, making a nominating contest inevitable, the strength of the no-party movement weakened. Nevertheless, its force was still respectable when the Allison letter appeared. Democratic journals promptly seized the opportunity to charge that "Taylorism" had degenerated into "unadulterated Whiggism," and Democrats flocked back into their party.[36] The nonpartisan Taylor electoral tickets which had been selected in Louisiana, Alabama, and Pennsylvania were aban-

[34] *Lynchburg Virginian* quoted in *Richmond Enquirer,* 12 May 1848.
[35] *Baltimore Clipper,* 31 January 1848. The position was taken by other southern journals such as the *New Orleans Commercial Bulletin,* the Montgomery *Alabama State Journal* (hereafter cited as *Alabama State Journal*), the *Milledgeville Southern Recorder,* the *Nashville Whig,* the Nashville *Republican,* the *Richmond Republican,* and the *Louisville Journal.* In the North the New York *Courier* took the same stand.
[36] *Nashville Union,* 8 April 1848.

doned.[37] An independent Taylor organization continued to operate only in Maryland.

Taylor men hardly noticed the defection; they were much too busy lining up delegates in the state and district conventions that met during the spring months. In the slave states Old Zack's supporters made an almost complete sweep. In Texas, Arkansas, Missouri, Mississippi, Florida, and Georgia, where the whole slate was chosen at the state meetings, the party named solid Taylor delegations. In Louisiana and Alabama, where delegates at large were elected at the state meetings, and in Tennessee, where the state delegates were named by a legislative caucus, the party also named only Taylor men. The General also secured some support in the North: Illinois, Iowa, and, surprisingly, Maine Whigs each selected some known Taylor supporters as delegates to the national convention.[38]

Clay also won support during the spring. Vermont, Maryland, Michigan, and Wisconsin state conventions instructed their delegates to vote for him. In the slave states his supporters secured complimentary resolutions from both the Missouri and the Georgia conventions and elected several strong figures, among them John C. Langdon of Mobile, as district delegates. Moreover, several journals that favored Taylor also indicated a strong willingness to support Clay if he were nominated.[39]

When Whig politicians studied the results of the Taylor-Clay struggle in the spring of 1848, they saw much cause for alarm. Taylor's support, overwhelmingly southern, amounted to 90 or 100 votes; Clay's strength in New England, New York, the border states, and the upper Northwest amounted to 80 or 90 votes. There were also about 100 delegates pledged to other candidates or uncommitted; most of these came from the block of four states stretching from New Jersey to Indiana. The possibility of a deadlocked convention became very apparent. Reaction was almost spontaneous; party leaders, particularly northerners, began to talk about compromise candidates. Their attitude was well expressed by James Harvey when he pointed out that the violence and bitterness

[37] *Charleston Mercury,* 23 November 1847; *Washington Union,* 30 March 1848; New York *Courier,* 10 March 1848; *New Orleans Commercial Bulletin,* 24 February 1848; Mueller, *Whigs in Pennsylvania,* p. 145; James K. Greer, "Louisiana Politics, 1845–1861," *Louisiana Historical Quarterly* 12 (1929): 555–59 (hereafter cited as "Louisiana Politics").
[38] James Love to Crittenden, 20 May 1848, Crittenden Papers; *Newark Advertiser,* 17 April 1848; Nashville *Republican,* 2 February, 31 March 1848; *Savannah Republican,* 18 April 1848; *Boston Atlas,* 12 May 1848.
[39] *Richmond Enquirer,* 20 April 1848; Nashville *Republican,* 24 April, 26 May 1848; *Baltimore Clipper,* 12, 15 May 1848; *Georgian,* 12, 20 May 1848; *Savannah Republican,* 10 May 1848.

of the war between friends of Clay and those of Taylor had "stimulated the conviction in the minds of all sober and reflecting men" that it was the duty of the coming convention "to lay them both aside" for another.[40]

Congressional leaders most often mentioned Crittenden in that connection. Although there was no doubt that he would have been an excellent choice, Crittenden never took his own chances seriously. All his hopes were bound up in the Taylor movement, which he refused to desert; any mention of his own name drew from him only refusals.[41] Thus his candidacy remained latent.

In the East an effort was made to focus attention on Daniel Webster. "Black Dan" was not a strong candidate. He had received nominations from Whig conventions in Massachusetts and New Hampshire, where he had always been hailed as the "greatest, and wisest, and ablest man" in the Union, and his chief editorial supporters (the *Courier* and the *Atlas* of Boston) boasted that "he could poll more votes in the Ohio Valley" than Harrison had and could carry every state that Clay had won in 1844, as well as New York and Georgia.[42] However, his chances outside the orbit of Faneuil Hall were slight. Webster's nemesis was Clay; to make any headway, he would have to eliminate the Kentuckian. It was with this objective that his Empire State supporters joined the Taylor movement in New York City in the early months of 1848; they hoped that a revelation of Taylor's strength in a Clay stronghold would induce the Kentuckian's followers to desert their beloved leader and swing their strength to Webster. But the Clay forces, sure of their power, refused to take the bait. This episode, combined with rumors that Webster would be willing to accept a vice-presidential nomination on the Taylor ticket, served only to create the impression that the Squire of Marshfield was ready to form a coalition with any candidate who offered him sufficient inducement.[43]

McLean and Corwin were much more significant in the speculations of northern Whig leaders. Although the Judge's candidacy, perhaps more noticed during the second winter of Polk's administration than that of any other Whig, had been almost submerged in the Taylor flood, a few faithful followers had managed to keep their hopes alive. They had

---

[40] Harvey to McLean, 12 April 1848, McLean Papers.

[41] Crittenden to G. B. Kinkaid, 10 January 1847, in Coleman, *Crittenden*, 1: 268.

[42] *Boston Atlas*, 2 May 1848. See also 25 March, 15 April 1848.

[43] Fuess, *Webster*, 2: 185; Baltimore *Republican*, 24 January 1848; Mower to McLean, 25 February 1848, McLean Papers. Webster considered the "stalking horse" effort ill advised (Webster to R. M. Blatchford, 30 January 1848, in *Webster's Writings*, 16: 491–92).

concluded that the wisest policy for the time was to "lie low" until plans to win over elements opposed to Taylor could be put quietly into effect.[44] Accordingly, little was heard from the McLean men till the autumn of 1847, when reports of his nomination by Whigs in Detroit revealed that he was once more in the running.[45] Simultaneously, his friends began to talk about substituting Seward for Mangum on the pre–Buena Vista ticket, and ex-Senator Tom Ewing was sent to Washington to work on congressmen.[46] By winter McLean's correspondents were again reporting a favorable trend in New England, as well as in Ohio, where Calvary Morris disclosed that a majority of the state central committee had indicated their preference for him.[47]

But McLean had two formidable opponents to eliminate in Ohio— Clay and Corwin. Against the Kentuckian, whose adherents one McLean supporter described as "aristocratic, brow beating, dogmatical, selfish, dictatorial simpletons," McLean's Ohio managers tentatively tried the tactics of the Webster men in New York; they were no more successful. But they wasted little time in lamentations, since the problem presented by Corwin's candidacy was much more pressing.[48]

Although the Wagon Boy had lost the support of many antislavery Whigs because of his Carthage speech in September 1847, he remained a potential candidate. His supporters, moreover, remained determined to give him a solid base by securing the endorsement of the Ohio Whigs. To carry out their purpose, they directed their attack against the orthodoxy of McLean's Whiggery and against his failure to announce a position on slavery.

McLean was and always had been, one partisan charged, "a Loco Foco of the worst sort." His political views "were nearly the same as they were when he left Jackson's cabinet."[49] Had he ever announced his allegiance to the Whig cause or, for that matter, had he ever proclaimed himself a Whig? Had not his followers indicated a hostility to Clay, a certain sign that McLean's Whiggery was lukewarm? Besides, was he not an "Old Hunker"? What sympathy could he have with the young men of the party or with the new issues that had arisen since he had

[44] Teesdale to McLean, 13 September 1847, McLean Papers.
[45] *Chicago Democrat*, 4 September 1847.
[46] Mower to McLean, 13 September 1847, Miner to McLean, 25 December 1847, McLean Papers.
[47] Harvey to McLean, 5 December 1847, Morris to McLean, 22 December 1847, Leonidas Jewett to McLean, 7 December 1847, ibid.
[48] Mower to McLean, 3 January 1848, D. B. Adger to McLean, 15 January 1848, ibid.
[49] J. L. Miner to William Miner, 16 February 1847, ibid.; Giddings to Sumner, 2 June 1847, in Julian, *Giddings*, p. 208.

donned the ermine? How did he stand on the war? What, moreover, were his views on slavery? Had he not supported the slaveholders in the case of *Prigg* v. *Pennsylvania,* and would he not call to his council those "old men" of the party who would advise a "continuation of the practice of unconditional submission to the slave power"? Why then should he be given the support of the Ohio Whigs? Was not Corwin, whose Whiggery and antislavery sentiments were unexceptionable, the man to follow?[50]

The vigor of this campaign soon showed itself in letters sent to McLean. His friends urged him to express his views "to quiet the clamor that is afloat."[51] McLean responded on 7 January 1848 with a letter on the Mexican War. In accordance with Whig argument, he condemned it as a conflict "unnecessarily and unconstitutionally commenced"; he demanded that Congress end it at once by defining the terms upon which peace should be made and by presenting them to the president with a threat to suspend any appropriations necessary to carry the war deeper into enemy territory if these terms were not offered to the Mexicans without delay. Steps should also be taken, he declared, to liquidate the war debt by a system of direct taxation, which would show the nation what it had paid for military glory. Adoption of "such a system of taxation would wind up the Mexican War in sixty days."[52]

But the announcement of these views did not clarify McLean's position on slavery; Corwin leaders, recognizing the significance of the omission and conveniently forgetting the attitude of their own candidate, did not hesitate to proclaim that McLean was opposed to "any declaration similar to that embraced in the Wilmot Proviso." Although his friends renewed their pressure for a statement on the point, the Judge refused to respond.[53]

The showdown between the two Ohioans occurred at the Whig State Convention in Columbus on 19 January 1848. The contest in that meeting was unexampled for its bitterness. Before the delegates had gathered, McLean's managers had recognized that they would not be able to control the convention and that the Corwin men would outnumber the supporters of any other contender. They determined, therefore, to seek the assistance of all anti-Corwin forces in order to block a nomination. In a furious contest within the committee on resolutions, the

---

[50] See Detroit *Free Press,* 6 December 1847, 7 April 1848; Elizur Wright to McLean, 2 January 1848, McLean Papers.

[51] Wright to McLean, 2 January 1848, McLean Papers.

[52] *Niles' Register* 73 (5 February 1848) : 354.

[53] Galloway to McLean, 10 January [1848], Chase to McLean, 10 January 1848, McLean Papers.

anti-Corwin coalition drew first blood; the Corwin men then transferred the fight to the floor of the convention. There, the "Miami tribe"—led by Robert McBretney of the *Xenia Torchlight,* John D. Campbell, and Governor William Bebb, and backed by the majority of delegates from the Western Reserve—waged an acrimonious battle for an immediate nomination. The coalition won again. Corwin men then sought to carry a resolution for an April convention, but in spite of threats to mark as fair targets for future revenge all who opposed such action, the coalition carried the day a third time. As a last resort, angry Corwin leaders demanded passage of a resolution approving the position of their candidate on the Mexican War; after a "perfect row," they won over enough of the coalition to secure its adoption.[54]

Although the endorsement was hardly a victory, it established Corwin once again as a prominent figure in the race for the Whig nomination. Among others, it attracted the attention of the Weed-Greeley-Seward triumvirate in New York.

The maneuverings of the three New Yorkers in the winter and spring of 1848 bewildered many northern Whigs. Weed had been among the first to recognize Taylor's potential as a candidate and to extend support. By August 1847, however, his enthusiasm for the General had cooled; in September he announced that since Old Zack's letters appeared to have been written for the purpose of showing he was not a Whig and would not accept a party nomination for the presidency, he, "being a Whig and in favor of a Whig candidate only," could not advocate Taylor's candidacy.[55] So sudden a change of position at a moment when Taylor was riding high offered much material for speculation; before long, political gossips concluded that Weed's shift had been made in order to boost Seward's chances for the vice-presidential position on a Clay ticket.[56] But there was evidence against that conclusion. Even though Clay sentiment in New York was very strong, Weed made no effort to promote or even to endorse Clay's candidacy during the whole preconvention campaign; nor did Seward show any eagerness for the vice-presidency—on any ticket.[57]

Such negative evidence could be discounted, of course, since Greeley was wildly enthusiastic about Clay, and his support could presumably

[54] Wright to McLean, 16 January 1848, Teesdale to McLean, 4, 7, 17, 19, 20 January, 1 February 1848, ibid.

[55] *Albany Evening Journal* quoted in New York *Courier,* 11 September 1847.

[56] Adger to McLean, 25 January 1848, McLean Papers; Robert Tyler to Buchanan, 18 November 1847, in Auchampaugh, *Robert Tyler,* p. 10; Baltimore *Sun,* 17 November 1847; *Boston Post,* 2 February 1848.

[57] Seward to Weed, [May 1848], in Frederic Bancroft, *Life of William H. Seward* (New York, 1900), 1: 159; Greeley to Clay, 28 April 1848, Clay Papers.

influence the selection of Seward as a running mate. But again there were indications, chiefly from well-informed opponents, that Greeley did not support Clay as fervently as his public statements would lead casual observers to believe. His purpose, it was charged, was rather to "kill off" Taylor by advocating Clay and then to drop the Kentuckian for some other candidate who would satisfy the free states' electorate better than any man from Dixie.[58] McLean's friend John Teesdale revealed that Greeley had written a letter to Governor Bebb confessing that he flaunted Clay's name from the *Tribune* masthead "in order, if possible, to prevent Taylor's nomination" and to enable the opponents of Taylor, if it were thought "inadvisable to run Clay, to unite upon . . . some other civilian."[59] Such an attitude hardly indicated a conspiracy to secure a vice-presidential post for Seward.

There were other possible explanations for the actions of Weed and Greeley. Undoubtedly, both Weed, who had supported Taylor, and Greeley, who had opposed Taylor, were concerned about how the General's nomination might affect the Whig party in the North. Taylor was essentially a slaveholders' candidate; his nomination, opposed by all the antislavery forces of the North, would certainly disrupt the Whig party. No one recognized that possibility better than New York politicians, who were watching the Democratic party in the Empire State tear itself apart over the issue of slavery in the territories and who knew that the Whig party was strongly infused with antislavery sentiment. A Taylor nomination invited political disaster for the party.

In addition, Weed and to a lesser extent Greeley were engaged in a battle for control of the Whig party in New York. At the time, Weed appeared to have a firm hand on the party helm, but his opponents were many and strong. Some of his strongest opponents, such as the editors of the New York *Courier,* were passionate Taylor men. Presumably, if the General carried the nomination and the election, these men would have enough influence under a Taylor administration to control Federal patronage in New York and to secure domination of the Whig party there.

Weed, of course, could have continued or renewed his support of Taylor and thus insured himself a place of influence in the General's administration. But even if he discounted the possibility of a party

[58] New York *Courier,* 25 January 1848. See also *Richmond Enquirer,* 31 January 1848; John Bell to William B. Campbell, 13 April, 23 May 1848, in St. George L. Sioussat, ed., "Letters of John Bell to William Campbell, 1839–1857," *Tennessee Historical Magazine* 3 (1917): 210–11; Teesdale to McLean, 23 September 1847, McLean Papers; Toombs to John Thomas, 1 May 1848, in Phillips, *Toombs, Stephens, and Cobb Correspondence,* pp. 104–5.
[59] Teesdale to McLean, 9 February 1848, McLean Papers. See also Stevenson to Clay, 19 June 1848, Clay Papers.

rupture, he must have recognized that his influence upon Taylor would have been diluted, because he would have had to share it with his opponents in New York; in that case his hold on the party would have been seriously threatened.[60]

Fears of a Whig party split, an electoral defeat in New York, and a loss of party control in that state all dictated support of some candidate other than Taylor. Since enthusiasm in New York for Clay was high, it seemed politically expedient to support a movement on his behalf. Weed did not oppose such a movement; Greeley openly endorsed it. But both must have recognized that Clay was not a winner; his support, both southern and northern, was too diffused to achieve the coalition needed for victory. They needed another candidate. The close connection of the two editors with Seward led some to the obvious conclusion that they were grooming him for the post, but most evidence of such a design appears only in the correspondence of the highly suspicious McLean men.[61]

Actually, Weed and Greeley were looking elsewhere, and their attention fastened on Ohio. A month after the state convention Greeley informed Congressmen Caleb B. Smith of Indiana and Joshua R. Giddings of Ohio that Tom Corwin was his man.[62]

At that time the choice seemed reasonable, since Corwin appeared to be the strongest northern candidate. Ohio was his without doubt: all over the state both district and county conventions were declaring him their favorite; Clay men, such as Thomas B. Stevenson, and Clay conventions, still uncertain as to Clay's intentions, indicated that Corwin was their choice if the Kentuckian retired. In Indiana John D. Defrees of the *State Journal,* although publicly supporting Taylor, disclosed that he would rather see Corwin in the presidency than any other man except Clay. New York Whigs and Massachusetts Websterians expressed similar sentiments.[63] By March, Corwin appeared to be on the crest of a rising movement. At almost the same moment, however, his candidacy collapsed. The reasons were obvious. While his prospects were good in Ohio, his following in other states was too small to swing them into line.

[60] Hints of this interpretation of the Weed-Greeley maneuvers are in Van Deusen, *Weed,* pp. 142–70; a fuller account is in R. J. Rayback, *Fillmore,* pp. 160–86.

[61] Mower to McLean, 19 April 1848, McLean Papers.

[62] Greeley to Smith, 18 February 1848, Smith Papers.

[63] Holt, "Party Politics in Ohio," 38: 267; *Pennsylvanian,* 27 March 1848; Teesdale to McLean, 6 March 1848, McLean Papers; Defrees to Smith, 20 December 1847, Stevenson to Smith, 6 March, 10 April 1848, Smith Papers; *New York Tribune,* 8 April 1848.

He was fundamentally a second-choice candidate, a condition that did not spell success.[64]

The most immediate beneficiary of Corwin's declining position was McLean, who had made advances since the Ohio State Whig Convention. In January, rumors were heard from New England that the Whigs of New Hampshire and Massachusetts, "who had evinced a partiality for Mr. Webster," would make a demonstration for McLean. By spring the *New Hampshire Statesman,* the *Salem Gazette,* the *Boston Whig,* and Governor George N. Briggs of Massachusetts were counted among his supporters, and acute observers were lending credence to reports that Vermont and Maine would join their sister states to give McLean almost the entire vote of the section after a complimentary ballot to Clay, Taylor, and Webster. Black Dan himself was said to favor such a course. Equally heartening news came from Indiana. Late in February Caleb B. Smith shifted his allegiance from Corwin to McLean; other politicians followed. In April the *Indianapolis State Journal* dropped Taylor with the caustic comment that the General had not proved himself a Whig, and it threw its support to McLean. When Quakers, Methodists, and antislavery groups hastened to add their strength to the trend, reports of a stampede to McLean among Hoosiers became highly credible.[65]

Nevertheless, the situation in Ohio remained an obstacle. McLean had made some gains in the state after the convention of 19 January, chiefly among Liberty men who, strangely, began to use his condemnation of the Mexican War as a reason for his nomination. Indeed, E. S. Hamlin of the abolitionist *Cleveland True Democrat* pressed McLean's candidacy so strenuously that Teesdale feared his support would alienate conservatives. Further gains probably were made when Jacob Brinckerhoff announced his support.[66]

On the other hand, Corwin men refused to lend their aid, even after it became apparent that their chief was out of the running. Expediency played a part in their refusal: they feared that a McLean nomination

[64] Wright to McLean, 21 February 1848, Mower to McLean, 13 March 1848, McLean Papers.

[65] Baltimore *Sun,* 31 January 1848; *Boston Post,* 2 May 1848; *New Hampshire Patriot,* 2 March 1848; *Indiana State Sentinel,* 15 April 1848; Smith to McLean, 29 March, 22 April 1848, Dowling to McLean, 17 March, 10 April 1848, Mower to McLean, 14, 25 February 1848, Defrees to McLean, 16 April 1848, John H. Sanders to McLean, 12 January 1848, John H. Bradley to McLean, 20 April 1848, McLean Papers; Bradley to Smith, 9 April 1848, Smith Papers; Dunlap Ludlow to Chase, 3 June 1848, Chase Papers.

[66] Teesdale to McLean, 12 May 1848, Chase to McLean, 26 May 1848, McLean Papers.

would defer or make impossible the election of another Ohioan for several terms. John D. Campbell made another objection: McLean's "Whiggism" was too *"uncertain—vacillating—and unreliable"* to satisfy Corwin's followers.[67]

Clay men also refused to join McLean's camp. Aside from the fact that they hoped for a Clay victory, they had other reasons for opposition, which were expressed by Thomas B. Stevenson. "My hostility to him is incurable," he declared, "because it is founded on evidences of his utter unworthiness. . . . No act of John Tyler's life is more dishonorable in my opinion, than acts *I know* of against McLean. I believe him utterly destitute of moral honor, where his ambition is involved; and as to his political principles, if you can show me they are of the Whig School, you know more than I do. . . . McLean would sacrifice the Whig cause in a moment for any chance of an *election.*"[68]

In the face of such opposition any attempt to swing these hostile elements to the Judge seemed not only futile but "preposterous." Nevertheless, the frequent outside advice, from Greeley, among others, that victory in Ohio was imperative if success was to be achieved elsewhere, moved McLean men to heroic efforts. They approached Corwin leaders such as Governor Bebb, Columbus Delano, Robert C. Schenck, and James M. Root; they attempted to convince local editors of McLean's availability; they established a state organization; they tried to set up a newspaper in Columbus; and they even asked Corwin by letter and by envoy to pledge his support to McLean.[69]

McLean's agents were completely unsuccessful with Corwin and with Corwin's followers. For a short time the Wagon Boy appeared to waver. His own preferences inclined him to Clay; if secondhand reports can be trusted, he had almost decided in February to declare for the Kentuckian as the only man who could thrust back the Taylor movement. During April 1848, however, it was reported that he would announce for McLean; on 19 May the *Lebanon Western Star,* generally regarded as Corwin's personal journal, declared for the Judge—a declaration which many regarded "as certain evidence of the Wagon Boy's conversion." A few days later, however, Stevenson informed Clay that this evidence was incorrect. The *Western Star* had acted on its own. Corwin was for Clay first and Webster second; if a civilian were not "deemed available," he would go for Scott. Evidently Corwin had not strayed from the position

[67] Campbell to Smith, 4 May 1848, Smith Papers. See also Corwin to Smith, 10 May 1848, W. H. Bennett to Smith, 8 February 1848; John Woods to Judge Leavitt, 29 February 1848, McLean Papers.

[68] Stevenson to Smith, 10 April 1848, Smith Papers.

[69] Ibid.

he had reached earlier in the year, when he had declared that he would support a McLean movement only if he were "demented" and wished "to scatter the Whig party of Ohio to the winds."[70]

Meanwhile, Corwin men had turned their attention to other candidates. At first it seemed that Corwin's considerable following would swing to Clay; in March numerous reports indicated the development of a powerful Clay movement in southern Ohio.[71] The trend was short-lived; Whigs in the northern regions of the state refused to join it, objecting to the Kentuckian's attitude toward slavery. As long as the Mexican War lasted, they accepted the position he had taken in his Lexington resolutions as sound doctrine. The annexation of New Mexico and California changed the situation; they began to demand as the price of their support an unequivocal statement of his hostility to the extension of slavery. But repeated entreaties from Ohioans failed to alter Clay's conviction that any letters on the subject would "do more harm than good."[72] Thus, at the very moment that Clay was announcing his availability and was securing the endorsement of New York's Whig caucus, Corwin men were turning away from him. The man to whom they turned was Winfield Scott.

Although General Scott's "political suicide" in the summer of 1846 had apparently ended the possibility that he would ever again be regarded seriously as a candidate, his friends were numerous, his ability was great, and his character was colorful. He could not be kept in the background for any length of time. By December 1846 some of his supporters were "beginning to hope again," and, as Teesdale informed McLean, it was beginning to look "as if he might be the most formidable competitor for the nomination, notwithstanding the evidence of gross indiscretion which displayed itself in the correspondence with Marcy."[73] Then the overwhelming force of the Taylor movement again pushed Scott out of the limelight; it even carried off some who had remained loyal through his previous trials.

But the victories Scott won at Cerro Gordo and Veracruz—in themselves much more brilliant than any Taylor had won—soon brought some who had "become seized with the Taylor mania" back into the fold,

[70] Teesdale to McLean, 12 February 1848, Mower to McLean, 12 February, 24 April 1848, Whittlesey to McLean, 22 April 1848, Chase to McLean, 20 May 1848, Miner to McLean, 20 May 1848, McLean Papers; Stevenson to Clay, 22 May 1848, Clay Papers; Stevenson to Smith, 6 March 1848, Smith Papers.

[71] Teesdale to McLean, 26 February, 2, 6 March 1848, Wright to McLean, 3 March 1848, McLean Papers.

[72] Stevenson to Clay, 8 April 1848, Clay Papers; Clay to Stevenson, 12 April 1848, in Colton, *Clay's Works*, 3: 462.

[73] Teesdale to McLean, 29 December 1846, McLean Papers.

and a few influential papers in Pennsylvania and Ohio, among them the *Harrisburgh Telegraph,* raised his name to their mastheads.[74] At the time, close observers reported that Scott could not hope to supersede Taylor, for the simple reason that his victories were no more "than [what] a majority of the people expected from him, as a scientific military leader," while Taylor's escapades had all the appearance of miracles.[75] Nevertheless, the signs of growing Scott sentiment during the latter part of 1847 indicated that the impossible might be achieved.

What made Scott potentially important was the location of his strength in the more populous states of the Union. From both New York and Pennsylvania came reports of a steady movement in his direction among elements that previously had been silent; it was a movement based on the recognition that Scott was a greater military figure than Taylor, and on the fact, pointed out by Greeley, that Scott was "not afraid" to avow his Whiggery and knew what a tariff was.[76] His candidacy also showed signs of vigor in several Clay strongholds; the *New York Express* and the *Pittsburgh Gazette* designated him as their first choice after Clay. At the same time, Scott secured the approval of Websterian journals such as the *Boston Transcript;* Whigs of the Western Reserve also began to show a marked interest in his possibilities.[77]

In late April 1848, after northern politicians had had time to take stock of the preconvention situation and to start considering compromise, Scott's candidacy burst again into full bloom. Teesdale, making another tour of Ohio, discovered that Corwin's followers had gone over to General Scott almost en masse and that followers of Clay and even of McLean had succumbed to the lure which Scott's growing military reputation and his lack of political commitments presented.[78] In Indiana, generally regarded as certain for McLean, friends of Caleb B. Smith urged him to drop the Judge, whose nomination would mean "death to [Smith's] future hopes," in favor of Scott. In Pennsylvania the Whig State Convention named an avowed Scott man, Acting Governor William F. Johnston, as one of the delegates at large to the national meeting;

---

[74] Harvey to McLean, 11 May 1847, ibid.; *North Carolina Standard,* 26 May 1847; Baltimore *Sun,* 5 May 1847; *Newark Advertiser,* 19 May 1847.

[75] Harvey to McLean, 13 June 1847, McLean Papers.

[76] Greeley to Clay, 30 November 1847, Clay Papers.

[77] *Washington Union,* 1 February 1848; Ullman to Clay, 12 July 1847, Clay Papers; Harvey to McLean, 28 October 1847, McLean Papers; *Charleston Mercury,* 25 November 1847; Detroit *Free Press,* 2 October 1847; *Nashville Union,* 25 May 1847; Dan R. Tilden to Smith, 6 February 1848, Smith Papers.

[78] Leavitt to McLean, 23 February, 4 May 1848, Teesdale to Miner, 26 February, 9, 31 March 1848, Teesdale to McLean, 23 March, 12, 26, 29 April, 2 May 1848, McLean Papers.

the "most influential Whigs in the state," firm Clay men and old friends of McLean, suddenly deserted their former favorites and announced a preference for Scott. Similar movements appeared in New York among congressmen such as Weed's friend Washington Hunt and among journals such as the *Rochester Democrat*. Even among Maryland and North Carolina Whigs there was evidence of sentiment for Scott. By mid-May the opinion among the habitués of the nation's capital, who had the impression that the "whole West" was ablaze with Scott fever, was that he would become the "northern" candidate for the presidency at the Whig National Convention.[79]

But Scott had two major obstacles in his way—Weed and Greeley. Neither looked with favor on his candidacy. While Weed remained quiet, the editor of the *Tribune,* though recognizing that Scott was the most formidable of northern candidates in the field, acted to prevent his nomination. Greeley circulated among New York Whigs a copy of a pro-Nativist letter which Scott had written for a Baltimore newspaper under the pseudonym of "Americus" in 1844. Party leaders promptly recognized the potency of such a weapon in the hands of their opponents; in New York the Scott fever cooled noticeably.[80]

Greeley also took steps to bring out McLean to counter Scott's influence. In mid-April Mower, who seemed finally to have wormed his way into the confidence of the editor, disclosed that Greeley was moving "everything in his power" to secure the nomination of the Judge as a compromise candidate after Taylor and Clay had "used themselves up," and that he was even trying to patch up an old quarrel between McLean's chief editorial supporter, Judge Wright, and Weed in order to obtain Weed's assistance—"equal to that of two states"—in the struggle. Other sources disclosed that Greeley was also using his influence among Websterians and that he would swing the majority of the New York delegation into McLean's column at the convention just as soon as Clay could be dropped.[81]

[79] D. Maguire to Smith, 6 May 1848, E. W. McGaughey to Smith, 23 May 1848, Smith Papers; Mower to McLean, 19 April 1848, Darragh to McLean, 2 March 1848, Harvey to McLean, 12 April 1848, Smith to McLean, 22 April 1848, McLean Papers; Morehead to Clay, 3 May 1848, Clay Papers; Hunt to Weed, May 1848, in Weed, *Autobiography,* p. 461; *Cleveland Plain Dealer,* 18 March 1848; *North American,* 15 March 1848; *Albany Atlas,* 13 April 1848; *Boston Atlas,* 23 March 1848; Detroit *Free Press,* 25 May 1848.
[80] Greeley to Clay, 28 April 1848, Clay Papers; Dowling to McLean, 26 April, 1 May 1848, Whittlesey to McLean, 11 May 1848, McLean Papers.
[81] Mower to McLean, 20 April 1848, Smith to McLean, 1, 28 May 1848, Teesdale to McLean, 10 May 1848, McLean Papers; "Theodore" to Smith, 9 May 1848, Smith Papers.

When the Whig delegates began to gather for their national convention in Philadelphia in June, the result was clearly in doubt. Taylor's strength had not changed since mid-April; he could count on about 90 or 100 votes, primarily from the slave states. Clay's support still numbered 80 or 90 votes, though not all of them were as firm as they had earlier appeared. Corwin had faded. Webster had little chance. McLean had no firm base; his hopes rested on the unsecured Indiana delegation, on the Websterians, and on the possibility of aid from an unstable Greeley. Only Scott had developed strength since early spring, but he could count on only about 50 votes, not enough to spell victory.

Chapter Ten

The Rumble of
Antislavery Revolt

While Democratic and Whig aspirants battled for convention delegates in the spring of 1848, antislavery elements in both parties were also developing plans of action. New York's Barnburners produced the most spectacular series of events by indulging in a bitter feud with the Hunkers over the legitimate method of choosing delegates to the national convention.

After they had adjourned at Herkimer in October 1847, the Barnburners issued a call for a state convention to meet in the same city on 22 February to name a delegation which would represent New York at Baltimore. The Barnburner-controlled legislative caucus of the Democratic party immediately recognized that the call was an innovation and was subject to attack on "legal" grounds. Accordingly, the caucus summoned the convention to meet instead at Utica on 16 February. The managers of the Herkimer meeting, quickly recognizing the problem, accepted this second summons.[1]

The Hunkers arose in great wrath to denounce the call as unlawful, pointing out that the Syracuse convention had adopted resolutions which provided for the summoning of state conventions by the party's central committee and for the election of delegates by congressional districts. A "handful of legislators . . . representing only 15 of 59 counties" could not presume to overrule the decisions of the party's sovereign body. The *Albany Argus* insisted that the summons to Utica was "a design to endorse the Herkimer treachery," a scheme "to divide the democratic party" and give victory to the Whigs.[2]

In mid-December 1847 the state central committee named at Syracuse issued a call for another convention to be held at Albany on 26 January.[3] This action brought a counterattack from the Barnburners, who with the *Buffalo Republic* of 8 January denounced the call as a "brazen-faced usurpation of power, without parallel in the history of the Democratic party of the state," and pointed out that for sixteen years state conventions had been called by the caucus and, what was more, that the central committee which issued the summons had no legal standing since another appointed in 1846 was still in office.

It was in this spirit that two conventions met in Albany and in Utica to proclaim their differences. The Hunkers, numbering ninety-three delegates from only four-fifths of the counties in the state, drew up an address that made reconciliation impossible.

The hostility of the Barnburners, they maintained, had its origin in the destruction of their grip upon state patronage by the Hunker-supported constitutional convention of 1846. Revenge on the purehearted men, the Hunkers, who had sought to return control of the state to the people had become the Barnburners' object. They were seeking to accomplish that revenge by deserting the party they no longer ruled, "because it refused to adopt the Wilmot Proviso," although they knew the measure would be carried out in time without the political agitation that threatened to shatter the foundations of the Union. Barnburners also knew that the principles they maintained would not be accepted by the coming Democratic National Convention. It was obvious, therefore, that they hoped to be cast out of that body in order to "claim the honor of political martyrdom" and make themselves "more formidable for mischief in the approaching great struggle between the democratic party and its enemies." They had, in fact, become members of the Whig party, the Hunkers claimed; as such, no true Democrat could uphold them.[4]

Three weeks later at Utica the Barnburners issued their reply. Making little attempt to justify their movement, they insisted that they were Democrats in the truest meaning of the word. They favored a strict construction of the constitutions of the Union and of New York; they were determined to uphold "the independent sovereignty of the several states in all their reserved rights"; they were pledged to guard "against any encroachments by the General Government upon the rights of the individual"; they were resolved to maintain the sacred principles of "free trade, freedom from public debt, freedom of worship, freedom of speech, and freedom of the press." They were also resolved to protect the independent treasury, to battle against any measure designed to distribute among the states the proceeds from the sale of public lands, to

---

[1] *Albany Atlas,* 19 November, 17 December 1847.
[2] *Albany Argus,* 22, 27 November, 1 December 1847.
[3] Ibid., 18 December 1847.
[4] *Niles' Register* 73 (19 February 1848) : 290-91.

keep the public domain out of the hands of speculators, to maintain peace with all the world so long as it could be maintained "without a sacrifice of national character," and to aid in "a vigorous prosecution of the existing war with Mexico."

They also announced a determination to stand by the Wilmot Proviso. At the same time, they declared a willingness to recognize the differences of opinion within the party and denied any desire to prescribe the Proviso as a a test in the coming presidential canvass. Nevertheless, they warned prospective candidates that any attempt to comply with southern tests—the Alabama Platform—would earn their hostility.

"The Democratic party of New York," they concluded, "moves on without fetters upon its action that selfish and sinister influences have hitherto caused. It invites to its ranks the just, the virtuous, and the true. It will welcome them to a standard which is unfurled after rare defeats, with redoubled energy and the hope of more enduring ascendency. On it are inscribed 'Free trade, free labor, free soil, free speech, and free men.' . . . We should be glad to unite with our brethren of other States on these terms."[5]

However, the Barnburners recognized that they needed more than brave words to create a movement; they needed a candidate to rally the faithful. They carefully examined the possibilities.

With unerring judgment they recognized early in 1848 that the leading aspirant for the Democratic nomination was Lewis Cass, a man whom many of them detested not only because he had helped defeat Van Buren at the 1844 convention, but also because, as the *Buffalo Republic* expressed it, he was "a Senatorial vaulter" who expressed opinions one day only "to abandon them on the next," a man who "seemed to delight in frequent exhibitions of ground and lofty tumbling for the amusement of the Southern portion of the Confederacy," a man unworthy of the presidency since his selfish ambitions had "induced him to abandon the cause of freedom, and . . . enlist on the side of the propagandists of slavery."[6]

They gave less thought to Buchanan. Some regarded him as one who had taken a hand in Van Buren's defeat at the 1844 convention, but more important was the prevailing suspicion that the Pennsylvanian was

[5] O. C. Gardiner, *Great Issue* (New York, 1848), pp. 75–90, 92–94.

[6] *Buffalo Republic*, 7 January 1848. Similar expressions came from the antislavery Democrats of Pennsylvania, Ohio, Illinois, Wisconsin, and Michigan (*Albany Atlas*, 3 February, 3, 22 May 1848; Preston King to Welles, 31 January 1848, Welles Papers; *Mobile Register*, 19 May 1848; Smith, *Liberty and Free Soil Parties*, pp. 121–23; Holt, "Party Politics in Ohio," 38: 272–73; *Racine Advocate*, 2 February 1848).

an earnest opponent of the Wilmot Proviso, that he was "in favour of the extension of Slavery in order to bring Slave labour in competition with Free Labour," which, among other things, would have a "bad effect among the working classes."[7]

Vice President Dallas was also a possible candidate. It was true that he was weaker in Pennsylvania than had been expected. At the same time, he was a sterling Democrat; his deciding vote on the Walker Tariff had confirmed that reputation. Moreover, he had won the favor of such antislavery champions as John Wentworth and, like the Barnburners, he appeared to have earned the hostility of President Polk. On the other hand, his Pittsburgh speech had been greeted somewhat too enthusiastically by southerners.[8]

Levi Woodbury's name loomed large in the Barnburners' considerations. He was favored in New England, he had earned the support of isolated groups of antislavery men, and he had taken no public position on the slavery issue. At the same time, there were nagging rumors and reports which indicated that he had embraced the Alabama Platform.[9]

Barnburners also considered six lesser lights, five of them surrounded by some halo of military glory. Most prominent was Secretary of the Treasury Walker.[10] Although he was a Mississippian and had led the southern contingent at Baltimore against Van Buren, he had been born in Pennsylvania, where he was closely connected through George M. Dallas with the old Jacksonians. He had conducted the complicated problems of wartime finance with considerable ability, and he had not been involved in any of the squabbles that had divided the party.

Among the military figures was Sam Houston, senator from Texas. An old-time Jacksonian with considerable experience in administration, the hero of the movement for Texas independence, he appeared a peculiarly available choice—capable, through skillful dramatization of his eccentricities, of offsetting the appeal of General Taylor. Two other southern war chiefs, William O. Butler of Kentucky and John A. Quitman of Mississippi, whose names were more often associated with the vice-presidency, were also available. Both had excellent war records,

[7] John McGrath to Buchanan, 19 March 1848, Buchanan Papers.

[8] *Buffalo Republic,* 29 November 1847; Baltimore *Sun,* 17 April 1848; Philadelphia *Times,* 18 May 1848. The Barnburners apparently never recognized that Dallas was part of the effort to prevent Van Buren's nomination in 1844. Although carefully hidden, the Dallas faction's anti–Van Buren maneuverings between 1841 and 1844 can be discerned. Some hint of this movement is in Shenton, *Walker,* pp. 33–49; and Sellers, *Polk,* pp. 53–55, 61–66, 76–92.

[9] Baltimore *Sun,* 10, 14 February 1848; *Washington Union,* 24 February 1848.

[10] *Pennsylvanian,* 20 January 1848.

and Butler owned a name famous in the annals of the nation's military history. Both had civil experience, Butler in Congress and Quitman as chancellor and acting governor of Mississippi. It was rumored, moreover, that Butler was opposed to the further extension of slavery.[11]

From the free states there were Franklin Pierce of New Hampshire and General William Worth of New York. Pierce had served ten years in Congress, had countless friends throughout the Union, and had taken a distinguished part in the war. Not very colorful, he was nevertheless a possible compromise candidate. Worth was handicapped by a total lack of civil employment; he had lived all his adult life in army garrisons. But the brillance of his Mexican War career—probably more brilliant than commonly realized, for he was the real "Hero of Buena Vista"— could easily be used to drown any criticism. His residence in New York, where he had early won followers as prominent as Moses Beach of the *New York Sun,* was not to be forgotten.[12]

However, none of these minor candidates was actually available. Walker, because of precarious health, declined to run and evidently lent what influence he had to his relative Dallas; Houston had few outright supporters and would have to combat a charge of bigamy; Butler showed no desire to enter the race; Quitman had been a nullificationist; Pierce was involved in Woodbury's candidacy; and Worth had injured his reputation by becoming involved in an intrigue to discredit General Scott.[13]

During the month before the national convention Barnburners also directed their attention to men such as Thomas Hart Benton, William Allen, and Henry Dodge, former governor of Wisconsin Territory and more recently a United States senator. Of these, Benton was the most attractive because, as the Baltimore *Sun* maintained, he "would take the democratic vote in New York in preference to anyone. He would take all the votes that Silas Wright could have got, had he lived. He would stand in Mr. Wright's place, successor to his principles, and with even more than his popularity."[14] Allen had the approving friendship of Benton, Blair, and Van Buren, all of whom believed that he was "radical in his

[11] *Niles' Register* 72 (5 June 1847): 210; Coleman, *Crittenden,* 1: 249, 257; Henry Gourdin to Calhoun, 4 February 1848, in Jameson, *Calhoun Correspondence,* p. 1160.

[12] *Chicago Democrat,* 5 October 1847; *New Hampshire Patriot,* 20 April 1848; *Baltimore Clipper,* 16 August 1847; Baltimore *Sun,* 17 May 1848.

[13] *Mississippian,* 18 February 1848; Nichols, *Pierce,* p. 174; *Baltimore Clipper,* 15 May 1848.

[14] Hammersley to Welles, 8 November 1847, Welles Papers; Baltimore *Sun,* 28 April 1848.

politics . . . and honest"; they had disclosed a willingness to put their influence behind his candidacy.[15] Sentiment for Dodge was chiefly western, finding expression in the columns of such journals as the *Chicago Democrat,* the *Iowa Sentinel,* and the *Cincinnati Signal.* Barnburner papers such as the *Buffalo Republic* approved of him because of "his well known adherence to the radical principles of his party."[16] None of these men, however, revealed any interest in a movement in his favor. Benton repeatedly declined to allow his name to be considered, and there were rumors that all three had decided to climb upon the Cass bandwagon. Bewildered and desperate, Barnburner leaders turned to Van Buren. Would he allow his name to be used at the convention?

The question came as no surprise to Van Buren. Ever since the death of Silas Wright, many Barnburners, aware that their lack of a leader had seriously weakened their position within the Democratic party, had concluded that it might be necessary to thrust Van Buren's name into the contest. A radical Democrat, possessing a name still potent in party ranks, thoroughly respected for his political acumen, and disliked by many southerners, he appeared to be a logical leader of a northern Democratic movement, particularly after it became known that he was in favor of the Wilmot Proviso. He had revealed that fact to his closest friends early in 1847; later in the year he had informed Peter V. Daniel of Virginia, associate justice of the United States Supreme Court, that Silas Wright in his Titus letter had "described the position I occupy and the views I entertain on the subject in terms more felicitous than any I could compose."[17]

In late 1847 many Barnburners, former followers of Silas Wright, and antislavery Democrats in other northern states began to announce that they would support the ex-president at the Baltimore convention.[18] But Van Buren had little desire to step into his dead friend's shoes. When Samuel P. Collins, editor of the *Wilkes Barre Pennsylvania Farmer,* asked permission to place him before the public, he refused the request.[19] Nevertheless, his name continued to be mentioned. Old and

---

[15] Van Buren to Blair, 6 November, 29 December 1847, Blair Papers; James W. Taylor to John Van Buren, 18 April 1848, Van Buren Papers.

[16] *Buffalo Republic,* 21 April 1848.

[17] Van Buren to Peter V. Daniel, 13 November 1847, Van Buren Papers. See also Butler to Van Buren, 28 November 1847.

[18] Maynard to Van Buren, 30 August 1847, Wilmot to Van Buren, 6 October 1847, Radebaugh and William Need to Van Buren, 18 December 1847, ibid.; *Buffalo Republic,* 9 September, 8 October 1847; Baltimore *Sun,* 23 September 1847.

[19] *Niles' Register* 73 (13 November 1847): 172. See also Van Buren to Wilmot, 22 October 1847, Van Buren Papers.

influential friends such as Frank Blair, Gideon Welles, John M. Niles, Marcus Morton, former attorney general of Pennsylvania Henry Simpson, William Allen, former United States senator from Ohio Benjamin Tappan, Thomas Hart Benton, former United States senator from North Carolina Bedford Brown, and even Senator Bagby of Alabama indicated approval. In the spring of 1848 various Barnburners, among them Senator John A. Dix, began to plead with him to reconsider his decision,[20] but it was not until his son John addressed him that Van Buren made a reply.

John Van Buren's letter to his father was written shortly before the Barnburner delegation was scheduled to gather for a conference on strategy in New York City on the eve of the Baltimore convention. Its tone clearly revealed the Barnburners' sense of desperation. The delegation, he pointed out, had to have a candidate; if it did not, "you, [James S.] Wadsworth, [Azariah C.] Flagg & other irregular regulars" would vote for the nominee of the Baltimore convention.

> My notion is that [Preston] King, Wadsworth & Dr. [John P.] Beekman should advise [the delegation] to present your name on their own responsibility as the choice of the democracy of this state. Claim the candidate for New York . . . & if defeated assume that the proviso is made the test of exclusion against a man who has said nothing [sic] on the subject . . . bolt the convention if it is rejected & nominate old Taylor at Utica in the fall if he answers my letter satisfactorily . . .[21] or nominate any honorable democrat who is willing to run. . . . Your agency in the matter would be merely a letter to Dr. Beekman reaffirming all your positions, but responding to his inquiry whether notwithstanding all this you would feel at liberty to decline if nominated at Baltimore, that you would not.[22]

Van Buren was ready with his reply;[23] it was foremost a lesson in practical politics. Until recently, he pointed out, northern Democrats had not understood that the "slave question" had an "unavoidable tendency" to "break the party as a national one." Nor had they recognized the need of raising the issue. As a result the South had been able "to turn Wilmot

[20] John A. Dix to Van Buren, 7 April 1848, Niles to Van Buren, 18 April 1848, Van Buren Papers.

[21] The use of General Taylor's name was probably suggested by James W. Taylor of the *Cincinnati Signal* (J. W. Taylor to John Van Buren, 18 April 1848, ibid.).

[22] John Van Buren to Martin Van Buren, 30 April 1848, ibid.

[23] Martin Van Buren to John Van Buren, 3 May 1848, ibid. See also my article, "Martin Van Buren's Desire for Revenge in the Campaign of 1848," *Mississippi Valley Historical Review* 40 (March 1954) : 707–16.

and King's proposition ag[ainst] them and their friends in most of the free states." But this adverse situation had been overcome by the Barn-burners' more temperate speeches. "The calm, dispassionate and friendly spirit in which the discussion has been carried, the clearness with which the necessity of its being now raised, the emphatic demonstration of the constitutionality and justice of your positions, and the overriding con-cern which has been manifested for the integrity of the Party as long as that could be secured with honor have all served to turn the tables upon your opponents."

Van Buren insisted:

> To keep public sentiment on this course, to silence the South and bring the free States in line with N York for the future (the great and only practicable object) there must be no departure by our Delegates at Baltimore from the course which has proved so suc-cessful thus far. A single rash and unadvised step which would give the Democracy of the other free States reason to assume that you are indifferent to the general success of the party, that you used this subject for private ends, to revenge past injuries or indulge personal piques might be fatal to your usefulness and future success.

Then Van Buren turned his attention to the suggestion "of having the friends you name bring me forward upon their own responsibility but backed by a declaration from me that if nominated I would not decline." He declared that

> nothing could be more cruel to me or more destructive to the standing you and your friends in this State have acquired. Can you possibly suppose that the declaration that they did this on their own responsibility only and without previous knowledge on my part would gain credence in any quarters? . . . The whole country would with one voice set it down as an idle pretense. . . . It would satisfy all that your enemies did you no more than justice when they charged upon you insincerity in regard to the slave question and that you had only let the cat out of the bag when she could no longer be concealed without destruction to the object to obtain which she had been bagged. Dismiss this idea therefore from your mind and suppress it if you find that it has entered the mind of others.
>
> The course . . . of political agitation in this State for the last four or five years has been to render my re-election impossible. . . . When this has become to all appearances certain, it would be ex-ceedingly unjust to me to drag my name into the canvass for any purpose. Be assured once for all that I have not the slightest desire to occupy that place again, but a great deal of unavoidable

repugnance. I owe my party friends a debt of gratitude and am willing to do any consistent act to advance their views, but upon this I feel a degree of delicacy about my position and am so well satisfied with it as it stands that I cannot consent to have it frittered away by experiment.

As Van Buren recognized, his reply did not solve the Barnburner delegation's problems. What were they to do if their delegation were refused admission into the convention? That something of this sort would be attempted they had deduced from the statements of such men as Yancey, who, in an address at Montgomery in January 1848, had urged southerners to attend the national convention if only to unseat northern Provisoists, and from the tone of Cass journals such as the Detroit *Free Press,* which demanded the ejection of the New York radicals from "the counsels of the party."[24] What, moreover, should be their reaction to any attempt to seat both delegations from New York— a formula suggested by several southern, western, and Pennsylvania newspapers? Supposing that they were admitted and that an anti-Provisoist were nominated, were they to give him their support?

To all these problems Van Buren gave careful attention and lengthy replies. He advised the members of the Barnburner delegation to prepare themselves with the facts necessary to show their right to admission and to present their claims "with dignity and force and in a spirit which shall not evince on the one hand a craving desire for admission or on the other such a show of indifference as will give countenance to the imputation that you are bent upon the dissolution of the party."

If the convention either refused them admission or sought to neutralize it by also admitting the Hunker delegates or by imposing any condition which would place the Barnburners "on an inferior footing," they should "have nothing further to do with the Convention—make an address to their constituents placing this rejection distinctly upon the ground of opposition to the extension of Slavery to free territories, disavow all connection with the nomination that is made and recommend the selection of a State Candidate. . . . Then take Genl Taylor if he is in a state to be taken by you, or some other person."

If, on the other hand, the delegates were admitted on "an equal footing," they should give their support to the preliminary resolutions which had been normal at previous conventions. However, if any unusual resolution were proposed, encouraging disunity in New York or raising "a suspicion that new security ought to be given for our fidelity

[24] *Albany Atlas,* 22 January 1848; Detroit *Free Press,* 29 April 1848.

to the nomination," such a movement should be met with an additional resolution "calling for a distinct disavowal of the ground taken by the Alabama, Virginia, Georgia and Florida Conventions."

If the convention got "amicably to business," the Barnburner delegates would have a "difficult and delicate duty to perform." They knew that Cass, Buchanan, Dallas, and Woodbury would be the leading candidates. If they were "unwilling to unite in recommending to the support of the people any one of them, . . . they should in good faith . . . avow their determination in this regard" before the convention made a choice.

However, Van Buren made clear, "I would not recommend that course." Instead, he suggested, as each of the "objectionable" names was brought forward, "I would state to the Convention without hesitation the objections to these Gentlemen, and the . . . certainty that neither of them could possibly get the vote of this [state]." Three men, Cass, Buchanan, and Dallas, had submitted "to the test imposed by Southern States"; the Utica convention had declared that it could not support those who made such a submission. The fourth candidate, Woodbury, had probably done the same thing in "more objectionable form." He was the candidate of South Carolina; however, it would be better to have "the S[outh] Carolinian himself than the echo of his State in the person of a Northern man."

The delegates could add that if a "fresh man" not implicated in the agitation were wanted, they could give him the vote of the state; if called upon, they could name "Benton, Shunk, Dodge, or Gov [Hugh J.] Anderson of Maine."

If with this "full knowledge" the convention persisted in nominating one of the objectionable candidates, Van Buren continued, "our delegates ought . . . in fairness submit to the nomination, unite in recommending it to the support of the people and turn the responsibility for the loss of the election to those who make it."

There was one final point. The delegates had to be prepared for "the renomination of Mr. Polk." If that occurred, they had to be ready "to leave the Convention in a body"; their determination on that score had to be "openly announced." Polk's renomination stood upon "far different ground" from other nominations because it involved considerations "of State character and State feelings" which could not be "compromised or overlooked." His renomination would have to be regarded as the culmination "of a design entertained at least as far back as the organization of his Cabinet." It would be "an act of bad faith, dishonorable and forever degrading to the . . . Democratic Party to which its supporters in N York can never consent to be made a party." Moreover, there was another reason for New York to object to Polk. Among Barnburners there were "not ten out of a thousand" who did not attribute the "dissensions in the Democratic ranks in this State to the action of Mr. Polk." They were convinced that his actions in regard to them were taken in "the full belief" that New York would present Silas Wright as a candidate to succeed him, and that his actions were intended to weaken Wright's position "and the power of his friends." They had refrained from pressing upon the country the "injustice" which had been done them, chiefly because they were unwilling to provoke political distractions during wartime. But if Polk were nominated, they would have "no alternative but to withdraw from the Convention and sustain their belief . . . before the country by such means as are in their power. Justice to the State and justice to the memory of that departed worthy imperiously require that the friends of Silas Wright would discharge this sacred duty without regard to the consequences."

Van Buren's advice apparently met with the instant approval of Barnburner leaders; indeed, it probably voiced their own judgment, hitherto unspoken for fear that it would have seemed too rash. Backed by the calm and considered views of their old chieftain, it became a course of action to be announced to the nation.[25] Shortly after Van Buren's letter reached his son, Barnburner newspapers began to warn the party that revolt was possible if their delegates did not receive complete recognition. The *Buffalo Republic* announced that either exclusion from the convention or a failure to reject the "conservative disorganizers" would bring action demonstrating that Barnburner rights could not "be foully wronged with impunity."[26] Moreover, failure to nominate an acceptable candidate would compel New York to present its own nominee and might even provide the impetus, according to the *New York Globe*, that would "LEAD TO THE FORMATION OF THE THIRD PARTY" already threatening in other quarters.[27]

The third-party movement into which Barnburners warned they might be forced to merge had been developing all through the early months of 1848. The obvious ringleader was Chase, who, despite the defeat of his

[25] Whether the Barnburner delegation, even if it had been admitted as New York's sole delegation, would have supported Cass as Van Buren recommended remains problematical. One of Buchanan's informants in New York City reported on 13 May 1848, after Van Buren's letter reached his son but before the meeting of the Barnburner delegation, that the Barnburners "are determined to defeat Gen. Cass if he is nominated by the Baltimore convention. They are sworn to do this." He also indicated that he was *"astonished* to hear them go on about Cass" (J. P. Brawley to Buchanan, 13 May 1848, Buchanan Papers).

[26] *Buffalo Republic,* 13, 20 May 1848.

[27] *New York Globe* quoted in *Albany Argus,* 19 May 1848.

plans at the Liberty party convention, had never given up his scheme for a great Wilmot Proviso league. Coincident and subsequent developments served to strengthen his determination to push his original plans to their conclusion. Something of his attitude was revealed in a letter he sent to Sumner in December 1847. He suggested that there was great likelihood that "the friends of freedom" would be "tricked out of the fruits of their labors by dextrous management of the Presidential Canvass." Efforts would be made "to keep both parties together upon their old platforms" and to select candidates acceptable to slaveholders. Taylor, a slaveholder himself, was the leading Whig candidate. Cass and Woodbury, who would "give any desired pledge to the Slaveholders," were the leading Democrats. While there was considerable opposition to these men, it was hardly powerful enough to secure nominations for other candidates. Proslavery nominations seemed inevitable. What could be done to capture the elements whom these nominations would alienate? Chase asked, "Cannot a great convention of all antislavery men be held at Pittsburgh, say next May or June, and put a ticket in nomination which will at all events receive votes enough to carry the nominee into the House, with a reasonable fair prospect of their election by the people in 1852? I have a good deal of faith in a movement of this kind."[28]

That a coalition movement would find support in major party ranks was readily apparent. In New Hampshire a coalition had already formed under the leadership of Hale. In Maine, Whigs and abolitionists had combined to carry the state legislature in 1846, and it was reasonable to believe that such success would not be easily forgotten. In Connecticut an ominous quiet, engendered, as many believed, by the feeling "that the next Presidential canvass would produce a new organization and make friends out of old opponents," seemed to foretell a willingness to join an antislavery coalition.[29] Sumner was certain the Barnburners could also be counted upon. "I have assurances on which I rely," he wrote Giddings in November 1847, "that they are in *earnest*. Preston King says that he does not care whether the presidential candidate is a Whig or a Democrat, *but he must be a Wilmot Proviso man*." Besides, there was evidence that John Quincy Adams had received a letter from Albany asking him to join with Van Buren "in a call for an antislavery convention to nominate a Northern candidate."[30] In Ohio, Whigs were openly threat-

---

[28] Chase to Sumner, 2 December 1847, in *Chase Correspondence,* pp. 126–27. See also Chase to Sumner, 22 September 1847, 19 February 1848, pp. 123, 129.

[29] Hammersley to Welles, 4 July 1847, Welles Papers.

[30] Sumner to Giddings, 1 November 1847, in Julian, *Giddings,* p. 212. Later it was admitted that Van Buren had not authorized such a movement (Sumner to Giddings, 1 December 1847, p. 214).

ening to cut party ties rather than become "accessory to the extension of slavery."[31] In Indiana, local meetings were demanding that a great national convention, to be called the "people's association," be summoned to consider the claims of various aspirants for the presidency and to select the one upon whom the "whole antislavery strength" could be united.[32]

The Macedonians would prove hostile, but they had already indicated their dislike for the regular Hale-King ticket. Their second meeting was held late in January 1848 at Auburn, New York. After a long session of fervent speeches which indiscriminately damned the Liberty party, religious organizations, and all mankind for recreancy to the principles of humanity and which urged antislavery men to become "slavestealers" if they could do nothing else for the cause, they readopted the Nineteen Articles and renominated Gerrit Smith, with the Reverend Charles E. Foote of Michigan as his running mate in place of Elihu Burritt. A third meeting was called to meet in Rochester in June.[33] The Macedonians were already lost; their absence from an antislavery coalition would hardly be noticed.

There might also be objections from Liberty party diehards, but the mass of Liberty men could be expected to concur wholeheartedly in the movement. Even Hale, Chase believed, would not stand in the way, for it was quite possible that he might become the antislavery nominee.[34]

A canvass of the situation in Ohio early in the spring of 1848 revealed that both Whigs and Democrats were anxious to see some movement made before the meeting of the national conventions; as one of Chase's agents pointed out, they wished to force the nomination of a man favorable to "the free territory issue."[35] Therefore, on 17 May 1848 Chase himself issued a call, backed by the signatures of three thousand men from all parties, for a "Free Territory Convention" in Columbus on 21 June.[36]

[31] Cleveland True Democrat, 10 January 1848; Smith, Liberty and Free Soil Parties, p. 127.

[32] Cincinnati Herald, 9 February 1848.

[33] Wilson, Slave Power, 2: 112–13. See also Goodell, Macedonian Address, pp. 3–5, 13. At the June meeting Smith and Foote were again endorsed (Niles' Register 74 [5 July 1848] : 8).

[34] Chase to Sumner, 2 December 1847, in Chase Correspondence, p. 127; Cincinnati Herald, 19 April 1848.

[35] George W. Ells to Chase, 8 April 1848, Chase Papers.

[36] Cincinnati Herald, 17 May 1848. Objections to the call came chiefly from antislavery men who were backing McLean. Their opposition was explained by William Miner: "Suppose Judge McLean to be the nominee of the Whig convention. The meeting must either adopt or reject him. If they adopt him, that instant he loses all hopes of Southern support, without which no Whig can be elected. . . . If

Meanwhile, plans for a similar convention were being developed by the Conscience Whigs in Boston.[37] In late 1847 various Conscience Whigs held discussions with Liberty party leaders and learned that the two groups could work together. With a watchful eye on events developing between the Barnburners and the Hunkers in New York, several Conscience Whigs entered the district contests to elect delegates to the Philadelphia convention. The results and the political maneuvers that followed were disappointing; they revealed that some potential supporters of a Provisoist position were tying their fortunes to Daniel Webster's nearly hopeless candidacy and that some Websterians, among them the *Boston Atlas,* were beginning to slip into the Taylor camp. The future became immediately obvious: Taylor would be nominated; therefore preparations for a reaction to his nomination were necessary. Encouraged by Chase, eight men (Charles Francis Adams, Stephen C. Phillips, Charles Sumner, E. Rockwood Hoar, Edward L. Keyes, Francis W. Bird, Henry Wilson, and Edward Walcutt) met in the editorial offices of the *Boston Whig* on 27 May to map out a campaign.[38] They decided that if the Philadelphia convention named Taylor "or any candidate not opposed to the extension of slavery," an "organized opposition" should at once be started with a call for a statewide meeting of Provisoists at Worcester.[39]

Thus, before the national conventions met, the groundwork had been laid for revolt. Barnburners in New York still appeared slightly hopeful that the delegates in Baltimore would prove amenable to reason. They were prepared, in return for recognition as the legitimate delegation from the Empire State, to allow the Democracy almost full latitude in nominating any candidate except Polk, provided always that no southern test were applied. For the sake of party unity they would not press their Provisoist demands. At the same time, they were mentally prepared to revolt if their minimum conditions were not satisfied. Conscience Whigs were likewise ready to remain with their party. Their support, however, was contingent upon the nomination of an antiextensionist—a harder

---

the . . . convention reject our nominee then we lose N. York and perhaps Ohio" (Miner to Chase, 22 May 1848, Chase Papers).

[37] The latest accounts of the developments among Conscience Whigs, all substantially the same, are in Frank O. Gatell, " 'Conscience and Judgment': The Bolt of the Massachusetts Conscience Whigs," *Historian* 20 (1959): 18–25 (hereafter cited as "Conscience and Judgment"); Donald, *Sumner,* pp. 140–69; and Duberman, *Adams,* pp. 134–38.

[38] Chase to Sumner, 25 March 1848, Chase Papers.

[39] Wilson, *Slave Power,* 2: 124–25; Pierce, *Sumner,* 3: 165.

condition than the Barnburners imposed, a condition which few expected to be met. Meanwhile, in Ohio, Salmon P. Chase prepared for what he considered inevitable—an organization to spearhead the antislavery movement which would spring from the reactions to the national conventions meeting at Baltimore and Philadelphia.

Chapter Eleven

Baltimore & Philadelphia

In Baltimore, where "wave after wave of parched Locofocoism" began to gather at the taverns as early as 15 May, preconvention talk centered on the New York feud. Wild rumors, passed by reporters, delegates, and the ubiquitous hangers-on, filled the smoke-laden atmosphere of the city's hostelries (where many tried to sleep eight to a room): the Barnburners had patched up their quarrel with the Hunkers; they were eager to be rejected in order to go home and nominate Old Zack; Walker had signed over the Federal patronage to secure their support; Cass was trying to bag the Utica delegates with promises of lucrative positions; the Barnburners had announced that they would support Woodbury and Butler; they had agreed to aid Polk if he would restore Blair to the

editorship of the "court journal"; they would accept no one but Van Buren. And all the while, gallons of "mint-juleps, sherry cobblers and brandy-sodas" eased the arid tonsils and lifted the weary tongues of the gossipers, for whom time had suddenly ceased.[1]

Underneath this feverish atmosphere there were some real developments. Friends of Buchanan approached both the Barnburner and the Hunker delegations. What they learned was not very heartening. There appeared to be Barnburners willing to support the Pennsylvanian, but as one friend reported to him, they wanted "to *know that your friendship are* [*sic*] with them and that you will not deceive them if you are elected as they say president Polk did." The Hunkers knew only that "it would not do to nominate Gen. Cass," because his nomination would destroy the Democratic party in New York. Neither element was willing to make the shadow of a commitment.[2]

Meanwhile, the Cass forces, along with "a set of scoundrels" from Pennsylvania (presumably Dallas supporters), had gone to work on the Virginia delegation, considered safe for Buchanan. Apparently holding out the bait of a vice-presidential nomination for a Virginian, Secretary of the Navy John Y. Mason, they succeeded before the convention met in winning a majority of the oversized delegation.[3]

Woodbury's friends were also active. On the advice of Fernando Wood they apparently made no overtures to the New York factions, hoping that Woodbury's public silence on the issue of slavery would be favorably interpreted.[4] Actually, they were more concerned with the southern delegations. As the convention approached, the pressure from the South on Woodbury to make a public declaration had increased. Woodbury, however, remained cautious. The most he would do was to write a letter to Yancey. He pointed out that he had not made public his views on "any of the political questions that . . . agitated the country," because his views were already known to most people and because his official position made such publication "of doubtful propriety." He expressed regret that "my friends cannot now be satisfied after deliberate consideration as to my constitutional opinions when they have been made known on so many occasions. . . . They stand on record . . . as opinions that belong to the school of strict construction—as the opinions that hold firmly and faithfully to all the compromises of the constitution." He assured Yancey that whatever his future "post of duty" he would attempt to apply his "long cherished principles . . . with the same respect to the reserved rights of the People of the States and fidelity to the whole constitution & the whole Country" that he had shown in the past.[5]

His meaning was obvious: the South knew his views on the subject "full well," and it had to be satisfied "without a committal" which would cost northern votes. According to one correspondent who had previously despaired over the attitude of Virginia, North Carolina, Georgia, and Louisiana delegates, Woodbury's letter had "a glorious effect."[6]

On Monday, 22 May, the convention opened its sessions under the stern eye of Judge C. W. Bryce of Louisiana in the close confines of the Universalist Church.[7] Almost immediately settlement of the New York feud became the major issue. Judge Francis H. Cone of Georgia made

---

[1] *New York Tribune,* 27 May 1848.

[2] Brawley to Buchanan, 13 May 1848, Buchanan Papers.

[3] Virginia had four delegates from each district; at their caucus they agreed on the unit rule. The original vote inside the delegation was Cass, 26; Buchanan, 22; Woodbury, 20. On their second ballot Cass received a majority (Richard Pollard to Buchanan, 25 May 1848, Robert Tyler to Buchanan, 22 May 1848, ibid.; Buchanan to Tyler, 13 July 1848, in Auchampaugh, *Robert Tyler,* p. 17).

[4] Fernando Wood to Woodbury, 9 May 1848, Woodbury Papers.

[5] Woodbury to Yancey, 15 May 1848, ibid.

[6] Whitney to Woodbury, 13 May 1848, Clapp to Woodbury, 10, 19 May 1848, ibid.

[7] Unless otherwise noted, the proceedings of the convention are based on the report in *Niles' Register* 74 (2 August, 22 November, 29 November 1848) : 69–77, 324–29, 348–49. Contemporary newspaper accounts vary only slightly.

the first move with a proposal to refer the quarrel of the two factions to the Committee on Credentials. Barnburners, led by Samuel J. Tilden and Preston King, objected. They denounced the motion as a "monstrous proposition," a plot designed to bury the question in a secret committee room where logrolling and intrigue, rather than a regard for the facts, would decide the issue. In turn, they each insisted that the parties to the quarrel be given a hearing before the bar of the house. Their protests went unheeded. The convention passed the Cone motion, supported in an unctuous oration from Senator Dickinson, by a voice vote; it appointed a committee, containing at least one member who announced that he was opposed to the admission of the Barnburner delegation, to settle the issue.[8]

For the moment, quiet prevailed, and the convention turned to routine matters. J. M. Commander, in spite of the fact that he had been elected in a meeting that did not even represent a congressional district, was given the right to cast South Carolina's nine votes.[9] Only Cass supporters objected. Andrew Stevenson of Virginia, former Speaker of the House, was elected permanent chairman. A short, sharp debate on the majority necessary for nomination resulted in the adoption of the two-thirds rule.[10] Then the meeting adjourned to rest nerves frayed with expectancy.

On the evening of the second day, 23 May, bitter controversy erupted. General Benjamin C. Howard of Maryland reported that the Committee on Credentials had decided not to hear the claims of the New York delegations until each contending party pledged itself "to abide by the decision of the convention" and agreed to support the nominees by all honorable means.[11] When the Hunker delegates complied, Howard, after consulting the committee, announced that their action entitled them to cast the votes of New York.

[8] Robert J. Moses of Florida made the announcement and requested that he be permitted to withdraw from the committee. The convention refused to hear him, and he retained his seat.

[9] *Charleston Mercury,* 5 May 1848.

[10] The two-thirds rule was adopted by an almost solid vote of the slave states—Delaware, Maryland, and Missouri excepted—as well as Maine, New Hampshire, Connecticut, New Jersey, Michigan, Illinois, and Iowa.

[11] Precisely what happened in the committee is difficult to determine. One report is that the committee favored admission of the Barnburners by a vote of 19 to 7 (Doctor Jonathon M. Foltz to Buchanan, 24 May 1848, Buchanan Papers). Another indicates that the vote was in favor of the Hunkers, 16 to 8 (Sutherland to Buchanan, 25 May 1848). A third report, which lists members of the committee, indicates that the test proposed was decided by a majority of one vote, 14 to 13 (*Cleveland Plain Dealer,* 26 May 1848).

In a moment the hall was a seething mass of angry delegates, each trying to be heard above the uproar made by his neighbor. When order was restored, Churchill C. Cambreleng calmly renewed the Barnburner request to be heard. He secured support from Isaac Toucey, senator from Connecticut, and from Yancey, who undoubtedly recognized that the establishment of such a precedent could be applied to him as well as to the Barnburners. Yancey announced that he had no sympathy for the principles of the Barnburners, but that he was determined to give them a fair hearing. "I deny the right of the committee to apply a test to either of the delegations from New York," he declared. "With all due deference to the committee, I must say they have transcended their authority. What right have the thirty respectable gentlemen . . . thus to impose a test in the name of the six or seven hundred delegates here assembled?" he asked. "If to abide the decisions of this body be the test of democracy, then there is a species of democracy of which I have never heard. . . . Had the committee asked, Are you in favor of the independent treasury and free trade? Are you opposed to internal improvements by the general government? Or applied any other test of principle, it would have been a different case. But I say boldly and fearlessly, that their test is an anti-Democratic test! To no foe of mine would I commend it." Thus passionately supported by one of the Barnburners' most violent opponents, the request was honored by the convention.

On the third day, 24 May, Dickinson, Foster, and James R. Doolittle for the Hunkers, and M. J. C. Smith, King, and Cambreleng for the Barnburners laid their cases before the governing body of the Democratic party in short speeches often interrupted by hisses and cheers. Both sides sought to prove the legitimacy of their claims on grounds already presented through the New York press. In addition, Hunkers stigmatized their opponents as political abolitionists, a charge the Utica delegates indignantly denied, though they did admit, through King, that they were "uncompromisingly opposed to the extension of slavery into new states and new territories" and that they would not remove the Proviso from their creed.[12] After four hours of oratory Yancey submitted a resolution declaring the Hunker delegates the legitimate representatives of New York because the Barnburners had "shown themselves to be factious Whigs in disguise and abolitionists" who had made the

[12] One correspondent suggested that King's short speech cost the Barnburners their seats: "At one time today the Barnburners had all on their side & would doubtless have been admitted, but for an abolitionist speech of Mr. King which has prostrated them forever" (Doctor Foltz to Buchanan, 24 May 1848, Buchanan Papers).

Wilmot Proviso, a measure designed to strangle the South, the "corner-stone of their edifice." The convention hastily adjourned for dinner.

When it reconvened, Yancey withdrew his motion, and the convention turned its attention to a resolution introduced by Thomas W. Barclay of Ohio, which provided that both delegations be seated and jointly cast the 36 votes of their state. Amid considerable confusion Barclay's resolution was adopted by the narrow margin of two votes, 126 to 124. To avoid further controversy the convention adjourned until the next morning, when Hunkers and Barnburners alike made known their dissatisfaction by announcing that they would take no further part in the proceedings.

Helpless to resolve the New York problem, the convention turned its attention to nominations.[13] At the very opening of the roll call Senator Turney momentarily stopped the proceedings to read a message from President Polk announcing that he was not a candidate for renomination and requesting that his ofttimes expressed desire to retire to private life at the end of his administration be observed by the assembly.

Only three names were placed in nomination—Buchanan, Cass, and Woodbury. The first poll revealed that Cass was far in the lead with 125 votes of 251 cast; Buchanan received 55 and Woodbury 53 votes. Dallas, Worth, and Calhoun secured 18 scattered votes. The poll contained some surprises. Cass was stronger than expected in the West, capturing 94 of the 117 votes of that area, including Louisiana, which was supposed to go for Buchanan; he had also made progress in the eastern border states, securing 26 votes in Delaware, Maryland, and Virginia, which had also been counted for Buchanan. His strength was negligible in the East. Buchanan's strength, at least 30 votes below expectations, was based primarily in Pennsylvania, New Jersey, and North Carolina. Woodbury received almost the whole vote of New England, but his southern vote, 15 ballots scattered among six states, was disappointing. Neither Alabama nor Georgia was solidly for him; Commander had cast South Carolina's vote for Calhoun, and Florida had not voted.

Only a slight shift in strength occurred on the second ballot. Cass picked up 8 votes from Woodbury in both New England and the South, but Woodbury secured South Carolina. On the third ballot Cass gained 23 votes, including 13 from Buchanan in North Carolina and Iowa and 9 from Woodbury in New England and Georgia. On the fourth ballot

[13] Thirty years later Senator William Allen of Ohio claimed that he had been offered the nomination by a Cass–Van Buren delegation which visited him during the night (Reginald C. McGrane, *William Allen: A Study in Western Democracy* [Columbus, Ohio, 1925], pp. 128–29). It appears more likely that the incident he recalled occurred in 1844.

New Jersey joined the bandwagon along with fifteen more delegates from New England and the South to give Cass 179 votes and the nomination. Cass had 25 of 76 northeastern votes and 154 of 174 southern and western votes.

Wild and enthusiastic applause followed the announcement of the result until M. J. C. Smith of the Barnburner delegation arose. A hush, almost ominous in its suddenness, fell upon the assembly. Smith delivered a sharp protest against the entire proceedings.[14] When he finished, his fellow delegates rose as one man and stalked from the hall, displaying a wrath so lurid, according to Henry B. Stanton, "that the delegates from the back states" were frightened "almost out of their wits."[15] Their action so upset the convention that it promptly adjourned.

When it reassembled that evening, the Barnburners' withdrawal still appeared to weigh heavily on the delegates. Their reaction took the form of a resolution by Thomas M. Foreman of Georgia inviting the Hunker delegation to cast New York's votes; the Hunkers refused, and the dispirited assembly turned its attention to the vice-presidential nomination. Six names were placed before the convention: William O. Butler of Kentucky, already mentioned as a possible running mate for Cass, Buchanan, Woodbury, or Dallas; John A. Quitman of Mississippi, the southern extremists' candidate; Benjamin C. Howard, Maryland's favorite son, who promptly withdrew; John Y. Mason, for whose nomination the Virginia delegation had deserted Buchanan; William R. King of Alabama, a Buchanan supporter; and General James J. McKay of North Carolina, chairman of the House Ways and Means Committee.

The first ballot revealed that the contest was between Butler and Quitman, who polled 114 and 74 votes respectively. In the Northeast the count was 47 for Butler, 14 for Quitman; in the Northwest, 24 for Butler, 27 for Quitman; in the Southeast, 11 for Butler, 14 for Quitman; in the Southwest, 32 for Butler, 19 for Quitman. The vote revealed that Butler was favored by eastern supporters of Woodbury and Buchanan and that Quitman's strength was based on the westernmost states, north and south. On the second ballot Butler received 169 votes, the necessary two-thirds, when northern delegates, who had voted for King, and the Virginia delegation, which withdrew Mason, swung into his column.

On the next morning, their spirits somewhat rejuvenated by the Hunkers' announcement that their delegation would sustain the nomina-

---

[14] *Niles' Register* 74 (13 December 1848) : 377.
[15] Henry B. Stanton, *Random Recollections* (New York, 1887), p. 162 (hereafter cited as *Recollections*).

tions, the delegates prepared for a battle over the platform, which rumor whispered would be contested by several southern extremists. The resolutions, reported from committee by Benjamin Hallett of Boston, contained little new or startling. All the principles "avowed on former occasions" were renewed and reasserted: the limited power of the Federal government; opposition to "a general system of internal improvements"; opposition to any policy designed to "foster one branch of industry to the detriment of another"; opposition to a national bank, an institution of "deadly hostility to the best interests of the country, dangerous to republican institutions and the liberties of the people, and calculated to place the business of the country within the control of a concentrated money power, and above the laws and will of the people"; opposition to any attempt by the Federal government "to interfere with or control the domestic institutions of the several states"; opposition to any measure designed to distribute among the states the proceeds of the sale of public lands; and opposition to any attempt to restrict the president's veto power, by which he was enabled to suspend the passage of any bill which could not secure "the approval of two-thirds of the Senate and the House of Representatives," until the judgment of the people could be heard.

Further resolutions avowed a determination to maintain the Jeffersonian principles which had made the nation "the land of liberty and the asylum of the oppressed," affirmed the justice and necessity of the Mexican War, commended the "unconquerable courage . . . daring enterprise . . . unfaltering perseverance and fortitude" of the officers and soldiers who carried the nation's arms against the foe, welcomed France into the growing sisterhood of republics, and pointed with pride to the achievements of James K. Polk. Finally, revealing the true bias of the assembly, the resolutions condemned the efforts of abolitionists and others "to induce Congress to interfere with questions of slavery, or to take incipient steps in relation thereto," as actions calculated to lead to the "most alarming and dangerous consequences."

A tremendous wave of applause swept the convention at the conclusion of the essentially, and significantly, negative report. Few were quick enough to recognize that the resolutions were a defense of past achievements and of the status quo, and not a program for the future, before Yancey rose with the announcement that he wished to present a protest from three members of the Committee on Resolutions. They had no objections to the platform, Yancey declared, but they understood that the party nominee entertained the opinion that while Congress had no right to interfere with the question of slavery in the states or territories, the people inhabiting a territory did have the right. The majority report had not made the party's position clear; it had left to the people the job of finding an exposition of the views of the party "in the avowed opinions of their nominee." This course the minority conceived to be wrong.

"It has been the pride of the Democracy," Yancey maintained, "that it has ever dealt frankly and honestly with the people. It has scorned to conceal its political opinions. It has made it a point of opposition to the Whig party, that it frequently goes before the people with a mask upon its brow, and has appealed to the masses to rebuke that party for a course so offensive to truth, and so unfair to them. Our country's institutions must find their surest support in an intelligent public opinion. That public opinion cannot be intelligently informed as to our views upon these institutions, if we refuse to avow them, and dare not advocate them." It was useless to deny that the question of slavery extension did not press for decision. Ten of the "sovereign non-slave-holding States" had already expressed opinions upon it. It was likewise idle to call the question an abstraction. If abstract in any sense, it was only so in those states which owned "not a dollar" of slave property and therefore had "not a single political right to be curtailed." For them opposition to the South on this point was "purely a question of moral and political ethics."

It was far different for southerners. They owned the property which the enactment of the Proviso would prevent them "from carrying with them to the territories." They had a "common right" in those territories, from which they were to be excluded "unless they chose to go there without this property." Up to this time they had been considered as political equals in the Union, with the "same power of expansion and progress" which had distinguished all its classes. If, then, the delegates refused to meet this issue and permitted the views of its nominee "to stand implicitly" as the opinions of the convention, they would be pronouncing in substance "against the political equality of the people—against the community of interest in the Territories . . . against the right of one half of the people of the Union to extend those institutions" which their forefathers had recognized when framing the articles of the Union. In order to obviate such a construction, the minority asked leave to present an amendment:

> *Resolved,* That the doctrine of non-interference with the rights of property of any portion of the people of this confederation, be it in

the States or in the Territories, by any other than the parties interested in them, is the true republican doctrine recognized by this body.

Without such a resolution, Yancey added, there was great danger that South Carolina, Florida, Georgia, and Alabama would refuse to support the Democratic ticket, thus giving the election to the Whigs; he himself would be among those who would bolt the party.

A scene of considerable confusion followed this last announcement. Dozens of delegates sought the floor, shouting and gesticulating. All, however, were drowned by cries of "question," and the Yancey amendment was put to a vote. The convention, which had already revealed its unwillingness to strain the slavery issue too far, rejected the amendment by the decisive count of 216 votes to 36.[16] The Florida delegation along with Yancey and another Alabamian promptly left the hall amid the catcalls and hisses of their former friends. After the unanimous adoption of the platform and a loud cheer for the nominees, the rest of the delegates followed their fellows into the "bright sunshine of the Baltimore streets." Within four days Cass accepted the nomination, resigned his seat in the Senate, and started the journey to his home in Detroit by way of Philadelphia, New York, and the Mohawk Valley.

Before he reached Philadelphia, the Whigs had already begun to gather for their own convention. They came in vast groups, "ten thousand from New York alone." One delegate reported that the city's "streets were thronged—Chestnut Street especially was almost walled up with men; and all seemed mad with excitement on politics—such gesticulating and jabbering you never saw or heard." As in Baltimore, the hotels were quickly "crowded to overflowing . . . beyond any possibility of admitting new comers; the boarding houses were full and private families largely quartered on."[17]

Reports of last-minute developments spread rapidly through the city. Taylor men, conspicuously younger than the average conventioneers, were strongly confident; well-disciplined, they met all the trains and preached Taylor's availability to incoming delegates. There were rumors that Webster would throw his strength to Taylor in return for the vice-presidency or the State Department. Clay, on the other hand, was "doomed"—even Greeley admitted it; the Ohio delegation had "abandoned" him. But the spirit of "illiberality and vindictiveness" evinced on

[16] The resolution secured the votes of South Carolina, Florida, Georgia, Alabama, and Arkansas, and one vote each from Maryland, Kentucky, and Tennessee.

[17] Malcolm C. McMillan, ed., "Joseph Glover Baldwin Reports on the Whig National Convention of 1848," *Journal of Southern History* 25 (August 1939): 371.

both sides suggested that a third candidate was necessary. Crittenden's name was often mentioned. McLean was also being considered; Indiana and Iowa, it was known, would vote for him on the first ballot, but Weed exhibited a violent opposition and was working for Crittenden or John M. Clayton so that Seward could get the vice-presidency. Scott was also being boomed; a few believed that he would take second place on a Clay ticket. There were also rumors that Pennsylvania, New York, and Ohio would unite on Scott as the northern candidate on the second or third ballot. Even antislavery men were quietly looking in his direction. Indeed, the antislavery element was too quiet; it was almost like the calm before a storm. There were rumors, too, that Clay might join any anti-Taylor revolt. Harmony, at any rate, could not be expected.[18]

Nor was there much evidence of harmony on 7 June, when the delegates—regular, alternate, and supernumerary—crowded into the narrow confines of the Chinese Museum where, according to the correspondent of the *Tallahassee Floridian,* the "confusion and uproar" were indescribable. "It looks," he reported, "no more like a deliberative assembly than a mass meeting before it comes to order."[19] Amid the tumult the convention proceeded to organize. It named John M. Morehead, ex-governor of North Carolina, as permanent chairman, selected a committee on credentials, and for the rest of the day wrangled over the right of Louisiana to cast the vote of Texas.[20]

On the following morning the dispute over the Louisiana–Texas issue was resumed, interspersed with long arguments over other delegate problems. How would states with an excessive number of delegates determine their votes? How could states with an insufficient number of delegates cast the votes of their missing districts? Could a man residing in one district cast the vote of another district which had named no delegate? Meanwhile, the galleries remained in a state of confusion "occasioned by the pressure of the crowd and the struggle constantly going on for favorable positions." The gallery began to bicker with

[18] Joseph L. White to Clay, 26 May 1848, Edwin Bryant to Clay, 27 May 1848, Greeley to Clay, 29 May 1848, C. C. Langdon to Clay, 29 May 1848, James Harlan to Clay, 2 June 1848, Clay Papers; "Theodore" to Smith, 31 May 1848, Smith Papers; M. Huntingdon to McLean, 3 June 1848, Harvey to McLean, 2 June 1848, Dowling to McLean, 7 June 1848, Mower to McLean, 5 June 1848, McLean Papers; Hunt to Weed [June 1848], in Thurlow Weed, *Memoirs of Thurlow Weed,* ed. Thurlow Weed Barnes (Boston 1884), pp. 167–68 (hereafter cited as *Weed's Memoirs*); *Pennsylvanian,* 6 June 1848; *North American,* 2 June 1848.

[19] *Floridian,* 24 June 1848.

[20] Unless otherwise noted, the proceedings of the convention are based on the report, less adequate than that of the Baltimore convention, in *Niles' Register* 74 (29 November, 6 December 1848): 349, 354–58.

delegates, applauding and hissing speakers "as they would clowns in a circus" and bringing proceedings to a standstill. It was not until midafternoon that some measure of order was restored. Louisiana was given the right to cast the votes of Texas, each state was authorized to determine its own method of counting votes, and the supernumerary delegates were allowed seats on the floor.

On the evening of the second day the impatient delegates turned their attention to nominations. Six names were placed before the convention: Taylor, Clay, Scott, McLean, Webster, and Clayton. Almost immediately Samuel Galloway of Ohio withdrew McLean's name, a somewhat unexpected move since the Judge appeared to have Indiana in his pocket and much residual strength in New England.[21] A moment later the withdrawal was forgotten when Judge Lafayette Saunders of Louisiana arose to explain Taylor's long-discussed relationship to the Whig party.

General Taylor, Saunders declared, had taken no part in bringing his name before the country; that action had been taken by his friends. Under such circumstances he did not think it was "proper" to withdraw his own name; that action would also have to be taken by his friends. It was General Taylor's opinion that his friends at the convention were "bound to abide its decision and to sustain the nominee *'heart and soul.'* " He himself would "hail with entire satisfaction the nomination by the convention of any other but himself." In case the convention chose another and his friends withdrew him, it would be "their act and not his," but one in which he would "cheerfully acquiesce."

Prolonged cheering followed the announcement; only when the chairman threatened to adjourn the assembly was some measure of order restored and the roll call of states begun for the first ballot. As the voting proceeded, a great silence fell on the hall; even the chattering in the galleries subsided. Slowly the realization that Taylor was taking the lead began to impress Clay men. Delegates who had been counted for the Kentuckian voted for Taylor or Scott, and cries of "treachery" echoed in different parts of the hall. The result, read "amid a silence that could be heard," revealed Taylor leading with 111 votes against 97 for Clay, 43 for Scott, 22 for Webster, and 6 scattered. Taylor's strength was overwhelmingly in the slave states, from which he secured 85 of their 108 votes; only Delaware and Maryland failed to give him any votes. From the Northeast he secured only 17 of 112 votes, and from the Northwest only 9 of 56. Clay's greatest strength was in the Northeast,

[21] Galloway informed McLean that he would have received only 17 votes on the first ballot (Galloway to McLean, 14 July 1848, McLean Papers). Evidently McLean's managers—and perhaps McLean himself—did not want the Judge to be a loser.

from which he secured 61 votes; he secured 23 votes from the South and a disappointing 13 from the Northwest. Scott secured 11 votes from the Northeast and 32 from the Northwest. Webster's vote came from three New England states.

After the second ballot, which showed a loss of 11 votes for Clay to the benefit of both Taylor and Scott, the Kentuckian's frantic managers secured an adjournment until the next morning.

During the night, according to Oliver Dyer, the convention's official reporter, Clay's managers threw away all chances of recovering any lost ground. "Instead of trying to win back the dissenters by proper appeals and arguments," Dyer later declared, "they vehemently assailed them, and wounded their self love by vituperative denunciation." Taylor's friends, on the other hand, talked only of the "controlling interests" of the Whig party and the welfare of the country. "They didn't care . . . for any particular individual"; all they wanted was a winner. They assured every listener that "every delegate had a right to his own opinion" and a right "to vote for whomsoever he believed to be the best man to bear the Whig standard in the coming close and desperate fight." Such talk, Dyer commented, "was deliciously soothing to the delegates whom Clay's friends were anathematizing, and kept them securely in line for Taylor . . . or Scott. It did more, it made them partizans against Clay, and set some of them to work to bring their colleagues into coalescence with themselves."[22]

When the convention met again on Friday morning, the air was tense with apprehension. Men spoke in hushed voices and appeared to walk on tiptoe. "The 'aye' on the motion to ballot," Dyer recalled, "was given in such suppressed tones that its effect was like that of the pianissimo of a grand orchestra." The roll call began and proceeded to Connecticut, which under the leadership of Truman Smith had voted solidly for Clay on the first two ballots.[23] Rumors had circulated during the morning that Smith had gone over to Taylor, and when his name was called, the excitement was intense. He responded in clear, penetrating tones: "Zachary Taylor!" As if ready for a signal, "the Palo Alto men burst out with repeated cheers and nearly stampeded the convention." With the announcement of the result—Taylor 133, seven votes short of nomination, Clay 74, Scott 54, and Webster 17—another scene "of the stormiest confusion" occurred. "Some of the delegates cheered till they

[22] Oliver Dyer, *Great Senators of the United States Forty Years Ago* (New York, 1889), pp. 74–75 (hereafter cited as *Great Senators*).

[23] In view of the fact that Truman Smith has always been listed as one of the Young Indians who supported Taylor, this development is rather strange. Was Smith really a Young Indian, or had he been playing a double game?

were exhausted. Others leaped upon seats and chairs, yelling themselves hoarse trying to get a hearing. Horace Greeley . . . and General James Watson Webb . . . ran back and forth between the reporters' table and the platform, shouting and gesticulating like mad men—Webb with his hat on the back of his head and his coat tails flapping in the breeze which he occasioned, and Greeley with the knot of his neck tie under his left ear and the ends floating over his shoulder."[24]

Of Taylor's gain of 22 votes since the first ballot, 15 votes came from former Clay supporters in eight states scattered from Massachusetts to Indiana. Almost all of Scott's increase also came from former Clay supporters.

The result of the next ballot was already foreseen: the Clay forces broke. Although some shifted to Scott, a small stampede to the Taylor bandwagon became evident before half the states had been called. With difficulty, Taylorites suppressed their mounting jubilation until the results were known. It was finally disclosed that Clay had been deserted by all but 32 delegates, 20 from the mid-Atlantic states; Webster still claimed about 14 delegates in New England; Scott's total increased to 63 votes. All the rest, a total of 171 delegates, which included 102 votes of 108 from the slave states, had joined Taylor. A long period of tumult followed as member after member arose to demonstrate support.

Among those who received recognition was Charles Allen of Massachusetts. Choking with rage, he shouted his opposition: "I think I know something of the feeling of my state, and I say that we can not consent that this should go forth as the unanimous vote of this convention." Loud cries of "Sit down!" "Order!" "Hear him!" "Go on!" momentarily drowned his voice. Then came words as clear as a bell: "The free states will no longer submit. I declare to this convention my belief that the Whig party is here and this day dissolved."[25] Cheers and hisses rose in a deafening combination from the now thoroughly excited convention. Member after member jumped to his feet to demand the floor, but the chairman gaveled the convention to order and called for nomination of candidates for vice president.[26]

First to be nominated was the wealthy Massachusetts cotton manufacturer Abbott Lawrence, who had long been the candidate of the Taylor

[24] Dyer, *Great Senators,* pp. 75–76.

[25] Wilson, *Slave Power,* 2: 136.

[26] For the contest over the vice-presidential nomination, I am following the account in the *North American,* 10, 11 June 1848. It agrees substantially with accounts in the New York *Courier,* 10, 11 June 1848; the *National Intelligencer,* 10, 13 June 1848; and Wilson, *Slave Power,* 2: 137–41. However, it varies from the accounts in *Niles' Register* 74 (6 December 1848) : 354–58; and Gatell, "Conscience and Judgment," pp. 25–26.

men and, it was rumored, had promised to contribute $100,000 to the campaign fund if he secured the nomination.[27] His name, however, brought murmurs of rage from the anti-Taylor men, and someone shouted, "We will not have King Cotton on both ends of the ticket."[28]

Amidst the turmoil John A. Collier of New York obtained the floor. In a low, clear voice he identified himself with the anti-Taylor forces, revealed the sorrow and bitterness of Clay's friends, and announced that he had a peace offering to present, which, if accepted, would reconcile the supporters of all the defeated candidates and prevent a fatal breach in the party. Then, to the astonishment of the convention, he nominated Millard Fillmore, former congressman, Silas Wright's opponent for governor in 1844, and at the time of the convention comptroller of New York.[29] Rapidly the names of Andrew Stewart, John Sargent, and Thomas M. T. McKennon (all congressmen from Pennsylvania), Seward and Hamilton Fish of New York, John M. Clayton of Delaware, ex-Senator George Evans of Maine, and Robert C. Winthrop of Massachusetts were added to the list. After the names of Seward and Winthrop were withdrawn, the balloting began.

The first result revealed that Collier's unexpected appeal to the convention had been effective. Fillmore received 115 votes, Lawrence 109 votes, and twelve others a scattered 53 votes. Fillmore secured 10 votes from New England, 30 from the mid-Atlantic states, 44 from the Northwest, and 31 from the South. Lawrence had 28 votes from New England, 6 from the mid-Atlantic states, 10 from the Northwest, and 64 from the South. On the second ballot Fillmore captured most of the scattered votes as well as those of some Lawrence supporters to win the nomination, 173 votes to 87.[30]

Almost immediately ex-Governor Joseph Vance of Ohio was on his

[27] Weed, *Autobiography,* p. 578; *New York Day Book,* 13 October 1848, cited in Van Buren Papers.

[28] Dyer, *Great Senators,* p. 79.

[29] Collier's action at this point had several motivations. He was an opponent of Weed, whose power in New York he hoped to limit in order to further his own ambitions to become either governor or senator. Collier expected that Weed would support Seward for vice president or else that he would support Lawrence to gain influence in the Taylor camp so that Seward could become a cabinet member or senator. If either course proved successful, the Weed-Seward combination would control New York Whiggery. Collier acted primarily to reduce the Weed-Seward influence. His nomination of Fillmore was intended to do two things: to remove Fillmore as a potential senator and to secure Fillmore's aid in the next New York senatorial contest. Fillmore repaid the debt, but Collier was unsuccessful (R. J. Rayback, *Fillmore,* pp. 177–86). That New York was not united behind Collier's effort was evident on the first ballot; the delegation cast 22 votes for Fillmore and 14 votes for seven other candidates, including Lawrence.

[30] *North American,* 10 June 1848.

feet to ask that the action of the assembly be given a unanimous vote of confidence. Turning particularly to the delegates from Massachusetts, New York, Pennsylvania, and his own state, who had refused to join in the demonstrations following Taylor's nomination, he begged them to "think well" before they withdrew from the "true church," an action that their very countenances seemed to foretell. After delegates from New York and Pennsylvania had responded in a conciliatory vein, Louis Campbell of Ohio arose. He had come there, he said, the firm opponent of Taylor. Like his senior colleague, however, he had learned that it was right to yield preferences for men, "but never for principles." If, then, the convention wished to preserve harmony, it would be necessary to reassert party doctrines or at least to adopt a resolution declaring that it was the duty of Congress to prevent the introduction and to declare unlawful the existence of slavery in any territory then possessed or thereafter acquired. Without such a declaration, which Campbell then formally proposed, the party would be hopelessly divided.[31]

A storm of hisses and cheers, mingled with loud cries of "question," immediately swept the hall and continued through the roll call that followed. When the announcement was made that the resolution had been defeated, the din redoubled and hostilities threatened to break out on the floor. Cooler delegates brought about some semblance of order, but not before Henry Wilson, who had mounted a table in the center of the floor, could shout: "I will go home: and, so help me God, I will do all I can to defeat the election of your candidate."[32] With these words still ringing in their ears, the excited delegates adjourned to carry their battle to the country, but like the Democrats, the Whigs marched into the fray with banners tattered by their own shots.

[31] Wilson, *Slave Power,* 2: 135.
[32] Ibid., p. 136.

Chapter Twelve

Free Soil, Free Speech, Free Labor, & Free Men

Before the Philadelphia convention adjourned, the nation had begun to turn its attention to the antislavery Democrats, among whom the news of Cass's nomination was greeted with marked hostility. As might be expected, reaction was strongest in New York, where the Barnburner delegates, determined to make no compromise with the "lords of the lash," had returned immediately after their withdrawal from the Baltimore convention. Greeted by a gigantic throng at the New York City railway station, they had repaired to Central Park; with twelve thousand listening and shouting, they displayed their indignation and announced their determination to fight for their principles. A few days later the delegation summoned the Democracy of the state to repudiate the nomination which Cass had purchased at "the price of the most abject subserviency to the slave power" and to select their own "democratic presidential candidate" at a convention in Utica on 22 June.[1]

Thus ignited, the revolt was fanned to a high flame by outraged Barnburner journals,[2] and it spread like wildfire through the state. Everywhere town meetings gathered to denounce Cass as a "trading, trafficking, unprincipled politician" ready to "barter away . . . the rights of freemen to gratify his ambition";[3] they would welcome the opportunity to express their contempt for him at the polls.[4] So widespread and so savage were these manifestations that some Whigs gleefully predicted that Cass would "scarcely get the support of a Corporal's guard in the State of New York." The *National Era,* organ of the Liberty party, proclaimed: "The Baltimore Convention has accomplished a feat which will long be remembered among the remarkable events in the political history of the country. It has broken up the Democratic party of the nation."[5]

Outside New York, similar signs of hostility to Cass were not so evident; for the most part, antislavery Democrats nursed their disappointment and anger in a silence only occasionally broken by the vehement protests of some party journal such as the *Wheeling Times,* which denounced Cass as "one of the greatest political prostitutes of the age."[6] Nevertheless, as the *Portland Advertiser* declared, "the feeling manifested in New York" existed all through the free states and needed only "worthy leaders to come forth and give it expression."[7] That claim was soon substantiated in Illinois and in southeastern Wisconsin. In Chicago, Wentworth's *Democrat,* despite the taunts of the city's Whig organ, refused to hoist the Cass flag to its masthead, and the district convention which nominated Wentworth for Congress renounced all allegiance to the Baltimore ticket.[8] In Wisconsin, leadership was provided by the editors of the *Racine Advocate* and the *Southport Telegraph,* both of whom proclaimed their reprobation of the Cass candidacy and succeeded in gathering a huge meeting of the "Democrats of Racine and Vicinity" to elect delegates to the Barnburner meeting in Utica.[9]

Meanwhile, news of Taylor's nomination also produced a strong and even more widespread reaction among Whigs. Clay Whigs were rabidly bitter. The Kentuckian himself revealed a keen disappointment in his letters to Thomas B. Stevenson, from whom he sought information upon the "unexpected course of the Ohio delegation," whose support, despite repeated warnings from the editor of the *Cincinnati Atlas,* he had counted upon. Stevenson was unable to satisfy his "historic curiosity,"[10]

[1] *Albany Atlas,* 2 June 1848.

[2] Of eleven Democratic dailies in New York, eight repudiated the Cass nomination: *New York Evening Post, New York Globe, Brooklyn Eagle, Albany Atlas, Troy Budget, Utica Democrat, Rochester Advertiser,* and *Buffalo Republic.* Two-thirds of the weeklies followed suit. Only one Barnburner paper, the *Hudson Gazette,* supported Cass (*New York Tribune,* 10 June 1848).

[3] *Buffalo Republic,* 27 May 1848.

[4] *Albany Atlas,* 1–22 June 1848; *Buffalo Republic,* 30, 31 May, 1–22 June 1848. In New York City the General Committee of Tammany Hall endorsed Cass by a vote of 24 to 12, but it failed to call for the customary ratification meeting (Butler to Van Buren, 31 May, 1 June 1848, Van Buren Papers). One meeting to repudiate Cass drew a crowd of ten thousand (*New York Tribune,* 10 June 1848).

[5] Edwin Bryant to Clay, 27 May 1848, Clay Papers; *National Era,* 8 June 1848.

[6] *Wheeling Times* quoted in *Richmond Enquirer,* 8 June 1848.

[7] *Portland Advertiser* quoted in *Boston Atlas,* 7 June 1848. See also *Sandusky Mirror* quoted in *Buffalo Republic,* 31 May 1848; John Lane to Van Buren, 10 June 1848, Henry F. Watson to Van Buren, 11 July 1848, John Case to John Van Buren, 7 June 1848, Van Buren Papers; *Cincinnati Signal* quoted in *Niles' Register* 74 (5 July 1848): 9–10.

[8] *National Era,* 22 June 1848.

[9] *Racine Advocate,* 31 May, 7, 14 June 1848.

[10] Stevenson to Clay, 19 June 1848, Clay to Stevenson, 14 June, 5, 14 August 1848, in Colton, *Clay's Works,* 3: 465–66, 470, 471; Stevenson to Clay, 19 June, 10 August 1848, Clay Papers.

nor could any of his other correspondents agree on the man responsible for his loss of the Buckeye State.[11]

Among the Clay rank and file, however, the question of responsibility for Ohio's "perfidious action" was not important. More significant was their determination "to be revenged" upon the chosen candidate and the "stock jobbing politicians" who had dethroned their beloved chieftain.[12] Some, such as David Graham of New York, begged Clay, "as an act of justice" to his faithful friends, to withhold any expression of approval. "Let those who have taken Gen. Taylor, 'upon their own responsibility,' (to use his own words), elect him if they can, upon the like responsibility," Graham pleaded. "But by all that is just, let no appeal to the generosity of your nature, to aid them, avail to disarm your friends of the power they possess and will surely exercise, to punish the corruption of those who have betrayed them."[13]

That punishment might be attempted was disclosed by the actions of a number of editors and politicians who had supported Clay. Chief among them was Greeley. The *Tribune* editor had revealed his bitter disappointment at Taylor's nomination on the night the Philadelphia convention adjourned, when carpetbag in hand he had entered the office of the *North American,* where several Taylor delegates had gathered to celebrate. "On seeing who was present," Oliver Dyer reported, "Greeley scowled . . . turned around, and started for the door." Stopped by Editor Morton McMichael's courteous query as to his destination, he snarled that he was "going home." When told that there were no trains that night, Greeley snapped, "I don't want any train. I'm going across New Jersey afoot."[14] Though he obviously did not carry out his threat, Greeley refused to declare for Taylor when he returned to New York City and sulkily retired to his editorial tent.[15] Several of his New York brethren took more spectacular action: the editor of the *Poughkeepsie Journal* kept the Clay flag flying, and the *New York Day Book,* known and honored by contemporaries as "the tartar from the old wine casks of

---

[11] Joseph Van Trump maintained that ex-Governor Vance was the culprit. John Minor Botts, however, suspected that Vance was only a "cats-paw" for Corwin; he claimed that Corwin had persuaded the Ohio delegates to support Scott in order that the convention might elect Taylor and so enrage the Ohio Whigs that they would gladly join in the nomination which Corwin planned to secure from the Free Territory convention in Columbus (Van Trump to Clay, 26 July 1848, Botts to Clay, 23 August 1848, Clay Papers). Both Van Trump and Botts ignored the obvious sentiment for Scott in Ohio before the convention; Botts's reasoning was proven false by Corwin's support of Taylor.

[12] Stevenson to Clay, 9 September 1848, ibid.

[13] Graham to Clay, 9 June 1848, ibid.

[14] Dyer, *Great Senators,* pp. 81–82.

[15] *New York Tribune,* 17 June 1848.

conservatism," appeared in a deep band of mourning with the announcement that the Whig party had been "DISSOLVED BY MUTUAL CONSENT."[16]

There were other manifestations of rebellion. From central New York
a Quaker reported that trying to convince the Whigs in that section to
vote for Taylor was harder than sailing up "Niagara Falls in a corn
basket."[17] The *Keene Sentinel* in New Hampshire, Horace Everett of
the *Windsor Journal* in Vermont, and the *Pittsburgh Chronicle* in
Pennsylvania all proclaimed an undying opposition to Taylor. In Cincinnati the penurious Stevenson resigned his post with the *Atlas* and
announced that he would rather starve before he would lift his pen on
behalf of the Whig nominee. A Michigan editor, announcing his repudiation of the Philadelphia nomination, described the new principles of
the Whig party in unintelligible doggerel:

> Sound the hewgag, strike the tonjon
> Beat the Fuzguzzy, wake the gonquong
> Let the loud Hozanna ring
> Bum tum fuzzelgum dingo bim.[18]

In the slave states there were also signs of opposition. Reports from
Maryland, Kentucky, and Georgia revealed that many Whigs had determined to cast their votes for Cass rather than support a man who had
been pushed into the title role by the enemies of Henry Clay. In
Mississippi one outraged Whig begged the Almighty God to rain "eternal shame" on the heads of every delegate to "that Convention of
Judases" who had shared in the betrayal of the venerable leader of the
party. In Tennessee, Parson Brownlow announced: "We shall not hum-
ble our pride, principles and honor in the dust by falling into the support
of any such man as Zachary Taylor has shown himself to be. . . . IF WE
HAD ANY ASSURANCE THAT TAYLOR WOULD DIE as soon as he is elected,
and Mr. Fillmore would take his place, we would support the ticket. As
it is, WE WILL NOT."[19]

---

[16] *Buffalo Republic,* 14 June 1848; *Albany Argus,* 22 June 1848; *New York Day
Book* quoted in *Cincinnati Herald,* 21 June 1848.

[17] *Albany Evening Journal* quoted in *Richmond Enquirer,* 29 July 1848. Seward's
editorial friend, the *Auburn Advertiser,* declared: "It would be hypocrisy in us not
frankly to admit that in placing the name of Gen. Taylor in that position [at the
masthead] we perform the most mortifying and unwelcome duty of our editorial
life" (*Albany Argus,* 14 June 1848). See also B. Hubbard to Lucius Lyon, 20 June
1848, Lucius Lyon Papers.

[18] *New Hampshire Patriot,* 22 June 1848; *Boston Post,* 20 June 1848; *Cleveland
Plain Dealer,* 15 June 1848; Stevenson to Clay, 12 June 1848, Clay Papers; *Indiana
State Sentinel,* 1 July 1848; *Detroit Free Press,* 11 July 1848.

[19] Baltimore *Republican,* 12 August, 2 September 1848; Joseph H. Lumpkin to
Cobb, 22 August 1848, in Phillips, *Toombs, Stephens, and Cobb Correspondence,* p.

Antislavery Whigs, meanwhile, spent less effort in making threats and uttering lamentations; they were rapidly developing plans for rebellion. The movement was generated by the action of fifteen delegates and alternates from Maine, Massachusetts, New York, New Jersey, and Ohio who had attended the Philadelphia meeting and had met immediately after its adjournment in the lecture room of the Chinese Museum. There, they decided to ask the Ohio Free Territory Convention to issue a call for a national antiextension meeting in Buffalo early in August.[20]

That the summons would receive a hearty approval soon became evident from the wave of Taylor repudiations that swept antislavery strongholds. New England became a hive of activity. In Massachusetts a dozen prominent journals of both the Conscience and the Webster wings announced their opposition to Taylor. Their attitude was well expressed by a Whig convention in Natick: "We are not," it announced, "so far degraded as to give the lie to all our past professions; to acknowledge ourselves knaves, hypocrites, slaves and fools for the sake of a Whig victory; and we do therefore repudiate the nomination of Zachary Taylor, and will do our utmost to defeat his election."[21] In such an atmosphere the long prepared and newly revised call of the Conscience Whigs for a convention of antislavery men was issued from the offices of the *Boston Whig*. Addressed to the people of Massachusetts, the summons denounced Taylor as a candidate whom "no northern Whig" was bound to support, because he was *"not a Whig"*; acquiescence in his nomination would be "treachery to the cause of Freedom" and would lead to the "utter prostration of the interests of Free Labor and the Rights of Freemen."[22] The convention was to meet in Worcester on 28 June.

The situation in Ohio was similar. Within a week after Taylor's nomination every county and eight of twelve Whig papers in the Western Reserve repudiated the ticket and demanded an antislavery candidate. The reaction of the region was voiced by the *Cleveland True Democrat*: "As we anticipated the Whigs have nominated Zack Taylor for president! This is the cup offered by slaveholders for us to drink. We loathe the sight. We will never touch, taste or handle the unclean

---

117; *Savannah Republican,* 12 July 1848; *Mississippian,* 30 June 1848; *Jonesboro Whig* quoted in *Nashville Union,* 18 July 1848.

[20] The men involved were Louis O. Cowan and Samuel Bradley of Maine; Charles Allen, Henry Wilson, and Daniel W. Alvord of Massachusetts; Isaac Platt, John C. Hamilton, and Robert Colby of New York; Horace N. Conger of New Jersey; and Louis D. Campbell, Samuel Galloway, John C. Vaughan, Stanley Mathews, John Burgoyne, and H. B. Hurlburt of Ohio (Wilson, *Slave Power,* 2: 142–43; Mathews to Chase, 12 June 1848, Chase Papers).

[21] *Boston Post,* 9, 15 June 1848.

[22] Hoar, *Autobiography,* 1: 146–48.

thing. We ask the Whigs of Cuyahoga County to live up to the pledge they have made."[23] Comparable demands arose in the Miami Valley; indeed, antislavery men throughout the state appeared to be ready for the political revolt which they hoped would be organized at the Columbus or the Utica convention.

On 21 June, nearly a thousand Ohioans of all parties gathered at the state capital; from chairman Nathaniel Sawyer's first call for order they made it evident that they had come prepared for rebellion. Wasting little time on oratory, they immediately adopted a long series of vigorous resolutions in which they announced themselves to be the "Friends of Freedom, Free Territory and Free Labor, willing and desireous to cooperate with any party thoroughly resolved and inflexibly determined to permit no further extension of slavery." Because the candidates selected at Baltimore and Philadelphia at the dictation of the slaveholders refused to announce antiextension views, the Ohioans found themselves forced to summon the "Freemen of every State and Every Party" who held antislavery opinions and who were therefore opposed to "the election of Lewis Cass and Zachary Taylor to meet at Buffalo on the 9th of August," where they would counsel together and "present for the suffrages of the American people, candidates worthy of Freemen, determined to remain Free."[24]

On the day following the Columbus convention the Barnburners, meeting at Utica, added their voices officially to the growing chorus of revolt. Since the day their delegation had stalked out of the Universal Church in Baltimore, they had been subjected to great pressure from men such as Benton, Allen, and Blair, who sought to keep them within the Democratic fold or at least to confine their quarrel to the state contest.[25] Within their own ranks Flagg and Dix disclosed that they were gravely apprehensive of the efficacy of any separate political organization.[26] But all attempts to restrain the Barnburners' younger leaders

[23] Cleveland True Democrat, 10 June 1848.

[24] Cincinnati Herald, 28 June 1848.

[25] Benton to Van Buren, 29 May 1848, Van Buren Papers; Benton to Cass, "rec'd June 10, 1848," Cass Papers (Clements) ; Thomas H. Benton, Thirty Years View (New York, 1856), 2: 723; Smith, Blair Family, 1: 231.

[26] Flagg's reasoning provides an interesting example of a Democrat torn between practicality and principle: "I am so incredulous . . . in regard to democratic cooperation from other states that I cannot be reconciled to the policy of a nomination. . . . If the free states are prepared for a grand rally in favor of freedom at this time I have seen no evidence of it, save in this State. And here we can stand by our principles in our State nominations as effectually as to ask other States to support a national nomination and get very little cooperation. But if a suitable person willing to be a candidate can be found I am content. . . . If there is to be a nomination, it is to be regretted that it had not gone out from Baltimore, with the odor of nationality about it. Then the radicals everywhere would have met

were made in vain. Psychological factors in themselves made reconciliation impossible, as Van Buren explained to Blair. "New York has too
recently humiliated herself before the democracy of other States or
rather has been too grossly humiliated by them to adopt measures which
seem to contemplate reconciliation on her part," he pointed out. "She
cannot afford to have her invitations to the people of honor and fidelity a
second time flouted."[27]

At the same time, moreover, Barnburner leaders were receiving encouragement from other quarters. In New York the rank and file of
their own faction appeared resolved to yield no ground, and there was
much evidence that a great bloc of New York Whigs was ready to join
them "to make the slave question the great issue of the future."[28] From
outside New York came similar words of cheer. In New England,
according to several of John Van Buren's informants, it was common to
hear both Whigs and Democrats remark, "I shall wait to see what the
Barnburners of New York do before I determine for whom my vote
shall be given this fall. If they nominate a man of the right stamp in
other respects and in favor of the principles of the Wilmot Proviso I
shall go for *him*."[29]

From the Western Reserve the *Cleveland True Democrat* added its
word of support. "For our part," it declared, "we feel a deep sympathy
with the Barnburners' movement. We like their cardinal principles—
FREE SOIL—FREE LABOR—NO MORE SLAVE STATES—NO FURTHER EXTEN-
SION OF SLAVERY. They are all good, and if faithfully carried out will
inevitably lead to the adoption of the whole routine of Liberty principles.
We bid them—God speed—and not only bid them so, but should no
course be opened of more effectually and speedily rescuing our country
from the thralldom of slavery and slave power, we shall not hesitate to
contribute our mite, however feeble, for their success."[30] With such
encouragement, as a Rochester Barnburner pointed out, the Utica movement "could not have been checked by as many . . . men . . . as could
stand between this [city] and the North River."[31]

---

the Cassites and disputed the endorsement of the Baltimore nomination" (Flagg to
Van Buren, 19 June 1848, Van Buren Papers). See also Parke Godwin, *Biography
of William Cullen Bryant* (New York, 1883), 2: 43; Welles to Van Buren, 5 June
1848, Van Buren Papers.

[27] Van Buren to Blair, 22 June 1848, Blair Papers.

[28] Willis Hall to Clay [June 1848], in Colton, *Clay's Works*, 5: 564.

[29] William Jordan to John Van Buren, 13 June 1848, "Amicus" to John Van
Buren, 27 May 1848, Alfred Babcock to John Van Buren, 20 June 1848, Van Buren
Papers.

[30] *Cleveland True Democrat* quoted in *Cleveland Herald,* 5 June 1848.

[31] Alison Gardner to John Van Buren, 24 June 1848, Van Buren Papers.

Thus it was an enthusiastic horde of Barnburners which gathered at Utica under the eye of Colonel Samuel Young, along with a handful of New York Whigs and a score of delegates from local Democratic camps in Massachusetts, Connecticut, Ohio, Illinois, and Wisconsin, to plan the destruction of Cass and the slave power.[32] Its first attention, once the group organized, was given to the selection of a presidential ticket.

Before the convention several men had been mentioned as possible candidates. One was Zachary Taylor. The Whig nominee had early attracted the consideration of such Barnburner sympathizers as James W. Taylor of the *Cincinnati Signal* and Frank Blair. It was probably the Cincinnatian who brought his "whilom correspondent" to the attention of his New York friends. At the time of the first Utica convention, held in February, rumors that Taylor would be the nominee of the "bolters" had become common knowledge.[33] Whether or not he had been given serious consideration by the Barnburner leaders at that time is unknown, but there is evidence that he was thought about in the period that followed. John Van Buren went so far as to ask the General if his *Signal* letter meant that he favored the Wilmot Proviso.[34] Knowledge of this action became public. It was inevitable, therefore, that Taylor should become a prominent figure in the pre-Utica speculations; he was not, however, considered among Barnburners themselves. Although John Van Buren was still suggesting Taylor as a possible nominee in early May, the Barnburners had dropped him before the meeting at Baltimore; his reply to John Van Buren had been unsatisfactory.[35] Moreover, his nomination by the Whigs had identified him with the slave power.

A more prominent candidate was John A. Dix, New York's junior senator. Despite urging from Van Buren and even threats to "trample him underfoot" if he did not consent to run, Dix refused to allow his name to be placed before the convention.[36] Franklin Pierce of New

[32] O. C. Gardiner, *Great Issue* (New York, 1848), p. 117. Further evidence of support came in the form of telegrams from Chicago—signed by Mayor Wentworth, Timothy Hoyne, Isaac N. Arnold, and "one hundred others"—and from Lafayette, Indiana.

[33] Smith, *Blair Family,* 1 : 224; James W. Taylor to Van Buren, 2 November 1847, Van Buren Papers; *Albany Argus,* 22 February 1848; Baltimore *Sun,* 21 February 1848.

[34] Thomas B. Stevenson, a close friend of the editor of the *Signal,* informed Clay early in April 1848 that a Barnburner agent had sounded the General in order to discover if his *Signal* letter meant that he favored the Wilmot Proviso. A little later John Van Buren admitted that he was the agent (Stevenson to Clay, 8 April 1848, Clay Papers; John Van Buren to Martin Van Buren, 18 April 1848, Van Buren Papers).

[35] Mower to McLean, 5 June 1848, McLean Papers; Joseph L. White to Clay, 26 May 1848, Clay Papers.

[36] Dix, *Memoirs,* 1 : 233, 240.

Hampshire was also approached to no avail.[37] Inevitably, therefore, Barnburner leaders turned again to Van Buren.[38]

Van Buren's reply to them in a long letter was read to the Utica convention by Benjamin Butler. Van Buren reiterated his "unchangeable determination never again to be a candidate for public office." At the same time he sympathized completely with the objectives of the Utica convention, commending the Barnburners for withdrawing from the Baltimore meeting, which had heaped "outrage" and untold "indignities" upon them, and agreeing that the decisions of the Democratic convention were in no way binding upon New York. The question of slavery, he recognized, was the chief issue; on this point he agreed entirely with the enlightened opinion of the nation. Nor was there the shadow of a doubt in his mind regarding the authority of Congress to prevent the further extension of slavery. Indeed, he had made the same declaration years before:

> Whilst the candidate of my friends for the Presidency, I distinctly avowed my opinion in favor of the power of Congress to abolish slavery in the District of Columbia, although I still was, for reasons which were then, and are still satisfactory to my mind, very decidedly opposed to its exercise there. The question of power is certainly as clear in respect of the Territories as it is in regard to the District; and as to the Territories my opinion was also made known in a still more solvent form, by giving the executive approval required by the Constitution, to the Bill for the organization of the Territorial Government of Iowa, which prohibited the introduction of slavery into that Territory.

Holding such views, he could not sanction the judgment of the Baltimore convention that the Constitution conferred no power on Congress to exclude slavery from the territories, unless he avowed himself to be "in favor of the Extension of Slavery in the abstract." "I do therefore, unhesitatingly approve the course you pursue, in withholding your votes from Governor Cass, and shall do so myself," he concluded. "If no other candidates than those before the country are presented I shall not vote for President."[39]

A great round of applause followed Butler's reading of the letter. Ovation after ovation shook the fragile hall. Without any hesitation the assembled multitude, disregarding his express refusal to stand for the

---

[37] Butler to Pierce, 16 June 1848, Pierce Papers.

[38] Samuel Waterbury et al. to Van Buren, 16 June 1848, Van Buren Papers.

[39] *Niles' Register* 74 (13 December 1848): 377–80; Gardiner, *Great Issue*, pp. 110–16. See also Van Buren to Dix, 20 June 1848, Van Buren Papers.

office, unanimously acclaimed Van Buren as their candidate for the presidency. With the same unity and dispatch it named former Governor Henry Dodge of Wisconsin as his running mate.[40]

Then the convention turned to the task of constructing a platform. As finally adopted, the platform revealed a desire to maintain the appearance of party regularity and to reflect past principles; at the same time it revealed a recognition and an approval of growing forces within the nation and a determination to push new principles to a conclusion and to join with forces going in the same direction.

The first part of the platform justified and approved the course of the Barnburner delegation at Baltimore and argued that New York, because of its exclusion, owed no obligation to the nominations made there. Moreover, it announced that the doctrines and opinions avowed by the Baltimore nominee upon the subject of congressional power over slavery in the territories "totally disqualified him to receive the support of the Democracy" of New York; the convention found it "utterly impossible . . . to yield him such support." In such circumstances New York had the right to present its own candidate.

Another portion of the platform announced the Barnburners' determination never to abandon the great principles "of liberty, justice, and benevolence proclaimed in the Declaration of Independence, . . . expounded in the inaugural address of Thomas Jefferson, and illustrated in the great measures of the several democratic administrations." It also announced their opposition to "unnecessary public debts, funding schemes, high taxes, however masked, standing armies, profuse expenditures of the public treasuries . . . and special legislation."

However, it also recognized the wisdom of a movement toward a new internal improvements plank, which was becoming more popular in both Whig and Democratic ranks in western New York and along the Great Lakes: "We think Congress has the power to make appropriations for the protection of the commerce with foreign nations, and among the Several States, by the improvement of harbors and rivers." It also approved a movement developing in the East for land reform: "The public lands of the United States should not be sold in large quantities to speculators; but should . . . be sold in small quantities to actual settlers . . . at a price to them not exceeding the cost and expense of acquiring, surveying and giving title to the same."

[40] Dodge's only rival was Marcus Morton, who had refused to be a candidate (Morton to Flagg, 17 June 1848, in Darling, *Political Changes,* pp. 349–50). A week after his nomination, of which he was never officially informed, Dodge declined it (*Niles' Register* 74 [12 July 1848] : 19).

The major part of the platform was devoted to the slavery issue. Taking as their text the words of their keynoter, Martin Grover—who had emphasized that the question before them was not whether "black men" were to be made free, but whether "white men" were *"to remain free"*—the delegates proclaimed the reasons for their hostility to the spread of slavery:

> While we . . . disclaim all right to interfere in any way with the institution as it exists, we yet feel ourselves . . . compelled to declare . . . that we regard domestic slavery . . . in the slaveholding states of this Republic, as a great moral, social and political evil—a relic of barbarism which must be necessarily swept away in the progress of Christian civilization, and which, therefore, ought not to be established, in the virgin soil of the territories.

In addition, they were alarmed by "the false degradation of labor" which occurred in "slave countries" where free labor was in effect "excluded from all those branches of industry usually carried out by slaves." Therefore, to permit the introduction of slavery into territories where it did not exist "would perpetrate an act of gross injustice against all the free laborers" of the nation and of "overpopulated Europe," because it would bar them from engaging in "that useful labor" which was essential not only to their "subsistence, health and comfort" but also to their "highest happiness" and their "moral and intellectual elevation." Introduction of slavery into such territories, moreover, would greatly retard "the accumulation of national wealth and the progress of civilization," because it would preclude the use of the "energy" and the exercise of the "intelligence and inventive skill" which resulted "from the competition of freemen."

For these reasons they were "uncompromisingly opposed to the extension of slavery by any action of the federal government to territories now free." The power to prohibit the introduction of slavery into the territories "was clearly delegated to Congress by the Constitution"; in their view "the highest consideration of patriotism, the strongest sentiments of justice and humanity, consistent with . . . professions of democratic principles, and a proper respect for the enlightened opinion of mankind" required that this congressional power "be exercised in favor of freedom."

Finally, the delegates requested and authorized the former Baltimore delegates to attend and take part in "any convention of the free States, or of any of them," which might be called "for the purpose of collecting and concentrating the popular will in respect of the question of the Presidency."[41]

Less than a week after the Utica convention, on 28 June, a third great antislavery convention gathered at Worcester with Samuel Hoar in the chair. The assembly was attended by some five thousand Conscience Whigs and a handful of Democrats from Massachusetts, who were able to travel on the railways at half fare, and a few out-of-state visitors such as Giddings and John Bigelow, a "live Barnburner" from New York City; they listened to nearly a dozen speakers, including Sumner, who vigorously flayed Taylor as the nominee of "an unhallowed union . . . between cotton planters and flesh mongers of Louisiana . . . and cotton spinners and traffickers of New England." In its final action the multitude summoned "the lovers of Freedom from both parties" in the commonwealth to join in Buffalo their own six delegates and other antislavery forces in the "revolution against . . . tyranny."[42]

Reports of the proceedings in Columbus, Utica, and Worcester sent waves of militant enthusiasm coursing through the North. Throughout New England, antislavery Whigs and Democrats took immediate action. In Massachusetts, Whigs held so many meetings that Charles Francis Adams, who at Worcester had been named chairman of a committee to organize the "Buffalo movement," was forced to establish an informal "speakers' bureau" to satisfy the demand; in a short while he was sending oratorical talent to every New England state and even to New York.[43] Democrats in the Bay State were not far behind Whigs. Leadership was assumed by Marcus Morton[44] (an old friend of Van Buren, the collector of the Port of Boston, and a sympathizer with Barnburner objectives) and by Amasa Walker, John Boles, and Nathaniel Morton —all of whom had been at Worcester. A score of local Democratic meetings in rural areas pledged allegiance to "free soil," and half a dozen county journals struck the "black flag of the slaves" to hoist the banner of "Van Buren and Freedom."[45] Vermont's radical Democrats

[41] *Niles' Register* 74 (20 December 1848): 386–87; Gardiner, *Great Issue,* pp. 118–20.

[42] *Sumner's Works,* 2: 75–88; Pierce, *Sumner,* 3: 165–66; *Niles' Register* 74 (5 July 1848): 9; Gatell, "Conscience and Judgment," pp. 26–34; Duberman, *Adams,* pp. 140–45.

[43] *New York Tribune,* 1 July 1848; Gatell, "Conscience and Judgment," pp. 34–35, 40–42.

[44] Morton's thinking and activity are best outlined in Darling, *Political Changes,* pp. 347–52.

[45] *Boston Post,* 3, 6, 12, 14, 25, 27 July 1848; *Boston Times,* 7 July 1848; Hoar, *Autobiography,* 1: 145.

(led by the editor of the *Bennington Gazette*), the Hale Democracy of New Hampshire, and factions in Maine, Connecticut, and Rhode Island also joined the parade.[46]

Yankee Liberty men responded in like manner. Although some revealed misgivings about the purity of Barnburner objectives and about the Barnburners' readiness to join an antislavery coalition and although the Boston *Emancipator* warned against "new alliances" that would mean a "falling back or letting down in any position" the party had taken, by the end of July every Liberty organization in New England had bowed to amalgamation. Even the *Emancipator* changed its attitude. "Of one thing we are certain," it declared late in the month, "and that is that the Liberty men can make no better disposition of their time and services this year, than in attending the Buffalo Convention and urging the nomination of Mr. Hale."[47]

New York also witnessed coalition activities on several fronts. Some Barnburners apparently worried about affiliating too closely with abolitionists, but the overwhelming majority looked toward Buffalo with high hopes.[48] In Whig ranks both the large, recalcitrant Clay contingent, centered in Manhattan and Albany, and the antislavery "wooly heads" in the vicinity of Syracuse lent the movement their support.[49] Much encouragement was given by Greeley, who, despite indecision as to his own future conduct, advised "Whig dissenters" to cast their lot with his ancient enemy, Van Buren.[50] Abolitionists at first held back. To dissuade amalgamation the Executive Committee of the American and Foreign Anti-Slavery Society issued an address of warning:

> Non-extension is not abolition, though included in it; and it will be time to consider overtures of coalition from fellow citizens who have recently awakened to see the disastrous policy of Slavery extension, when they shall have embraced the great anti-Slavery principles we avow. . . . Till then we owe it to our able and chosen candidates, and to our party to be united—neither to propose or listen to any set of men . . . who from policy do not embrace the truth in the anti-Slavery question, or . . . who content themselves with merely

[46] *Niles' Register* 74 (9 July 1848): 38; *Buffalo Republic*, 19, 21, 26 July, 3 August 1848.

[47] Tuck to Hale, 21 June 1848, Lewis Tappan to Hale, 8 July, 2 August 1848, Samuel Lewis to Hale, 10 July 1848, Hale Papers; Boston *Emancipator*, 5, 28 July, 2 August 1848.

[48] Tuck to Hale, 21 June 1848, Hale Papers.

[49] *Albany Atlas*, 4 August 1848; *Albany Argus*, 8 August 1848; *Syracuse Journal* quoted in *Niles' Register* 74 (19 July 1848): 38.

[50] *New York Tribune*, 1 July 1848.

making efforts to stay the progress of an evil which we banded together . . . to destroy.[51]

Although the orthodox men who controlled the Liberty party machinery gave heed to the address, the rank and file turned a deaf ear; their demands for fusion swept the whole organization to Buffalo. Indeed, the enthusiasm in New York even brought the announcement that a Macedonian delegation would attend the convention.[52]

Throughout the Northwest the movement for independent action grew with equal rapidity. In Ohio, despite Giddings's announced distrust of the "leading Locos of New York," Whigs and Democrats everywhere joined to send representatives to Buffalo. So great was the rush to antislavery conventions that the *National Era* declared: "We cannot find room for even brief notices of all the Free Soil meetings in Ohio. The people there seem to be cutting loose *en masse* from the old party organizations."[53] In Indiana, hitherto relatively untouched by third-party appeals, and in Michigan, editors hastened to tear Cass and Taylor banners from the mastheads of their papers, while statewide conventions and scores of local meetings named Buffalo delegations and resolved "to bury all political animosities and strike hands for the one great cause of Free Soil and Free Labor."[54] Northern Illinois and southeastern Wisconsin witnessed scenes of similar activity. In Chicago vast throngs of Whigs and Democrats marched the streets chanting the name of the Utica nominee. Every county of the region saw members of the major parties uniting in the movement to "bar slavery" forever from the western plains. Signs of antislavery attitudes also began to appear in Iowa.[55]

Among political abolitionists of the Northwest, union with antiextensionists found hearty response in all areas. Ohio Liberty men pointed the way. Under the leadership of Chase their state convention had shared the deliberations of the Free Territory meeting at Columbus and afterward had indicated a willingness to join the Buffalo movement. Backed

[51] Ibid., 8 July 1848.

[52] *National Era,* 6, 27 July 1848. In the East there were also some "Van Buren and Free Soil" demonstrations in Jersey City; Norristown, Wayne County, and Pittsburgh in Pennsylvania; and Baltimore (*Buffalo Republic,* 10, 15 July, 3, 4 August 1848; *Niles' Register* 74 [16 August 1848] : 109).

[53] Giddings to Follett, 26 July 1848, in Hamlin, "Follett Papers," 10: 32–33; *Cincinnati Herald,* 5 July 1848; *National Era,* 20 July 1848.

[54] *Indiana State Sentinel,* 29 July 1848; William Failey to James S. Wadsworth, 7 July 1848, Van Buren Papers; *Detroit Advertiser,* 5 July, 10 August 1848; *National Era,* 10 August 1848; *Buffalo Republic,* 14, 31 July 1848.

[55] *National Era,* 20 July 1848; *Buffalo Republic,* 11 July 1848; *Racine Advocate,* 19, 22 July, 2 August 1848.

by the *Cincinnati Herald,* which condemned old-guard warnings as "too transcendental for . . . common sense," amalgamation spread rapidly through local organizations of the state.[56] By mid-July the whole Liberty party of Ohio appeared resolved on "union with the Friends of Freedom."[57] Indiana, Illinois, and Michigan abolitionists quickly followed in the wake of their Buckeye State brethren.[58] In Wisconsin, apparently, fusion at first had little appeal. The opinion of Liberty men was voiced by the *Milwaukee Freeman:* "We regard this movement as an abandonment of the Liberty party. We wash our hands of all participation in the business." But such views ran contrary to the trend; late in July a state convention called by Charles Durkee to prevent the isolation of the party in Wisconsin, named delegates to the Buffalo convention with instructions to "sustain no candidates" except those who were "not only pledged against the extension of slavery" but were also "committed to the policy of abolishing it."[59]

As might be expected, the question of who would carry the northern banner in the upcoming contest became as important as the actual movement toward Buffalo. From the first, Van Buren's name loomed largest. Some reasons were obvious: As a former president, Van Buren had greater prestige than any other person connected with the movement; as the candidate of the Utica convention, he claimed the support of the largest single contingent of delegates to the forthcoming convention; as various demonstrations indicated, his name drew antislavery Democrats into the movement. In addition, the feeling developed that the Barnburners would not cooperate if the Buffalo convention failed to nominate him;[60] since their cooperation was highly desirable, many resigned themselves to his inevitable nomination.[61]

But there were many Whigs and Liberty men who mistrusted both the Barnburners and Van Buren. Some of the mistrust was based on old

[56] *Cincinnati Herald,* 28 June, 19 July 1848.

[57] *National Era,* 6, 13 July 1848.

[58] Smith, *Liberty and Free Soil Parties,* pp. 134–35.

[59] *Milwaukee Freeman,* 9 June 1848 in Smith, *Liberty and Free Soil Parties,* p. 136; *Racine Advocate,* 2 August 1848.

[60] In an exchange of letters Tilden informed Chase that the Barnburners would be willing to go along with the Buffalo convention on the vice-presidential nomination. "As for the presidency," he continued, "it will not under any circumstances, be practicable to change the position of the Democracy of this State. Their conviction on this subject would be irresistable, whatever might be the desires of leading men" (Chase to Tilden, 19 July 1848, in Bigelow, *Tilden Letters,* 1: 50–52; Tilden to Chase, 29 July 1848, in *Chase Correspondence,* pp. 469–70).

[61] Stanton to Chase, 6 June 1848, Chase Papers; Sumner to Whittier, 12 July 1848, in Pierce, *Sumner,* 3: 168; Tuck to George G. Fogg, 5 August 1848, Amos Tuck Papers; S. P. Parsons to Hale, 6 July 1848, Hale Papers.

prejudices. Samuel Lyman of Massachusetts charged that the Barnburners were more in favor of "free plunder than of free soil." Richard Henry Dana expressed the attitude another way: "All we ask is that we be not required to vote for a man identified with everything we have opposed through life; whose name we have rebelled against, who all our public men have opposed on both personal and political grounds."[62] There were others from localities as wide apart as Maine and Indiana who believed Van Buren's candidacy would be "almost if not quite fatal" to the cause because it would drive away "just the persons we want with us."[63]

The chief objection to Van Buren appeared to be against the "servile stamp" of his administration and particularly against his "rather superfluous reaffirmation" of an old pledge to veto any bill abolishing slavery in the District of Columbia, which, one Liberty partisan maintained, had all the appearance of an insult gratuitously thrown into the face of would-be supporters.[64] So intense was the feeling on this matter among Conscience Whigs of Massachusetts and among abolitionists in general that Gamaliel Bailey of the *National Era* and Charles Francis Adams each took it upon himself to suggest that Van Buren clarify his position.[65] But Van Buren, who objected to making any statement on the issue because it would appear that he was trying to "gather votes," refused to be drawn out.[66] In his reply to Adams, "the most enigmatic thing conceivable,"[67] he merely acknowledged Adams's "fair criticism" and made no attempt to clarify his position, because he was not an aspirant.[68]

The candidates of the anti–Van Buren element were Hale and McLean. Naturally, Hale was supported by members of his own party,

[62] Lyman to Palfrey, 30 July 1848, Dana to Jared Willson, 20 July 1848, in Gatell, "Conscience and Judgment," p. 43.

[63] A. Willey to Chase, 10 July 1848, H. C. Stewart to Chase, 24 July 1848, Stanton to Samuel Lewis and Chase, 3 July 1848, Chase Papers; Rufus Elman to Hale, 7 July 1848, Hale Papers; Charles Francis Adams, Jr., *Charles Francis Adams* (Boston, 1900), p. 90.

[64] Willey to Chase, 7 July 1848, Sumner to Chase, 7 July 1848, Chase Papers.

[65] Adams to Van Buren, 16 July 1848, Gamaliel Bailey to Van Buren, 2 August 1848, Van Buren Papers. See also H. H. Van Dyck to Van Buren, 17 July 1848, William F. Channing to Van Buren, 13 August 1848.

[66] Van Buren to Blair, 26 July 1848, Blair Papers.

[67] Adams quoted in Gatell, "Conscience and Judgment," p. 43.

[68] Van Buren to Adams, 24 July 1848, in *Reunion of Free Soilers of 1848* (Boston, 1877), pp. 25–26. The desire to secure Barnburner aid and the mistrust of Van Buren caused some Liberty men and some Whigs to consider John A. Dix as a possible presidential candidate (Tuck to Fogg, 5 August 1848, Tuck Papers; Duberman. *Adams,* p. 146).

who, with the Boston *Emancipator,* pointed out that he was "first in the field"; they questioned the expediency of deserting him for "any new men set up by an alliance of half-fledged antislavery Whigs or Democrats," especially when such an alliance was "begotten through some mere party prejudice or disappointment, founded on no true regard for the slave."[69] But Hale himself was apparently willing to withdraw.[70]

McLean's backers came chiefly from Ohio. Whigs such as Edward Wade, E. S. Hamlin, and Giddings, and Liberty leaders such as Chase were among his supporters; each regarded him as "emphatically right" on the Free Soil issue, though some had reservations about his position on abolition.[71] Conscience Whigs in Massachusetts such as Charles Francis Adams, Stephen C. Phillips, Sumner, and Henry B. Stanton, who had not warmed to McLean as a suitable Whig candidate, also focused their attention on him, mostly as a possible counterweight to Van Buren.[72]

Chase, Giddings, and Sumner each importuned the Judge to allow his name to be presented at Buffalo.[73] McLean proved reluctant, and he had good reasons. Friends reminded him that he would ruin his chances of achieving his long-sought goal, a Whig presidential nomination in 1852, if he identified himself with the Buffalo movement.[74] He also recognized that the Barnburners were exhibiting a firm determination to nominate Van Buren and that some of his own more influential supporters—Chase, Sumner, and Stanton—were willing to aid them.[75]

Political expediency caused their shift to the Van Buren banner; its rationale was well explained in a letter Chase received from a New York abolitionist. "The Barnburners are in earnest," he pointed out, "but they have prejudices and obstacles to contend with which are imperfectly understood at a distance." Chief of these was their need to preserve the appearance of regularity. "Under their present organization," Chase's informant explained, they have "the advantage of the regular party

[69] Boston *Emancipator,* 28 June 1848. See also *Niles' Register* 74 (19 July 1848): 38; Lewis Tappan to Hale, 8 July, 2 August 1848, Hale Papers. Hale supporters usually suggested Giddings, John A. Dix, or John Van Buren as the vice-presidential candidate.

[70] Hale to Lewis Tappan, 6 July 1848, Hale Papers.

[71] Chase to Giddings, 10 March 1848, in *Chase Correspondence,* p. 132.

[72] Sumner to Chase, 12 June 1848, Chase Papers.

[73] Chase to McLean, 2 August 1848, Giddings to McLean, 13 July 1848, Sumner to McLean, 31 July 1848, McLean Papers. McLean supporters usually suggested Benjamin F. Butler, John A. Dix, or John Van Buren as a running mate.

[74] Whittlesey to McLean, 24 July 1848, ibid.

[75] Chase to McLean, 2 August 1848, Sumner to McLean, 31 July 1848, Stanton to McLean, 28 July 1848, ibid.

usages—by this they have and will if rightly used take the great body of the party with them and keep them for any purpose or measure, but should another nomination than Mr. Van Buren be made . . . the great body of the party will return again to their former servile associates, coerced by the cry that they have been led into federal ranks."[76] To prevent such a loss, Chase and others had begun to talk of a Van Buren–McLean ticket.[77]

But second place on any ticket was a position that McLean would never accept. Late in July he informed several of his Cleveland followers that he would not run. "The great and exciting question of slavery extension as it bears upon my position on the bench," he wrote, "the use of my name in the present canvass and the rejection of it by the Ohio delegates to the National Convention, the relation which Mr. Van Buren maintains to the public, have all been deliberately considered, and I am brought to the conclusion that I ought not to go before the Buffalo Convention as a candidate for the Presidency."[78] Then McLean wavered. A few days later he informed Chase that he would not necessarily refuse the nomination if a "general upheaval" should occur in his favor.[79] Although his supporters knew that no such upheaval would come, they persisted in their hope of giving him second place. E. S. Hamlin telegraphed him, asking for complete liberty to use his name in the convention. But McLean refused to give assurance that he would accept even a nomination for the presidency if it were offered.[80]

A motley horde of political nonconformists descended upon Buffalo during the sweltering days of early August. By train, steamer, and canal boat, on horseback and afoot—a vast army, numbering no less than twenty thousand—they thronged into the city[81] to attend the birth of a

---

[76] E. Harrington to Chase, 5 August 1848, Chase Papers.

[77] Significantly, some Barnburners had earlier suggested the same ticket. See Bradford R. Wood to McLean, 3 July 1848, McLean Papers; *New York Globe* quoted in *Indiana State Sentinel,* 10 July 1848.

[78] McLean to James A. Briggs et al., 28 July 1848, in *Ohio State Journal,* 21 August 1848; *Niles' Register* 74 (13 September 1848) : 165.

[79] McLean to Chase, 2 August 1848, in Holt, "Party Politics in Ohio," p. 326. See also McLean to W. H. V. Denny, 31 July 1848, McLean Papers.

[80] Chase to McLean, 12 August 1848, Hamlin to McLean, 17 August 1848, McLean Papers. Before anyone except the Ohioans knew of McLean's indecision, Sumner, who had urged him to allow his name to be presented, apparently decided that the Judge would not run and impulsively approached Edward Everett as a possible vice-presidential candidate. Everett refused (Donald, *Sumner,* p. 167 note 7).

[81] Rather lengthy accounts of the scene at Buffalo are in *Buffalo Republic,* 8–12 August 1848; *Albany Atlas,* 10–12 August 1848; Gardiner, *Great Issue,* pp. 128–45; and Oliver Dyer, *Phonographic Reports of the Proceedings of the National Free Soil Convention* (Buffalo, 1848), pp. 3–35.

new party. Antislavery men of every stripe were there: Macedonians, orthodox abolitionists who talked of Hale's virtues, Liberty party politicians of the Chase brand, McLean men, Great Lakes Democrats, New York Barnburners and their allies from New England, and Conscience Whigs of Massachusetts, the Western Reserve, and Wisconsin. Mingling with this crowd were Clay men by the hundreds, intent upon striking down the military chieftan who had dethroned their idol at Philadelphia;[82] northern Negroes, some of them fugitives, holding conference with delegates from Maryland, Virginia, and Delaware; Democratic advocates of river and harbor improvements; and Land Reformers.

The latter two groups had appeared because their particular demands, like those of the antislavery men, had been rejected by or had received no consideration from the two major parties. The greater number of the advocates of river and harbor improvements were inhabitants of the Chicago area. Without exception they were Democrats who had been thoroughly angered by Polk's veto of two bills which would have provided the funds necessary to improve the snag-filled western rivers and the poorly protected harbors of the Great Lakes. Their attitude toward the problem had been expressed in the resolutions of the River and Harbor Convention held in July 1847 in Chicago, where Whigs and Democrats from all over the Union had demanded the appropriation of public monies to remove the "peculiar dangers to the navigation of the lakes . . . and the western rivers."[83] During the following year Democratic state conventions in Michigan and Wisconsin and all the major Democratic journals in the Great Lakes area had renewed the demand.[84] Newspapers such as the *Chicago Democrat,* moreover, announced that the Chicago platform would be applied as a test to every man who aspired to the presidential chair.[85] When news that Cass had been nominated in Baltimore reached the region around the lower end of Lake Michigan, internal improvements champions instantly recalled the terse, two-sentence letter that Cass had sent to William Whitney when asked to attend the Chicago convention: "I am much obliged to you for your kind attention in transmitting to me an invitation to attend the Convention on Internal Improvements, which will meet in Chicago in July.

[82] It appears that some Clay Whigs expected to support Van Buren; others thought it possible that Clay himself might be named (J. G. Proud to Clay, 11 June 1848, Botts to Clay, 3 July 1848, Clay Papers). Tuck was willing to support Clay (Tuck to Fogg, 5 August 1848, Tuck Papers).

[83] Proceedings of the convention are in *Niles' Register* 72 (26 June, 17, 24, 31 July, 7 August 1847): 266–67, 309–10, 331–33, 344–46, 365–67.

[84] Baltimore *Sun,* 28 June 1847; Detroit *Free Press,* 13 September 1847; *Daily Wisconsin,* 14 April 1848.

[85] *Chicago Democrat,* 13 July 1847.

Circumstances, however, will put it out of my power to be present at that time."[86] This rebuff was enough to turn many against Cass; when the Barnburners in Utica expressed favor for their program, advocates of river and harbor improvements joined the movement to Buffalo.

Land Reformers had first appeared as an organized force in national politics with the creation of the National Reform Association under the leadership of George Henry Evans, in New York City early in 1844. Their avowed object was "to establish the right of the people to the soil" through legislation giving away the public lands to actual settlers.[87]

Evans aimed his campaign primarily at workingmen. Land reform would drain excess laborers from eastern manufacturing areas; trade unions could aid the movement by transporting the penniless to the West. In turn, their removal would create both a labor scarcity and an excess of housing in the East. Workingmen who remained behind would be rewarded by higher wages, better working conditions, and lower rents. From its beginning, labor leaders were attracted to the movement; a dozen working mechanics sat on the first central committee of the National Reform Association. The labor press, ranging from the *Lowell Operative* to the *Cincinnati Nonpareil,* backed the movement.

In 1845 the National Reform Association merged with the New England Workingmen's Association. Thereafter the two organizations, joined by delegates from "industrial councils" that were being established in eastern cities, met in annual session as the Industrial Congress.[88] Evans became editor of their journal, the *Working Man's Advocate.*[89] In the following year the Land Reformers created their first ripple in national politics when they spread through the country a circular titled "Vote Yourself a Farm." It was a trenchant appeal to the landless and the near-landless to form a new party with but a single aim: "to limit the quantity of land that anyone may henceforth monopolize and inherit; and . . . to make the public lands free to actual settlers only, each having the right to sell his improvements to any man not possessed of other land."[90]

[86] *Niles' Register* 72 (17 July 1847) : 310.
[87] New York *Working Man's Advocate,* 6 April 1845. The proposal was not a new one; the National Trades' Union had advanced a similar proposition in 1835.
[88] The "industrial councils" of the late 1840s were originally organizations of local labor associations, comparable to the citywide "unions" of trade associations of an earlier period and to the city federations and central bodies of a later period. Weak as labor organizations, they were quickly joined by a variety of reform elements which sometimes dominated them.
[89] John R. Commons, "Horace Greeley and the Working Class Origins of the Republican Party," *Political Science Quarterly* 24 (1909) : 480.
[90] John R. Commons, *Documentary History of American Industrial Society* (New York, 1910), 7: 305–7.

Coincidentally, Land Reformers began to ask candidates for public office to pledge themselves to use their influence "to prevent all further traffic in the Public Lands of the States and of the United States, and to cause them to be laid out in Farms and Lots for the free and exclusive use of actual settlers."[91] Thereafter the "free land" issue made moderate progress. Conservative eastern journals such as the *Buffalo Commercial Advertiser* condemned "the idea . . . of making a man virtuous, happy and industrious" by giving away the public domain to needy settlers as a "preposterous scheme," "at war alike with philosophy and divine revelation."[92] At the same time men such as Hale, Greeley, and Wentworth, along with such journals as the *Philadelphia Times,* the *Cleveland Plain Dealer,* and the *Cincinnati Herald,* became champions of land reform.[93] Their attitude was expressed in Wentworth's *Chicago Democrat:*

> The time has come when the voice of labor must be heard. It will not answer now to summarily lay its petition on the table. Man must in the end triumph and Capital must be his slave. The fact that the voice of the laborer is crying in our fields, is evidence that a fresh necessity has established an additional right. . . . As soon as the freedom of the public lands, in limited quantities shall have been secured to actual settlers, Land Limitation and Homestead Security in the States must inevitably follow. Then every man will labor in his own land; then will the desire of the first settlers of this continent be perfected; and we will indeed be a free and happy people. The present dominion of Capital tends to the tenant system, under which Republicanism is impossible. This system tends to separate classes in society; to the annihilation of the love of country; and to the weakening of the spirit of independence. . . . We are a republic. If we desire to continue so, let us pass the public lands into the hands of the people: let us give to those who are unable to buy, *without money and without price,* that which the fact of birth entitles them to. By this means we strike at the last foothold of the *"Money Monopoly"*—the Monopoly of the Soil.[94]

With such influential backing the Land Reformers gradually spread their organization through the North. Everywhere local industrial congresses, labor associations, and mass meetings announced their support; by the summer of 1847 the National Reform Association declared that it

[91] Ibid., p. 312.

[92] *Buffalo Commercial Advertiser* quoted in *New York Tribune,* 14 February 1846.

[93] Boston *Emancipator,* 18 July 1848; *New York Tribune,* 15 October 1845, 31 January, 2 May 1846; Philadelphia *Times,* 15 October 1847; *Cleveland Plain Dealer,* 24 September, 8 October 1847; *Cincinnati Herald,* 11 August 1847.

[94] *Chicago Democrat* quoted in *New York Tribune,* 19 February 1848.

would nominate as its national ticket those candidates "introduced to their notice, by a political organization having the cause of human rights at heart."[95] In June 1848 the annual meeting of the Industrial Congress made it known that only the Liberty League had complied with its demands; accordingly, it nominated Gerrit Smith and William S. Waite of Illinois as its standard bearers.[96]

The Macedonians were not the only political element interested in the program of the Land Reformers. At the Ohio Free Territory Convention, E. S. Hamlin of the *Cleveland True Democrat* introduced and secured approval of a resolution recognizing "as valid the interpretation of the doctrine of free soil" which assured "to actual settlers, under suitable limitations, the free grant of reasonable portions of the Public Domain, as permanent homes for themselves and their children."[97] Barnburners were also attracted to the movement. Early in 1848 their representatives in the New York Assembly cast their votes for a resolution instructing senators and congressmen "to use their best efforts to obtain the passage of a law to protect the sale of . . . public lands, and to cause them to be surveyed into lots of limited quantities for the use of actual settlers."[98] In Utica they also announced a free-land plank.

In mid-July, moreover, in a letter to Alvan E. Bovay, chairman of the National Executive Committee of the Industrial Congress, Van Buren hinted that he was not unsympathetic. Since he did not wish to create the impression that he was again seeking the presidency, he declined to give a direct opinion; however, he did point out that he regarded "the public domain as a trust fund belonging to all the states to be disposed of for their common benefit." In making such a disposition, Congress should act upon the principle that the people had "a greater interest in any early settlement and substantial improvement of the public lands than in the amount of revenue" which might be derived from them, and that "to accomplish this object the accumulation of large tracts in a few hands, should be discountenanced, and liberal facilities afforded for the acquisition of small portions" by citizens "in good faith desireous of possessing them as homes for themselves and their families."[99] It was the promise held forth in such resolutions and statements, a promise of success in wider fields, that brought the Land Reformers to the Buffalo convention in August.

[95] *New York Tribune*, 12 June 1847; *Voice of Industry*, 25 June 1847.

[96] *New York Tribune*, 1 July 1848. Waite later declined the nomination (*Niles' Register* 74 [12 July 1848] : 19).

[97] Hamlin to Chase, 14 May 1848, Chase Papers; *Cincinnati Herald*, 28 June 1848.

[98] *Albany Atlas*, 8 January 1848.

[99] Ibid., 26 July 1848.

Out of this heterogeneous mass a new party was to be formed. Agreement on a platform promised to be a formidable task, for chances of disagreement smoldered in every question. Would Barnburners, reluctant to be tagged as abolitionists, and politically wise Whigs accept a platform more radical than the Wilmot Proviso? Would old-line Liberty men accept anything less than their full party creed? How would Democrats and Whigs settle their differences over the tariff? Would the demands of delegates from the Great Lakes for river and harbor improvements arouse the old Democratic-Whig cleavage on the internal improvements issue? Would Whigs accept the free-land plank pressed by eastern laboring and agrarian interests?

Friction over nominations seemed no less inevitable. Barnburners seemed determined to accept no one but Van Buren, but there was an ominous antipathy to him in Whig and Liberty ranks. The determination of old-guard Hale men to accept none but their candidate was equally foreboding. The intrigues of Taylor and Cass politicians, scattered throughout the conglomerate multitude, were not calculated to resolve any discord.[100]

Despite the heterogeneity and the seeming undertone of dissonance, only harmony pervaded the throng that gathered beneath torchlights for a convention eve rally in Buffalo's public park, where they listened with marked enthusiasm to a dozen orators who denounced the evils of slavery and called for a united front against the common foe.

The reasons for this unity, amazing even to the leaders of the Free Soil movement, are readily ascertainable. While each of the elements present harbored fears, prejudices, and predilections, they all had one cause in common—the advancement of the democratic ideal. Full recognition of human rights and dignities and the betterment of the welfare of the common man were their goals. Those ideals can be readily seen in the principles of each faction. Most advanced were the abolitionists with their program of personal liberty for all men, slavery for none, white or black. Although less advanced, the Barnburners were determined to prevent the extension of an institution that was a complete denial of democracy and to dedicate the unblighted western plains to the free laborer who, in himself and in his labor, epitomized the democratic concept. Among Conscience Whigs, whose original opposition both to slavery itself and to its extension was based upon ethical and religious

---

[100] Most of the intrigues were apparently intended to convince the "honest unsuspecting free soil men" that they were being used by Barnburner "gamesters" and "sick Whigs" for their own selfish aims (*Buffalo Republic*, 8 August 1848; *Cleveland Plain Dealer*, 9 August 1848; Detroit *Free Press*, 12 August 1848; *National Era*, 23 August 1848).

grounds, something of the spirit of both the abolitionists and the Barnburners appeared. Some of the Conscience Whigs of Massachusetts
hoped also to curb the power of the textile manufacturers, whose ties
with southern planting interests made them chary of interfering with
property rights, however odious morally, for the benefit of human rights.

Advocates of river and harbor improvements sought to lighten the
farmers' and the businessmen's marketing burdens, to give them full and
complete opportunity to develop their holdings and investments. Land
Reformers were intent upon improving the welfare and status of workingmen whose advance was being limited by an apparently excessive
labor supply. Simultaneously, they sought to preserve and to increase
land ownership, which to them was a highly necessary prerequisite to
democracy. They aimed at keeping the western lands out of the hands of
the great landlords and speculators by giving land to the needy poor, who
would thereby achieve the self-sufficiency and self-respect due to all
members of the nation. Freedom of opportunity for the free man was
the common desire of the elements gathered at Buffalo. The leavening
quality of this ideal tempered old differences and gave birth to a new
party.

The harmonious spirit that pervaded the torchlight meeting was still
apparent when "an immense concourse" began to assemble as early as
half-past eight on the morning of 9 August under the tent which had
been erected in the park. Within a few moments, according to Oliver
Dyer, "every available seat and foothold on the ground was occupied."
After hours of listening to speeches—during which the staging erected
for reporters "went down with a tremendous crash, capsizing ink, paper,
tables, reporters and all, . . . rasping the epidermis, . . . and committing
sundry other outrages of similar nature"—the assembly came to order at
noon under the gavel of Nathaniel Sawyer of Ohio.[101] It was immediately evident that the immense throng of milling delegates—who
"seemed to think because they were Free-soilers . . . they had a perfect
right to take any possession, place, or seat they might choose"—would
be too unwieldy to transact business with any degree of efficiency.[102] A
solution of the difficulty was proposed by Preston King, chairman of a
hastily constituted Committee on Organization. With shouted unanimity
it was promptly adopted.

[101] In later years a tradition grew that the chairman had sat under a picture of an
old barn, bearing the legend "let it burn for conscience' sake" (James A. Woodburn, *Political Parties and Problems in the United States* [New York, 1914], p.
72 n). None of the contemporary accounts mentions such a picture.
[102] Dyer, *Free Soil Convention,* pp. 3–5.

King's plan provided for two assemblies: "a mass convention . . . of all persons who had come to Buffalo for Free Soil," to meet in the "Oberlin tent" that had been set up in the park; and a "select, representative, deliberative" body, the Committee of Conferees, to decide on the "main questions" and refer them to the tented assembly for ratification. The Committee of Conferees was to consist of six delegates at large from each state represented and three from each congressional district, chosen so as to give "equal representation to each of the three former political parties"; the provision was faithfully carried out.[103] With this preliminary business settled, the mass meeting elected Charles Francis Adams permanent chairman and relaxed for a long session of fervent speechmaking.[104] The "delegated convention" adjourned to deliberate behind the closed doors of the Universal Church; Chase was named chairman, and a Committee on Resolutions headed by Benjamin F. Butler was appointed.

Almost nothing is known of the deliberations of the Committee on Resolutions. It was carefully constructed to contain all political elements, and its report reflected a clear effort to reconcile differences. Butler placed the report before the Committee of Conferees on the second day.

They had come together, the report declared, "as a union of freemen . . . forgetful of past political differences, in a common resolve to maintain the rights of free labor against the aggressions of the slave power, and to secure free soil for free people." They repudiated the candidates named at Baltimore and Philadelphia "under the slaveholding dictation," because neither could be supported by the opponents of slavery extension "without a sacrifice of consistency, duty, and self-respect." Those nominations had demonstrated the necessity of a union of the people "under the banner of free democracy" to declare their "independence of the slave power, and . . . a fixed determination to rescue the federal government from its control."

Accordingly, they resolved "to plant" themselves "upon the national platform of freedom, in opposition to the sectional platform of slavery." While they proposed "no interference by Congress with slavery within the limits of any state," they insisted that it had been "the settled policy of the nation not to extend, nationalize, or encourage, but to limit, localize, and discourage slavery" since the introduction of the Jefferson proviso in 1784. They were determined to return to this policy. The

[103] Richard H. Dana III, *Speeches in Stirring Times and Letters to a Son* (Boston, 1910), p. 152 (hereafter cited as *Speeches*).

[104] The endurance and enthusiasm of the mass meeting must have been boundless. Oliver Dyer recorded forty-three speeches in two long days.

Federal government had "to relieve itself of all responsibility for the existence or continuance of slavery" wherever it possessed "constitutional authority to legislate on that subject"—an obvious reference to the District of Columbia—and Congress had to enact legislation to prevent "the extension of slavery into territory now free." They accepted the responsibility which the "slave power" had forced upon them. "To their demand for more slave States and more slave territory" their calm and final answer was "no more slave States and no more slave territory."

In order to satisfy the desires of elements present in the convention who were not primarily antislavery, the report also contained other demands: cheaper postage, the retrenchment of the expenses and patronage of the Federal government, the abolition of all unnecessary posts and salaries, and the election by the people, so far as practicable, of all civil officers in the service of the government. It called upon Congress to provide for river and harbor improvements in the interest "of the safety and convenience of commerce with foreign nations or among the several States," recommended to the favorable consideration of the nation "as a wise and just measure of public policy" the "free grant to actual settlers . . . of reasonable portions of the public lands," and advocated a tariff that would "raise revenue adequate to defray the necessary expenses of the federal government, and to pay annual installments" on the national debt.[105] The report concluded with a now famous call to battle: "We inscribe on our banner, 'Free Soil, Free Speech, Free Labor, and Free Men,' and under it will fight on, and fight ever, until a triumphant victory shall reward our exertions."[106]

Adopted by the Committee of Conferees with vociferous and excited unanimity, the report was then presented to the mass convention. Awesome silence, broken only by the fluttering of the tent flaps, descended on the assembled host during the reading. When the last words rang through the tent, a thundering roar of cheering voices announced mass concurrence.

Inspired by the acclaim given their initial efforts, the delegated convention retired to choose candidates. When the convention opened, many had feared a struggle among the supporters of Van Buren, Hale, and McLean that might have broken up the meeting. But no conflict oc-

[105] According to E. S. Hamlin, the tariff resolution created more discussion than any other: "Hon. Jo[seph L.] White from New York City was on the Committee and was very anxious that a resolution on the tariff should be adopted which would afford the Clay Whigs of N. Y. an excuse for uniting with us. He was satisfied with the resolution as adopted" (Hamlin to McLean, 17 August 1848, McLean Papers).
[106] Dyer, Free Soil Convention, pp. 19–20; Gardiner, Great Issue, pp. 138–40.

curred. Word that McLean's name would not be presented removed one possible problem.[107] While some rancor against Van Buren persisted, there was a noticeable lessening of earlier antipathy.[108] The growing spirit of political affinity was recorded by George W. Julian:

> In common with my Whig associates, I had all along felt that I could not support Mr. Van Buren under any circumstances; but the pervading tone of earnestness in the Convention, and the growing spirit of fraternity had modified our views. We saw that several of the great leaders of the Liberty party were quite ready to meet the Barnburners on common ground. It seemed very desirable to profit by so large a body of helpers, and to profit by their experience and training in the school of politics. Mr. Van Buren had certainly gone great lengths as the servant of the slave power, but . . . if nominated by the anti-slavery men of the free States, and equally committed to their principles, it was altogether improbable that he would again lend himself to the services of slavery. Besides . . . it was part of the work of earnest anti-slavery men to forget party measures and prejudice for the sake of the cause, and to cultivate the virtues of hope and trust rather than the spirit of doubt and suspicion, in dealing with a man who was now ready to unfurl the flag of freedom.[109]

A similar change of view apparently occurred among the Barnburners, the objects of abolitionist and Whig suspicions and mistrust. Though none of them recorded their party's attitude, the Barnburners evidently set aside their own qualms over an appearance of regularity and over too close an identification with abolitionism; they merged wholeheartedly into the movement. According to Chase and Hamlin, they even indicated

---

[107] I can find no evidence in contemporary sources for the frequently repeated statement that Chase "withdrew" McLean's name, for his name was never presented. Knowledge that he would not be presented must have circulated without any announcement.

[108] This feeling was illustrated in a story told by Henry B. Stanton. During his speech nominating Van Buren, as Butler was graphically describing how the ex-president, absorbed in bucolic pursuits at his farm, had leaped a fence to show a visitor a field of sprouting turnips, "a tall, gaunt delegate from Ohio . . . slowly and spirally elevated himself like a jackscrew," and shouted "in shrill piercing tones: 'Damn his . . . turnips. What does he say about the abolition of Slavery in the Deestrick of Columby!'" (Stanton, *Recollections,* p. 164; Dyer, *Great Senators,* pp. 100–101).

[109] George W. Julian, *Political Recollections: 1840–1872* (Chicago, 1884), pp. 59–60 (hereafter cited as *Political Recollections*). See also excerpts from the diary of Albert G. Hunt, in Albert B. Hart, *Salmon Portland Chase* (Boston, 1899), pp. 99–100; and Stanton to Hale, 20 August 1848, Leavitt to Hale, 22 August 1848, Hale Papers.

a willingness to accept McLean if the convention selected him, and they were "exceedingly disappointed" when they learned that his name would not be presented.[110]

With such sentiment acting as a binding force, the Committee of Conferees lost little time in completing its labors. A round of eulogistic oratory placed Van Buren, Hale, Giddings, and Charles Francis Adams in nomination. Then Butler read a letter from Van Buren, in which the former president pointed out that his nomination at Utica had been made against his wishes and that he had yielded because the use of his name was needed "to enable the ever faithful democracy of New York to sustain themselves in the extraordinary position into which they had been driven by the injustice of others."

But the convention at Buffalo was a different matter. "If wisely conducted," it could be "productive of more important consequences than any which has gone before it, save, only, that which framed the Federal Constitution." It was a convention wholly unlike any other because it was composed of individuals "who have, all their lives, been arrayed on different sides in politics . . . and who still differ." They had come together determined to suspend "rival actions on other subjects" in order to unite their common efforts to prevent the "introduction of human slavery into the extensive territories of the United States, now exempt from that great evil." With this objective he "cordially" concurred. As for his own prospects, he wanted to make clear his recognition that the delegates might conclude that their objective could best be promoted "by the abandonment of the Utica nomination." They might hesitate, however, if they thought such a course would "not be agreeable" to him. It was on this point that he wanted to "protect" them against the "slightest embarrassment" by assuring them, "sincerely and very cheerfully," that "so far from experiencing any mortification from such a result, it would be most satisfactory to my feelings and wishes."[111]

Van Buren's letter made a deep impression on the conferees; it revealed that the Barnburners were willing to abandon their own separate movement and to allow free and open voting. When the prolonged cheering that followed Butler's reading of the letter subsided, Henry B. Stanton announced that he had been authorized to inform the convention that Hale would withdraw as the Liberty party candidate and would "cheerfully abide" by the decision of the convention.[112]

[110] Chase to McLean, 12 August 1848, Hamlin to McLean, 17 August 1848, McLean Papers.

[111] Niles' Register 74 (16 August 1848) : 109–10.

[112] Hale had evidently authorized Stanton and Giddings to take the action (Leavitt to Hale, 22 August 1848, Hale Papers).

Almost immediately the conferees took an informal poll of preferences. It revealed a majority in favor of Van Buren, who secured 244 votes, against 183 for Hale and 42 scattered among Giddings, Adams, and William W. Ellsworth.[113] According to a Whig contemporary, Van Buren's total was cast by the full Democratic contingent, about half the Whigs, and a handful of Liberty men, among them Chase and Stanton.[114] Hale's support came chiefly from his own party adherents, many of whom had no desire to see him nominated. The scattered count consisted of Whig votes which "would have been given to Mr. Van Buren on an actual ballot."[115] So clear was the preference for the former president that Joshua Leavitt, after quickly consulting other abolitionists, moved and secured Van Buren's nomination by acclamation.[116]

After a short adjournment the conferees turned to the vice-presidency. Since the Liberty party had no candidate and since Van Buren was an eastern Democrat, political expediency suggested that second place on the ticket should go to a western Whig.[117] To expedite the matter, Charles Sedgewick of Massachusetts moved that the roll call, which normally began with Maine, start with the western states. Ohio named Giddings and then withdrew him when the other western states announced that their choice was Charles Francis Adams. The ex-president's son, still in mourning for his father, was named by acclamation.[118]

The mass convention approved the ticket with a deafening acclamation; then in a tumultuous din it adjourned to march through the streets of Buffalo, with torches flaring and drums beating, behind a banner that succinctly summarized its campaign position:

'87 and '48
JEFFERSON AND VAN BUREN
No Compromise

[113] There were 19 states, including Delaware, Maryland, and Virginia, and 118 congressional districts represented for a total of 468 votes. A majority was 235.

[114] "I voted for Mr. Van Buren because I believed he was the only candidate who could be regarded as sure of carrying a single state, & was the best man to knock to pieces the main prop of Slavery, the *Northern democratic party,* & because no one doubted that he would be the nominee & I thought it wise that he should have a fair majority on the first trial. Many Liberty men did the same & for the same reasons" (Stanton to Hale, 20 August 1848, Hale Papers).

[115] Dana, *Speeches,* p. 138. See also Charles Francis Adams, Jr., *Richard Henry Dana* (Boston, 1890), 1 : 140.

[116] Leavitt to Hale, 22 August 1848, Hale Papers.

[117] "The Whigs urged their claims. They said the Liberty party had got the platform—the Barnburners the candidate for president—& they ought to have the vice president. The Liberty men generally conceded this" (Stanton to Hale, 20 August 1848, ibid.).

[118] Duberman, *Adams,* pp. 150–51.

A few days later Van Buren announced that he would accept the standard placed in his hands. At the same time, in answer to the most pointed criticism of his past policies, he assured his new friends that he had not meant in his letter to the Utica convention to repeat the declaration that he would withhold his approval from a bill for the abolition of slavery in the District of Columbia. He declared:

> The circumstances by which the question is now surrounded are widely and materially different from what they were when the declaration was made, and because, upon a question of expediency, circumstances must control. At that time the apprehension was honestly entertained, that there was danger of a servile war, in consequence of the extent to which the agitation of this question had been pressed. Participating in this apprehension, and believing that such a declaration, in advance of any action of Congress upon the subject, would have a salutory influence in allaying the excitement, and warding off the danger which menaced the peace of the slave-holding states, I did not hesitate to make it. Whilst on the one hand, all grounds for this apprehension have passed away, we are on the other, threatened with a subversion of the spirit and character of our government, through the successful encroachments of the slave power. If, under such circumstances, the two branches of the National Legislature should decide that a due regard for the public interest requires the passage of such a law, I should not, if President, think it within my line of duty, to arrest its passage by the exercise of the veto power.[119]

The Buffalo convention was really the climax of the presidential campaign of 1848. It was, of course, the first deliberate and conscious attempt to create a political party (aside from a one-idea party) in American history. But more significantly it marked the moment when men of vastly different and hostile political principles and attitudes were able to submerge their differences and hostilities to pursue a common goal—prevention of the extension of slavery into the territories. Moreover, once Martin Van Buren had been nominated and had accepted his nomination, Free Soil became inexorably the major issue of the campaign. The convention had made it impossible to evade or ignore that issue.

[119] *Niles' Register* 74 (27 September 1848): 201–2. Adams's acceptance speech is in Gardiner, *Great Issue*, pp. 150–51.

Chapter Thirteen

Slavery: The Issue

By the time the Free-Soilers had completed their organization, both major parties had entered the third month of their campaigns. Among regular Democrats the Cass nomination had met with high approval. The rejoicing was particularly evident in the Northwest, where journals such as the *Cleveland Plain Dealer* greeted the news in big, bold headlines proclaiming "THE GREAT WEST TRIUMPHANT"; the *Illinois State Register* reported that "no nomination" had ever been "hailed . . . with more cordial and genuine joy and enthusiasm."[1] The Detroit *Free Press* summarized the reasons for this western enthusiasm in ten succinct statements:

> *Firstly.*—Because Lewis Cass drafted the law under which Aaron Burr was tried for treason. . . .
> *Secondly.*—Because Thomas Jefferson . . . upwards of fifty years ago had confidence sufficient in Lewis Cass to make him Marshal of the territory of Ohio.
> *Thirdly.*—Because Lewis Cass, in the last war with our implacable enemy, Great Britain, was the first man who entered Canada. . . .
> *Fourthly.*—Because Lewis Cass has proved himself an able negotiator, inasmuch as he completed twenty one treaties with the Indians, none of which has ever been disputed by that wild, wandering and indominatable race.
> *Fifthly.*—Because . . . Andrew Jackson . . . called Lewis Cass to his counsels, by making him Secretary of War.
> *Sixthly.*—Because Lewis Cass, when our minister to France, circumvented and annihilated the wiles and schemes of our inveterate foe when the quintuple alliance was being formed under the influence of Great Britain, which would have left our shipping at the mercy of English cruisers, and would have deprived us of our rights to the highway of nations.
> *Seventhly.*—Because Lewis Cass . . . boldly, fearlessly, and honestly advocated our right to territory up to 54 40. . . .

Eighthly.—Because Lewis Cass is the candidate of that party which has always been the consistent advocate of human rights, of freedom of opinion, and of liberty of conscience.

Ninthly.—Because that party has guaranteed to adopted citizens the same rights, protection, and privileges which it has and does to citizens of native birth, and because it scattered to the four winds of heaven the odious alien, gagging and sedition laws.

Tenthly.—Because . . . he will not submit to the foreign dictation of Great Britain.[2]

In the southwestern states, which had supported Cass almost unanimously at the convention, the rejoicing was equally enthusiastic.[3] Even Whig papers such as the Nashville *Republican* admitted that the Democrats had nominated a candidate over whom it would be "worth while to achieve victory."[4]

Along the Atlantic seaboard the jubilation appeared a little strained in some quarters. The reactions of two friends of Howell Cobb were probably typical. While one announced himself fully satisfied that Cass was a "perfect embodiment of progressive democracy" and was opposed to the Whig principle of "putting the people in ward, to save them from their pretended ignorance and folly," the other declared himself "reconciled" but "not very much delighted."[5] Farther north, in Pennsylvania and New Jersey, editors who had supported Buchanan announced a wholehearted acceptance of the decision made at Baltimore; even some antislavery organs succumbed. One of them, the *New Brunswick Times,* excused itself with this announcement: "It is true that Gen. Cass does not advocate the Wilmot Proviso, but he is a democrat. On every cardinal point of the democratic creed he is known to be right, and we have no wish to introduce other issues in this election."[6] In New York,

[1] *Cleveland Plain Dealer,* 26 May 1848; *Illinois State Register,* 13 June 1848. See also *Daily Wisconsin,* 26, 27, 30 May 1848; *Iowa Capitol Reporter,* 31 May 1848.

[2] Detroit *Free Press* quoted in *Louisville Journal,* 8 August 1848. The lack of any reference to contemporary issues was not unusual.

[3] *Mobile Register,* 5 June 1848.

[4] Nashville *Republican,* 31 May 1848. In Mississippi the first reports from Baltimore indicated that the Democrats had nominated Woodbury and Quitman, which the *Vicksburg Sentinel* described as a "perfect hurricane of a ticket" (*Vicksburg Whig,* 7 June 1848). The *New Orleans Commercial Bulletin,* which called the Cass-Butler nomination a "kangaroo ticket" because all its strength was in its hind legs, maintained that Woodbury would have been a stronger candidate than Cass (1 June 1848).

[5] Thomas to Howell Cobb, 5 June 1848, T. R. R. Cobb to Howell Cobb, 31 May 1848, in Phillips, *Toombs, Stephens, and Cobb Correspondence,* pp. 106, 107. See also Crallé to Calhoun, 3 June 1848, in Jameson, *Calhoun Correspondence,* p. 1170; *Richmond Enquirer,* 29 May 1848; *Georgian,* 8 June 1848.

Hunker papers such as the *Albany Argus* predicted that Democrats would "come with alacrity to the support of the nomination" because it was made in "the accustomed and regular manner."[7] In New England, Cass's birthplace, the Michigander's nomination was everywhere hailed as "scarcely less a compliment . . . than would have been that of another of her distinguished sons."[8]

Among Whig regulars Taylor's nomination had been no less joyfully received. In the southern states the great mass of Clay men and all but a handful of Clay leaders rallied to the party's tattered banner. Many who confessed that their "hearts were not in it" nevertheless decided to follow their "judgment," which told them that the victory of any Whig was preferable to four more lean years.[9] Even the *Jonesboro Whig,* which preferred Taylor dead to Taylor alive, agreed to vote for the General "at a venture."[10] Equally cheering was the reaction among anti-Taylor men of the North. In New England, Websterian journals such as the *Boston Atlas* announced : "It matters not to us now, that we had other preferences. It matters not that he was not our choice, nor the choice of Massachusetts. We feel bound in honor, Massachusetts having taken part in the Convention, to abide the result, and to award it our full, free and untiring support."[11] The more outstanding McLean men hardly hesitated before putting their shoulders to the Whig wagon.[12] Even Tom Corwin, who had privately expressed the opinion that Taylor's qualifications consisted in "sleeping forty years in the woods, and cultivating moss on the calves of his legs," decided to contribute his aid because he thought the nation needed "the United *Whig* strength . . . to save it from the certain ruin, that must follow the adoption of the present dogmas, of the Loco Foco party."[13]

---

[6] *Pennsylvanian,* 26 May 1848; *New Brunswick Times* quoted in *Nashville Union,* 22 June 1848.

[7] *Albany Argus,* 30 May 1848.

[8] *Boston Post,* 27 May, 5 June 1848. See also *New Hampshire Patriot,* 1 June 1848. Several Whig journals commended the nomination (New York *Courier,* 30 May 1848; *National Intelligencer* quoted in *Cleveland Herald,* 31 May 1848).

[9] See J. Morrison Harris to Clay, 5 September 1848, Thomas A. Burke to Clay, 29 June 1848, Clay Papers; Lewis Condish to Crittenden, 12 June 1848, Crittenden Papers; *New Orleans Commercial Bulletin,* 21 June 1848; *Vicksburg Whig,* 28 June 1848.

[10] Quoted in *National Intelligencer,* 17 August 1848.

[11] *Boston Atlas,* 9, 12, 14, 17, 20 June 1848.

[12] Harvey to McLean, 9 June 1848, Whittlesey to McLean, 12 June 1848, Mower to McLean, 12 June 1848, Miner to McLean, 13 June 1848, McLean Papers.

[13] Stevenson to Clay, 22 May 1848, Clay Papers; Chase to Sumner, 20 June 1848, in L. Belle Hamlin, ed., "Selected Letters of Salmon P. Chase: February 18, 1846 to May 1, 1861," *Quarterly Publication of the Historical and Philosophical Society*

There was one element, however, upon whom the news of Taylor's acceptance of the Philadelphia nomination fell like a sodden blanket— the Maryland Independents. They were the last statewide organization of nonpartisan Taylor men; they had remained fiercely loyal to Old Zack through all efforts to prove him a Whig. Their faith had been badly shaken, however, when they learned of Judge Lafayette Saunders's statement indicating that Taylor's friends would withdraw him from the race if he failed to secure the Philadelphia nomination.

For a while the hopes of the Independents were buoyed by the widespread rumor in Democratic newspapers that Taylor had "repudiated the statements made in his behalf by the Louisiana delegation" and that he had not only denied "their right and authority to make such a representation" but had also reiterated "his former declaration that he would not be a candidate of a party."[14] But after three of his friends (Baillie Peyton, Logan Harton, and Alexander C. Bullitt) published "a card" denying the rumor on Taylor's authority, the Maryland Independents formally disbanded.[15] Their reaction was expressed by the *Baltimore Buena Vista*: "We regard [Taylor's action] as an abandonment of every pledge on which he had been called to act. We deem it a desertion of his position. . . . Finding him thus unreliable on one thing, we know no reason for supposing we can rely on him in anything. . . . We now abandon his support."[16] This was the final blow to any Whig hopes of

---

of Ohio 11 (1916): 138; *Ohio State Journal*, 8 August 1848; Corwin to Greene, 15 June 1848, in Hamlin, "Greene Papers," p. 28. Stevenson was half amused at Corwin's party regularity: "I expect you will . . . have to take the stump in Ohio. . . . If there were not so much to commiserate in the conception I should amuse myself by the fancy of seeing the author of a certain anti-war speech . . . pounding, grinding, compounding and igniting brimstone, charcoal & saltpeter for the edification of those who thought themselves enlightened, purified, and rendered better men by the aforesaid speech" (Stevenson to Corwin, 29 June 1848, in Colton, *Clay's Works*, 3: 468).

[14] *Baltimore Clipper*, 6, 10, 13 June 1848; Baltimore *Republican*, 17 June, 1 July 1848.

[15] The rumor that Judge Saunders's declaration was not authorized seems to have started with a Colonel John Winthrop of New Orleans after he interviewed Taylor. The story is neatly summarized in the *Albany Argus*, 5 July 1848, from information taken from the *New Orleans Crescent*, the *New Orleans Mercury*, the *New Orleans Courier*, and the *New Orleans Delta*. The "card" is in *Niles' Register* 74 (12 July 1848): 19. Taylor did not know at first what Judge Saunders had said in Philadelphia (Taylor to Wood, 22 June 1848, in *Taylor Letters*, pp. 158–59). But he had obviously approved Saunders's action, both before and after the statement (Taylor to Allison, 25 June 1848, pp. 162–64).

[16] *Washington Union*, 25 July 1848. Taylor tried to explain his action to the Maryland Independents but revealed no concern over their withdrawal of support (*National Intelligencer*, 23 September 1848; Taylor to Allison, 8 August 1848, in *Taylor Letters*, pp. 164–65).

capitalizing on Taylor's nonpartisan appeal. Thenceforth, as one wit remarked, Old Zack was "a Whig and a quarter over."[17]

Neither party, however, wasted much time counting those safely in the fold or lamenting those irrevocably lost; when the first flush of jubilation had passed, both organizations settled down to the serious business of winning. Time gave the Whigs the opportunity to open their campaign with the warning that a Democratic victory meant more wars of conquest, more shedding of the blood of American youth.[18] "The election of Gen. Cass," the *Boston Atlas* of 31 July declared, "will be followed by wars of aggression on weak neighboring republics, bringing as their inevitable result, acquisition of territory, amalgamation with a barbarous, hostile population, further extension of slavery, Standing Armies to strike down the Liberties, and a Public Debt to paralyze the enterprize of the wealthy and forge chains for the free limbs of an honest, industrious people." On the other hand, in spite of the fact that he had led the American army in its invasion of Mexico, Taylor was a "MAN OF PEACE." He had approved neither the war nor "the conquest and annexation that were intended to follow it."[19]

Democratic journals greeted this salvo with ridicule. The *Pennsylvanian*'s message to the electorate was typical:

> They are to remember, in the first place, that General Taylor was *not* nominated because he has been a successful military leader, whose sword, terrible in war, scourged the enemies of our country, and avenged insults upon our flag in the blood of the offenders! They will please bear in mind, that when he voluntarily marched from Corpus Christi to the Rio Grande, he did so, not for purposes of war, but led by the soft persuasions of peace; and, that when he cut his way through opposing thousands at Palo Alto and Resaca, he did so, not to spill blood or to vindicate our national honor, but to coax and flatter the stubborn Mexicans. They will further recollect, that when he captured Monterrey, he did not do it with bomb-shells, but with prayers, and that when he marched into the streets with his cannon, and fired from the heights into the town, his intentions were amicable and merciful. And above all the "Whig" Quakers and peace advocates . . . must not forget that at the battle of Buena Vista General Taylor was no warrior. When he told Bragg to give the Mexicans "a little more grape" it was, they are begged to bear

[17] *Richmond Enquirer*, 2 August 1848.

[18] See *Savannah Republican*, 31 May 1848; *North American*, 13 June 1848; Nashville *Republican*, 26 June 1848.

[19] *Boston Atlas*, 7 July 1848. See also *Savannah Republican*, 20 June 1848; *North American*, 20 June 1848; Nashville *Republican*, 25 June 1848.

in mind, in the spirit of generosity that gives to the poor even when the store is exhausted. . . . For General Taylor hates war, and there is no danger of his being in such a hurry to protect his country from outrage and invasion. He leaves that to such sanguinary people as Mr. Polk and Gen. Cass.[20]

Ridicule was followed by an attack upon Whig hypocrisy. Many a Democratic journal pointed out the inconsistency between Whig professions and Whig actions.[21] The *New Hampshire Patriot* of 15 June explained:

From the beginning, they have denounced the war as the most atrocious of crimes, as unholy, unjust, wicked, cruel and awful; and now they have taken as their standard bearer a man who has been foremost in prosecution of the "bloody work" which they have so unsparingly denounced—a man who was never heard of here except with the "bloody details of death and carnage." . . . They have declared that every man engaged in the war *was guilty of deliberate murder;* and yet they all now support the very "head-butcher" of the whole, as some of them have called him! . . . Denouncing all acquisition of Mexican territory as unjust, impolitic, and dangerous to our national existence, they have selected for a candidate a man who has declared himself in *favor of annexing seven of the great provinces of Mexico to our country.* . . . Poor, unprincipled, time-serving federalism is thus forced to belie all its professions.

The political sins and peccadilloes of the two major candidates also received attention. Both were quickly stigmatized as "Federalists": Cass, so the charge ran, because he had worn the "Black Cockade" while he had lived in Delaware during the period of the undeclared war with France;[22] Taylor because his supporters in the Whig party were "political descendents in a direct line from those who supported . . . the odious alien and sedition laws" and had "hatched treason" at the Hartford convention.[23] Both, moreover, were indicted for the crime of feeding too plentifully at the public treasury: Cass because he had received more

[20] *Pennsylvanian,* 14 June 1848.
[21] *Boston Times,* 9 June 1848; *Boston Post,* 26 June 1848; Philadelphia *Times,* 13 June 1848; *Washington Union,* 8 June 1848; Detroit *Free Press,* 13 June 1848; *Louisville Democrat,* 18 October 1848; *Nashville Union,* 6 July 1848; *Mobile Register,* 14 July 1848.
[22] *Louisville Democrat,* 31 May 1848; *Nashville Union,* 15 June 1848; *Georgian,* 7 July 1848.
[23] *Richmond Enquirer,* 20 August 1848. The *Boston Post* pointed out that Harrison Gray Otis, a Hartford convention Federalist, favored Taylor (3 October 1848).

than $60,000 in excess of his salary while governor of Michigan Territory; Taylor because he had received over $70,000 in allowances during his army career, "exclusive of quarters and salary." Taylor was also drawing "six hundred and ninety one dollars and thirty three cents" every month for "doing nothing but superintending his cotton plantation."[24]

In the western states, where all land speculators were thoroughly hated, much publicity was given to the charge that Cass had once been a partner in a land speculating company operating from Detroit and, to make his crimes even worse, that he had defrauded his partners when the time came for a division of the company's ill-gotten spoils. To reinforce the indictment, Henry A. Wise's ten-year-old accusation that the Democratic candidate had been "engaged in speculating in the public lands while Secretary of War" was exhumed and paraded before the electorate.[25]

Cass's approval of a rather barbarous "White Slave Law"—providing that "any vagrant . . . could . . . be delivered over to any constable, to be . . . hired out for the best wages"—which the Michigan territorial legislature had enacted in 1818, earned the excoriation of indignant Whig humanitarians, many of whom conveniently forgot that William Henry Harrison had signed an even more harsh measure and that similar laws could be found in the statute books of their own states.[26] Further evidence of the Michigander's "disgraceful character" was provided in George D. Prentice's charge that Cass had "erected the first distillery ever established in Detroit" and had "sold whiskey to the Indians at *thirty dollars per gallon*."[27] His antirepublican bias was proven by the fact that he had admired Louis Philippe, the recently dethroned king of France, a charge which Democrats countered by pointing out that the organ of British interests in New York City, the *Albion,* and the *London Times* were both opposed to Cass's election.[28]

The attitude of both candidates toward Mexican War volunteers provided another point of attack. Cass had introduced a bill by which the volunteer's clothing allowance of $3.50 per month, with which he bought

[24] *Illinois State Register,* 28 July 1848; *Washington Union,* 29 September 1848.

[25] *Louisville Journal,* 20 July 1848; *Louisville Democrat,* 5, 7 August 1848; *Richmond Enquirer,* 11 August 1848; *New Orleans Commercial Bulletin,* 31 July, 22 August 1848.

[26] *North American,* 23 June 1848; *Vicksburg Whig,* 9 August 1848; *Nashville Union,* 22 August 1848; *Floridian,* 29 July 1848.

[27] Detroit *Free Press,* 19 September 1848.

[28] *New Orleans Delta,* 12 June 1848; *Washington Union,* 3 August 1848; *Illinois State Register,* 11 August 1848; Baltimore *Republican,* 15 June 1848.

his clothing from high-priced private dealers, would be reduced to $2.50 with the privilege of buying at cost from the government stores. Whigs charged that Cass had maliciously sought to lower the wages of men who had gloriously sustained their country's honor.[29] These charges were indignantly denied by the Democracy, whose journals in turn maintained that Taylor had monstrously slandered the volunteers, in particular that he had called the Second Indiana Regiment "a damned set of thieves and robbers" and had declared that "all officers of the N[orth] C[arolina] regiment ought to have been dishonorably discharged and the privates shot." To add a sectional complaint, northern journals charged that he had deliberately stationed northern troops "in unhealthy and inactive positions" so that the glory of carrying the arms of the nation could be won by southern regiments.[30]

Although such charges were reiterated all through the campaign, their political value soon diminished. Instead, the attitude of the candidates toward slavery extension, an issue that both major parties would have preferred to avoid, quickly and inexorably came to dominate the discussion of each candidate's merits. It was upon this point that the greater part of the contest was waged, with both parties conducting appropriately sectional campaigns.

As on other issues, northern Whigs opened with the charge that Cass had "surrendered himself unconditionally to the South" and was therefore "odious to all friends of the Wilmot Proviso."[31] By nominating Lewis Cass, the *North American* of 27 May proclaimed, "the Convention has repudiated the Wilmot Proviso,—has utterly rejected, annulled and trampled it under foot, and given to the republic . . . a candidate . . . who has solemnly proclaimed, as his, a principle which allows the South the option of making every new territory herafter to come into the Union a slave state, without allowing any opposite equal privilege to the North." Proof of the charge could be found in a private letter Cass had written to a Detroit friend, R. S. Wilson, on 19 February 1847:

> The Wilmot Proviso . . . would be death to the war, death to all hopes of getting an acre of territory, death to the administration, and death to the Democratic party. It was not so intended. It no doubt originated with proper feelings, but things have now come to

[29] *Washington Union*, 22 June 1848; *Nashville Union*, 4 July 1848.

[30] *Indiana State Sentinel*, 12 July 1848; *Daily Wisconsin*, 26 July 1848; Detroit *Free Press*, 4 August 1848; *Nashville Union*, 12 August 1848; Baltimore *Republican*, 12 September 1848; *North Carolina Standard*, 2 August 1848.

[31] New York *Courier*, 26 May 1848.

such a pass that its adoption will produce these effects. It is distinctly avowed by the Southern members of Congress that they would not vote for any measures for the promotion of the war, nor would they ratify any treaty if this provision becomes law. . . . I hope the appropriation will pass without any proviso.[32]

Even more evidence of his hostility to the Proviso could be produced: Cass had voted to strike it from the Three Million Bill and had even promised the editor of the *Washington Union* to veto any Proviso measure.[33]

On the other hand, northern Whigs argued, Taylor stood on exactly opposite ground. With him in the executive chair, slavery would be limited to its existing boundaries. Not one enslaved black would step into the virgin territories of the West, not one chain would scar its unblemished wilds. It was true that Old Zack was a slaveholder; however, as Caleb B. Smith of Indiana, among hundreds of others, pointed out, Taylor had pledged himself in the Allison letter to "leave the legislative department of the government" decide the momentous issue. He would "not arrest the action of that department by the tyrannical exercise of the veto power." His election, with the pledges he had given the country, would leave to Congress full power to prevent the extension "of the foul institution." If this were not sufficient evidence of his antislavery principles, Truman Smith of Connecticut could produce a letter to prove that Taylor had declared he would "neither veto the Wilmot Proviso, nor would he intrigue against it, nor do anything to embarrass its passage through the two houses of Congress."[34]

Northern Democrats denounced all the charges and claims against Cass as a pack of lies. "There is not a line or word, written, or uttered by Gen. Cass, in favor of extending slavery into territories now free," the *Boston Post* of 9 August maintained. "His administration," the *Cleveland Plain Dealer* announced, "will never be used to give countenance to so obnoxious a measure as will carry slavery into the territories." Was he not a northern man, born and reared in New England, the very seedbed of the antislavery movement? As for the Nicholson letter, in all confidence, it had been "designed to cheat the South and get the nomina-

[32] The Detroit *Free Press* finally printed the letter on 29 August 1848.

[33] *Washington Union*, 10 August 1848.

[34] *Richmond Enquirer*, 24 July 1848; Truman Smith to *New Haven Journal*, quoted in *Washington Union*, 1 September 1848. See also *Boston Atlas*, 11, 18 July, 9 October 1848; *Ohio State Journal*, 12 June 1848; *Cleveland Herald*, 18 July, 14 August 1848; *National Era*, 6 July 1848; *Indiana State Journal*, 13 July 1848. Democratic journals in the South carefully reprinted these indications of Taylor's Provisoist sympathies.

tion." Was this unfair to the southerners? "Damn them!" Wasn't it "their *turn* to be cheated?"[35] Equally important, the *Daily Wisconsin* of 20 June reminded its readers, "Gen. CASS lives in the West—and feels with it. We want a President who will appoint Northern men in the *new* territories, and they will *enforce existing local laws against* slavery, which will keep those territories as they should be—the refuge and asylum of freemen."

As for Taylor, northern Democrats insisted, that was another matter. Was it reasonable to suppose that he, a southern slaveholder, would neglect the welfare of his section and prevent the extension of the peculiar institution? A glance at the statements of his southern supporters would quickly dispel any illusions on that score. What could one believe when journals such as the Nashville *Republican* exclaimed, "A Louisiana Planter in favor of the Proviso! The INTOLERABLE ABSURDITY of such a proposition scarcely permits us to treat it with any seriousness," or when men such as Sargent S. Prentiss declared, "We require no pledge from Gen. Taylor. The holder of a southern plantation—the owner of three hundred wooly heads—need not give the guaranty of any pledge"? Did this not prove that the Whig candidate was no antislavery man? How, then, could the Whigs have the brazen temerity to claim Taylor would not veto the Proviso, especially when, as everyone knew, he had informed the New York Barnburners that his Allison letter had not pledged him to allow a law or any kindred measure for the restriction of slavery "to pass unchecked"? If Taylor were an antislavery man, would Hope H. Slatter, the notorious slave dealer of Baltimore, have closed his market and taken the stump for Taylor, would Taylor's flag have been raised over the Washington "nigger pen" when news of his nomination flashed through the nation?[36] The very idea was mockery.

[35] *Cleveland Plain Dealer,* 6 June, 18 July 1848; *Indiana State Sentinel,* 23 September 1848; Chase to John Van Buren, 19 June 1848, in Bigelow, *Tilden Letters,* 1: 53.

[36] *New Hampshire Patriot,* 13 July, 28 September, 5 October 1848; *Boston Times,* 25 October 1848; *Boston Post,* 29 August, 31 October 1848; *Rochester Democrat* quoted in *New York Tribune,* 15 July 1848; *Cleveland Plain Dealer,* 15 June, 18 August 1848; Detroit *Free Press,* 29 June, 18 July 1848; *Indiana State Sentinel,* 26 July 1848; *Daily Wisconsin,* 23 June 1848. One writer let his imagination run wild when he declared that "Hell itself" was on Taylor's side, for it was known that "every hater of God's humanity" would take to the stump in his favor, every gale of freedom that swept over the hills of the North would be "blighted by his touch"; that he would "swear [to] do the bidding of his brothers, the slaveholders . . . and from his throne of human skulls . . . send forth the mandate for the extermination of Mexico, and the putting of patriarchal thumb screws, bull whips, and chains and iron fetters on the hands and feet of twenty million slaves"; that "man made in the image of God" would be sold "high in the shambles" (*Cleveland Plain Dealer,* 24 June 1848).

Southern Whigs, as might be expected, used the same arguments as their northern Democratic opponents, adding some twists of their own. Cass, they maintained, boasted that he never had been a slaveholder, that he detested slavery, and that he would be delighted to see it abolished.[37] Equally important, he was the champion of the doctrine which gave the "mongrel tribes" of the territories "an undoubted and inalienable right" to say whether slavery should exist there or not.[38] This was "a monstrous doctrine," the *Savannah Republican* of 25 July declared:

> The true position is, that neither Congress or the territorial legislature has the right to exclude us from the new territory. It is a question which belongs entirely to the people of these territories when they come to form their State Constitutions, preparatory to their admission into the Union, and not to the hybridous squatters who may wander over that region. The idea of insulting the South by giving these ignorant and worthless Mexicans—a mongrel race of Indians, negroes, mulatoes, meztizoes, half-breeds and every imaginable shade and species of humanity, such unheard of and unconstitutional power, is absurd and preposterous in the largest sense of those terms. It is a doctrine too monstrous to be tolerated—an ostracism too degrading to be endured.

It proved that Cass sought the "political conquest of the South," the destruction of its institutions, and the "imprisonment of slavery" within its existing limits.[39]

A man with such doctrines could not receive southern support, not even if he were a "northern man with southern principles." The slave states had had their fill of these Democratic doughfaces. Van Buren had been hailed as one, and now he was the head of a powerful party that had been organized "as the basis of opposition to and invasion of Southern rights!"[40] Indeed, even southern Democrats could no longer be trusted to protect and defend the interests of the South. Witness the fact that Polk, "the great boast of Southern democracy," had sanctioned a bill for the government of Oregon Territory "with the infamous Proviso in it, and that too, notwithstanding EVERY Southern member in the House . . . voted against it."[41] If Polk could "desert the South in its utmost need, . . . what can we expect from Mr. Cass,"[42] a man who had presented to the Senate a resolution from the legislature of his home

[37] *New Orleans Bee* quoted in Detroit *Free Press,* 16 September 1848.
[38] *Vicksburg Whig,* 4 October 1848.
[39] *Savannah Republican,* 22 September 1848.
[40] *New Orleans Commercial Bulletin,* 7 July 1848.
[41] *Savannah Republican,* 22 August 1848.
[42] Nashville *Republican,* 6 September 1848.

state announcing "that hostility to the extension of human slavery is now and ever has been one of the Principles of the Democratic creed"?[43]

On the other hand, southern Whigs claimed, Taylor's election would bring slavery "under the protection of his eagle eye and his giant arm."[44] Any assertion that he would not veto the Proviso was "monstrous . . . entirely at war with the character of the man and the tenor of his whole life," the *Natchez Courier* maintained.[45] His hatred of that "unclean thing," the Proviso, had been proven time and again.[46] In a letter to "a citizen of Tuscaloosa, Alabama," he had made it clear that his *Signal* letter had not been sent with the intention of approving any of the views held by the editor of the *Signal:*

> The letter itself . . . was not intended for publication, but simply written as a matter of courtesy. . . . For this object it was entirely sufficient; though under the belief that it would never go beyond this point, it is quite possible that it may not have been prepared with that care and critical accuracy which appears to be so much required by politicians.—It was simply my desire on that occasion . . . to express my respect for opinions which I believed to be honestly entertained, and, so long as thus held, my approval of his [the *Signal* editor's] maintaining them.[47]

Further proof of Taylor's southern position could be found in his reply to a communication of Dr. David Pannill, Taylor elector from Orange County, Virginia: "If after . . . the many public evidences of my hostility to that measure, to say nothing of my extreme southern location, and of the fact I own some one hundred working slaves; there are those who will yet persist in saying I would favor it, then I must despair of setting them right."[48] Such direct testimony could not be controverted, slave state Whigs maintained. To the South it meant that Taylor was "far more acceptable than any other man" in the Union, for, as the *Savannah Republican* of 12 June expressed it, "He is a Southern man and a Slaveholder—one of ourselves."

Southern Democrats, in turn, used much the same arguments as northern Whigs. Cass, they maintained, held the true southern ground on the question of slavery in the territories. In his Nicholson letter he had proven himself to be the "firm and avowed opponent" of the

[43] *Savannah Republican*, 13 September 1848.
[44] *Matamoros Tribune* quoted in *Albany Atlas*, 7 July 1848.
[45] *Natchez Courier* quoted in *Boston Post*, 29 August 1848.
[46] Detroit *Free Press*, 3 November 1848.
[47] *Tuscaloosa Monitor* quoted in *Cleveland Plain Dealer*, 9 August 1848.
[48] Detroit *Free Press*, 3 November 1848; *Richmond Enquirer*, 2 October 1848.

"distracting and pestiferous" Proviso and had revealed that he was "opposed to the exercise of any jurisdiction by Congress over the matter."[49] He would therefore veto "any bill either excluding or recognizing slavery in any territory."[50] His doctrine, they admitted, did not prevent the territorial legislatures from dealing with the question of slavery. This, however, was all to the good, since as matters stood slavery was forbidden in the southwestern territories both by Mexican and by international law; until some power did act, "not a slave" could be taken there. By recognizing the rights of the territorial legislature, Cass had discovered the only method by which the prohibition could be annulled and slavery could be permitted to enter the Southwest.[51]

Whig statements that Cass was opposed to southern interests were obviously false, southern Democrats maintained. If they were not, why did the Florida legislature, controlled by Whigs, declare that "a just and correct interpretation of the Constitution" vested "exclusive jurisdiction over the persons or individuals" in the "Territorial as well as the State Legislatures"—that the "people of the territory alone" (while they remained a territory) and the people of the state (when they should ask to be admitted as a state) had the right "to say whether the institution of slavery" should exist "within the limits of such Territory or State"?[52] Moreover, if Cass was a Wilmot Proviso man, why did not the Barnburners of New York support him?[53] The truth of the matter was that Cass was the "only" safe candidate for the South, both because his opinions were "coincident with those entertained by the people of the Slaveholding States"[54] and because he was the candidate of that party which had always extended its protection to southern institutions, "even at some sacrifice of individual feeling and preference."[55]

On the other hand, southern Democrats claimed, Taylor was "committed beyond redemption" to the antislavery party, the northern Whigs, among whom he was played up not as a southern candidate, but as the "champion" of the Wilmot Proviso.[56] "He is supported at the North as

[49] *Richmond Enquirer*, 6 June 1848.

[50] *Louisville Democrat*, 28 September 1848.

[51] *Georgian*, 20 June 1848.

[52] *Floridian*, 23 September 1848.

[53] *Georgian*, 24 July 1848. See also Jefferson Davis to H. R. Davis, October 1848, in Dunbar Rowland, ed., *Jefferson Davis—Constitutionalist: His Letters, Papers, and Speeches* (Jackson, Miss., 1923), 1: 216.

[54] *Richmond Enquirer*, 6 June 1848.

[55] Louis McLane to Calhoun, 1 July 1848, in Boucher and Brooks, *Calhoun Correspondence*, pp. 446–47. See also Cobb to a Charleston Committee, [4] November 1848, in Phillips, *Toombs, Stephens, and Cobb Correspondence*, p. 134.

[56] *Mississippian*, 22 September 1848.

the ENEMY OF THE EXTENSION OF SLAVERY," the *Mobile Register* of 18 October declared. "His advocates there 'out Herod' the free soilers in their denunciation of the distinctive institution of the South, and they repeat in every form of speech and writing, the assertion that he is 'pledged' to act with them. . . . To all this General Taylor opposes no denial. By his silence he admits the assertion. *He must therefore be taken for what he is said to be and treated accordingly.*"

If there was any doubt that Taylor was an antislavery man, one needed only to glance at the *Signal* letter, which had placed him "in an attitude of hostility to the rights of the South," pledging him irrevocably to that odious measure, the Wilmot Proviso.[57] If he had expressed any later opinion binding himself to veto the Proviso, the *Athens Southern Banner* knew not where to find it.[58] Some of his own supporters in the South, men such as Congressman Meredith P. Gentry of Tennessee, admitted that Taylor would not check the passage of the firebrand measure, since such an action would aggravate their northern Whig brethren.[59] In such a situation was it not logical to infer "that should Congress adopt the Wilmot Proviso, or any other aggression on the South," he would "allow Congress" to do what it pleased ?[60]

The entrance of the Free-Soilers into the campaign in early August was greeted almost joyfully by northern Democrats and Whigs. A little weary of abusing each other, they turned the full force of their oratory and editorials upon the new party. Much of the violence in their attack was undoubtedly the result of a realization that the "Free Democracy" would carry off critical portions of their own supporters. Invariably, regular journals of both parties were most bitter in those regions where the antislavery forces were strongest.[61] Their attack was an application of the "divide and conquer" technique. They sought to emphasize the differences within the new party, to point out the incongruities in its makeup, and to attribute its formation to ulterior motives, to ambition or the desire for revenge, rather than to any desire to advance a political ideal.

They aimed a large amount of abuse at Van Buren. He was an "apostate," the "leader of the fiends of disunion who would rather rule in hell than serve in heaven," a "traitor," a "hypocrite," a "sorehead," an

---

[57] *New Orleans Delta,* 11 September 1848.

[58] *Athens* (Ga.) *Southern Banner* quoted in *Floridian,* 7 October 1848.

[59] *Nashville Union,* 7 November 1848.

[60] *Richmond Enquirer,* 23 October 1848.

[61] Detroit *Free Press,* 17 August 1848; *Indiana State Sentinel,* 2 September 1848; *Mississippian,* 25 August 1848; Marcy to Wetmore, 8 September 1848, Marcy Papers; Giddings to Chase, 20 September 1848, Chase Papers.

"ingrate," an "assassin," and the "Judas Iscariot of the nineteenth century." He was motivated by a need for "revenge" for his defeat in 1844, by "a wolfish desire" to destroy Cass, and by "an overweening and disappointed ambition."[62] By "his cold ingratitude and treachery," the *Pennsylvanian* declared, "he has fallen lower than plummet ever sounded —the weight of his turpitude has even dragged him beyond the awful abyss where contempt turns to pity." The Baltimore *Republican* predicted that his name would be "remembered only to be despised." One of Stephen A. Douglas's correspondents maintained that he could not "find power of language" to reflect his feelings for "the man" upon whom the Democracy of the Union had "for years heaped honors, dignity and wealth," who "on the brink of the grave, in a spirit of malevolent vengeance" drew from "beneath his hypocrite cloak, an assassin's stilleto to stab . . . his party."[63]

Nor were his followers spared. Adams was a "political huckster," Palfrey a "Judas," Sumner a "transcendental lawyer," Wilson a "Jesuit" and a "jackel," John Van Buren a "jolly, roistering, swearing, dare devil of a fellow, fond of women, wine and fun, without any particular regard to the *quality* of either." The rest of the Free-Soilers were "low blackguards," "whelps," "malcontents," "antediluvians," "infidels," "political vipers," "eleventh-hour proselytes of freedom," "pentitents with stained hands," "zealots with turned coats," "lousy curs," "hyenas," and a "heterogeneous melange of incongruous anamolies [*sic*]."[64] George W. Julian recorded the experience of many an antiextensionist when he described his own:

> I was subjected to a torrent of billingsgate which rivaled the fish market. Words were neither minced nor mollified, but made the vehicles of political wrath and the explosions of personal malice. The charge of abolitionism was flung at me everywhere. I was an "amalgamationist" and a "wooly head." I was branded as the "apostle of disunion" and the orator of "free dirt." It was a standing

[62] The attacks on Van Buren began after the Utica convention and continued through the campaign (*Boston Times,* 31 August 1848; *Boston Post,* 11 September 1848; *Boston Atlas,* 13 September 1848; *New York True Sun* quoted in *Niles' Register* 74 [5, 12 July 1848] : 9, 19; *Pennsylvanian,* 20 September 1848; *Washington Union,* 5 July 1848; *Cleveland Plain Dealer,* 27 June 1848; Detroit *Free Press,* 12 July 1848; *Louisville Democrat,* 19 July 1848; Edward M. Shepard, *Martin Van Buren* [Boston, 1899], pp. 428–29).

[63] *Pennsylvanian,* 21 July 1848; Baltimore *Republican,* 24 June 1848.

[64] Pierce, *Sumner,* 3: 177–78; *New Hampshire Patriot,* 21 September 1848; *Boston Atlas,* 30 June, 19, 22 August, 4 September, 21 October 1848; *North American,* 6 September 1848; Detroit *Free Press,* 9 August 1848; *Mobile Register,* 25 August 1848.

charge of the Whigs that I carried a lock of the hair of Frederick Douglass, to regale my senses with its aroma when I grew faint . . . I was threatened with mob violence by my own neighbors.[65]

When revilement of individual Free-Soilers became tiresome, orthodox journals turned their descriptive abilities upon the Barnburners. Their aim was to make Free-Soilers and potential Free-Soilers suspicious of these "allies," to breed discontent and division within the new party. The diatribe of the *Cleveland Herald* was typical:

> There never was a partisan faction more unprincipled in its aims, or more villainously unscrupulous in its means, than are the Barnburners. It will not be denied that the Barnburners uttered one syllable against the enormities of slavery so long as they were undisturbed in the possession of the spoils of office. No scheme for the perpetuation and security of slavery was ever suggested by the ambition of the South, which did not receive the warm, unswerved, unqualified support of the entire of these corrupt confederates.[66]

To prove this contention, regular Whigs and Democrats in the free states dug back into the past of Little Van to parade before the public the dark shades of a proslavery career. They reminded the electorate that he had supported a proposition at the New York Constitutional Convention of 1821 to require Negroes to hold a $250 freehold in order to vote.[67] As secretary of state, he had urged Spain to make peace with Colombia and Mexico in order to prevent their attack on Cuba to abolish slavery; he had also urged the American agent in Mexico to oppose the "baneful spirit of emancipation, designed to be introduced and propagated in the island of Cuba."[68] As vice president, he had voted for a bill to "ransack the mails" to prevent abolitionist literature from being distributed in the South.[69] As president, he had approved the reenslavement of the unhappy Amistead captives.[70] Above all, he had entered the White House as "the inflexible and uncompromising opponent of every attempt, on the part of Congress, to abolish slavery in the District of Columbia, against the wishes of the slaveholding States."[71] Such acts

---

[65] Julian, *Political Recollections,* pp. 65–66.

[66] *Cleveland Herald,* 29 August 1848. See also *Albany Argus,* 7 August 1848; *North American,* 21 September 1848.

[67] *Boston Times,* 3 October 1848.

[68] *Boston Atlas,* 18 August 1848.

[69] *New Hampshire Patriot,* 31 August 1848.

[70] *Cleveland Plain Dealer,* 6 September 1848.

[71] *Albany Argus,* 8 July, 20 August 1848; *Boston Atlas,* 16 August–30 October 1848; *New Hampshire Patriot,* 31 August 1848.

were seen as sufficient proof that Van Buren had no genuine sympathy for the antislavery movement.

Besides, Van Buren was an undesirable candidate on other counts. In the election of 1812 he had supported De Witt Clinton against Madison; he had also been an opponent of the war with Britain.[72] There were creditable rumors that he was an infidel and an atheist.[73] He was supported by radical, agrarian locofocos whose principles were "at war with the safety of . . . civil and religious institutions—fanatics of the Cobbett calibre" who were "willing and ready to let down the flood gates of anarchy and misrule" whenever they secured power.[74] Respectable, God-fearing, home-loving citizens could have no association with such a rascal crew.

Free-Soilers frequently returned this attack in kind, hurling back their defiance in terms fully as opprobrious.[75] But they recognized that vituperation could not aid their campaign. Their object was to prove to the electorate that the Free Soil party had a common ideal, that the leaders of the movement, despite past disagreement over policy, were seeking the advancement of human rights. To do so, they were forced to cling more closely to immediate issues. They made little mention of Van Buren's antislavery record—his support of the admission of Missouri as a free state, his vote against extension of the slave trade to Florida, his personal opposition to the annexation of Texas. They reconciled apparent inconsistencies in his record on slavery by explaining that his former course had been that of a conservative, a protector of vested interests. Protection of these interests, however evil, had been his duty as an officer of the government. By no stretch of the imagination did this mean that he had ever favored an extension of that evil.[76] Besides, as Sumner pointed out to Boston Whigs:

> The candidates selected as exponents of the principles . . . expressed in the Buffalo Platform have claims upon your support, in forgetfulness of all former differences of opinion. They are brought forward not because of the *Past,* but *the Present.* . . . It is not for the Van Buren of 1838 that we are to vote, but for the Van Buren of *to-day*—the veteran statesman, sagacious, determined, experienced, who, at an age when most men are rejoicing to put off their armor,

[72] *Boston Times,* 30 June 1848; *Albany Argus,* 30 October 1848.
[73] Robert Everett to Van Buren, 11 October 1848, Van Buren Papers. The charge was also made that Van Buren owned a plantation and slaves.
[74] *Boston Atlas,* 24 October 1848.
[75] *Buffalo Republic,* 14 August 1848; *Albany Atlas,* 9 September 1848.
[76] *Buffalo Republic,* 22 September 1848; *Daily Wisconsin,* 15 September 1848.

girds himself anew and enters the lists as the champion of Free-dom.[77]

Could as much be said for the Whig or Democratic candidates? Free-Soilers asked. Was it logical to suppose that Taylor, himself a slaveholder, would not be devoted to the preservation of the slave power? To doubt it would be folly, the *Racine Advocate* insisted.[78] As for Cass, whom Silas Wright had described as a "perfect timeserver and demagogue," a man "afraid of his own shadow in civil office," had he not pledged himself publicly to veto any bill prohibiting the extension of slavery?[79] Did the free-state electorate believe for a moment that the arguments which northern Taylor and Cass papers were using to prove their favorites were opposed to extension could be used in the slave states? The very idea was preposterous. The southern press, as the Free Soil press revealed by repeated reprints of southern editorials, claimed that its favorites were proslavery men and scoffed at statements to the contrary as "the very quintessence of absurdity."[80] Could northern freemen, friends of liberty, place their consciences and their principles in the hands of such men?

The response to the Free Soil nominations and to arguments in the north soon made it evident that there was a very large block of voters who could not. Antislavery ferment, which had languished during the Buffalo meeting, broke out with redoubled vigor. Ratification and organization meetings, ranging from school district assemblies to state conventions, were held from Bath, Maine, to Dubuque, Iowa; a hundred established journals hoisted the names of the Buffalo candidates, and scores of new campaign journals appeared to expound Free Soil dialectics to the electorate.[81]

Everywhere state and congressional Free Soil tickets appeared and prominent men took to the stump for Van Buren and Adams. In Massachusetts, where thousands flocked to the new party, a convention —including men such as Sumner, Joshua Leavitt, Stanton, Henry Wilson, John A. Andrew, Anson Burlingame, Charles Allen, Richard Dana, the Hoar brothers, Palfrey, Nathaniel Morton, John Boles, Abner C. Phillips, and Amasa Walker—named Stephen C. Phillips and John

[77] *Sumner's Works*, 2: 143–44.
[78] *Racine Advocate*, 11 October 1848; *Albany Atlas*, 22, 26 August 1848. See also *Cincinnati Herald*, 2 August 1848; *Sumner's Works*, 2: 155; Dana, *Speeches*, pp. 147–57.
[79] *Albany Atlas*, 14 October 1848.
[80] Ibid., 1 September 1848.
[81] *National Era*, 24 August, 7, 14 September 1848; Smith, *Liberty and Free Soil Parties*, p. 154.

Mills, a former Democrat, to head its state ticket.[82] The Cambridge Clay Club publicly announced that it would support Van Buren to the last man.[83] In other New England states Hale, who had withdrawn as the Liberty candidate, Amos Tuck of New Hampshire, Jacob Collamer of Vermont, and Senator Niles of Connecticut led antiextension movements.[84]

In New York, excitement reached a fever pitch. Enthusiastic young crusaders who formed "Jefferson Leagues" and "Northern Lights Associations" rallied the rank and file to huge torchlight meetings; hundreds of Free-Soilers of every variety—Barnburners, Conscience Whigs, Clay Whigs, Land Reformers, Liberty men, and Anti-Renters—united in a common desire to advance the cause of human rights, stumping the state for a ticket headed by the party's gubernatorial candidates, John A. Dix and Seth M. Gates.[85] Free Soil electors were named in both New Jersey and Pennsylvania, where David Wilmot led the movement for Van Buren.[86]

Throughout the Northwest the scenes were the same. In Ohio, Chase, Vaughan, Giddings, Brinckerhoff, Charles Cist, Tappan, Samuel Lewis, and James M. Root kept the state in a furor. Enthusiasm for the Free Soil ticket in the Western Reserve was so zealous that the most sanguine observers confessed astonishment.[87] The spirit of the campaign throughout the state was probably best summarized by Thomas B. Stevenson when he told Crittenden that the Wilmot Proviso was "stronger in Ohio than Whiggery, democracy and military glory all combined."[88] In Michigan the Detroit *Free Press* reported a "concerted plan to desert Taylor." First the Buena Vista Club in the capital repudiated him for Van Buren, and then a whole bloc of counties in the south-central part of the state followed suit under the leadership of James W. Gordon, who was prominent enough to have been mentioned as a possible vice-presidential candidate on the Taylor ticket, and Austin Blair, Whig leader in the state legislature. Democratic Provisoists in the same district, led by

[82] Wilson, *Slave Power*, 2: 157; Pierce, *Sumner*, 2: 171.
[83] Dexter Reynolds to Van Buren, 4 October 1848, Van Buren Papers.
[84] *Cleveland Herald*, 5 September 1848; Niles to Welles, 8 October 1848, Welles Papers; S. B. Parker to Van Buren, 25 August 1848, Van Buren Papers; *Niles' Register* 74 (13 September 1848) : 165.
[85] *Albany Atlas*, 7 September 1848; Edward O'Connor to Van Buren, 29 August 1848, J. W. Edwards to Van Buren, 16 August 1848, Van Buren Papers.
[86] Cornelius Holderman to Chase, 4 October 1848, Chase Papers; *New Jersey Free Soil Convention* (New Brunswick, N. J., 1848), p. 3; *Pennsylvanian*, 15 September 1848; Going, *Wilmot*, p. 329.
[87] Chase to Van Buren, 21 August 1848, Van Buren Papers; Hamlin to McLean, 17 August 1848, McLean Papers.
[88] Stevenson to Crittenden, 7 September 1848, Crittenden Papers.

Flavius J. Littlejohn, unhesitatingly joined the parade.[89] In Indiana, where Whigs and Liberty men dominated, in Illinois, where Democrats dominated, and in Wisconsin, where no single element dominated, lively campaigns brought thousands into the fold. In Iowa a "People's Convention" named Free Soil electors.[90]

The Liberty party all but vanished. In several states it was formally dissolved; in others it remained a mere name. Everywhere, in spite of grumbling from diehards such as Lewis Tappan and in spite of some movement toward the Macedonians, its leaders and forces succumbed to the blandishments of the new movement.[91] Even men as orthodox as the editor of the *Emancipator,* who refused to haul down Hale's flag until the Liberty candidate had withdrawn from the field, and Sherman M. Booth of the *Milwaukee Freeman,* who had led a contingent that threatened to vote for "the *man* of this nation, Gerrit Smith," became strong supporters of Van Buren.[92] Their attitude was described by the *National Era:* "The Liberty party, as such, no longer operates—its candidates have been superceded, with their own consent, by others. . . . With this result we are entirely satisfied. In our judgment, no more efficient movement could have been made, and in view of the exigency, no better candidates selected."[93]

Not only old-line Liberty men but even the nonpolitical Garrisonians were infected by the Free Soil virus. The editor of the *Liberator* himself found much in the new party that he could commend. Though he pronounced the free-territory issue to be "weaker than a spider's web," he nevertheless hailed the movement as a "cheering sign of the times." Those who had left the Whig and Democratic parties "for conscience sake," he wrote to Samuel May, "deserve our commendation and sympathy. It is our duty to show that there is a higher position to be attained by them. . . . This can be done charitably, yet faithfully. On the two old parties, therefore, I would expend—*pro tempore* at least—our heaviest

[89] Detroit *Free Press,* 26, 30 August 1848; Floyd B. Streeter, *Political Parties in Michigan* (Lansing, Mich., 1918), pp. 87–88, 90–93 (hereafter cited as *Michigan Parties*).

[90] Smith, *Liberty and Free Soil Parties,* pp. 144–45; Cole, *Era of the Civil War,* p. 95.

[91] A rump convention of the Liberty party, calling itself the National Liberty Party, met at Buffalo on 14 August. There were 104 delegates present, including Beriah Green and Elizur Wright. The convention endorsed the Macedonian ticket (Ralph V. Harlow, *Gerrit Smith: Philanthropist and Reformer* [New York, 1939], pp. 183–84). See also *National Era,* 24 August 1848.

[92] Boston *Emancipator,* 6 September 1848; *Milwaukee Freeman,* 2 August 1848, in Smith, *Liberty and Free Soil Parties,* p. 146.

[93] *National Era,* 24 August 1848.

ammunition." Garrison's followers appeared to find Free Soil even more commendable than did their chief. As early as 25 August the editor informed his readers that "a number of those" who had previously disdained the use of the ballot were preparing "to vote . . . for Martin Van Buren"; in spite of repeated warnings against such "temptation," he was forced to admit, as election day approached, that "the Free Soil fever has carried off multitudes of abolitionists, and it is to be feared that many of them will never recover themselves."[94]

The same fever was felt even in the South. Delaware, Maryland, Virginia, North Carolina, Kentucky, and Missouri Provisoists named full Free Soil electoral tickets. In North Carolina the movement won the support of William H. Heywood, a close friend of Polk, who had created a nationwide sensation by resigning his seat in the United States Senate rather than voting against the Tariff of 1846 as he had been directed by the North Carolina legislature. In Maryland and Missouri the Free-Soilers were led by ex-Governor Thomas Francis and by Montgomery Blair. Even more amazing was a movement in Louisiana, where a handful of men under the leadership of Thomas G. Mackay met in Lafayette, in defiance of the mayor's warning, to create a Van Buren club and to announce their complete sympathy with the Free Soil platform.[95]

These manifestations of rapidly mounting Free Soil strength in the month after the Buffalo meeting alarmed northern Democrats and Whigs alike. Unable to check the growth of the movement through ridicule and abuse, they began to cast about for other means. During late July members of both major parties in the North and the South expressed the hope that the passage of the "Clayton Compromise" might bring to an end the agitation for Free Soil. The bill, providing for the establishment of territorial governments in Oregon, New Mexico, and California, left the question of whether a slaveholder could carry his property into these territories to the courts and the question of whether to establish slavery in any new state to the territorial convention that

[94] *Liberator,* 26 May, 14 July, 25, 28 August, 8, 29 September, 27 October 1848; Francis J. and Wendell P. Garrison, *William Lloyd Garrison, 1805–1879* (New York, 1889), 3: 235 n, 236.

[95] Wilson, *Slave Power,* 2: 159; *Niles' Register* 74 (20 September, 18 October 1848): 191, 247–48; *National Era,* 24 August, 7, 28 September 1848; *North Carolina Standard,* 11 October 1848; *Cleveland Herald,* 5 September 1848; *New Orleans Delta,* 21 August 1848; Greer, "Louisiana Politics," p. 560. One Louisianian informed Van Buren that the sugar planters of Louisiana were in favor of "Free Territory" because more "slave territory would bring more sugar lands into cultivation and produce an injurious competition" (Alexander Walker to Van Buren, 28 August 1848, Van Buren Papers).

would draw up a constitution preparatory to the territory's admission to the Union.[96]

The Clayton Compromise was attacked by Provisoists and by southern extremists. The *New York Tribune* called it a "political trick." If the bill passed, it argued, "we shall have an immediate organization of each territory, under influences most hostile to free labor and free soil. Slaves will be carried there and the territorial judges will pronounce the whole a fair business transaction." Then the Supreme Court would simply defer a decision until "slavery" had become strong enough to organize state governments and apply for admission into the Union. "After that the court may decide as it sees fit; slavery will take care of itself."[97] On the other side, the Nashville *Republican* opposed the measure because it secured for the South "not a single right except the right of litigating a right of property in the Supreme Court."[98]

More moderate elements subscribed to the tangled opinion of the *Augusta Republic,* which read "the Compromise Bill with real joy," because it would narrow "the gulph" that divided North and South and threatened to get "wider, and deeper, and hotter." If the measure failed, the nation would be "turned upon a storm-lashed sea, with no compass or friendly stars" to direct its course.[99] Other newspapers, such as the Philadelphia *Times,* endorsed the bill because with its passage "the fancied and real importance of the Barnburning movement" would "instantly sink to zero."[100]

The Clayton Compromise was approved by the Senate on 27 July by a vote of 24 to 22. Two days later all hopes for settling the issue of slavery in the territories were dashed when Congressman Alexander H. Stephens's motion to lay the bill on the table—tantamount to a rejection—passed the House by a vote of 112 to 97.[101]

[96] *Niles' Register* 74 (16 August 1848) : 108.

[97] *New York Tribune* quoted in *Niles' Register* 74 (26 July 1848) : 56. See also *New York Evening Post,* 20 July 1848; *Albany Atlas,* 20 July 1848.

[98] Nashville *Republican,* 16 August 1848. See also *Richmond Whig* quoted in *Richmond Enquirer,* 1 August 1848. Robert Toombs called the measure the "Euthanasia of State Rights" (Pleasant R. Stovall, *Life of Robert Toombs* [New York, 1892], p. 61).

[99] *Augusta Republic* quoted in *Richmond Enquirer,* 9 August 1848. See also *Boston Times,* 29 July 1848; *Albany Argus,* 26 July 1848; *Richmond Enquirer,* 1 August 1848.

[100] Philadelphia *Times,* 20 July 1848. The *Daily Wisconsin* of 9 August 1848 suggested that passage of the measure would have the opposite effect: "The Free Soil agitation would have been *far more intense, had the bill passed.* . . . The cry of REPEAL would have been a far more powerful rallying cry than any other tocsin that could have been sounded."

[101] The measure passed the Senate by the following count: in favor—7 northern

Although disappointment over the result was widespread, party leaders in the North wasted little time grieving. By September they developed more subtle strategies. The new tactics of the Democrats were simple: they seized upon Free Soil as their own property. The strategy was tersely summarized by the *Geneva* (Ill.) *Gazette:* "General Cass is not only in favor of 'free soil' . . . but is in truth the only *real free soil* presidential candidate in the field."[102] The *Boston Times* went even further. "We say that the democracy will continue to support Cass and Butler," it announced; "indeed, there is no other ticket which presents anything like so strong claims to the support of those men who are *really in favor of free soil.*"[103]

Reconciling such statements with the Cass formula that Congress had no power over slavery in the territories presented no great problem. Greene C. Bronson, associate justice of the New York Court of Errors, provided a ready solution when, in reply to a Barnburner overture for an alliance, he announced that he was utterly opposed to the extension of slavery into any territory where it did not exist. However, he did not think it "either necessary or expedient" to call upon Congress to legislate on the subject. "The relation of master and slave," he explained, "does not exist by the law of nature, nor has the claim of the master, like the right to property in general, been recognized by all civilized communities." In short, slavery could not exist where there was no "positive law" to uphold it. It was not necessary that slavery be forbidden; it was

---

Democrats, 1 northern Whig, 10 southern Democrats, 6 southern Whigs; against—10 northern Democrats, 8 northern Whigs, no southern Democrats, 4 southern Whigs. It failed in the House by the following count: in favor (against tabling)—21 northern Democrats, no northern Whigs, 49 southern Democrats, 27 southern Whigs; against (for tabling)—31 northern Democrats, 73 northern Whigs, no southern Democrats, 8 southern Whigs (*Niles' Register* 74 [2 August 1848]: 80). Analysis of the vote shows that the North was essentially against the measure: its vote was 29 in favor (including only 1 Whig) and 122 against. The South was essentially in favor: its vote was 92 in favor (every southern Democrat) and 12 against (all Whigs). Blame for defeat of the measure was placed upon the 8 southern Whigs who voted to table it in the House. A correspondent informed Van Buren that Robert Barnwell Rhett believed the 8 southern Whigs had acted against the measure because "they thought that by leaving the affair open Genl. Taylor would carry every Southern State against Genl. Cass, and that at the North the latter would be completely broken down by his equivocal position on the subject and the Buffalo nominee and Genl. Taylor together would sweep all the States" (Gilpin to Van Buren, 28 July 1848, Van Buren Papers).

[102] *Geneva* (Ill.) *Gazette* quoted in *Illinois State Register,* 15 September 1848. See also *Cleveland Plain Dealer,* 3, 25 October 1848; *Boston Post,* 5 September 1848; *New Hampshire Patriot,* 26 October 1848; *Daily Wisconsin,* 21 September, 17 October 1848; *Racine Advocate,* 31 August 1848.

[103] *Boston Times* quoted in *Vicksburg Whig,* 4 October 1848.

enough that it was not specially authorized. "If the owner of slaves removes with, or sends them into a country, state, or territory, where slavery does not exist by law, they will from that moment become free men." State laws had no extraterritorial authority: "A law of Virginia which makes a man a slave there, cannot make him a slave in New York, nor beyond the Rocky Mountains." Since Bronson entertained no doubt about the correctness of his legal interpretation—which automatically made all territories free territories—he declined to join the Free Soil movement.[104]

Bronson's "positive law" formula was made public in mid-August and was soon adopted by the Democracy as its own. Thenceforth, from Maine to Illinois, Democratic orators and the Democratic press blazoned it before the electorate as the doctrinal position of true Free-Soilers. One of its best expressions, repeated ad infinitum, was developed by the *New Hampshire Patriot*:

> The Democracy of New Hampshire are *all* for Free Soil; they will do as much and go as far to keep free the territories now free, and to prevent the extension of slavery as any other men. . . . They are told by the most eminent jurists of the land, however, that slavery cannot extend itself to free territory without the aid of *positive law;* and while they will never assist in the enactment of such a law, but will ever oppose it by all legal means, they at the same time give to the country the proof of their sincerity by supporting a man who is pledged by the history of his whole life, pledged by all his interests, associations, and feelings, and *pledged by a solemn and public promise to* VETO *any law that may be passed by Congress for such a purpose.* Gen. Cass declares that *Congress has no constitutional power to pass such a law,* and if they should pass one he is bound by oath to *veto it.*[105]

Under such circumstances, northern Cass men pointed out, it was rank madness for Democratic advocates of Free Soil to desert their party, to throw away their votes, and by their action to secure the election of Taylor.

Northern Whig tactics took a somewhat different turn. Some party meetings and newspapers hoisted banners for "Taylor, Fillmore & Free Soil,"[106] but their major effort was directed toward convincing the

---

[104] *Pennsylvanian,* 10 August 1848.

[105] *Boston Times,* 18 September 1848; *Albany Argus,* September–October 1848; *Cleveland Plain Dealer,* 25 October 1848; *Indiana State Sentinel,* 16 September 1848; Eli Nichols to Chase, 6 November 1848, Chase Papers; *New Hampshire Patriot,* 10 August 1848.

[106] *Albany Argus,* 6 September 1848; *New York Tribune,* 9 September 1848.

electorate that only the "Whigs of the North" could "rightfully claim the appelation of the *Free soil party*."[107] Like the Whig Young Men of New York City, they appealed to their brethren to stand by those who had "never compromised, never traficked, never betrayed, the free spirit of the North, rather than the noisy new converts to free soil and free labor, who never ceased to truckle to the South until she had spurned them with contempt from her councils and refused longer to repay subserviency by offices and honors."[108] Closely coupled with these appeals were Whig warnings that support of Free Soil candidates would only result in a repetition of the "same third party swindle" that had been worked on the nation in 1844.[109] On this point Seward's admonition to the Whigs of the Western Reserve who proposed to abandon their party was typical. "You expect to establish a new and better party, that will carry our common principles to more speedy and universal triumph," he declared, but "you will not succeed in any degree, now or hereafter, because it is impossible. . . . Seceding Whigs can only give success to the party of Lewis Cass."[110] Abraham Lincoln stumped Massachusetts and Illinois with the same message.[111]

Immeasurable assistance was given these tactics when Webster came out of semiretirement at Marshfield. The Bay State orator had revealed not a little displeasure at the news of Taylor's Philadelphia victory, but instead of making a public announcement of his position, he had sulkily retired to his home.[112] Encouraged by his silence, antislavery Whigs hinted that he might throw his lot in with the Buffalo movement. After Van Buren's nomination Webster's close friend Ebenezer Rockwood Hoar urged him to support the Free Soil ticket. "One word from you,"

[107] Resolutions of the Massachusetts Whig Convention (*Boston Atlas*, 14 September 1848).

[108] *Georgian*, 30 August 1848. See also Wells to Niles, 5 September 1848, Welles Papers; *New York Tribune*, 23 September, 14 October 1848; *North American*, 1 September 1848; *Cleveland Herald*, 14 August 1848; *Detroit Advertiser*, 10 October 1848.

[109] *Milwaukee Sentinel*, 18 September 1848.

[110] William H. Seward, *Works of William H. Seward*, ed. George E. Baker (Boston, 1884), 3: 294-95. Seward advanced a similar argument at a meeting in Boston (3: 286-90).

[111] Albert J. Beveridge, *Abraham Lincoln, 1809-1858* (Boston, 1928), 1: 469-77.

[112] At the time of the nomination Webster wrote to his son: "These northern proceedings can come to nothing useful, to you or to me. . . . If the Conscience men at Worcester, were to ask to put me on their ticket, what would it all come to? I could not consent to that with so little show of strength as they now put forth. On the other hand, suppose I acquiesce in Genl. Taylor's nomination. He will or will not be chosen. If chosen . . . it may be for *your* interest not to have opposed him" (Daniel Webster to Fletcher Webster, 19 June 1848, in *Webster's Writings*, 16: 496-97).

Hoar pointed out, "would blow out of existence this Taylor faction . . . throughout the North, in twenty-four hours. Any token of assent would make you the acknowledged leader of the 'free soil men.'" But Webster had no confidence in the movement. "I would much rather trust General Taylor," he replied, "than Mr. Van Buren even on this very question of slavery, for I believe that Gen'l. Taylor is an honest man, and I am sure he is not so much committed on the wrong side as I know Mr. Van Buren to have been for fifteen years."[113]

With such thoughts in his mind it was only a matter of time before Webster made his position public. On 1 September, much to the delight of regular Whigs, he pledged his support for Old Zack from the steps of his Marshfield estate. He knew that it "would be idle to conceal the fact" that Taylor's nomination had not been "satisfactory to the Whigs of Massachusetts," because they believed "that it was not wise, or discreet, to go to the army for the selection of a candidate for the Presidency." He knew also that the Philadelphia nomination had been dictated by a "sagacious, wise, and far-seeing doctrine of availability." In such a situation what were the Whigs of Massachusetts to do?

What was the alternative presented? The contest, as Webster saw it, was between Taylor and Cass. He explained:

> In my opinion there is not the least probability of any other result. . . . I know that the enthusiasm of a new formed party, that the popularity of a new formed name, without communicating any new formed idea, may lead men to think that the sky is to fall, and that larks are suddenly to be taken. I entertain no such expectation. I speak with no disrespect of the Free Soil party. I have read their platform, and though I think there are some unsound places in it, I can stand on it pretty well. But I see nothing in it both new and valuable. . . . If the term Free Soil party, or Free Soil men, designate those who are fixed and unalterably fixed, in favor of restriction of slavery . . . then I hold myself to be as good a free soil man as any of the Buffalo convention. . . .
>
> The gentlemen at Buffalo have placed at the head of their party Mr. Van Buren, a gentleman for whom I have all the respect that I ought to entertain for one with whom I have been associated in some degree, in public life for many years. . . . But really, speaking for myself, if I were to express confidence in Mr. Van Buren and his politics on any question, and most especially this very question of slavery, I think the scene would border on the ludicrous, if not on the contemptible. I never proposed anything in my life of a general

[113] Hoar to Webster, n.d., in Hoar, *Autobiography*, 1: 149–50; Webster to Hoar, 23 August 1848, in *Webster's Writings*, 16: 298–99.

or public nature, that Mr. Van Buren did not oppose. Nor has it
happened to me to support any important measure proposed by him.
If he and I were now to find ourselves together under the Free Soil
flag, I am sure that, with his accustomed good humor, he would
laugh. If nobody were present, we would both laugh at the strange
occurrences and stranger jumbles of political life that should have
brought us to sit down cozily and snugly, side by side on the same
platform. That the leader of the Free Spoil party should have so
suddenly become the leader of the Free Soil party would be a joke
to shake his sides and mine.

Besides, Webster concluded, Van Buren had not the slightest chance to
emerge victorious from the contest. The real choice was between Cass
and Taylor; between those two, no Whig could hesitate.[114]

The action of Horace Greeley was equally important. Late in September, shortly after he was given a Whig nomination to Congress, he
announced that he would support Taylor. The reasons for his action fit
very neatly into the pattern of Whig strategy. "While I frankly avow
that I would do little . . . to make Gen'l Taylor President," he declared,
"I cannot forget that others stand or fall with him . . . to whom I
cannot now be unfaithful." The fate of the Free Soil issue gave him
some trouble. He argued, however, that Van Buren could not win. Every
Whig ballot cast for Van Buren therefore became "in effect half a vote
for Cass," who he was certain would never keep "slavery out of California and New Mexico." Taylor, on the other hand, had been pledged not
to veto antiextension legislation; thus, Greeley concluded, the "triumph
of Free Soil" made it necessary to "support Whig nominations."[115]

Not only northern Democrats and Whigs but also southern Whigs
appropriated Free Soil to their own ends. They pointed out that the
great growth of the antislavery movement in the North was a clear
indication that the contest there was really between Van Buren and
Taylor. They had evidence from northern newspapers that Cass's prospects were diminishing every day; there were even reports that a great
Van Buren–Cass coalition was being planned "to prevent the election of
a southern man" in New York, Vermont, Connecticut, and Massachusetts.[116] Credence had to be given these reports, the *Vicksburg Whig*
argued, because of the character of the Free Soil leaders. "If a man were
asked to name the shrewdest and most sagacious politican in the world,
without a moment's hesitation he would give you 'Martin Van Buren.'

[114] *Webster's Writings*, 16: 123–29. Webster later made a similar speech before
the Massachusetts Whig Convention in Abington (16: 373–79).
[115] *New York Tribune*, 7 October 1848.
[116] *Vicksburg Whig*, 1 November 1848.

There is no question, that such a man would never stake his earthly all upon this movement, without strong indications of success." Therefore, if the South seriously deprecated the election of Van Buren, there was "but one way to prevent such a result." It had to support Taylor because "every Southern vote cast for Cass" would assist Van Buren.[117]

Coincident with this development in the southern Whig campaign, slave state Democrats discovered a vulnerable point of attack in the Whig vice-presidential candidate, Millard Fillmore. From the start of the campaign they had charged that Fillmore was an antislavery man, but they had little documentary evidence to prove their contentions. His vote against gag rule number 21 in 1838 was exhumed, and he was charged with introducing petitions to abolish slavery in the District of Columbia.[118] Such accusations, however, did not go far to prove Fillmore an abolitionist. Whigs could readily point to the fact that Henry A. Wise of Virginia, a Cass supporter, had also opposed the gag rule.[119] Moreover, they could produce a relatively satisfactory explanation of Fillmore's conduct in bringing antislavery petitions before the House in the form of a letter to John Gayle, governor of Alabama: "The rule upon which I acted was, that every citizen presenting a respectful petition to the body that by the Constitution had the power to grant or refuse the prayer of it, was entitled to be heard; and therefore the petition ought to be received and considered. If right and reasonable the prayer of it should be granted, but if wrong or unreasonable it should be denied."[120]

Early in September southern Democrats exploded a bombshell in the Whig camp by publishing a letter which Fillmore had sent to the Erie County Antislavery Society ten years before:

> Your communication . . . as chairman of the committee appointed by "The Antislavery Society of the County of Erie" has just come to hand. You solicit my answer to the following interrogatories.
>
> *1st.* Do you believe that petitions to Congress on the subject of slavery and the slave trade ought to be received, read and respectfully considered by the representatives of the people?

[117] Ibid., 30 August 1848. See also *Savannah Republican,* 19, 21 August 1848; *New Orleans Commercial Bulletin,* 2, 11 September 1848; Nashville *Republican,* 12 October 1848.

[118] *Richmond Enquirer,* 15, 17 June, 15 August 1848; *North Carolina Standard,* 12 July 1848; *Georgian,* 23 June, 29 July, 19 September, 17 October 1848; *Floridian,* 1, 29 July, 2 September 1848; *Nashville Union,* 29 July 1848; *Mobile Register,* 4 August 1848.

[119] *Savannah Republican,* 6 July 1848; *Vicksburg Whig,* 12 July 1848.

[120] Millard Fillmore, *Millard Fillmore Papers,* ed. Frank H. Severance (Buffalo, N. Y., 1907), II: 279–80; *Mobile Register,* 1 September 1848; *New Orleans Commercial Bulletin,* 2 September 1848.

2d. Are you opposed to the annexation of Texas to the Union, under any circumstances, so long as slaves are held there?

3d. Are you in favor of Congress exercising all the constitutional power it possesses to abolish the internal slave trade between the states?

4th. Are you in favor of immediate legislation for the abolition of slavery in the District of Columbia?

I am much engaged, and have no time to enter into an argument, or to explain at length my reasons for my opinion. I shall therefore content myself for the present by answering all your interrogations in the AFFIRMATIVE, and leave for some future occasion a more studied discussion on the subject.[121]

Published throughout the South without a word of comment,[122] the "Erie County letter"—when coupled with the not impertinent suggestion that confinement in the White House might prove as fatal to Taylor as it had to William Henry Harrison and thus bring Fillmore into the executive chair—became the Democrats' chief weapon against the Whig ticket. Unanswerable, it confronted Whigs wherever they turned, and, as Robert A. Toombs reported late in September, "It gave an excuse to all Democrats who wanted to go back to their party to abandon Taylor."[123]

[121] *Washington Union,* 1 September 1848.

[122] *Richmond Enquirer,* 2 September 1848; *Georgian,* 6 September 1848; *Louisville Democrat,* 7 September 1848; *North Carolina Standard,* 6 September 1848; *Charleston Mercury,* 9 September 1848; *Mobile Register,* 18 September 1848.

[123] Toombs to Crittenden, 27 September 1848, in Phillips, *Toombs, Stephens, and Cobb Correspondence,* p. 128.

Chapter Fourteen

Final Complications

The intense preoccupation of all political parties with the problem of slavery did not completely preclude consideration of other issues. It was the northern Democrats, undoubtedly conscious that their party position on various economic issues of the past had won them power, who most often reminded the electorate that other issues besides slavery were involved in the outcome of the election. They warned that the silence of their opponents upon these questions did not mean that the old platforms had been abandoned. "The man who believes that the old issues between the two great parties in this country are not involved in the present contest is grossly deceived," the *New Hampshire Patriot* of 22 September maintained:

> It is true that the federal and abolition organs . . . so pretend; and in so doing they exhibit more tact and shrewdness than honesty; for who does not know that, upon a fair, candid, open presentation of the great fundamental questions which have so long divided the people of this country, the result would be the disgraceful and overwhelming defeat of all these factions arrayed against the Democracy? Well aware of this, it is the policy of all those factions to keep these issues out of sight, to induce people to believe that they are not involved in the approaching election, to divest their attention entirely from them, and to occupy their minds wholly by other less important and collateral questions.

Repeated offerings of such bait, however, brought only slight response from the Whigs. In the South their campaign continued its old refrain. It was well described by one of Howell Cobb's correspondents:

> Their speeches consist of three parts—miscellaneous abuse of Cass and the Democrats, comments on the dangers to slavery, and the impossibility of trusting any Northern man, exemplified by the course of Van Buren—and lastly a glorification of Old Taylor's battles. I have never heard one of them advance a principle—save

only that Congress ought to decide all questions, as per Allison
letter. . . . They refuse to acknowledge that they are for any of the
old Whig measures—won't tell what they are for, and go it blind for
Taylor as a slaveholder and a hero.[1]

Northern Whigs were less wary of revealing their stand upon the
issues which had divided American parties for two decades, but their
arguments for the most part were confined to localized campaigns. An
example was the old tariff problem.

Whigs had begun a campaign on the tariff immediately after the
passage of the Walker Act of 1846. In Massachusetts and Pennsylvania,
particularly, party journals, predicting calamity, had raised a cry for
"repeal" and "restoration" of the Tariff of 1842.[2] In Pennsylvania even
Democrats had added their voices to the swelling cry. "REPEAL is the
word!" the Philadelphia *Times* exclaimed. "Take it up Democrats! echo
it men! echo it miners and laborers! shout it mechanics! There shall be
no rest, no reposing until the British Tariff Bill is repealed."[3] So
powerful was the demand that all but a handful of Keystone State
Democrats were thrust from office in the congressional election of 1846.

It was not long, however, before events proved that the Whigs were
false prophets. They had predicted that the Walker Tariff would lower
the rates of wages, throw thousands out of employment, induce general
disaster and incalculable individual suffering, lessen the value of property, depreciate the value of agricultural products, check public and
private improvements, and plunge the states into the "inky pot of
repudiation."[4] As early as January 1847 it became evident that both
Federal revenues and agricultural exports were rising rapidly; Whig
"calamity howlers" gave up in despair. The tariff issue disappeared from
the political forum.

But it reappeared in Massachusetts and Pennsylvania during the
presidential campaign of 1848. Once again, Whig journals in those states
predicted future ruin. Much of their argument was directed toward the
farmer. They admitted that the tariff had not been disastrous for him,
but, they insisted, prosperity had resulted only because there had been a
grain shortage in Europe. Now, however, the *North American* pointed
out, "The plague is virtually over. The crops of Great Britain and
Ireland promise to be as fruitful as our own; and on the continent of

[1] W. W. Hull to Cobb, 22 July 1848, in Cole, *Whigs in the South,* p. 132.
[2] *Boston Atlas,* 31 July, 4–6 August 1846; *North American,* 24, 31 July, 4 August
1846.
[3] Philadelphia *Times,* 29, 30 July 1846.
[4] *Richmond Enquirer,* 11 October 1847.

Europe the year has been one of fecundity. . . . Our surplus is not wanted there." What were the American farmers to do? Could they sell their products at home? Obviously they could not, since the "glorious market" which the protectionists had sought to secure for the agriculturists "by filling the country with workshops and factories, and filling those with the life and bustle of prosperous industry"—that home market which was growing fast because of the Tariff of 1842—had vanished "under the deadly influence of the free trade law of 1846." Not until that market was restored by the repeal of the Walker Tariff could "farmers flatter themselves that their abundant crops" were to be "sources of prosperity."[5]

Nor was the outlook in industry any more hopeful. "The important manufacture of iron," the *Boston Atlas* maintained, "is pretty nearly ruined, and the day is not distant if the present policy is continued, when the capital invested in that business will be a dead loss, and the labor employed in it will have to seek employment elsewhere." Cotton factories which had once given "fair dividends to capital and high wages to labor" had been running for a year "at a loss," with nothing better in view. "Every branch of domestic industry" was "withering away before the Sirocco policy of the Polkish democracy." Only if Taylor were elected could the nation expect to have a tariff law which would "protect the labor of the country, and give the market of America to the workmen of America."[6]

The Democrats' reply to this attack upon their measures was chiefly statistical. The *Pennsylvanian* of 26 October pointed out that the iron industry, far from being ruined by the Walker Tariff, had actually found new business. Its domestic market had increased by $4 million between 1845 and 1847, while exports in the same period had increased from $863,000 to $1,132,000. The textile industry, moreover, was exporting its products to the whole world—"a queer sort of destruction," the *New Haven Register* remarked.[7]

But this sort of argument over the tariff was confined almost entirely to Massachusetts and Pennsylvania. In the South only the Nashville *Republican*, which dutifully reprinted attacks upon the Walker Tariff by northeastern journals, seemed concerned with the issue. Southern Democratic journals usually confined their rare observations on the subject to

[5] *North American*, 8 August 1848. See also 3 August, 19 October, 8 November 1848.
[6] *Boston Atlas*, 21 July 1848. See also 3 October 1848; *North American*, 12 July 1848; Charles H. Delevan to Crittenden, 31 October 1848, Crittenden Papers.
[7] *New Haven Register* quoted in *Washington Union*, 18 October 1848.

a condemnation of Fillmore as "the self-styled author" of the Tariff of 1842. In the West, comment was equally infrequent. The Detroit *Free Press,* one of the few newspapers to take notice, warned that the object of a protective tariff was "to benefit the rich at the expense of the poor, and to build up a set of manufacturing aristocrats, to draw the life's blood from the hardworking portion of the community." The *Daily Wisconsin* occasionally reminded its Democratic readers that the Free-Soilers had "dropped their Free Trade principles."[8]

The internal improvements issue was also brought into the campaign. However, the argument on the subject, which had once been nationwide, was now confined almost entirely to the Great Lakes area. There the campaign of the Whigs was directed against Cass's unfortunate letter to the Chicago River and Harbor Convention, which Whig journals paraded before the electorate day after day without a word of comment in type either so large as to require a quarter column or so microscopic that the whole letter could be crammed into a single line.

Against these tactics the Democrats could only protest that Cass had voted for every river and harbor bill since he had entered the Senate and that he had refused to attend the Chicago meeting because it had been arranged to further the interests of such Whig politicians as Tom Corwin.[9] To prove their contention, they used the words of prominent Whigs such as Richard W. Thompson of Indiana, who admitted that the Democratic nominee had always favored internal improvements; they gave much publicity to the declaration of the *Racine Advocate,* which supported Van Buren, that opposition to Cass on account of his letter to the Chicago meeting was not "fair," since the convention had been "looked upon with distrust by many people" and besides had "proved itself a humbug."[10]

In turn they asked if the Whig candidate had ever uttered "a word, or given a vote in favor of a single river or harbor."[11] The Detroit *Free Press* of 28 June regaled its readers with an invented letter which Taylor might have sent to the Detroit Common Council in reply to a question about his opinion on the issue:

> Your favor has been received, and in reply to the resolution of the "Common Council" (by the way, does "Common Council" mean a

[8] Nashville *Republican,* 7, 14 August 1848; *Georgian,* 4 August 1848; Detroit *Free Press,* 27 July 1848; *Daily Wisconsin,* 15 September 1848.
[9] Detroit *Free Press,* 17 June 1848; *Cincinnati Enquirer,* 12 June 1848; *Cleveland Plain Dealer,* 28 June 1848.
[10] *Indiana State Sentinel,* 20 September 1848; *Racine Advocate,* 7 June 1848.
[11] *Daily Wisconsin,* 3 July 1848.

meeting of the people, or is it a legislative body? you didn't inform me) asking my opinion in relation to the improvement of Lake Harbors. I don't know how big your lakes are, but if boats can run on them, the harbor ought to be made good. I should be in favor of improving the harbor at Baton Rouge, and the clearing out of *snags* (that I suppose means Allygators) but I somewhere read that there were no snags or allygators in the North. I don't see how the government can make these improvements—it appears to me that the owners of steamboats and vessels . . . should make the improvements.

I notice you don't say, in your esteemed favor, anything about me being a candidate for President! I know Michigan is a loco-foco state, but I am you know, not a candidate of a party, but of the people.

Upon the other issues that had once divided Whigs and Democrats there was very little discussion. Very little attention was given to the Independent Treasury System. The *North American* pointed out that "every day's experience" with the new financial structure demonstrated its "utter absurdity." Every "intelligent merchant or man of business" knew that any scheme whereby specie was withdrawn from circulation and revenues were locked up in "iron vaults" was "calculated not only to derange the whole machinery of trade, but to depress every interest connected with moneyed operations." The farmer, the mechanic, and the workingman, it contended, "are especially the sufferers by this wretched experiment; for, constituting the great mass of the community, and depending upon their own labor for subsistence, whatever disturbs the money market operates directly to their disadvantage, in the depreciation of prices, in the reduction of wages, and in the diminution of employment." Except, however, for an occasional declaration that Taylor's election would bring about the repeal of the detested "locofoco invention," few Whig journals made any reference to the issue at all. For the most part they appeared content to relegate the nation's banking structure to the limbo of "obsolete" problems.[12]

Similar treatment was given the old land issue. Hardly a word was uttered by either major party in favor of or against their once cherished principles. In the North, however, attention turned to the rapidly developing land reform movement.

Officially, the land reform banner was carried through the campaign by the Macedonians. Free-Soilers had bid for that right in their Buffalo platform, but their offer had been rejected because, as one ardent group

[12] *North American,* 30 September, 4 October 1848.

of disciples informed Van Buren, their free-land plank had not been "clear and decided enough for *National Reformers*." It had neither acknowledged "the *natural* right to Land," nor had it demanded the prohibition of the *"unlimited* sale thereof to the monopolists and speculators," thus "leaving an open door for the continuance of the evils paramount to chattel slavery with all its horrors combined."[13]

Nonetheless, Free-Soilers made an effort to become the special champions of free land during the campaign. Wherever their assemblies met, planks demanding the "appropriation of the public domain in limited quantities to actual settlers, and to actual settlers only" were adopted.[14] In the East the Barnburners aimed their efforts particularly at workingmen, coupling their advocacy of land reform with reminders that Martin Van Buren was "the author of the TEN HOUR SYSTEM." They also reiterated their old argument that permitting slave labor in the territories would degrade free labor and would prevent the laboring man from entering the new territories. A vote for Van Buren and Free Soil was a vote to "elevate and dignify labor."[15]

Free Soil candidates for congressional and legislative positions, particularly those with Democratic and Liberty party backgrounds, eagerly took the land reform pledge. Some, such as George W. Allen, a nominee for Congress in northern Ohio, even tried to shift the main goal of the party by centering their campaigns on the dangers involved in land monopoly rather than on the wrongs of Negro slavery.[16] Free Soil efforts had some obvious effects: during the campaign a number of land reform journals deserted the hopeless prospects of Gerrit Smith and joined the forces of Free Soil.[17]

The two major parties divided expectably on the issue. To northern Whigs the land reform movement spelled anarchy and "agrarianism"— the mid-nineteenth-century term of condemnation for all movements that threatened vested interests. The *National Intelligencer*'s reaction on 15 August was typical. "The next step . . . after prodigally wasting the birth right of the People in the Public Lands," it maintained, "will be to divide the property of all those who have earned it among those who prefer the easier method of living by their wits, to counteract by

---

[13] Rochester National Reform Association to Van Buren, 22 August 1848, Van Buren Papers. See also Cole, *Era of the Civil War*, p. 89; George F. Stephenson, *Political History of the Public Lands from 1840 to 1862* (Boston, 1917), pp. 136–37; *Iowa Capitol Reporter*, 13 September 1848.

[14] *North American*, 1 September 1848; *Racine Advocate*, 1 November 1848.

[15] *Albany Atlas*, 7 November 1848; *Buffalo Republic*, 9 October 1848.

[16] *Ohio State Journal*, 29 August 1848.

[17] *National Era*, 5 October 1848.

legislation the ordinances of Providence, and confound all its distinction between industry and indolence, between carefulness and prodigality, and between virtue and vice."

To Democrats, particularly in the Northwest, the new issue presented a challenge to be met. Many of the party's local conventions adopted free-land planks, and congressional nominees took the land reform pledge. In Ohio, Sam Weller, the gubernatorial candidate, pushed the policy of the National Reform Association with a vigor that rivaled the energy of all but its most fanatical disciples.[18]

Another issue, nativism, was brought into the campaign, mildly in the South, more strongly in the North. Whigs and Democrats both sought to turn it to their advantage by charging that the nominee of the other party was hostile to foreigners. Whigs, however, were at a great disadvantage. Their only talking point was the fact that Cass had voted against an appropriation of Federal funds for the relief of famine-stricken Ireland, a measure introduced into Congress by Crittenden.[19]

On the other hand, Democrats and Free-Soilers could not only point out that the Whigs were the traditional enemies of newcomers, an attitude they had inherited from the Federalists, but also they could and they did remind the foreign born that Taylor had first been nominated by the "church burning" Native Americans of Philadelphia and that every Nativist newspaper in the Union had endorsed him.[20] They frequently recalled that the *Philadelphia Sun,* one of the semiofficial organs of the Nativist party, had editorially claimed Taylor as one of its own kind and had refused to recognize him as a Whig, and that General Henry A. S. Dearborn, the Nativist candidate for vice president, had withdrawn in favor of Fillmore.[21] Did this not prove, Democratic journals asked, that Taylor and the Whigs had sold out to the Nativists? If further evidence were wanted, the foreigner needed only to look at the *Boston Courier,* which had denounced the Irish as "wild hordes of a semi-barbarous population," or at the *National Intelligencer,* which defended the "infamous and tyrannical course pursued by the British Government in Ireland."[22] Did this not reveal that "Whiggery and

[18] Holt, "Party Politics in Ohio," 38: 296–97.

[19] *North American,* 28 October 1848; *New Orleans Commercial Bulletin,* 6 November 1848.

[20] *Cleveland Plain Dealer,* 7 July 1848; *Albany Argus,* 15 June 1848; *Albany Atlas,* 10 October 1848; Detroit *Free Press,* 18 October 1848; *Richmond Enquirer,* 2 November 1848.

[21] *Louisville Democrat,* 23 June 1848; *Pennsylvanian,* 19 June 1848; Philadelphia *Times,* 3 July 1848; *Illinois State Register,* 14 July 1848; *Iowa Capitol Reporter,* 18 October 1848.

[22] *Boston Times,* 18 July, 24, 30 August 1848; *Boston Post,* 1 November 1848.

Orangeism" were synonomous? Could Irishmen and Catholics, or any foreigners for that matter, vote for the candidate of such a party—a party that condoned oppression and would refuse asylum and comfort to fugitives from tyranny?

One final complex of issues was brought into the campaign. It started with William Lowndes Yancey. The Alabamian had walked out of the Baltimore convention while the hall was still ringing with his threat to lead his friends into Whig ranks. On his way home to Montgomery he stopped at Charleston, where he delivered a passionate indictment of the Democratic nominee, whom he charged with holding Provisoist opinions; forgetting his own threat, he called upon the South to unite in a convention to name candidates who would take the Alabama Platform as their guide.[23] Then he departed southward to arouse the Democracy to a realization of the South's danger.

Outside South Carolina Yancey received a cool reception. Many who had once declared that adoption of the Alabama Platform was the sine qua non of their supporting the Baltimore nominee now roundly condemned his course. The reaction of James C. Dobbin of North Carolina was characteristic. "I was provoked at Yancey's conduct in the convention," he informed Howell Cobb. "The introduction of his resolution was unnecessary. The resolution reported by the committee was comprehensive. There was no evidence that Cass had wrong views, and the adoption of Yancey's resolution squinted very much toward a suspicion of Cass and looked too much like pressing nice, hair-splitting distinctions on the subject upon our Northern democratic friends, whose liberality should be appreciated but not abused."[24] In Yancey's own state the two leading Democratic journals denounced him as a man "smitten with the ambition to become the John Van Buren of Alabama and the founder of a school of Barnburnerism for the South." In Mississippi the party organ at Jackson declared that nothing that the Democratic convention had done "was wiser and more patriotic" than the rejection of the Yancey "firebrand." The question, it maintained, had been "agitated for sinister purposes, by the bidders for abolition votes at the North, or the factionists at the South, who wished to gain political capital by claiming to be the peculiar champions of our domestic institutions." Such agitation could only work to the injury of the slave states.[25]

[23] *Charleston Mercury*, 12 June 1848.
[24] James C. Dobbin to Cobb, 15 June 1848, in Phillips, *Toombs, Stephens, and Cobb Correspondence*, p. 108. See also Henry R. Jackson to Cobb, 21 June 1848, pp. 110–11.
[25] DuBose, *Yancey*, pp. 215–16; *Mobile Register*, 3 July, 4 October 1848; *Mississippian*, 16 June 1848. Yancey himself early recognized the futility of his

It was therefore only in South Carolina that Yancey's plans made any headway. The situation there was ripe for such a development. Cass was *persona non grata* to the political powers of the state; that fact had been made clear by the *Mercury*'s denunciation of his Nicholson letter earlier in the year. The prevailing attitude had not changed when news of the Michigander's nomination reached Charleston. The *Mercury* and others immediately announced that Cass was "the least acceptable" of all those whose names had come before the convention:

> The proceedings of that body have fallen like the startling tones of an alarm bell on the ears of the South. Its nomination of Gen. Cass —its resolutions about slavery . . . fill us with apprehension almost to dismay. The opinions of Gen. Cass, promulgated in his late letter —that the inhabitants of a territory, before they are invested with the attributes of self government and sovereignty—tenants of the public lands, at the sufferance of the States—mere squatters, have the right to appropriate the territory that may be acquired . . . and to exclude from its limits the property of fourteen of the States— had been repudiated by the press and the people of the whole South. It is a doctrine too monstrous to be tolerated, an ostracism too degrading to be endured.[26]

Among men who held such views a distinct current toward Taylor set in, especially after it was learned that Isaac Holmes, a Charleston congressman closely identified with Calhoun, had declared his preference for the General. But Taylor's nomination by the Whigs made him too bitter a pill for many Democrats. For a moment the South Carolina Democracy wavered. Its position was fittingly expressed in a toast offered at a Fourth of July celebration in St. Paul's Parish: "General Cass and General Taylor: The two horns of a dilemma to Southern patriots. We want no statesman who has knuckled to abolitionists, or who marches under the banner of Whiggery."[27]

But by this time the seeds that Yancey had sown began to sprout.

---

plans; he wrote to Calhoun, "I greatly fear that we cannot make even a start in Alabama" (14 June 1848, in Boucher and Brooks, *Calhoun Correspondence*, p. 441).

[26] *Charleston Mercury*, 30 May, 2, 16 June 1848. Beverley Tucker in his bitterness over the convention described Cass in terms that the Barnburners also used: "A political mountebank, whose whole political life has been a succession of ground and lofty tumbling, and all sorts of clap trap exhibitions calculated for the taste of the rabble Democracy" (Tucker to Hammond, 12 June 1848, Hammond Papers). See also Lesesne to Calhoun, 5 July 1848, W. W. Harlee to Calhoun, 8 June 1848, Louis T. Wigfall to Calhoun, 10 June 1848, in Boucher and Brooks, *Calhoun Correspondence*, pp. 438–40, 454.

[27] *Charleston Mercury*, 8 July 1848.

Rumors that a southern party was in the making began to spread through the South; Littleton W. Tazewell of Virginia, Jefferson Davis of Mississippi, and Calhoun were proposed as standard bearers. The rumors had some foundation. Yancey himself suggested the names of Tazewell and Davis,[28] and there was evidence of Calhoun's interest in a movement that was nothing less than a rebirth of his earlier program.[29] Calhoun's connection with the movement, however, raised fears that it was an effort to place him in nomination. James H. Hammond categorically declared: "Mr. Calhoun in his desperation wishes to run as a third candidate, but the only effect of his persistence would be to bring Carolina into that contempt, at once, which assuredly waits her in a few years under his mad lead. . . . [He], as some others, think that you have but to say nigger to the South to set it on fire . . . and he hoped to be thus made an independent Slavery candidate."[30]

The movement for an independent southern candidate did not advance very far. By midsummer it had become clear that the movement would receive no support. South Carolinians were forced to choose between Taylor and Cass. On 20 July many of them met at Charleston to declare war on the North through an independent Taylor nomination:

> We regard the issue now made between the States of the Union, styling themselves the Free States, and the States in which the institution of domestic servitude exists, as paramount to all questions which can be presented. . . . In seeking one, under whose lead we shall look for the best guidance in our difficulties, we turn to General Taylor. . . . Under his administration we feel assured that the rights of the States will be respected and preserved, and we cordially concur in that nomination of him for the Presidency of the Union, which has been made by the people . . . irrespective of Parties, and independent of politicians.[31]

The assembly selected William O. Butler, the Democratic nominee for vice president, as Taylor's running mate.

In the weeks that followed, the Taylor boom in South Carolina rapidly assumed the proportions of a landslide. Although Calhoun declared his neutrality in a letter to the *Mercury*,[32] there was little doubt about the

[28] *New Orleans Commercial Bulletin*, 19 July 1848; Yancey to Calhoun, 21 June 1848, in Jameson, *Calhoun Correspondence*, p. 1177.

[29] See my article, "Calhoun's Presidential Ambitions," pp. 351–52.

[30] Hammond to Simms, 20 June 1848, Hammond Papers.

[31] *Charleston Mercury*, 21 July 1848.

[32] Calhoun's letter is dated 1 September 1848. See also *Niles' Register* 74 (18 October 1848) : 247.

stand of his closest political associates: almost as one man they enrolled behind the Taylor-Butler ticket. Even such prominent Calhoun foes as Hammond and the poet William Gilmore Simms joined the movement, which by 1 August appeared irresistable.[33]

But there were already indications that the movement could be turned. As early as June, two influential newspapers in Columbia, the *Palmetto State Banner* and the *South Carolinian,* had announced that they could accept the Cass doctrine on slavery in the territories: "We fear no flimsy territorial law—if the soil and climate are suitable for slave labor, slavery WILL BE introduced, in spite of any enactment which may be made on the subject by any miserable Mexican and Indian legislature which may convene in the Territories."[34] During July and August some of the state's lesser figures, such as James W. Walker and Andrew Pickens, who chafed under the dictation of the Squire of Fort Hill, began to turn to Cass as a way of breaking Calhoun's hold on the state.[35] To make the movement stronger, only leadership and a little luck were needed. Both were forthcoming. The leadership was secured when Robert Barnwell Rhett returned from Congress in mid-August determined to keep his state from supporting a man whom he believed to be tainted with all the hated Whig "consolidationist" heresies;[36] the luck was supplied by Taylor's interminable letters.

The Whig nominee's epistolary efforts had worried his friends before his nomination at Philadelphia, and his postconvention communications proved no less distressing.[37] When notified of his nomination by the Charleston meeting, he immediately penned two letters of reply, which were given to the public in late August. In one, written to William B. Pringle, he gratefully acknowledged his nomination by the Charleston Democrats;[38] in the other, addressed to the *Charleston News,* he reiterated his old nonpartisan stand:

> I never had any aspirations for the Presidency, nor have I now, farther than the wishes of my friends are concerned in the matter;

[33] Hammond to M. J. Keith et al., 14 August 1848, Hammond Papers. Hammond characterized Taylor's supporters as "broken down politicians" and included himself among them (Hammond to Simms, 13 August 1848).

[34] *Palmetto State Banner* quoted in *Mobile Register,* 30 June 1848; *South Carolinian* quoted in *Georgian,* 17 June 1848.

[35] Walker to Hammond, 21 July, 4, 22 August 1848, Simms to Hammond, 21 July 1848, Hammond Papers.

[36] Simms to Hammond, 29 August 1848, ibid.

[37] Taylor's propensity for saying the wrong thing politically led one of his supporters to advise him "to make no replies whatsoever" to any future inquiries (Ewing to Taylor, 22 July 1848, Thomas Ewing Papers).

[38] *Niles' Register,* 74 (13 September 1848): 165.

nor would I have it on any other terms, than I stated when the subject was first agitated, which is, that my acceptance must be without pledges or being trammelled in any way, so that I could be President of the whole Nation, and not of a party.

I have accepted the nomination of the Philadelphia Convention, as well as the nomination of many primary assemblies gotten up in various sections of the Union, in some instances irrespective of party; and would have accepted the nomination of the Baltimore Convention, had it been tendered on the same terms.[39]

In the North, where surprisingly scant attention had been given to the Charleston nomination of a Taylor-Butler ticket, the letters brought widespread reaction. Democratic journals, eager to sow dissension in Whig ranks, gleefully printed both letters. In addition they hastened to point out Taylor's inconsistencies by quoting from them. The *Baltimore Republican* of 23 October published one of the better and briefer juxtapositions of opposing claims:

GENERAL TAYLOR'S TWO FACES

1.

I am not an ultra Whig

I am a *decided* Whig

2.

I will not be a party candidate

I accepted of the Whig nomination with pride and pleasure

3.

I will not be the exponent of *any* party principles

I am a *Whig in principle,* and have made no concealment of the fact

4.

I have no concealments. I have no opinion *that I would not willingly declare* to my assembled countrymen

I have laid it down as a principle *not to give my opinions* upon the various questions of policy now at issue

5.

I accepted of the Whig nomination with pride and pleasure

I would have accepted of the Baltimore nomination had it been tendered to me

[39] *Washington Union,* 22 August 1848.

6.

I would prefer seeing Henry Clay in the office of President to any individual in the Union	I do not design to withdraw my name if Mr. Clay be the nominee of the Whig National Convention

7.

My own personal views were better withheld until the end of the war	All of my command knew I was a Whig, for I made no concealments of my political sentiments

8.

I fully coincide that every freeman has a right inherent to possess himself of the political opinions of a candidate	I *will not* promise what I would do or would not do, were I elected President of the United States

9.

I would not only *acquiesce,* but *rejoice,* if some other individual than myself should be elected as a candidate for the Presidency	It has not been my intention at any moment, to withdraw my name from the canvass whoever may be the nominee of either Whigs or Democrats

Among northern Whigs, particularly among unhappy Clay men of New York who had joined the Taylor forces only reluctantly, the two letters produced a profound sensation. In Albany the news caused the greatest consternation. Thurlow Weed, acting spontaneously, called a mass meeting; rumors that he was prepared to lead a party bolt swept through the city. Whether Weed intended such a maneuver is not clear; if he did, he was dissuaded by Fillmore, who readily recognized that his own political future was at stake. Fillmore also persuaded Weed against the introduction of any resolutions designed to stir up further excitement.[40]

At the meeting, which occurred on Saturday night, 24 August, at least a thousand Whigs gathered in the rotunda of the capitol. Demands for a new nomination were heard on every side. The *Albany Argus,* describing

[40] Accounts of events in Albany at this juncture vary. See *Albany Atlas,* 28 August 1848; *Albany Argus,* 28, 29 August 1848; Barnes, *Weed's Memoirs,* p. 169; Van Deusen, *Weed,* p. 163; R. J. Rayback, *Fillmore,* pp. 188–91; and my article, "Who Wrote the Allison Letters?" pp. 54, 67–70.

the scene, declared that "the name of Henry Clay was in every Whig mouth, and the revulsion of feeling in his favor . . . burst forth without restraint and with heartfelt enthusiasm."[41] However, heroic forensic efforts of Weed and particularly of John M. Collier persuaded the crowd to postpone action until the following Monday; by that time passions had cooled a bit, and Collier succeeded in convincing the crowd that the Charleston affair was "a proposition on the part of certain Democrats to drop Cass and go for Taylor, and not as had been supposed . . . a proposition on the part of southern Whigs to drop Fillmore."[42] Accordingly, the meeting referred the matter to the coming Whig State Convention.

Elsewhere in the state, however, the feeling of indignation was not so easily palliated. In Poughkeepsie and several other places Clay and Fillmore were nominated as the Whig ticket. In New York City, which Nicholas Dean described as on "the very brink of a party explosion," Clay clubs began to organize, and preparations were made for a giant Clay-Fillmore meeting at Vauxhall Gardens.[43] Clay's consent apparently was taken for granted.

Since the Philadelphia convention the disappointed old man had remained quietly at Ashland, refusing to take part in the canvass. Friends such as Morehead and Abbott Lawrence begged him to proclaim his approval of the Taylor nomination and thus to help the Whigs reunite their party. To all such appeals Clay returned decided and bitter refusals.[44] In spite of his bitterness, however, Clay was a regular Whig, and news of the New York movement in his favor gave him considerable concern. Accordingly, on 8 September he announced through the columns of the *New York Express:* "I am utterly opposed to the use of my name as a candidate for the Presidency. . . . I have given, and shall give, no countenance, or encouragement to any movement to bring my name as a candidate for that office before the public."[45] With that announcement

---

[41] *Albany Argus,* 28, 29 August 1848.

[42] Barnes, *Weed's Memoirs,* p. 169.

[43] *New York Tribune,* 9, 23 September 1848; *Niles' Register* 74 (13 September 1848): 165; Nicholas Dean to Clay, 5 September 1848, Clay Papers. A meeting to nominate Clay in Toledo, Ohio, was checked by the editor of the *Toledo Blade* (*Cleveland Plain Dealer,* 4 September 1848).

[44] Burnley to Crittenden, 17 July 1848, Crittenden Papers; Abbott Lawrence to Crittenden, 18 September 1848, in Coleman, *Crittenden,* 1: 324; Clay to James Harlan, 22 June 1848, Clay to Louisville Committee, 28 June 1848, Clay to Stevenson, 14 August 1848, Clay to White, 10 September 1848, in Colton, *Clay's Works,* 5: 565–74; Morehead to Clay, 22 June 1848, Clay to G. W. Curtis, 4 July 1848, Clay Papers.

[45] *Niles' Register* 74 (20 September 1848): 191. Clay repeated his determination in several private letters.

the Clay-Fillmore movement collapsed. The Vauxhall Gardens meeting in New York City was annulled, the Clay clubs were disbanded, and Clay leaders retired to their homes.

Although Taylor's managers were again able to breathe easily, they recognized, as Nicholas Dean remarked, that there was still "a deep current of grumbling and dissatisfaction."[46] Some gesture had to be made to win the good will of the Clay Whigs and to meet northern demands that Old Zack place himself on Whig grounds. His answer to this request came in the form of a second letter to Captain Allison dated 4 September 1848.[47]

In this second Allison letter Taylor explained that he was writing to correct certain impressions which the publication of portions of his communications, maliciously "riven" from their context, had created in regard to his relationship with the Whig party. He pointed out that when his name had first been mentioned in connection with the presidency, he was in command of the American army in the valley of the Rio Grande, and he had therefore believed it the better part of discretion to keep his political opinions quiet. Accordingly, he had resisted all nominations, whether made by Whigs, Democrats, or Nativists, until he was led to believe that his opposition "was assuming the aspect of defiance of popular wishes." After that he permitted himself to be announced as a candidate for the presidency and "accepted nomination after nomination in the spirit in which they were tendered." They were made, he maintained, "irrespective of parties, and so acknowledged."

However, "no one who joined in those nominations could have been deceived as to my political views. From the beginning until now, I have declared myself to be a Whig on all proper occasions. With this distinct avowal published to the world, I did not think that I had the right to repel nominations from my political opponents any more than I had the right to refuse the vote of a democrat at the polls."

It was under these conditions that the Whigs had tendered him a nomination, which he had accepted "with gratitude and with pride." He would have accepted a Democratic nomination on similar terms. "But in so doing," Taylor declared, "I would not abate one jot or tittle of my opinions as written down. Such a nomination, as indicating a coincidence of opinion on the part of those making it should not be regarded with disfavor by those who think with me; as a compliment personal to

---

[46] Dean to Clay, 5 October 1848, Clay Papers.

[47] The latest analyses of the authorship of the second Allison letter are in Hamilton, *Taylor*, pp. 117–24; R. J. Rayback, *Fillmore*, pp. 190–91; and my article, "Who Wrote the Allison Letters?" pp. 51–72.

myself, it should not be expected that I should repulse them with an insult. I shall not modify my views to entice them to my side; I shall not reject their aid when they join my friends voluntarily."

He had declared that he was not a party man, and he still held that resolution; it meant only that he was "not engaged to lay violent hands indiscriminantly upon public officers" whose opinions might be different from his, nor "to force Congress, by the Coercion of a veto," to pass laws to suit his peculiar desires. This, he understood, was "good Whig doctrine."[48]

In the northern states the communication had a much desired effect. Grumblings abated; many Clay Whigs who had remained undecided as to their course rejoined the party. As Truman Smith informed Crittenden late in September: "The 2d Allison letter has cleared away many if not most of the difficulties with which we have struggled in the free States. . . . General Taylor now stands before the country exactly where he should have placed himself last Jany and this would have saved us from a multitude of troubles to say nothing of possible defeat."[49]

In South Carolina the effect was exactly the reverse. There the Cass movement had been growing. Early in August the *Mercury,* which had been demanding some assurance that Taylor "regarded the right of the people of the Slaveholding States to hold Slaves in Territories as essential to the maintenance and security of slavery in the States,"[50] began to slide toward Cass. The first indication of its movement came after southern Whig votes defeated the Clayton Compromise, a measure the *Mercury* had supported as "an adjustment of the [slave] question, honorable and satisfactory to the South."[51] From then on it revealed a strong distaste for any association with Whiggery. On 21 August the *Mercury* announced that since southern Whigs by their action in Congress had failed to "afford any countenance to those who are inclined to support their candidate simply on the ground of his being a Southern man," it could see no reason why any southern Democrat should abandon his party to fraternize with the Whigs. Henceforth the *Mercury* would support the Democratic nominee.

The accession of the most influential journal in South Carolina gave a considerable boost to the Cass movement. After the publication of the second Allison letter a Cass wave swept through the state. One prom-

[48] *Niles' Register* 74 (27 September 1848) : 200–201.

[49] Smith to Crittenden, 23 September 1848.

[50] *Charleston Mercury,* 19, 21 June, 20, 21 July 1848; Lesesne to Calhoun, 5 July 1848, in Boucher and Brooks, *Calhoun Correspondence,* p. 450.

[51] *Charleston Mercury,* 2 August 1848.

inent figure after another, many of them Calhounites who had earlier shown a preference for the Whig nominee, returned to the Democratic camp. Even such Taylorites as Hammond began to doubt the wisdom of voting for a man who owned such "a damned rascally set of friends" outside of South Carolina; he admitted that if he had seen the second Allison letter a month earlier, he would "not have been a Taylor man."[52] The Cass tide was in full flood in early October, when South Carolina went to the polls to elect the legislature which would choose presidential electors. The result was an overwhelming victory for the Democratic nominee.

Defeat in the Palmetto State failed to worry Whig managers, for reports elsewhere in the South were beginning to reveal that Taylor would everywhere poll a vote heavy enough to sweep some Democratic states into the Whig column. Delaware, Maryland, North Carolina, and Tennessee, all normally Whig states, were certainties. Crittenden's capture of the Kentucky governorship by more than 8,000 votes put the result of the presidential contest in that state beyond doubt. Louisiana was also regarded as "safe beyond all question." Toombs reported "not much dispute" about Florida. In Georgia, where Whigs found Fillmore a lodestone, the contest was desperate, but here too Whigs anticipated victory "by a *narrow, close* vote." Only Alabama and the southwestern states of Mississippi, Missouri, Arkansas, and Texas were given up as hopeless.[53] Taylor, therefore, was sure of 66 electoral votes from the slave states against 38 votes for Cass, with Virginia's 17 votes in doubt but leaning toward the Democratic candidate. Except for Georgia, Democratic strategists came to the same conclusion.[54]

Information from the free states was equally heartening for Whigs. Cass was winning the entire electoral vote of the western states: Indiana, Michigan, Illinois, Wisconsin, and Iowa; not only were these states normally Democratic, but also some Whigs in the area were going for

[52] Hammond to Major Felder, 15, 18 September 1848, Hammond Papers. See also B. F. Whitmore to Hammond, 22 September 1848; *Charleston Mercury,* 30 September, 2, 6 October 1848; J. D. Wilson to Calhoun, 4 August 1848, in Boucher and Brooks, *Calhoun Correspondence,* p. 462.

[53] Crittenden to Ewing, 1 September 1848, Ewing Papers; Ewing to Crittenden, 24 September 1848, Toombs to Crittenden, 27 September, 5 October 1848, George E. Badger to Crittenden, 12 October 1848, Peyton to Crittenden, 21 October 1848, Crittenden Papers; Stephens to Crittenden, 26 September 1848, Toombs to Crittenden, 27 September 1848, in Phillips, *Toombs, Stephens, and Cobb Correspondence,* pp. 128–29.

[54] George S. Houston to Cobb, 23 September 1848, Alfred Iverson to Cobb, 17 October 1848, James F. Cooper to Cobb, 20 October 1848, in *Phillips, Toombs, Stephens, and Cobb Correspondence,* pp. 126, 130, 131.

Van Buren rather than Taylor. Maine, in spite of a strong Free Soil movement among Democrats, and New Hampshire, where the Free Soil trend existed about equally in both parties, were also counted in the Cass column. These western and New England states gave Cass a total of 49 votes. At the same time, however, reports from the East indicated that despite widespread disaffection among Whigs, Massachusetts, Rhode Island, Vermont, and Connecticut would all be in the Taylor column. New Jersey, where Free Soil was weak, was normally Whig. And New York, thanks to the Barnburners, was utterly safe for Taylor.[55] That provided him with 71 electoral votes from the North.

Only nine more votes were necessary for election. Everyone agreed that victory depended on the returns from Ohio, normally Whig, and from Pennsylvania, usually Democratic by a narrow margin. During the final month of the campaign both major parties and the Free-Soilers threw their strength into these two states.

In Ohio, Whigs worked with feverish desperation. Early in October, Seabury Ford, the Whig nominee, won the gubernatorial election over Weller by a margin so narrow—fewer than 350 votes—as to place the results in doubt for a week. Final returns revealed, moreover, that Ford's victory had been made possible only because he had won the Free-Soilers, primarily former Whigs, who had no candidate of their own in the field. Loss of these votes in November would make Cass a certain victor. Terrified, Whigs screamed for help, and from every side party leaders rushed to the rescue. Seward and Francis Granger of New York and a horde of Kentuckians descended on the state; Horace Greeley flooded Ohio with *Tribunes* "appealing with weeping and wailing and lamentation to the Buckeyes to come to the help of Old Zack." There were some charges that $20,000 of "foreign gold" was shipped in to bring Free-Soilers back to the Whig fold. As election day approached, however, Whigs gave up in despair.[56] All their hopes then turned toward Pennsylvania.

There, a state election had been held simultaneously with that in Ohio. With the aid of "foreign emissaries" and the Free-Soilers, the Whig

[55] Woodbridge to Crittenden, 12 September 1848, Truman Smith to Crittenden, 16 September 1848, Ogden Hoffman to Crittenden, 20 September 1848, Charles H. Delevan to Crittenden, 26 September 1848, R. W. Thompson to Crittenden, 21 October 1848, Crittenden Papers; A. E. Burr to Welles, 18 October, 1 November 1848, Welles Papers.

[56] Chase to Briggs, 27 September 1848, Chase Papers; Burnley to Crittenden, 18 October 1848, Crittenden Papers; Giddings to his daughter, 19 October 1848, Giddings-Julian Papers; *National Era,* 26 October 1848; *Cleveland Plain Dealer,* 23, 28, 31 October 1848.

gubernatorial candidate, William F. Johnston, was elected. At the same time, however, the Democratic nominee for canal commissioner won his post by a majority even greater than Johnston's, and the total vote cast for Democratic congressional candidates exceeded that of the Whigs.[57] Pennsylvania was indeed a doubtful state: the Free-Soilers there appeared to hold the balance. Both major parties redoubled their efforts, importing statesmen from outside to harangue the electorate. Democrats, recognizing their vulnerable point, began to circulate rumors that the party's chief rebel, Wilmot, had been induced to return to the fold.[58] Whigs, in turn, encouraged formerly Democratic Free-Soilers to remain firm and, according to Democratic journals, "put into operation all the arts and appliances known to federal tactics." Capitalists and employers "wielded all their power, and every threat and new bugbear known to the Whig policy of coercion were unscrupulously employed. Money was poured out like water."[59] Throughout the state the atmosphere grew steadily more feverish, with charges and countercharges, claims and counterclaims flying about so thick and fast that by election day neither of the major parties could be sure of victory. Only a heavy poll was certain.

[57] *North American,* 12 October 1848; *Pennsylvanian,* 21 October 1848; Truman Smith to Crittenden, 3 October 1848, C. B. Penrose to Crittenden, 24 October 1848, Crittenden Papers.

[58] That pressure may have been put on Wilmot may be inferred from Quaife, *Polk's Diary,* 4: 166. See also Henry Welch to Buchanan, 29 October 1848, Buchanan Papers.

[59] *Pennsylvanian,* 20, 25 October 1848. Use of money by a "not over-scrupulous committee" had been suggested as a means of achieving victory for Taylor in both Ohio and Pennsylvania as early as July ("Theodore" to Smith, July 1848, Smith Papers).

Chapter Fifteen

The Returns

It was nearly a week after election day before enough returns were gathered to reveal the outcome of the contest. During the interval, as reports from the "doubtful" states trickled in, it became evident that the Whig candidate would win "a splendid victory." The final tabulation confirmed the result. Of 2,878,023 votes cast, Taylor polled 1,360,967—47.28 percent of the popular vote. Cass secured 1,222,342—42.47 percent of the total. The electoral count was Taylor 163 votes, Cass 127 votes. Van Buren won 291,804 popular votes—10 percent of the total—but he failed by wide margins to carry any state.[1]

A broad analysis of the returns reveals that Taylor triumphed both in the North and in the South. In the North he secured 924,664 popular votes—45.56 percent of the total (almost 6 percentage points more than Cass)—and 97 of 169 electoral votes. He won the normally Whig states of Vermont, Massachusetts, Rhode Island, Connecticut, and New Jersey, and he took both New York and Pennsylvania from the Democrats. In the South his appeal was proportionately even greater. He secured 436,303 popular votes—more than 51.45 percent of the total—and 66 of 121 electoral votes. He carried the normally Whig states of the upper South: Delaware, Maryland, North Carolina, Kentucky, and Tennessee; he transferred two states, Georgia and Louisiana, from the Democratic to the Whig column; and he captured the new state of Florida.

A closer analysis indicates even more clearly the extent of Taylor's triumph. In the North he exceeded Clay's 1844 total by more than 13,000 popular votes, and in spite of all the forces making for division and alienation, he retained more than 95 percent of the Whig vote. In New England, where the party had feared the greatest loss, Taylor won four states and retained 91 percent of the Whig vote. Rhode Island Whigs, who gave him a 60 percent majority, held most firmly, followed by Maine Whigs (96 percent) and Connecticut Whigs (95 percent). He carried all three mid-Atlantic states, exceeding Clay's 1844 vote by more than 12,000 and increasing the Whig proportion of the popular vote by a

ELECTORAL VOTE IN 1848

NORTH	TAYLOR	CASS	SOUTH	TAYLOR	CASS
Maine		9	Delaware	3	
New Hampshire		6	Maryland	8	
Vermont	6		Virginia		17
Massachusetts	12		North Carolina	11	
Rhode Island	4		South Carolina		9
Connecticut	6		Georgia	10	
New York	36		Florida	3	
New Jersey	7		Kentucky	12	
Pennsylvania	26		Tennessee	13	
Ohio		23	Alabama		9
Indiana		12	Mississippi		6
Michigan		5	Missouri		7
Illinois		9	Arkansas		3
Wisconsin		4	Louisiana	6	
Iowa		4	Texas		4
	97	72		66	55
TOTAL				163	127

whole percentage point. In the Northwest, traditionally a Democratic stronghold except for Ohio, he did most poorly. But even here he increased Whig totals in southwestern Ohio and in most of Indiana. Moreover, he surpassed Clay's 1844 vote in Illinois and retained the Whigs' proportion of the state total.

His accomplishments were even greater in the South, where he gathered 47,116 more popular votes than Clay had won and increased the Whig proportion of the vote by more than 6 percentage points. Taylor's popular vote surpassed Clay's in every slave state. In three states, North Carolina, Kentucky, and Florida, he won by landslides; in Louisiana he won by a near landslide. Clay had never carried a southern state by such

[1] All statistical returns in this and the following two chapters have been taken from W. Dean Burnham, *Presidential Ballots, 1836–1902* (Baltimore, Md., 1955). I have made some minor corrections in arithmetic which produce small changes in the totals. I have also used some statistics, which are not in Burnham, from the *Whig Almanac, 1849*. In the contest for the control of Congress the Whigs did not fare so well as in the presidential contest. Of the 231 members of the House of Representatives in the Thirty-first Congress, there were 104 Whigs, 111 Democrats, 1 vacancy, and 15 Free-Soilers. The Free-Soilers were Tuck of New Hampshire, Mann and Allen of Massachusetts, Booth of Connecticut, King of New York, Howe and Wilmot of Pennsylvania, Sprague of Michigan, Julian of Indiana, Durkee of Wisconsin, and Campbell, Hunter, Crowell, Giddings, and Root of Ohio. There were also two Free Soil senators: Hale of New Hampshire and Chase of Ohio.

majorities. Except in Maryland the Whig proportion of the popular vote increased in every slave state. In the south-Atlantic area Taylor increased the Whig vote by nearly 4 percent and in the Southwest by 9 percent. In the strongly Democratic states of Alabama, Mississippi, and Arkansas (all of which he lost), increases in the Whig vote ranged from 14 to 23 percent.

It was indeed a splendid Whig victory, and the hordes of hungry Whig office seekers, who had been on a starvation diet for nearly a decade, had real cause for rejoicing.

Democrats found little in the returns to give them any cheer. Cass won the two traditionally Democratic states of New England, Maine and New Hampshire. The victory in New Hampshire was particularly gratifying. In spite of the divisions created by the Hale movement in that state, Cass's vote exceeded Polk's 1844 vote. He also increased the Democratic vote in Pennsylvania, Maryland, and Georgia. And he won the electoral vote of two other traditionally Democratic states, Virginia and South Carolina.

Most significant, perhaps, Cass maintained the party's hold on the West, where he carried eleven of fourteen states. He took Ohio from the Whigs and lost only one normally Democratic state in that section, Taylor's home state of Louisiana. Even there he increased the party's total vote. The sweep justified his title, *"The* Man of the Great West."

But such accomplishments were scant consolation. In the nation as a whole, Cass polled 116,122 fewer popular votes than Polk had received; in the states which had been in the Union in 1844, his total was less than Polk's by 157,419 votes. The Democratic party's proportion of the total vote dropped from 49.55 percent in 1844 to 42.47 percent in 1848, an overall decline of more than 14 percent.

For the Free Soil party, whose adherents had hardly expected to win, the returns revealed neither victory nor defeat. Van Buren polled nearly five times as many votes as Birney had won—291,804 against 62,016. His vote exceeded that of Cass in three states: Vermont, Massachusetts, and New York. But he did not win a single electoral vote.

More significant, Van Buren secured 14.33 percent of the popular vote in the free states, and he clearly affected the returns. In both New York and Ohio his vote shifted the electoral count: New York, traditionally Democratic in presidential elections, voted Whig; Ohio, traditionally Whig, voted Democratic.

Of the three northern sections, Van Buren made, proportionately, the greatest impression in New England, where he secured 77,785 popular votes, nearly 20 percent of the total cast for all candidates. A close

POPULAR VOTE IN 1844 AND 1848[2]

	1848			1844		
	TAYLOR	CASS	VAN BUREN	CLAY	POLK	BIRNEY
New England	171,196	144,519	77,785	186,653	177,730	25,652
Maine	35,125	39,830	12,096	34,342	45,722	4,839
New Hampshire	14,781	27,763	7,560	17,866	27,160	4,161
Vermont	23,122	10,948	14,337	26,770	17,994	3,894
Massachusetts	61,070	35,281	38,058	67,521	52,146	10,815
Rhode Island	6,780	3,646	729	7,322	4,867	—
Connecticut	30,318	27,051	5,005	32,832	29,841	1,943
Mid-Atlantic	444,035	323,904	132,632	431,184	442,477	19,097
New York	218,603	114,320	120,510	232,482	237,588	15,814
New Jersey	40,009	36,880	849	38,318	37,495	131
Pennsylvania	185,423	172,704	11,273	160,384	167,394	3,152
Northwest	309,433	342,236	81,177	293,073	306,029	17,261
Ohio	138,656	154,782	35,523	155,091	149,127	8,082
Indiana	70,300	74,558	8,033	67,866	70,183	2,108
Michigan	23,947	30,742	10,393	24,185	27,737	3,638
Illinois	52,853	55,915	15,702	45,931	58,982	3,433
Wisconsin	13,747	15,001	10,423		territory	
Iowa	9,930	11,238	1,103		territory	
South-Atlantic	185,135	170,752	208	172,496	172,429	6
Delaware	6,440	5,910	82	6,271	5,970	6
Maryland	37,743	34,487	126	35,994	32,733	—
Virginia	45,265	46,739	—	44,860	50,679	—
North Carolina	44,095	35,810	—	43,255	38,894	—
South Carolina		elected by legislature				
Georgia	47,511	44,792	—	42,116	44,153	—
Florida	4,081	3,014	—		territory	
Southwest	251,168	240,931	2	216,691	239,799	—
Kentucky	66,573	48,792	—	60,751	51,954	—
Tennessee	64,239	58,227	—	60,169	59,902	—
Alabama	30,482	31,173	—	26,002	37,401	—
Mississippi	25,821	26,550	—	19,876	25,892	—
Missouri	32,698	39,865	—	31,206	41,322	—
Arkansas	7,587	9,301	—	5,604	9,546	—
Louisiana	18,487	15,379	—	13,083	13,782	—
Texas	5,281	11,644	2		republic	
TOTAL NORTH	924,664	810,659	291,594	910,910	926,236	62,010
TOTAL SOUTH	436,303	411,683	210	389,187	412,228	6
TOTAL NATION	1,360,967	1,222,342	291,804	1,300,097	1,338,464	62,016
TOTAL VOTE		2,878,033			2,700,588	

[2] It should be noted that the Van Buren totals in this table are too low. There were Free Soil electoral tickets in Virginia, North Carolina, Missouri, and Louisiana. In the election of 1844 there were 11 "scattered" votes, which appear only in the total vote count. In 1848 there were 2,646 votes reported for Gerrit Smith (Connecticut, 24; New Jersey, 77; New York, 2,545) and 274 "scattered" votes that appear only in the total vote count.

analysis of the vote in that section reveals some interesting variations. Van Buren's appeal was about the same in Maine, where Taylor was unnaturally strong, and in New Hampshire, where the Democratic machine had been galvanized into a strong force by the Hale revolt. He averaged 13.7 percent in Maine and 15 percent in New Hampshire. In Vermont and Massachusetts he had greater strength. In Vermont he ran second, ahead of Cass, in six of the state's fourteen counties, and he won a plurality in two other counties; he averaged more than 29 percent of the vote. In Massachusetts he ran ahead of Cass in eight of the fourteen counties; in five counties he captured more than 30 percent of the popular vote, reaching a peak in populous Worcester County, which he carried with a plurality of 43 percent. Boston, however, which gave Taylor a 62 percent majority, gave Van Buren only 15 percent of its vote, little more than half of his 28 percent state average. South of Massachusetts Van Buren did not do so well. In Rhode Island, where no votes had been recorded for Birney in 1844, and in Connecticut, where abolitionism had not made a strong impression, he was a poor, even hopeless, third in almost every county.

From the middle Atlantic area Van Buren secured his largest popular total, 132,632 votes. Over 90 percent of that total came from New York. Of the Empire State's fifty-nine counties, he ran second in twenty-two and captured a plurality in eight others. His smallest proportion came from New York City, slightly more than 9 percent of the vote. (His 5,014 votes in the city, however, contrasted sharply with the 117 votes that Birney had received in 1844.) In the Hudson Valley–Lake Champlain area his support became steadily greater the farther it was removed from New York City, ranging from 11 percent in Rockland County, to 25 percent in Columbia County, to 28 percent in Franklin County on the Canadian border. But his greatest vote came from the central area marked by Delaware County in the southeast, St. Lawrence County in the northwest, Allegany County in the southwest, and Monroe County in the northwest; this area had been heavily populated by New Englanders, had been most thoroughly influenced by Charles Grandison Finney's religious revival, had supported the Anti-Masons, and had been strongly Democratic in the election of 1844. There, with rare exceptions, Van Buren secured at least one-third of the vote in every county, more than 40 percent in seven counties, and a majority in two counties, topped by a 59 percent vote in St. Lawrence County, home of Silas Wright and Preston King. In the far western counties of the state his proportion of the vote ranged from 17 percent in Erie County (Buffalo) to 33 percent.

Van Buren's brave showing in New York was not duplicated in the other mid-Atlantic states. He received only 1 percent of the vote in New

Jersey and 3 percent of the vote in Pennsylvania, his lowest proportions in any northern states. Pennsylvania gave him 11,273 votes, almost 60 percent of which were cast in the counties bordering on New York and Ohio. Even in these areas he won 25 percent of the vote only in Bradford and Tioga counties, part of Wilmot's congressional district. More characteristic was the result in Philadelphia, which gave him only 1.5 percent of its vote, and in Allegheny County (Pittsburgh), which gave him 4.5 percent of its vote.

The northwestern states gave Van Buren 81,177 votes, more than 11 percent of the votes cast in that section. The voting pattern there was highly varied. In Ohio he won 35,523 votes, but 44 percent of that total was concentrated in the eleven counties in the northeastern corner of the state, the Western Reserve. His vote in that area ranged from 19 percent in westernmost Huron County, to 38 percent in Cuyahoga County

INCREASE OR DECREASE IN VOTE BETWEEN 1844 AND 1848

	TOTAL	WHIG	DEMOCRATIC	LIBERTY-FREE SOIL
New England	3,484	−15,457	−33,211	52,133
Maine	2,148	783	−5,892	7,257
New Hampshire	917	−3,085	603	3,399
Vermont	−251	−3,648	−7,046	10,443
Massachusetts	3,927	−6,451	−16,865	27,243
Rhode Island	−1,039	−542	−1,221	729
Connecticut	−2,218	−2,514	−2,790	3,062
Mid-Atlantic	10,508	12,851	−118,573	113,535
New York	−29,833	−13,879	−123,268	104,696
New Jersey	1,871	1,691	−615	718
Pennsylvania	38,470	25,039	5,310	8,121
Northwest	55,157	−7,237	9,968	52,390
(+Wisc., Ia.)	(116,599)	(16,440)	(36,207)	(63,916)
Ohio	16,661	−16,435	5,655	27,441
Indiana	12,761	2,434	4,375	5,925
Michigan	9,522	−238	3,005	6,755
Illinois	16,213	6,922	−3,067	12,269
(Wisconsin)	(39,171)	(13,747)	(15,001)	(10,423)
(Iowa)	(22,271)	(9,930)	(11,238)	(1,103)

	TOTAL	WHIG	DEMOCRATIC	LIBERTY–FREE SOIL
South-Atlantic	4,068	8,558	−4,691	202
(+Fla.)	(11,163)	(12,639)	(−1,677)	(202)
Delaware	185	169	−60	76
Maryland	3,638	1,749	1,754	126
Virginia	−3,535	405	−3,940	—
North Carolina	−2,244	840	−3,084	—
South Carolina		elected by legislature		
Georgia	5,934	5,395	639	—
(Florida)	(7,095)	(4,081)	(3,014)	—
Southwest	18,691	29,256	−10,594	—
(+Texas)	(35,691)	(34,537)	(1,050)	(2)
Kentucky	2,660	5,822	−3,162	—
Tennessee	2,395	4,070	−1,675	—
Alabama	−1,744	4,480	−6,228	—
Mississippi	6,606	5,945	558	—
Missouri	35	1,492	−1,457	—
Arkansas	1,738	1,983	−245	—
Louisiana	7,001	5,404	1,597	—
(Texas)	(17,000)	(5,281)	(11,644)	(2)
TOTAL	91,908	27,971	−157,101	218,260
+ {Wisc., Ia., Fla., Tex.	(177,445)	(61,010)	(−116,204)	(229,788)

(Cleveland), to 55 percent in Giddings's home county of Ashtabula. He won a plurality in six counties and 33 percent of the popular vote of the whole area, running ahead of Taylor in normally Whig territory. But this large outpouring of Free Soil sentiment was not matched elsewhere in the state, where Van Buren's vote ranged from light to "respectable." Even in the Miami Valley, which included Cincinnati, he won only 8 percent of the vote.

In Indiana, which had never been seized by an antislavery fervor and where Van Buren received only slightly more than 5 percent of the total, his vote was also relatively concentrated. Forty-five percent of his 8,033 supporters cast their ballots in five sparsely settled counties near Chicago and in seven counties in the east-central area of the state.

In Illinois, Van Buren received 15,702 votes, about one-eighth of the total cast in the state, a proportion greater than he won in Ohio. He also secured more widespread support than in Ohio. Nearly 60 percent of his total came from eleven counties in John Wentworth's sprawling congres-

PERCENTAGE OF VOTE SECURED AND RETAINED

	1848 TAYLOR	1844 CLAY	Retained (%)	1848 CASS	1844 POLK	Retained (%)	1848 VAN BUREN	1844 BIRNEY
New England	43.5	47.8	91.0	36.7	45.5	80.6	19.7	6.5
Maine	40.3	41.6	96.8	45.7	53.8	84.9	13.7	5.6
New Hampshire	29.5	36.3	81.2	55.4	55.2	100.3	15.0	8.4
Vermont	47.9	55.0	87.1	22.6	36.9	61.2	29.6	8.0
Massachusetts	45.4	51.7	87.8	26.2	39.9	65.6	28.7	8.2
Rhode Island	60.7	60.2	100.8	32.6	39.9	81.7	6.5	—
Connecticut	48.5	50.8	95.4	43.3	46.1	93.9	8.0	3.0
Mid-Atlantic	49.1	48.4	101.4	35.8	49.5	72.3	14.6	2.1
New York	47.9	47.8	100.2	25.0	48.8	51.2	26.4	3.2
New Jersey	51.4	50.4	101.9	47.3	49.3	95.9	1.1	.1
Pennsylvania	50.2	48.4	103.7	46.7	50.5	92.2	3.0	.9
Northwest	42.5	47.5	89.4	47.0	49.6	94.9	10.4	2.7
(+Wisc., Ia.)	(42.2)			(46.6)			(11.7)	
Ohio	42.1	49.6	84.8	47.0	47.7	98.3	10.8	2.6
Indiana	45.9	48.4	94.8	48.7	50.0	97.4	5.2	1.5
Michigan	36.7	43.5	84.3	47.2	49.9	94.4	15.9	6.5
Illinois	42.4	42.3	100.2	44.9	54.4	82.5	12.6	3.1
(Wisconsin)	(35.1)			(38.2)			(26.6)	
(Iowa)	(44.6)			(50.4)			(4.9)	
South-Atlantic	51.8	50.0	103.6	48.0	49.9	98.2		
(+Fla.)	(51.9)			(47.9)				
Delaware	52.6	51.2	102.7	47.3	48.7	97.3		
Maryland	52.1	52.3	99.6	47.8	47.6	100.4		
Virginia	49.1	46.9	104.7	50.8	53.0	92.1		
North Carolina	55.1	52.6	104.7	44.8	47.3	94.7		
South Carolina			elected by legislature					
Georgia	51.5	48.6	105.9	48.4	51.3	94.3		
(Florida)	(57.5)			(42.4)				
Southwest	51.7	47.4	109.0	48.2	52.5	91.0		
(+Texas)	(51.2)			(48.7)				
Kentucky	57.7	53.9	107.0	42.2	46.0	91.7		
Tennessee	52.4	50.1	104.5	47.5	49.8	95.4		
Alabama	49.4	40.9	120.7	50.5	59.0	83.9		
Mississippi	49.3	43.4	113.8	50.6	56.5	89.5		
Missouri	45.0	43.0	104.6	54.9	56.9	96.4		
Arkansas	44.9	36.9	121.7	55.0	63.0	87.3		
Louisiana	54.5	48.7	111.9	45.4	51.2	88.6		
(Texas)	(31.0)			(68.9)				
TOTAL—North	45.76	47.96	95.26	39.90	48.77	81.40	14.24	3.26
(+Wisc., Ia.)	(45.56)			(39.99)			(14.33)	
TOTAL—South	51.92	48.57	106.80	48.07	51.42	93.78		
(+Fla., Texas)	(51.45)			(48.54)				
TOTAL—NATION	47.28	48.13	98.23	42.47	49.55	85.71	10.13	2.31

sional district in the northeastern corner of the state, where he won pluralities ranging from 34 percent to 46 percent in seven counties and a 58 percent majority in Lake County. Van Buren's support in that area was stronger than in any other area of the North. He secured another 15 percent of his Illinois vote in the Sixth Congressional District in the northwest and north-central part of the state. In one county, Henry, he won a majority.[3] South of the Illinois River he ran very badly.

Of the older states in the Northwest, Van Buren won his greatest proportion of votes in Michigan, nearly 16 percent, where Birney had also won a comparatively substantial total in 1844. As in Maine and New Hampshire his vote there was relatively even throughout the settled southern portions of the state with a few exceptions. He secured only 6 percent of the vote in Wayne County (Detroit),[4] but he won between 20 percent and 30 percent of the vote in the areas around Flint, Lansing, Jackson, Battle Creek, and Kalamazoo. In the new state of Wisconsin, Van Buren carried a greater proportion of the vote than in any other northwestern state, 26.6 percent. But here too his vote was concentrated. While he won a respectable vote in most settled portions of the state and carried three western counties by a plurality, he received 55 percent of his total state vote in the four counties in the southeastern corner of the state; in two he won a majority. In Iowa, Van Buren ran a distant third throughout the state.

[3] Burnham, *Presidential Ballots*, pp. 376, 908, reports "no return" from Henry County; I am using the returns reported in the *Whig Almanac* for Henry County.
[4] Although in 1848 the "city" did not have the great political importance of later years, the vote in the nation's major "urban" areas is interesting:

North	Taylor	Cass	Van Buren
Suffolk Co. (Boston)	8,895	3,173	2,132
New York City	29,070	18,975	5,290
Erie Co. (Buffalo)	7,647	3,360	2,381
Philadelphia (City and Co.)	31,229	21,508	877
Allegheny Co. (Pittsburgh)	10,112	6,591	779
Cuyahoga Co. (Cleveland)	1,776	2,368	2,594
Hamilton Co. (Cincinnati)	9,018	10,834	1,986
Wayne Co. (Detroit)	2,540	3,305	421
Cook Co. (Chicago)	1,708	1,622	2,120
South			
Baltimore	10,474	10,995	
Richmond	1,064	345	
Chatham Co. (Savannah)	843	739	
Louisville	2,336	2,020	
Davidson Co. (Nashville)	2,698	1,976	
St. Louis	4,827	4,778	
Mobile Co.	1,319	1,073	
Orleans Co. (New Orleans)	5,551	4,579	

Chapter Sixteen

The Reasons

As in all American elections the forces and factors that produced these results were many and complex. The most overwhelming and the most obvious, and yet the most easily overlooked in 1848, was the factor which losing candidates normally contemned as "blind obedience to party dictates." Described more positively and more kindly, the most important factor affecting the Free Soil election was party loyalty. By 1848 both the Whig party and the Democratic party had won the affection and allegiance of large numbers of people. These people voted for Taylor because he was the candidate of the Whig party and for Cass because he was the candidate of the Democratic party. They would have voted for any other candidate that Whigs or Democrats might have nominated, regardless of character or principle, because they were convinced that their party was right. They were the party regulars.

The strength of this element in the presidential election of 1848 was the largest single factor contributing to the results. In an election in which divisive forces were very powerful, the overwhelming majority in both parties remained loyal to party. Taylor retained 98.23 percent of the Whig vote in the whole nation and 95.26 percent of the Whig vote in the free states. Cass held 85.91 percent of the Democratic vote in the nation, 81.40 percent in the free states and 93.78 percent in the slave states.

However, party loyalty was hardly the only factor affecting the Free Soil election. Loyalty ranged from total to tenuous; even among people strongly loyal to party it was a quality that could be shaken or destroyed. It was a quality that needed to be nurtured, particularly among voters who had developed grievances. At the same time, retaining the loyalty of party regulars was not sufficient. It was also necessary to win the vote, if not the allegiance, of new voters and to take advantage of disaffection in the ranks of the opposition—disaffection caused either by the character of the candidate or by the failure of the candidate and the party to proclaim the "right" position on issues. The effort to win these voters, those whom a later age dignified as "independent voters," gave character and significance to the election of 1848.

In the South after the nominating conventions there were two disaffected elements: the Whigs with a strong affection for Clay, who were made bitterly unhappy by Taylor's nomination; and the proslavery extremists, chiefly Democrats, who had failed to secure a positive pledge of support for the principle that slaveholders had the right to carry their slaves into the territories. In the contest to win over these disaffected elements and any new voters, the Whigs won handily, though not completely.

Taylor won in the South, as the *Richmond Enquirer* pointed out, because of "the magic of his victories" in what the northern Whigs had earlier called "an unjust, unnecessary, unconstitutional, and damnable war," and "more than anything else" because "he was held up as a large slaveholder, and, therefore, true to the South."[1]

The appeal of Taylor's military glory in the South cannot be exaggerated. There had been little overt opposition and no moral objection to the Mexican War in the slave states; accordingly, southerners could appreciate the Old Hero's spectacular achievements without any feeling of guilt. Although his military appeal was strong everywhere, it was strongest in the southwestern states. Many years later Reuben Davis in his *Recollections of Mississippi and Mississippians* recalled the "zeal and fervor" of the campaign: "The Taylor banners were inscribed with the names of battlefields and flaming pictures of blood and carnage, and fervent appeals were made to the soldiers who had followed him to glorious victory. The Cass banners were full of civic honors and the victories of peace; but these triumphs showed dim and pale, contrasted with the livid glories of the battleflags of Taylor."[2] The *Mobile Register*, reflecting the southwestern scene, declared on 11 November that the "foremost" factor, "admitted by all," in the Whig victory was "the military popularity of Gen. Taylor. . . . The gallant deeds of the mighty captain shed a hallow [*sic*] of glory round his head, awakening the deepest enthusiasm, and dazing the eyes of his opponents." In the southwestern states of Alabama, Mississippi, Missouri, Arkansas, and Louisiana, Taylor exceeded Clay's 1844 total by 19,304 votes, an increase of 21 percent. The westerners' admiration for the manly character of Taylor's military exploits contributed largely to these results.

Even more important was Taylor's relationship to the slavery issue. Southern attitudes on the question of extending slavery to the territories varied greatly; they ranged from the belief that slavery was not adapt-

---

[1] *Richmond Enquirer,* 14 November 1848; *North Carolina Standard,* 15 November 1848.

[2] Reuben Davis, *Recollections of Mississippi and Mississippians* (Boston, 1889), p. 201.

able to the territories, which meant that the issue was unimportant and its solution impracticable, to the belief that it was necessary for the future of the institution and for the future of the southern way of life to impose slavery upon the territories. But whatever his attitude, the average southerner wanted a solution of the problem favorable to the South, the more favorable the better.

In the contest for votes the Whigs enjoyed most of the advantages. Taylor was a southerner and a slaveholder. He was ipso facto a man who would support southern solutions of the issue. Southern Whigs had only one real problem—vice-presidential candidate Millard Fillmore and his Erie County letter. Fillmore was a millstone; many Whig leaders feared that he would drag down the whole ticket—a fear that revealed how strong proslavery feelings were in some quarters. Their answer was to emphasize the fact that Cass was a northerner. No matter how favorable the Nicholson letter might appear to the South, Cass, like all northerners, was obviously tainted with abolitionism. Southern Democrats had little with which to counter these emotionally logical arguments. They could point to the fact that northern Whigs, by implication abolitionists in the southern mind, were supporting Taylor. They could charge that this support meant Taylor's southern managers were deceiving southerners about his proslavery position. But southerners found it easier to believe that it was Taylor's northern managers who were doing the deceiving. Democrats could also point out that Cass was opposed to the hated Wilmot Proviso. But southerners easily recognized that Cass's opposition to the Proviso did not make him a proslavery man, nor did it make him an advocate of a southern solution for the problem of slavery in the territories. By all odds Taylor was the better risk. Southerners responded to the logic of the situation by voting in larger numbers for Taylor than they had for Clay.

The Taylor campaign did not win over all Clay partisans, however. In the eastern seaboard states of Delaware, Maryland, Virginia, North Carolina, and Georgia, Taylor's totals were less than Clay's in 139 of 327 counties. In some counties the difference was miniscule; in about 30 percent there was a decline in the vote of both parties. In a majority of these counties, however, the returns clearly indicated pockets of anti-Taylor resistance. There was less of this attitude in the Southwest. Taylor's totals were lower than Clay's in 110 to 470 counties of that section; of these, 45 were in Missouri, where both parties conducted lackluster campaigns. In 90 percent of the counties that gave Taylor a lower vote than they had given Clay, the vote of both parties declined, indicating that there was some other factor in the South besides loyalty to Clay which affected the returns. The conclusion is inescapable. There were some Clay partisans, particularly in the Southeast, who refused to vote for Taylor. Nor did they vote for Cass; none of Taylor's managers was able to detect any movement in that direction. They simply did not vote.[3] However, the importance of the Clay partisans can easily be exaggerated. They formed but a small fraction of the whole number of voters in the South; they had no appreciable effect on the results.

The Taylor campaign did not win over all southerners who took an extreme position on the subject of slavery in the territories. This element, which had failed to rally behind Calhoun's early presidential movement, had nevertheless been attracted to the Calhoun doctrine that slaveholders had a right to carry their slaves into the territories. That doctrine had been given active expression in the Alabama Platform. Yancey had sought to persuade the Democratic convention to adopt the Calhoun doctrine; when he failed, he threatened revolt. But the revolt never materialized. There was no southern third-party movement pledged to advance slavery into the territories, because southerners were satisfied that Taylor was as good an advocate of southern interests as could be found. The proslavery extremists themselves recognized that fact in South Carolina, where they named a Taylor-Butler ticket. When the final test came, however, South Carolina pushed aside the knowledge that the Nicholson letter doctrine would give control of the territories to "squatters" who would bar slavery; the state cast its electoral votes for Cass. But the strong proslavery element elsewhere cast its vote for Taylor. His ability to attract these proslavery forces made Taylor's victory a "slaveholders' victory."[4]

In the North after the nominating conventions, there were many disaffected elements: Democrats who personally disliked Cass, Democrats made unhappy by their party's course on the tariff and on river and harbor improvements, Land Reformers, anti-Nativists, Whigs made bitter by Clay's "dethronement," and the antislavery element—Barnburners and other Provisoist Democrats, Conscience Whigs, and Liberty men. For both major parties in the North the task of holding, winning back, or winning over these dissidents and any new voters was infinitely more difficult and complex than it was in the South.

One force operated in the North as it did in the South—Taylor's

[3] The attitude of these Clay Whigs was expressed in various letters (Toombs to Crittenden, 27 September 1848, Meredith P. Gentry to Crittenden, 20 November 1848, Crittenden Papers; N. Dimock to Mangum, 23 October 1848, Mangum Papers).

[4] For other analyses of the southern vote see Cole, *Whigs in the South,* pp. 130–34; Herbert J. Doherty, Jr., *Whigs of Florida: 1845–1854* (Gainesville, Fla., 1959), pp. 27–28; Paul Murray, *Whig Party in Georgia: 1825–1853* (Chapel Hill, N. C., 1948), p. 138; Greer, "Louisiana Politics," p. 562.

military glory. While northern Whig leaders did not use the more blatant methods of their southern counterparts, Whig newspapers carefully kept Taylor's military record before the public in those areas where moral objections to the Mexican War had been slight. Democrats had little ammunition with which to counter the daily reminders of the Old Hero's victories. They could point to Cass's record in an earlier war; in the West they also emphasized his handling of Indian affairs, to the satisfaction of white settlers, and his championship of western interests. However, as in the South, Taylor's military exploits heavily outweighed Cass's civil accomplishments, particularly in those areas where the public admired rugged character and physical capability, the areas where the atmosphere was most like the frontier.

In the Northeast this area included Maine and Pennsylvania. Maine was New England's frontier; it was the only state in that section in which the Whig vote increased. Pennsylvania was the northeastern state most closely akin to the South and to the West; there the Whigs also increased their vote. They increased it, Hendrick B. Wright declared, because of the lure of "gunpowder." One of Buchanan's friends observed that the Whig increase was made possible by the "long bearded" vote: "They came to the polls not singly or in files but by regular battalions." It was, he maintained, "Taylorism and nothing else. . . . Jacksonianism and Harrisonianism over again" which gave the Whigs victory.[5] The same factor was responsible for the increase in Taylor's vote in almost every county of the Ohio Valley. Military glory gave Taylor his strongest appeal among lukewarm Democrats and new voters.

Nevertheless, military glory was not as powerful a force in the North as it was in the South. It could not win over all of what the *Pennsylvanian* of 9 November described as "a thousand interests—each animated by its own peculiar desire—each instigated by its own peculiar grief." It was these interests which "the great Democratic party had offended . . . some by failing to give them office—others by refusing to compromise its principles—others by bold repudiation of detested traitors—and others, by being made to appear as the foe of certain enterprises for the special protection of which it is the fashion of our opponents to believe all government has been instituted among men."

Among these factions were Democrats who believed in a protective tariff and in Federal aid for improvement of rivers and harbors. Outside of Massachusetts and Pennsylvania the tariff proved to be a very minor issue; neither major party emphasized it. In Massachusetts, argument on

[5] Wright to Buchanan, 13 November 1848, Hutter to Buchanan, 8 November 1848, Buchanan Papers.

the subject took on the nature of reflex action. And in Pennsylvania, where strong protectionists were already Whigs, it was doubtful that the issue cost Cass many, if any, votes. Indeed, the Democratic vote in Pennsylvania increased, hardly an indication of major defection. The river and harbor issue was most important in the commercial cities of the Great Lakes area: Buffalo, Cleveland, Detroit, and Chicago. Whigs' and Free-Soilers' reiteration of Cass's diffidence toward the issue may have cost the Democrats votes in each of these and in some smaller lake cities. In Buffalo, Detroit, and Chicago the Whig vote increased; in Cleveland and Chicago the large Free Soil vote undoubtedly included advocates of river and harbor improvements.

Land Reformers were not a large group in 1848; moreover, they were widely scattered through the cities and towns of the North. If they had any concentration, it was in New York, Ohio, and Illinois. The Whigs, antagonistic to the whole idea of land reform, made no effort to lure them to Taylor; nor did the Democrats try to win them over to Cass. However, Democratic candidates for Congress, particularly in Ohio, worked hard for the land reform vote, and Free-Soilers in New York and Illinois gave the free-land issue considerable attention. Although Gerrit Smith was the official candidate of the Land Reformers, it seems highly probable that the increase in the Democratic vote in Ohio was partially attributable to that element and also that Van Buren secured some of his New York and Illinois votes because of the Land Reformers.

Nativism, like the tariff, remained a minor issue. Whigs, whose candidate was openly supported by the eastern Nativists, could hardly hope to make an impression on immigrants of any nationality, and their attempts to do so were feeble. Democrats, relatively certain of holding the immigrant vote, contented themselves with reminding the electorate of Taylor's Nativist associations. This issue shifted few, if any, votes.

As in the South, the Taylor forces in the North never won over all the Clay partisans. They were hostile when the campaign began, and their disappointment and frustration were greatly exacerbated by the Charleston nomination of Taylor and Butler, which they interpreted as an effort to drop Fillmore, a "Clay supporter." Weed's efforts and the second Allison letter, aimed at convincing Clay partisans that Taylor was a real Whig, served to quiet the rampant discontent. When the test came, most Clay Whigs voted for Taylor. But analysis of the northern vote—greatly complicated by the defections of Whigs to the Free Soil party—along with contemporary observations, suggests strongly that many Clay Whigs stayed home on election day in Connecticut, in upstate New

York, and in central Ohio.[6] This stay-at-home group did not, however, appreciably affect the election results.

The most obvious and most important element of discontent in the North were the antislavery forces. It has been shown that they were a complex group with differing party backgrounds and with a wide range of philosophies upon the subject of slavery. For both major parties the task of winning these discontented forces was hindered by subtle factors. Among antislavery Whigs there was an anti–Mexican War group which found it morally difficult to vote for a "butchering" general. Among antislavery Democrats there existed a group which held Cass in contempt—the kind of contempt that the tough develop toward the soft. This group was by no means confined to Barnburner ranks; it existed in many parts of the North. But the most important obstacle that both major parties had to overcome was the existence of the Free Soil party, which gave to antislavery elements an alternative choice for president.

Whigs and Democrats responded to the challenge in much the same way. Both sought to impress the public with the insincerity of the Free-Soilers, and especially with the insincerity of the Barnburners and of Van Buren on the subject of slavery extension. They were called soreheads, seekers of revenge, and longtime minions of the slave power; their professed advocacy of the Wilmot Proviso was branded as false. Any who voted for Van Buren and Free Soil would be "gulled." By this tactic Whigs and Democrats alike hoped to convince their own rank and file that voting for Van Buren would actually advance the dark tide of slavery; they would accomplish more toward its confinement by staying within their own parties.

At the same time both Whigs and Democrats sought to prove that each major opposition candidate was opposed to the Wilmot Proviso and favorable to the expansion of slavery. Whigs, by quoting southern

---

[6] In Connecticut 2,514 Whigs and 2,790 Democrats who had voted in 1844 voted neither for Taylor nor for Cass in 1848; of these, 3,062 voted for Van Buren, leaving 2,242 who did not vote. In New York 13,879 Whigs and 123,268 Democrats who had voted in 1844 voted neither for Taylor nor for Cass in 1848; of these, 104,696 voted for Van Buren, leaving 32,451 who did not vote. Considering the antislavery sentiment in these states, it would be impossible to determine how many of the nonvoters were antislavery men who were simply unable to make a decision among the candidates. But many must have been Clay men. In the tenth and eleventh congressional districts of Ohio (Delaware, Franklin, Licking, Knox, and Richland counties) 5,110 Whigs and 3,115 Democrats who had voted in 1844 voted neither for Taylor nor for Cass in 1848; 1,157 of this number voted for Van Buren, leaving 6,968 who did not vote. Since the area was only mildly antislavery, it can be concluded that the Whigs who did not vote were more likely to have been Clay men than undecided antislavery men (Ewing to Crittenden, 24 September 1848, Crittenden Papers).

Democratic newspapers and by tying Cass closely to the policies of the proslavery Polk administration, not only made the point that Cass's "solution" to the territorial problem was a proslavery solution but also asserted that Cass would wage future wars to extend the boundaries of slavery. Democrats, by quoting southern Whig journals and by emphasizing Taylor's ownership of slaves, made the point that Taylor both logically and emotionally had to favor the extension of slavery.

To these arguments the Free-Soilers added one of their own: if either Taylor or Cass opposed the extension of slavery, there was no evidence of it. Neither had approved the Wilmot Proviso, which was the real test of an antislavery position.

This simple argument of the Free-Soilers made it necessary for both major parties to prove a more positive antislavery position. Whigs tried indirection. Taylor, they maintained, knew the horrors of war firsthand; because of this knowledge he was "a man of peace." Under his administration there would be no more wars to extend the boundaries of slavery. In his letter to the *Cincinnati Signal* he had announced his approval of the principles contained in the Proviso. Moreover, as a good Whig, he had pledged himself on numerous occasions not to veto any legislation which Congress might enact on the subject. Besides, the Whig party was the real Free Soil party; the Whigs were the true champions of the Wilmot Proviso, a fact proven by their votes in Congress. The Whigs' implication was obvious: with Taylor in the White House there would be no further extension of slavery.

Democrats tried a different tactic. They pointed out that Cass was a northerner. Born in New England, he had absorbed that section's abhorrence of slavery; a resident of Michigan, he held the westerners' common desire to keep the territories free. His Nicholson letter doctrine, moreover, reflected the western doctrine of self-determination, that the territories should decide the question of slavery for themselves. And there could be no doubt about the decision the territories would make. Slavery did not exist there. According to the highest legal authorities, it could not exist there until a positive law created it, and the territories would never sanction such an institution. The Democrats' implication, like the Whigs', was obvious: Cass was the champion of the true antislavery doctrine.

Undoubtedly, both Whigs and Democrats recognized that their arguments contained fundamental weaknesses. Taylor had actually repudiated the implication that he approved the Proviso. And it was not necessary, as the Democrats insisted, to create a law to sanction slavery; there was nothing, not even an international law, either to prevent slaveholders from carrying their peculiar property into the territories or, under the Nicholson letter doctrine, to prevent them from passing legislation giving protection to the slave institution.

The Whigs recognized more quickly the weakness in their efforts to prove their candidate an antislavery man. Ultimately they turned to using the arguments propounded by Tom Corwin. The senator from Ohio, as everyone knew, had been a passionate opponent of the Mexican War; moreover, he was an acknowledged opponent of slavery, though he deprecated the importance of the Proviso. Yet he had taken to the hustings on Taylor's behalf almost immediately after his nomination. Corwin's reasoning was simple and easy to understand. Taylor had to be supported because he was a Whig; he had to be supported in order to preserve the unity of the Whig party. Preserving Whig unity was paramount to all other interests—even to the great moral question of slavery—first, because it was the only way of keeping the Democrats out of control. Four more years of a Democrat in office would mean more wars of expansion, the firmer fastening of ruinous Democratic policies upon the nation. Second, preserving the unity of the Whig party was paramount because it was the only way of assuring a glorious future to the nation and because—this point was only hinted—it was the only sure way of preserving the Union itself.

In time other great Whig figures who were, who claimed to be, or who were reputed to be opposed to slavery extension adopted this argument, sincere in itself, yet a clear appeal to old prejudices and old loyalties. Among them were Daniel Webster, Thurlow Weed, Horace Greeley, and William H. Seward. Lesser figures such as Rufus Choate, John Davis, Thaddeus Stevens, Abraham Lincoln, and dozens of Whig editors followed the same line, to which they added the argument that a vote for Van Buren was half a vote for Cass, half a step against the unity of the Whig party.[7]

Northern Democrats were unable to produce either a comparable argument or a comparable cast of antislavery leaders to support Cass. They could maintain, though they did it much less forcibly than the Whigs, that the future of the nation depended upon the continued control of the administration by the Democratic party, but they could not argue for the unity of an already badly disrupted party. Nor did they have any strong antislavery leaders ardently supporting Cass. The best

[7] Thornton K. Lothrop, *William Henry Seward* (Boston, 1896), pp. 55–57; Claude M. Fuess, *Rufus Choate: Wizard of the Law* (New York, 1928), pp. 191–92; *Boston Atlas,* 29 June 1848; Woodley, *Stephens,* pp. 200–201; Going, *Wilmot,* p. 328.

they could produce were Thomas Hart Benton, William Allen, and Francis P. Blair, old friends of Van Buren, and such minor figures as Long John Wentworth and Hannibal Hamlin. None, however, campaigned strongly on behalf of the Democratic standard bearer.[8]

The problems of the campaign were entirely different for Free-Soilers. They had to win over and weld together an electorate with strong and diverse traditions, attachments, and prejudices, an electorate which had a subconscious philosophical unity, as the Buffalo convention had demonstrated, but which had only one clearly defined common aim: a desire to prevent the further extension of slavery.

It was not an easy task. Old loyalties were difficult to break down. Free Soil leaders tried to do this by pointing out that the old parties, important as they had been, were failing to meet new issues—particularly the great issue of slavery extension. Moreover, neither major party had nominated a candidate who could be regarded as opposed to slavery extension. In fact, it appeared more likely that the major parties' candidates, either because of personal involvement with the slave institution or because of ambition, were willing to see slavery extended. In such a situation party loyalty was misplaced loyalty. The great, overwhelming object was preservation of the freedom of the territories, both in order to prevent the extension of an immoral institution and in order to preserve the freedom of free men. To achieve this goal, it was necessary to abandon old parties and to join in the great crusade for Free Soil. But Free-Soilers were also faced with the task of proving their own honesty, particularly the honesty of the Barnburners and of Van Buren.

In retrospect there is little doubt that both the Barnburners and Van Buren favored the Proviso and Free Soil. The Barnburners, undoubtedly, had originally moved toward revolt because of political considerations. Long dominant in the councils of the Democratic party of New York, they had seen their preeminent position quickly eroded by a series of events: the party's failure to renominate Van Buren in 1844; Polk's failure to appoint one of their number to a cabinet position and his coincidental appointment of an arch-Hunker; their consequent "loss" of Federal patronage; Silas Wright's defeat for reelection in 1846 through the connivance of Polk and the Hunkers; and Wright's untimely death, which destroyed their hope of reasserting an influence on the national

---

[8] In a letter to the *New York Evening Post* Blair indicated that he would vote the Baltimore ticket "simply upon punctillio." "My heart," he declared, "is with Mr. Van Buren and his principles" (*Mississippian,* 18 August 1848). See also Cole, *Era of the Civil War,* pp. 59–60; and Charles E. Hamlin, *Life and Times of Hannibal Hamlin* (Cambridge, Mass., 1899), p. 181.

scene. This series of events in itself produced a strong determination to recover their former position.

The whole situation was then complicated by the introduction of the Wilmot Proviso. Barnburners quickly accepted it as their own; one of their number became its champion in the lame-duck session of the Congress. There was no evidence of an ulterior motive in this acceptance, for the Proviso had not yet become a cause of contention. The Barnburners' acceptance of the Proviso was actually a logical result of their long-standing championship of the principles of freedom and equality and of their opposition to the annexation of Texas. Free territories for free men was an appealing program. It was not until a resolution approving the principles of the Proviso was introduced into a party caucus that they learned of the Hunkers' opposition. The Proviso then became one more issue upon which the two factions of the party disagreed.

At this point the Proviso became inextricably connected with Barnburner efforts to recover control of the Democratic party in New York. Although some older leaders cautioned that the Proviso might widen the split between the two factions, Barnburners became determined to commit the party to its support. Their effort not only widened the gap, but because of the shock of Wright's death it also caused them to lose their campaign to win back party control.

Barnburners then turned without much hope to the national convention for recognition as the Democratic party of New York. Failing, they came back to New York determined upon vindication at the polls. While the Proviso had become an essential part of their creed and while they intended to emphasize it, their main aim was recovery of party control. But a metamorphosis occurred. Between the Barnburners' return from Baltimore and the Buffalo convention, the antislavery sentiment of the nation became more apparent. And the Barnburners, who had discerned very little antiextension sentiment outside their own ranks and had actually feared that their championship of the Proviso might hinder their campaign for recovery of party control, gave themselves more and more to the prevailing current. In Utica, after setting up their own organization, they agreed to meet with antislavery forces in other states for consultation. By the time of the Buffalo convention a complete change had occurred. Recovery of control of the party in New York had become secondary; their main aim had become the advancement of the principles of the Proviso. To achieve this end, as Liberty party leaders learned, the Barnburners were even willing to give up their candidate. They had become firm Free-Soilers.

Van Buren's position was no less clear. In his long public service he had revealed that he was no abolitionist and that he was unwilling to disturb the institution of slavery where it already existed because that in turn would disturb the peace and harmony of the Union. At the same time, he had revealed that he was opposed to the further extension of slavery. His actions were in the public record; his private communications also showed him favorable to the Proviso. He was a reluctant candidate for the presidency. Sixty-five years old, scarred by many a political battle, he wanted only the quiet of private life. He accepted the nominations of the Utica and the Buffalo conventions not because of any desire for revenge but because the Barnburners convinced him that he was the only alternative. In both cases he publicly pledged himself to Free Soil.

It was this analysis that the Free-Soilers used, in the cruder language of political persuasion, in their campaign to win votes for Van Buren and Free Soil. They used it particularly to persuade Whigs and Liberty men, among whom they continually emphasized the necessity to forget past principles and past actions and to act in the present, to vote not for the Van Buren of the past but for the Van Buren of 1848, the only presidential candidate publicly pledged to support the Proviso.

Assessment of the three-cornered contest for the antislavery vote shows that the Democratic argument was clearly successful in New Hampshire, where the party had had three years of experience in combating the Provisoist forces. It was probably also an important factor in Pennsylvania, where Provisoist sentiment was weak and where western and southern undercurrents were subtly strong. It was undoubtedly an influence in the Northwest, which was attracted by a "western solution" of the territorial problem.

Nevertheless, it was among Democrats that the Free Soil party made its largest advances. Conservatively calculated, 58 percent of the 291,000 Free Soil votes came from the Democratic rank and file. Nearly 60 percent of this Democratic vote was cast in New York. But even if the New York vote is subtracted from the totals, the number of former Democrats who voted for Van Buren is greater than the number of former Whigs or former Liberty men who voted for him. Close to half, perhaps more than half, of the Free Soil voters in Maine, Vermont, and Massachusetts had voted as Democrats in 1844. In the Bay State formerly Democratic Free-Soilers outnumbered formerly Whig Free-Soilers by more than two to one. In Illinois and Wisconsin more than 60 percent of the Free Soil voters were former Democrats.

This attraction to Free Soil was based on various factors. Although

SOURCES OF FREE SOIL VOTE[9]

	WHIG	%	DEMOCRATIC	%	LIBERTY	%
New England	17,400	22	34,300	44	25,300	32
Maine	600	05	6,500	54	4,900	40
New Hampshire	3,000	40	300	04	4,200	56
Vermont	3,300	23	6,700	48	3,800	28
Massachusetts	8,000	21	19,000	50	11,000	28
Rhode Island	500	71	200	28	—	
Connecticut	2,000	40	1,600	32	1,400	28
Mid-Atlantic	12,200	09	107,000	81	13,100	10
New York	11,000	09	99,500	83	10,000	08
New Jersey	200	32	500	62	100	16
Pennsylvania	1,000	09	7,000	63	3,000	27
Northwest	34,000	42	26,700	32	20,200	25
Ohio	23,300	66	4,000	11	8,000	22
Indiana	3,000	37	3,000	37	2,100	25
Michigan	3,400	33	2,900	28	4,000	39
Illinois	2,500	16	9,600	61	3,600	23
Wisconsin	1,400	13	7,000	69	2,000	19
Iowa	400	36	200	18	500	45
TOTAL	63,600	22	168,000	58	58,600	20

Van Buren was condemned as an "arch-traitor," he had been a Democrat. Therefore, to a Democrat, voting for him was not a disloyal act. Besides, almost the whole Free Soil party platform was an extension of Democratic party principles, and it was couched in Democratic party terms. "Free territories for free men" was Democratic party language.

The Free Soil party did not attract all antislavery Democrats, however. There were many whose sentiments on the subject were satisfied by the Cass doctrine. There were some (they were most obvious in Connecticut and New York)[10] who were so completely confused by the complexities of the arguments and by the political maneuverings that they stayed home on election day. There were some, such as Marcus

[9] I have secured these figures by interpolating Whig and Democratic losses since 1844 and adding the Liberty vote of 1844 (except in Wisconsin and Iowa, where I have used the 1846 totals). In making these interpolations, I have been generous to both the Whigs and the Liberty men, niggardly to the Democrats.

[10] See note 8 above; Burr to Welles, 18 October, 1 November 1848, Welles Papers.

Morton, who found themselves unable to campaign for Van Buren because his running mate was Charles Francis Adams, "the greatest iceberg in the Northern Hemisphere."[11] But in the last analysis the party found more Democrats, including Barnburners, who were willing to stand up and be counted for Free Soil than it found among the rank and file of other parties.

Relatively, however, Liberty men gave Free Soil even greater support. About 20 percent of the Free Soil votes came from the Liberty rank and file. This number represents the fairly solid support of the whole party. However, not all Liberty men voted for Van Buren. There were those who felt that Free Soil was too great a dilution of abolitionist principles, a step backward, and there were those who mistrusted Van Buren; these people either voted for Gerrit Smith, who reportedly received 2,500 votes in New York, or they stayed home. But the overwhelming majority had no such doubts. Many had Democratic party backgrounds; many, such as Salmon P. Chase, had been persuaded that a coalition of antislavery forces was a prerequisite to ultimate success. Like the original Liberty presidential candidate, John P. Hale, these Liberty men voted for Van Buren.

The Free Soil party made its poorest showing among Whigs. Although Whigs gave Van Buren about 22 percent of his vote, this number was only slightly larger than the number cast by Liberty men. Indeed, Whigs cast fewer votes for Free Soil than did Liberty men in at least eight states, including Massachusetts. They made a brave showing only in New Hampshire, where they had previously been organized under the banner of Hale's Independent Democracy, and in Ohio, where they contributed about two-thirds of the Free Soil vote, much of it concentrated in the Western Reserve. In fact, the Ohio Whig vote for Van Buren was more than a third of the Whig total cast for him.

Antislavery Whigs had the greatest trouble convincing themselves that the former Democrat Van Buren was a sincere Free-Soiler. And when formerly Whig Free-Soilers analyzed the returns in Massachusetts and even in Ohio, they emphasized the fact that "John P. Hale, Judge McLean or any other man would have received . . . more votes."[12] There can be no doubt that this anti–Van Buren feeling ran deep; even Charles Francis Adams shared it. However, it was not the only, nor even the major, factor involved in the disappointing Whig turnout. In Massachusetts, home of some of the more passionate antislavery Whigs, the Free Soil campaign took a not surprising turn. Among formerly Whig

[11] Duberman, *Adams,* p. 152.
[12] *Cleveland True Democrat,* 14 November 1848.

Free Soil leaders it became as much a campaign for control of the Whig Party as a campaign for advancement of Free Soil principles; in short, it reverted to the original aims of the Young Whigs.[13] This shift in purpose undoubtedly caused confusion in the Massachusetts electorate and reduced the appeal of Free Soil.

But most important was the Whig campaign to win over the "erring brethren." It suggested that the future of the territories did not depend on the president so much as it depended upon the Whigs, who everyone knew were opposed to slavery extension. With Tom Corwin as its guide, it raised the issue of the need for preservation of party unity in order to ensure the nation's future—a clear appeal to old loyalties. It "exposed" the fact that Van Buren was a Democrat and made it clear that the Free Soil program was a Democratic, even a radical, program, written in terms unfamiliar to Whigs. It emphasized that a vote for Van Buren would aid Cass to victory, thus continuing the hated Democratic "rule or ruin" policy.

This Whig argument was a stroke of genius. It appealed at once to antislavery sentiment, to loyalty, and to prejudice. Among some Whigs it created so much irresolution that they stayed home. But others throughout the North ("large numbers," according to Edward Pierce) gave Taylor their votes, ignoring his "slaveholding interests and associations," and "relying on his declaration in general terms against the exercise of the veto power."[14] These were the Whigs, according to tradition, whom Van Buren repelled. Actually, these were the Whigs for whom antislavery principles were weaker than old loyalties and prejudices, for whom the great moral principles involved in Free Soil were less important than Whiggery. These were the Whigs, treated very generously by historians, who enabled Taylor, a slaveholder, to carry the Northeast and to win the election.[15]

[13] Duberman, *Adams,* pp. 152–57.

[14] Pierce, *Sumner,* 3: 176.

[15] This interpretation of northern developments conforms more closely to the opinion at the time of the election than to the opinions of some, though not all, of the historians who later studied portions of the subject. See *New Hampshire Patriot,* 10 August 1848; Parker to Van Buren, 25 August 1848, Van Buren Papers; Duberman, *Adams,* pp. 152–57; Donald, *Sumner,* p. 166; Burr to Welles, 24 July, 18 October, 1 November 1848, Welles Papers; Mueller, *Whigs in Pennsylvania,* pp. 152–58; Smith, *Liberty and Free Soil Parties,* pp. 145–57; Holt, "Party Politics in Ohio," 38: 282–83, 303–6; Woodbridge to Crittenden, 12 September 1848, Crittenden Papers; Streeter, *Michigan Parties,* pp. 90–99; Cole, *Era of the Civil War,* pp. 57–60; John King to Lucius Lyons, 25 October 1848, Cass Papers (Clements).

Chapter Seventeen

The Significance of the Free Soil Election

The presidential election of 1848 was significant, as most presidential elections are significant, because of its effect on party structure, because of what it revealed of the people's attitude, and because of what it suggested concerning the future course of parties and of the nation's policies.

The Free Soil election revealed that both major parties were approaching, if they were not already in, a state of crisis. That conclusion is apparent from a careful examination of the election returns.

Whig managers could easily perceive that Taylor's "glorious victory" contained some alarming aspects. Despite his brave showing, Taylor secured a smaller proportion of the total popular vote than Clay had won in 1844: 47.28 percent against 48.13 percent. The decline occurred in the North. Although Taylor's vote in that section exceeded that of Clay, it was only because of new voters in the recently admitted states of Wisconsin and Iowa. In the older northern states Taylor's vote was less than Clay's by nearly 10,000 votes, and the Whig vote declined from 47.96 percent in 1844 to 45.76 percent in 1848.

More specifically, Taylor lost a substantial portion of the Whig vote in the five northernmost states: 19 percent in New Hampshire, 13 percent in Vermont, nearly 12 percent in Massachusetts, 15 percent in Ohio, and 16 percent in Michigan. He also suffered smaller, but significant, percentage losses in Maine, Connecticut, and Indiana. In New York, where he made a percentage gain, he nevertheless lost nearly 14,000 popular votes.

In the strong Whig states of Vermont, Massachusetts, Rhode Island, and Connecticut, and in the hopelessly Democratic states of New Hampshire and Michigan, such losses did not affect the results; however, they did reduce the party base for future elections. Whig losses in New York were more serious. Because of the Democratic division the losses did not matter in the 1848 election. But New York was normally closely contested; if the Whig party expected to win there in the future, it could not afford to lose any votes. Taylor's losses in Ohio were even more serious; they were large enough to cost him the state's normally Whig electoral vote. The loss was balanced by a Whig victory in Pennsylvania. But Pennsylvania was usually Democratic; the Whigs could not expect to hold it in the future.

Even without any attempt to examine the election results beneath the surface, it is obvious that in the North the Whig party was in serious trouble. Altogether, at least 46,000 of its members refused to vote for the party's candidate, and these defections cost the party one large state.[1] In the future it would take only a few more desertions in the North to reduce the party to an ineffective force.

The problem, of course, was slavery. Some who deserted were Clay partisans, but the overwhelming majority were opponents of slavery extension. But those who deserted on this score represented only one aspect of the problem. There were others, holding antislavery views, who, as Nicholas Carroll informed Mangum, "took Taylor as a choice of evils. The thinking men of the country under solemn protest voted for him & he is elected by those who abhorred his nomination, but finally determined in his favor so as to keep out Lewis Cass." The question for Whig politicians was: Could this element be held in the future, particularly if the Democrats nominated a man more clearly dedicated to freedom in the territories or if the Free-Soilers nominated a man more acceptable to wavering Whigs? The obvious answer was that the antislavery element that had voted for Taylor constituted a vast army of potential deserters; it could shift its allegiance at any time and cause the disintegration of the Whig party in the North.

But the Whig problem was not confined to the North; although not so obvious, it also extended to the South. Whig managers in that section quickly recognized that Taylor's victory there was the result of highly fortuitous circumstances which would be difficult, if not impossible, to repeat. The Whig victory was highly ephemeral. Most important, however, was the fact that the Taylor candidacy had probably conditioned the southern Whig electorate to expect that future Whig candidates would also be sympathetic to southern institutions and to the southern solution of the problem of slavery in the territories. The Whigs' failure

[1] This figure represents the number of Whigs who voted in 1844 but did not vote for Taylor in 1848; it is larger than the number which the Whigs "lost," because the latter figure represents the number of Whigs who did not vote for Taylor minus the votes that Taylor gained.

to name such a candidate in the future could produce several results: If Democrats at the same time named a candidate more sympathetic to the southern point of view, the Whigs would lose the election; if Democrats named a candidate unsympathetic to the South, there would be a southern political revolt, like that of the Barnburners, and the Whigs would lose the election. Moreover, if the Whigs did again nominate a southern candidate—and the southern Whig managers were acutely aware of this consequence—the northern antislavery element that had been loyal to the party might revolt. In short, the whole future of the party was obviously in jeopardy.

Whatever problems the presidential election presented to the Whigs, it created even greater ones for the Democrats. As with the Whigs, Democratic losses were greatest in the North. There Cass lost more than 150,000 votes in the states that had voted in 1844, a proportionate decline of 18 percent. While Polk had won a majority in five northern states and had barely missed in another, Cass carried only two states by a majority, New Hampshire and the new state of Iowa. Although the Democratic vote increased in New Hampshire, Pennsylvania, Ohio, Indiana, and Michigan, the Democratic proportion of the total vote declined in every northern state except New Hampshire.

The decline was greatest in the Northeast. In New England, where the party was already a minority, the Democrats lost more than 33,000 votes, a decline of nearly 20 percent. In two states of that section, Vermont and Massachusetts, the loss was a disastrous 35 percent. In the mid-Atlantic area Democrats lost nearly 120,000 votes, a decline of 28 percent. While most of this loss occurred in New York, where the Democratic vote dropped 48 percent, Cass also lost traditionally Democratic Pennsylvania. That loss cost him the presidency.

Even in the Northwest, which he carried, Cass suffered reverses from the 1844 vote. The Democratic proportion of the total popular vote there dropped 5 percent. Though Cass won Ohio, the Democratic proportion of the vote in that state declined. In his home state of Michigan he lost proportionately nearly 6 percent of the vote, and in strongly Democratic Illinois his vote dropped a spectacular 17 percent. The extent of disaffection in the section was reflected in Wisconsin, a new state which ordinarily would have been strongly Democratic; there Cass secured only 38 percent of the vote.

The Democratic decline also extended to the South. Cass lost about 15,000 votes in the states that had voted in 1844, a proportionate decline of 6 percent. Although he polled majorities in Virginia, Alabama, Mississippi, and Missouri, won landslide victories in Arkansas and Texas, and increased the Democratic totals in Maryland, Georgia, Mississippi, and Louisiana, the general picture was one of decline. In those states in which Cass polled majorities the Democratic proportion of the vote dropped—nearly 8 percent in Virginia, 16 percent in Alabama, 10 percent in Mississippi, 3 percent in Missouri, 13 percent in Arkansas, and 11 percent in Louisiana.

The conclusion, widely unrecognized, perhaps because of the Democratic party's temporary recovery in 1852, is inescapable. The returns revealed that the Democratic party was already in a state of dissolution. In the North at least 160,000 voters deserted the party's candidate, three times the number of Whig defections.[2] In the Northeast the desertion was so great that the party was apparently a hopeless minority in three states, with a constituency numbering only 23 percent of the voters in Vermont, 26 percent in Massachusetts, and 25 percent in New York. In the South nearly 18,000 voters deserted the party candidate; though less serious than in the North, these desertions strongly suggested that the party could lose its hold on Virginia and Alabama, as it had lost Georgia and Louisiana. And there were other signs of problems. Of the fifteen seaboard states where direct polls on the presidency were conducted, the Democrats carried only three. Of the eight traditionally Democratic states of the West, the party's proportion of the vote declined in every one.

As for the Whigs, so for the Democrats, the problem was slavery. Undoubtedly, Cass lost votes for other reasons as well: because of Taylor's military glory and because of Cass's alleged attitude on river and harbor improvements. But essentially he was the victim of the slavery problem both in the North and in the South. In the North he was not seen as a Provisoist, a fact which alienated tens of thousands of Democrats who voted for Van Buren; in the South he was not as sympathetic to the southern attitude as Taylor, a fact which cost him thousands of Democrats who voted for the Whig candidate. For Democratic managers it meant that the party was already being eroded from two directions. Moreover, there was greater danger in the future. There were many Democrats in the North who voted for Cass because they accepted the Nicholson letter doctrine in conjunction with the positive-law theory as an antislavery position; there were also many Democrats in the South who voted for Cass because they accepted the Nicholson letter doctrine as a proslavery statement.

Democratic party leaders were faced with a much more difficult

[2] This figure is obtained in the same way as the Whig figures in note 1 above.

problem than Whigs. Not only did they have to keep the allegiance of their already badly depleted rank and file, but they also had to win back a large portion of alienated Democrats in the North and in the South. To accomplish all this with one candidate in the next presidential contest would be impossible.

With both major parties facing possible disintegration because of the slavery issue, their future course was almost inevitable. Self-preservation, if nothing else, required that they find—and quickly—a solution to the problem of slavery in the territories. In a sense both parties found themselves in the same position in which they had been early in 1847, when they were confronted by two extreme views on the subject, that of Wilmot and that of Calhoun. Party leaders, recognizing the danger, had responded then. Southern Whigs had produced the Berrien-Stephens no-territory resolution, which Henry Clay had endorsed in his Lexington address. Among Democrats Buchanan had suggested an extension of the Missouri Compromise line, while George M. Dallas and Lewis Cass had proposed that the issue be left to the territories. However, for obvious reasons, neither party had advocated a real solution. Now a solution became imperative.

Fortunately—and this was the most immediately significant outcome of the Free Soil election—the electorate had provided a clue. It wanted a moderate solution of the problem of slavery in the territories.

This problem was the overwhelming issue of the presidential campaign of 1848. From the introduction of the Wilmot Proviso to the casting of ballots, it had affected every aspect of the campaign; in fact, it was the only issue that had affected the whole campaign. And the decision that the electorate made upon that issue was clear. The voters had rejected both the Wilmot Proviso and the Calhoun position as solutions of the problem. Although there were more northerners favorable to congressional legislation forbidding the extension of slavery than appeared in Van Buren's vote and although there were many southerners favorable to Calhoun's position (a number impossible even to estimate because of their absorption into the Taylor movement), the vast majority of voters rejected both alternatives. They asked for a solution in between the two extremes, a solution that would disrupt neither the parties nor the nation.

However, the electorate did not make clear the precise character of the solution it wanted. During the electoral campaign the people had been confronted with three moderating ideas: the Clayton Compromise, leaving the ultimate fate of slavery in the territories to the Supreme Court; the Nicholson letter doctrine, leaving the slavery question to the territories; and the Bronson doctrine, which theoretically prohibited slavery in the territories until the enactment of a positive law permitted its existence. All three ideas were vague, subject to varying interpretations, and leading logically to a variety of laws. The electorate did not choose among them. It left the choice and the solution to the new administration and to the new Congress. All it demanded was a moderate solution.

The Taylor administration and the famous Thirty-first Congress responded to this mandate. Their solution of the territorial problem was ingenious. Congress admitted California as a free state, which pleased the Provisoists and yet did no violence to the advocates of the Calhoun doctrine. Congress also organized the rest of the Mexican cession into two territories, New Mexico and Utah, without reference to slavery, and it provided that the issue of slavery would be decided by the territories when they were admitted to the Union as states. That solution, by avoiding a congressional decision between the merits of the extreme positions, avoided a disruption of both parties. It evaded the problem of whether the territories should be open or closed to slavery while they were in a territorial condition, and it left to the territories the problem of applying Bronson's positive-law doctrine at the time they applied for admission as states. Under such circumstances the territories as territories could go either way, an application of Cass's Nicholson letter doctrine, and they could make their final decision when they became states, a fair application of the Calhoun doctrine.

Thus the major immediate result of the election of 1848 was the enactment of three measures involving the territories secured from Mexico, a part of the so-called Compromise of 1850. They were moderate measures. Although they did not satisfy the whole electorate, as the Southern Rights movement of the spring of 1851 indicated, they were generally approved by the electorate in the "finality" election of 1852.

But there was more than immediate significance in the Free Soil election. The political developments and issues of the period from 1845 through 1848 had created a new movement constructed of three major elements: Liberty men, whose long-held attitude toward slavery as self-inculpative was one of moral indignation and indictment; Whigs, who inculcated some of the abolitionists' attitudes and found that "slavery preyed upon their conscience"; and Democrats, who concluded that the extension of slavery would be a threat to free labor, to free men, and to their cherished principle of equal opportunity for all men.

These elements, at first separately and then in the form of the Universal Antislavery League, which Salmon P. Chase envisioned and for whose consummation he deserves the largest credit, set out to make the problem of slavery in the territories the major, if not the only, issue of the presidential campaign of 1848. They succeeded remarkably well. Though they won no electoral votes, they attracted nearly 15 percent of the northern voters and put Free Soil in the mind of every candidate and every voter. Charles Sumner recognized the accomplishment in a post-election letter to Chase: "I feel we have cause for high satisfaction. We have found a large number of men through all the Free States, who are willing to leave the old parties and join in a new alliance of principle. The public mind has been stirred on the subject of slavery to depths never reached before."[3]

There was more to the accomplishment. Francis P. Blair suggested something of it in a letter to Van Buren: "Our forlorn hope has accomplished all that was wished. . . . Every Cass and Taylor man in the North was compelled to give adhesion . . . to the principle of no new territory to be added to our Africa."[4] Horace Greeley expressed the achievement more fully:

> By the self devotion of the Free Democracy, the danger of an Extension of Slavery under our National flag is well nigh averted. The struggle is by no means ended, but the nature of the end is made certain. By the proclaimed resolution of a part of the voters of the Free States that they will hold the Liberty of Men paramount to all questions of power or policy, the lagging majority have been brought measurably to the standard. "Van Buren and Free Soil" have triumphed in making even the venal and time-serving, lip-deep Free Soilers vociferous for "Taylor and Free Soil," or for "Cass and Free Soil." The cant about "sectional issues," "Union and compromise," etc. have been drowned in one universal shout for "Free Soil and No Compromise." The benefits of this will accrue to all parties through all time, but the honor is mainly due to . . . the self-forgetting, single-minded champions of Free Soil.[5]

Greeley's analysis, though not entirely accurate, was farsighted; it pointed to the real significance of the presidential election of 1848. The Free-Soilers' campaign in that election had made the further spread of slavery unthinkable and impossible.[6]

Moderating influences would still prevail. In the measures Congress

[3] Sumner to Chase, 16 November 1848, Chase Papers. The conclusion was recorded in many sources. See Conner to Calhoun, 28 September 1848, in Jameson, *Calhoun Correspondence,* p. 1183; Welles to [?], 18 September 1848, Welles Papers; *Albany Atlas,* 7 November 1848; *Daily Wisconsin,* 2 September 1848.

[4] Blair to Van Buren, 30 November 1848, Van Buren Papers.

[5] *New York Tribune,* 18 November 1848.

[6] *Boston Atlas,* 11 November 1848.

enacted in 1850, the principle of legal equality remained foremost: freemen and slaveholders were equally free to enter the territories acquired from Mexico. But the equality provided by law was more apparent than real. None of the measures encouraged slaveholders to transport their peculiar property into those territories. And slaveholders needed encouragement, or legal protection, to undertake the task; the Southern Rights movement of 1851 was a response to the recognition of that need.

Although a great majority of the electorate professed satisfaction with the "egalitarian" solution to the territorial issue written into the Compromise of 1850, it soon became clear that the northern electorate had not approved an extension of slavery. Less than six years after the election of 1848 Stephen A. Douglas introduced the Nebraska Bill, which provided for the application of the principle of equality to territory regarded as free since the adoption of the Missouri Compromise. Almost immediately a large portion of the northern electorate served notice that it did not really accept the principle of equality. It would not provide a legal opportunity to make free territory into slave territory. All the passions which the Free Soil campaign of 1848 had firmly embedded in the minds of northern voters were reawakened, and a second Free Soil movement began—a movement which brought about the disintegration and erosion of the Whig and Democratic parties that had threatened in 1848 and which created an enlarged Free Soil organization—the Republican party. That party carried out the mandate which the presidential campaign of 1848 had foreshadowed: it stopped the spread of slavery into the territories.

Note on Sources

This is not intended to be a formal bibliography, either enumerated or annotated. In the course of doing research on this book I consulted nearly 600 primary and secondary sources which I believed should have had some material relating to the presidential campaign of 1848. A surprisingly large number contained very little or nothing at all, even including the papers and biographies of men closely engaged in the contest. Of the sources used, I have cited approximately 275 in the footnotes. This note is intended only to indicate those that were most useful.

Not many historians have written MONOGRAPHS on the American political situation in the years between 1845 and 1848, and most of these monographs are confined to developments in single states. The more valuable ones included Arthur B. Darling, *Political Changes in Massachusetts: 1824–1848* (New Haven, Conn., 1925); Frank O. Gatell, " 'Conscience and Judgment': The Bolt of the Massachusetts Conscience Whigs," *Historian* 20 (1959): 18–45; Herbert D. A. Donovan, *Barnburners* (New York, 1925); Henry R. Mueller, *Whig Party in Pennsylvania* (New York, 1922); Charles M. Snyder, *The Jacksonian Heritage: Pennsylvania Politics, 1833–1848* (Harrisburg, Pa., 1958); Edgar A. Holt, "Party Politics in Ohio, 1840–1850," *Ohio Archeological and Historical Publications* 37 (1928): 439–591 and 38 (1929): 47–182, 260–402; Erwin H. Price, "Election of 1848 in Ohio," *Ohio Archeological and Historical Publications* 36 (1927): 188–311; Floyd B. Streeter, *Political Parties in Michigan* (Lansing, Mich., 1918); Arthur C. Cole, *Era of the Civil War, 1848–1870* (Chicago, 1922); Paul Murray, *The Whig Party in Georgia, 1825–1853* (Chapel Hill, N. C., 1948); Herbert J. Doherty, Jr., *Whigs of Florida, 1845–1854* (Gainesville, Fla., 1959); and James K. Greer, "Louisiana Politics, 1845–1861," *Louisiana Historical Quarterly* 12 (1929): 381–425, 555–610. Among the larger and very useful studies are Theodore Clark Smith, *Liberty and Free Soil Parties in the Northwest* (New York, 1897); Arthur C. Cole, *Whig Party in the South* (Washington, D. C., 1913); and Henry Wilson, *History of the Rise and Fall of the Slave Power in America* (Boston, 1874), vol. 2.

Of more than 200 BIOGRAPHICAL STUDIES of prominent and minor figures who participated in the campaign of 1848, the overwhelming majority contained nothing of value for this study. Some (about thirty) provided bits of information and are appropriately footnoted. Another score proved more useful. Among the older biographies, the more important ones included Frederic Bancroft, *Life of William H. Seward* (New York, 1900), vol. 1; Ann Mary Crittenden Coleman, ed., *Life of John J. Crittenden with Selections from His Correspondence and Speeches* (Philadelphia, 1871); Wendell P. and Francis J. Garrison, *William Lloyd Garrison, 1805–1879* (New York, 1889), vol. 3; Edward L. Pierce, *Memoirs and Letters of Charles Sumner* (London, 1893), vol. 3; Edward M. Shepard, *Martin Van Buren* (Boston, 1899). Of those published between the two world wars, the more informative included Claude M. Fuess, *Daniel Webster* (Boston, 1930), vol. 2; Charles B. Going, *David Wilmot: Free-Soiler* (New York, 1924); Eugene I. McCormac, *James K. Polk: A Political Biography* (Berkeley, Calif., 1922); Roy F. Nichols, *Franklin Pierce: Young Hickory from the Granite Hills* (Philadelphia, 1931); George R. Poage, *Henry Clay and the Whig Party* (Chapel Hill, N. C., 1936); William E. Smith, *Francis Preston Blair Family in Politics* (New York, 1933), vol. 1; and Francis P. Weisenburger, *Life of John McLean: A Politician on the United States Supreme Court* (Columbus, Ohio, 1937). Of more recent biographical materials, the better ones include Gerald M. Capers, *John C. Calhoun—Opportunist; A Reappraisal* (Gainesville, Fla., 1960); David Donald, *Charles Sumner and the Coming of the Civil War* (New York, 1960); Martin Duberman, *Charles Francis Adams, 1807–1886* (Boston, 1960); Brainerd Dyer, *Zachary Taylor* (Baton Rouge, La., 1946); John A. Garraty, *Silas Wright* (New York, 1949); Norman Graebner, "Thomas Corwin and the Election of 1848: A Study in Conservative Politics," *Journal of Southern History* 17 (1951): 162–80; Holman Hamilton, *Zachary Taylor: Soldier in the White House* (New York, 1951); Albert D. Kirwan, *John J. Crittenden: The Struggle for the Union* (Lexington, Ky., 1962); Philip S. Klein, *President James Buchanan* (University Park, Pa., 1962); Robert J. Rayback, *Millard Fillmore: Biography of a President* (Buffalo, N. Y., 1959); Charles G. Sellers, *James K. Polk, Continentalist: 1843–1846* (Princeton, N. J., 1966); James P. Shenton, *Robert J. Walker: A Politician from Jackson to Lincoln* (New York, 1961); Ivor D. Spencer, *The Victor and the Spoils: A Life of William L. Marcy* (Providence, R. I., 1959); Glyndon G. Van Deusen, *Thurlow Weed: Wizard of the Lobby* (Boston, 1947); and Frank B. Woodford, *Lewis Cass: The Last Jeffersonian* (New Brunswick, N. J., 1950).

AUTOBIOGRAPHICAL WORKS and memoirs of individuals involved in the
1848 campaign are not numerous; there are only about fifty in that
category. Nevertheless, there are a few of special value. These include
Myrta L. Avery, ed., *Recollections of Alexander H. Stephens* (New
York, 1910); Thurlow W. Barnes, *Memoirs of Thurlow Weed* (Bos-
ton, 1884); Harriet A. Weed, ed., *Autobiography of Thurlow Weed*
(Boston, 1883); Morgan Dix, comp., *Memoirs of John Adams Dix*
(New York, 1883), vol. 1; Oliver Dyer, *Great Senators of the United
States Forty Years Ago* (New York, 1889); George W. Julian, *Polit-
ical Recollections: 1840–1872* (Chicago, 1884); and Henry B. Stanton,
Random Recollections (New York, 1887).

A glance at the footnotes will quickly reveal that by far the greatest
amount of material came from the published works and private papers
of men involved in the campaign and from newspapers. Of the PUB-
LISHED WORKS OF CONTEMPORARIES, I have used the following more than
casually and sometimes very frequently: Richard H. Dana III, ed.,
Speeches in Stirring Times and Letters to a Son (Boston, 1910);
Works of Charles Sumner (Boston, 1875), vols. 1 and 2; *Writings and
Speeches of Daniel Webster,* National Edition (Boston, 1903), vols. 4,
13, 16, and 18; George E. Baker, ed., *Works of William H. Seward*
(Boston, 1884), vol. 3; John Bigelow, ed., *Letters and Literary Memo-
rials of Samuel J. Tilden* (New York, 1908), vol. 1; John B. Moore,
ed., *Works of James Buchanan: Comprising His Speeches, State Pa-
pers, and Private Correspondence* (Philadelphia, 1909), vols. 6–8;
Dwight L. Dumond, ed., *Letters of James Gillespie Birney: 1831–1857*
(New York, 1938), vols. 1 and 2; *Diary and Correspondence of Salmon
P. Chase* (Washington, 1903); L. Belle Hamlin, ed., "Selected Letters
of Salmon P. Chase: February 18, 1846 to May 1, 1861," *Quarterly
Publication of the Historical and Philosophical Society of Ohio* 11
(1916): 138–68; Hamlin, ed., "Selections from the Follett Papers,"
*Quarterly Publication of the Historical and Philosophical Society of
Ohio* 9 (1914): 69–100; 10 (1915): 1–33; 11 (1916): 1–35; Hamlin,
ed., "Selections from the William Greene Papers," *Quarterly Publication of the Historical and Philosophical Society of Ohio* 13 (1918): 1–
38; 14 (1919): 1–26; Chauncey S. Boucher and Robert P. Brooks, eds.,
Correspondence Addressed to John C. Calhoun, 1837–1849 (Washington, D. C., 1930); Richard K. Crallé, ed., *Works of John C. Calhoun*
(New York, 1854–1855), vols. 4 and 6; J. Franklin Jameson, ed., *Correspondence of John C. Calhoun* (Washington, D. C., 1900); Calvin
Colton, ed., *Works of Henry Clay: Comprising His Life, Correspondence and Speeches,* Federal Edition (New York, 1904), vols. 2, 3, and

5; J. G. de Roulhac Hamilton, ed., *Papers of William Alexander Graham* (Raleigh, N. C., 1960), vol. 3; Charles H. Ambler, ed., *Correspondence of Robert M. T. Hunter, 1826–1876* (Washington, D. C., 1918); Henry T. Shanks, ed., *Papers of Willie Person Mangum* (Raleigh, N. C., 1955), vols. 4 and 5; Milo M. Quaife, ed., *Diary of James K. Polk during His Presidency: 1845–1849* (Chicago, 1910), vols. 1–4; *Letters of Zachary Taylor from the Battlefields of the Mexican War* (Rochester, N. Y., 1908); and Ulrich B. Phillips, ed., *Correspondence of Robert M. Toombs, Alexander H. Stephens, and Howell Cobb* (Washington, D. C., 1913).

I have used very extensively the PAPERS deposited in the Library of Congress of the following men: William H. Allen, Francis P. Blair, James Buchanan, John C. Calhoun, Salmon P. Chase, Henry Clay, John M. Clayton, John J. Crittenden, Franklin H. Elmore, Thomas Ewing, Joshua R. Giddings and George W. Julian, Francis Granger, James H. Hammond, John McLean, Willie P. Mangum, William L. Marcy, Franklin Pierce (and photostats of Pierce's papers), Caleb B. Smith, Zachary Taylor, Martin Van Buren, Gideon Welles, and Levi Woodbury. I have also used the papers, deposited in the places indicated, of the following men: James Buchanan (Pennsylvania Historical Society), Lewis Cass (William L. Clements Library, University of Michigan; and Burton Historical Collection, Detroit Public Library), George M. Dallas (Pennsylvania Historical Society), Alpheus Felch (Burton Historical Collection), Azariah C. Flagg (Columbia University), John P. Hale (New Hampshire Historical Society), Lucius Lyon (Clements Library), Robert McClelland (Burton Historical Collection), James K. Polk (New York Public Library), John Teesdale (Ohio Historical Society), Amos Tuck (New Hampshire Historical Society), Henry N. Walker (Burton Historical Collection), and Elisha Whittlesey (Ohio Historical Society).

NEWSPAPERS were the largest single source of materials for this book. The list below, with exact masthead titles, contains those which were available to me for the whole period, for part of the period, or in scattered numbers.

From New England: *Boston Courier, Boston Daily Atlas, Boston Daily Times, The* (Boston) *Emancipator, The* (Boston) *Liberator, Boston Post, Boston Whig,* (Concord) *New Hampshire Patriot and State Gazette, Springfield* (Mass.) *Republican.*

From the mid-Atlantic states: *Daily Albany Argus, Albany Evening*

Atlas, Albany Evening Journal, Brooklyn Eagle, Buffalo Republic, New Brunswick (N. J.) *Times, Morning Courier and New York Enquirer, New York Evening Post, New York Express, New York Weekly Tribune,* (New York) *Voice of Industry,* (New York) *Working Man's Advocate, Newark Daily Advertiser,* (Philadelphia) *North American,* (Philadelphia) *Pennsylvanian,* (Philadelphia) *Spirit of the Times and Daily Keystone.*

From the Northwest: *Chicago Democrat, Chicago Journal, Cincinnati Herald-Philanthropist, Cleveland Herald, Cleveland Plain Dealer,* (Cleveland) *True Democrat,* (Columbus) *Ohio State Journal,* (Columbus) *Ohio Statesman, Detroit Daily Advertiser,* (Detroit) *Daily Free Press,* (Indianapolis) *Indiana State Sentinel,* (Iowa City) *Iowa Capitol Reporter,* (Milwaukee) *Daily Wisconsin, Racine Advocate, Sangamo Journal, Springfield Illinois State Journal, Springfield Illinois State Register.*

From the south-Atlantic states: *Augusta* (Ga.) *Republic, Baltimore Clipper, Baltimore Patriot,* (Baltimore) *Republican and Argus, The* (Baltimore) *Sun, Charleston Mercury, Columbus* (Ga.) *Times, Macon Telegraph, Milledgeville* (Ga.) *Southern Recorder,* (Raleigh) *North Carolina Standard, Daily Richmond Enquirer, Savannah Daily Georgian, Savannah Daily Republican,* (Tallahassee) *Floridian, Tallahassee Journal,* (Washington) *National Era,* (Washington) *National Intelligencer, Washington Union.*

From the Southwest: *The* (Jackson) *Mississippian, Lexington Observer and Reporter, Louisville Daily Democrat, Louisville Journal, Mobile Advertiser, Mobile Register and Journal,* (Montgomery) *Alabama State Journal,* (Nashville) *Republican-Banner, Tri-Weekly Nashville Union, Nashville Whig, New Orleans Commercial Bulletin, New Orleans Courier,* (New Orleans) *Daily Picayune, New Orleans Weekly Delta.*

Finally, I should note several other contemporary publications that proved useful. These include the *Congressional Globe,* 29th Cong., 1st sess.–30th Cong., 2d sess.; *American Whig Review: A Whig Journal;* De Bow's *Commerical Review of the South and West; Niles' National Register; North American Review;* Oliver Dyer, *Phonographic Report of the Proceedings of the National Free Soil Convention* (Buffalo, N. Y., 1848); O. C. Gardiner, *Great Issue* (New York, 1848); William Goodell, *Address of the Macedonian Convention, and Letters of Gerrit Smith* (Albany, N. Y., 1847); Lysander Spooner, *The Unconstitutionality of Slavery,* 2 vols. (Boston, 1845, 1847).

Index

Democrats with commitment to antislavery position, 243–44; nominated with Butler in South Carolina, 268–69; writes letters to William B. Pringle and *Charleston News*, 270–71; "two faces" of, 271–72; preelection prospects of, 276–78; vote for, analyzed, 279, 280–81, 282, 284–85, 286, 289–94, 303–5; and Free Soil, 295–310 passim

Taylor–Butler ticket, 269, 272–73, 291

Taylor Independents, 41, 45, 154, 157–58

Taylor support: in Kentucky, 148; in Virginia and North Carolina, 149; in Maine, Illinois, Iowa, Georgia, Florida, Alabama, Mississippi, Missouri, Arkansas, and Texas, 158

Taylor Whigs: motives attacked by Democrats, 46–48; insist that Taylor is a true Whig, 48; attack Clay, 1847, 145

Tazewell, Littleton W., 269

Teesdale, John, 163, 165, 168

"ten hour system," 265

Thompson, Jacob, 38

Thompson, Richard W., 263

Three Million Bill, 25–26, 239

Tilden, Samuel J., 65, 66, 67, 188

Titus letter, 74, 176

Tod, David, 78

Toombs, Robert A., 38, 130, 259, 276

Toucey, Isaac, 144, 189

Trumbull, Joseph, 2

Tuck, Amos, 58, 111, 249

Tucker, Beverley, 44

Turney, Hopkins L., 144

Two Million Bill, 23, 25

Tyler, John, 118, 148

Ullman, Daniel, 124

Unconstitutionality of Slavery, The, 100

universal reformers, 110

Utica (Free Soil) convention, June 1848: 206; nominates Van Buren, 209–10; platform of, 210–12

Van Buren, John: 75, 177, 207, 208, 245, 267; leader of Herkimer convention, 77

Van Buren, Martin: 11, 13, 14, 15, 17, 20, 33, 49, 67, 136, 137 n.21, 175, 176, 181, 182, 186, 207, 213, 222, 223, 226, 227, 241, 248, 249, 255, 256, 257, 263, 265, 277, 294, 309; campaign for renomination of, 1844, 61–62; and negotiations with Polk on cabinet post for New Yorker, 63–67; potential Democratic candidate, 176–77; antislavery position of, 176; rejects Barnburner overtures, 177–78; advises Barnburner delegation to Democratic Convention, 179–81; position of, on slavery in the District of Columbia, 207, 216, 227 n.108, 230; antislavery position and record of, 209, 247–48, 297, 299; presidential nominee of Utica convention, 209, 210; leading candidate for Free Soil nomination, 215; refuses to act like candidate, 216; presidential nominee of Free Soil party, 228–29; abused by Democrats and Whigs, 244–47; charged with proslavery career, 246–47; vote for, analyzed, 279, 281–87, 293, 294–302 passim

Van Buren, Smith, 65–67

Vance, Joseph, 199

Vaux, Richard, 45

Veracruz, battle of, 167

"Veritas," 30

"Vindicator affair," 31

Virginia, 139, 149

Virginia Resolutions, 28, 113

"vote-yourself-a-farm men," 89, 220

Wade, Edward, 217

Wadsworth, James S., 76, 177

Waite, William S., 222

Walcutt, Edward, 184

Walker, Amasa, 78, 212, 248

Walker, Henry N., 16

Walker, James W., 270

Walker, Robert J.: 139, 143, 174, 175, 186; potential presidential candidate, 13; named Secretary of the Treasury, 64

Walker Tariff, 174, 261, 262

Webb, James Watson: 34, 88, 198

Webster, Daniel: 7, 81, 165, 184, 194, 196, 197, 198, 296; quells mutiny at Faneuil Hall, 1846, 86–87; campaign of, in South, 1847, 95; opposition to, in Massachusetts, 95–96; opposes antislavery campaign, 96–97; preconvention support for, 159;